The
Renaissance Popes

The
Renaissance Popes

Statesmen, Warriors and the

Great Borgia Myth

GERARD NOEL

CARROLL & GRAF PUBLISHERS
New York

Carroll & Graf Publishers
An imprint of Avalon Publishing Group, Inc.
245 W. 17th Street
11th Floor
New York, NY 10011–5300
www.carrollandgraf.com

AVALON
publishing group incorporated

First published in the UK by Constable,
an imprint of Constable & Robinson Ltd, 2006

First Carroll & Graf edition, 2006

ISBN-13: 978-0-78671-841-2
ISBN-10: 0-7867-1841-2

Printed and bound in the EU

CONTENTS

Contents

ACKNOWLEDGEMENTS

I am most grateful to Ben Glazebrook with whom I discussed, at length, the basic theme of this book. He was then chairman of Constable and later, together with the incoming managing director and subsequent chairman, Nick Robinson, did me the honour of commissioning the book.

I owe a great debt to the leading contemporary English expert on the Borgia period, Professor Michael Mallett. We had many (for me) enlightening conversations on the subject in London and at his home in Leamington Spa. It is to him, moreover, that we owe the vital piece of information that, by exhorting false evidence under torture from those who served Alexander VI, Julius II was able to launch the Great Borgia Myth.

I record my great appreciation to Samantha Wyndham for her work and research on the artistic and architectural aspects of Renaissance Rome.

I am profoundly indebted to Dr Stella Fletcher for the valuable fruits of her extensive knowledge of the political history of the Renaissance period. She was also extremely helpful in tracing authorities and sources for this complex and controversial period.

Henry Hely-Hutchinson, a former professional proofreader, helped me considerably with his gimlet eye, at various stages in the book's composition and with his valuable suggestions. For this, I am most appreciative.

The extensive knowledge of Italian history possessed by Luigi Lucato proved immensely useful and interesting, as emerging from our many conversations on the subject. I am most grateful.

After all this help, and a writing period of over three years, I was left with a lengthy but unwieldy script, plus a mass of notes and overflowing material. In help toward reduction of this to a coherent form of the required length, I owe a very special debt to Michael Ward. His expert literary and editorial abilities have been essential elements, without which the final text might never have been completed.

ILLUSTRATIONS

INTRODUCTION

This book has been germinating in my mind for many years. I have long been interested in the Renaissance popes, about whom, as far as I know, no book exists that recounts sequentially the individual story of each. An inspiration for the book was the suggestion by a senior member of the English Catholic hierarchy that I should write about some good popes rather than, as has so often been done, the bad popes. The person in question has been a friend of mine since we were both students in Rome.

The patron of my college was Monsignor Montini, later Pope Paul VI, whom I got to know and whose biography I subsequently wrote. My interest in popes started at that time. An interest in the Renaissance popes came later. My hierarchical friend's suggestion about good popes gave me much food for thought. The Renaissance popes can hardly be called, in general, 'good popes'. My investigation of their lives, however, revealed something that (at least to me) was very clear, and extremely interesting – the pope who gave his family name to the Borgia Age, though presented as particularly bad, has in fact been gravely maligned. Thus, my book also attempts to rectify a grave historical misconception about the allegedly worst pope in history, and to demonstrate that Rodrigo Borgia, Pope Alexander VI, was by no means nearly as bad as traditionally painted.

I am well aware of the dangers of any revisionist writing of history. It is vulnerable from all sides. What I call the 'Great Borgia Myth' (see Part II), however, has ultimately become a source of its own weakness. When, after the successful launching of the myth, it began acquiring more and more invariably exaggerated and often grotesque accretions, it eventually became so swollen, gross and top-heavy as to be ripe for overthrow.

The myth began to be questioned seriously from the end of the nineteenth century onwards. Subsequently it was chipped away at by many authors, but surprisingly was not, for the time being, accorded detailed dissection in any single scholarly work. Then, in 1942, along came the publication in

English of a biography of Alexander VI by Orestes Ferrara that, for the first time, presented a completely different picture of his life. Why did it not, in due course, revolutionize the scholarly, let alone popular, perception of the Borgia period? The suggested answer is interesting. Ferrara's book never got as far as impinging on the popular view of the Borgias. As to its reception in scholarly circles, the situation is even more interesting.

The book was published at the height of the Second World War. Books at that time, at least in England, could only be published in an 'economy' form. Promotion by publishers was extremely limited. Book reviews of any kind, let alone studies in depth, were scarce. Moreover, Orestes Ferrara's book was published by a relatively obscure, though by no means undistinguished, publishing house, namely Sheed & Ward. Its founder and proprietor was the scholarly Australian, Dr Frank Sheed, who also translated Ferrara's book. Frank Sheed's publishing partner, Maisie Ward, was also his wife. She too was a profound student of Catholic history and theology, and a member of a prominent English Catholic academic family.

Largely because of the timing of the book's publication, it received a minimum of attention when it first appeared. This seemed, at the time, to be accidental. But was it so accidental that, as time went on, the book continued to be ignored? For academic believers in the Borgia myth, such silence was fortuitous but extremely advantageous. Why not let sleeping dogs lie? So it was that no answer ever appeared at the time to Ferrara's detailed dismantling of the Borgia myth. Nor, as far as I know, has any attempt ever been made to produce any such rebuttal. In the absence, therefore, of an adequate reply, the Ferrara thesis stands unchallenged. The Borgia myth, correspondingly, stands exposed. The section of this book devoted specifically to the myth is based largely on the findings of Ferrara. (See Part II, chapter 8.)

As to the other popes of the Renaissance period, my main objective has been not only to portray them as public figures of their time but, primarily, as *men*. I have included many facts about them not usually to be found in conventional biographies. Conversely, the complicated political details of their various pontificates have been simplified, as far as possible. For this, there are two reasons. The first is that, for the most part, the popes were figureheads who, though they gave a general direction to affairs, did not attend to day-to-day matters. These were dealt with by the Holy See's Curia, at that time the largest and most highly developed bureaucracy in the world. The popes, moreover, would never have had time for detailed attention to such matters, so all-consuming – in some cases – were their private interests and preoccupations. More attention has been given to these, in this book, than in most accounts of the period. Only thus, it is felt, can a rounded and balanced portrait be produced of this truly extraordinary gallery of men.

Another reason for avoiding excessive political detail is that it is, at times, so complicated that it can obscure the wood for the trees. In this work, therefore, the question tends to move away from the more usual one of 'what did they *do*?' (or, more exactly, 'what was done in their names?'). The more important question becomes, 'what were these popes like as men of flesh and blood?'

In examining the latter question, over many years, as wide a net as possible has been cast over the literary material available. This has included countless volumes gathering dust on the back shelves of numerous second-hand bookshops, from Hong Kong to Hay-on-Wye. Thus uncovered was a multitude of facts about the Renaissance popes that seldom, if ever, appear in mainstream biographies and histories.

So it was that I discovered, for example, the nature of Nicholas V's favourite (pornographic) reading; the polite exclusion by Aeneas Silvius Piccolomini (afterwards Pope Pius II) – from his own bed – of the alluring invitation of two English ladies in a hayloft; Paul II's fondness for melons, jewellery and pageboys; the interest of one of Innocent VIII's witch-hunting inquisitors in a collection of penises in a cardboard box; the delicate nature of Leo X's painful indisposition; the moribund appearance of Cardinal Farnese, whose apparently imminent demise persuaded his fellow conclavists to elect him as Pope Paul III; and many other matters of which little was hitherto known, including Alexander's taste for the simplest of diets. (How bored he must have been during all those alleged banquet-orgies.)

A drawback of this wide network of sources is the difficulty of being able, in every instance, to cite first-hand chapter-and-verse references for every statement. This would, in any case, be inappropriate in anything but a strictly academic study and impossible in a popular one. For this very reason, nothing is reported as fact that has not been thoroughly verified. Nothing has been consciously exaggerated, let alone invented. Rumours or legends are carefully identified as such, and duly qualified (*'on dit'*). This is more than can be said of many of the 'facts' adduced to blacken the name of Alexander VI, so many of which have passed into history and been accepted as gospel truth.

No attempt is here made to present a detailed introduction to the Renaissance period. This would be a major and lengthy undertaking, beyond the scope of this book. Along with the general observations appearing below, however, a few principles regarding late medieval Catholic theology might help to explain how an historical phenomenon such as the Roman Renaissance came, perhaps inevitably, to occur. Nicholas V (1447–55) is taken to be the first pope of the period in question, and Pius V (1566–72) to be the last. The pontiff dominating the period is, of course, Alexander VI (1492–1503), who gave his name to the Borgia Age and the subsequent myth associated therewith.

At the start of the Renaissance, in the fifteenth century, papal rule was in decline. With the exile of popes to Avignon and their consequent abdication of their responsibilities as bishops of Rome, the secular princes moved in. The princes made appointments to benefices, fixed clerical taxation and became involved in related matters. Unopposed, their power was pervasive – upon his election in 1447, Pope Nicholas V had to contend with the conflicting interests of Venice, Naples, Milan and Florence (the latter two being controlled respectively by the influential Visconti and Medici families).

Finding it increasingly difficult to stand unaided, the popes initiated a train of events that caused serious damage to the credibility of the Church. At Avignon they were well-placed geographically to lead western Christendom, but they lost control of the papal states. They were perceived as being in the pocket of the French kings, and were thus resented in the Italian states.

The Visconti family had ruled Milan since *c.*1300, obtaining their ducal title from the emperor in 1395, but the line ran out in 1447. Milan was a significant manufacturing centre, particularly famous for the production of armour, and commanded the southern end of transalpine trade routes. It also dominated its Lombard and Ligurian neighbours, including the marquisate of Mantua (ruled by the Gonzaga family from 1328) and the maritime republic of Genoa, the financial stability of which was countered by its governmental chaos.

Besides Genoa, four other republics survived in fifteenth-century Italy (all the other medieval communes having fallen under the sway of 'despots' such as the Visconti, Gonzaga and Este). One of them, Florence, became an important power through the absorption of a number of other cities, such as Arezzo, Pisa, Pistoia and Prato. Failure to absorb Lucca in the early 1430s contributed to the fall of the Albizzi faction and the rise of the Medici. While Siena sought to balance factions, the institutions of Florentine republican government were seriously undermined by the dominance of a single faction, first the Albizzi and then the Medici. Eligibility for office-holding became limited to an increasingly narrow elite, at the heart of which was the Medici faction. Power was determined by wealth. In 1427, the richest man in Florence was Palla Strozzi. When, in 1434, Cosimo de' Medici returned from a brief exile, Palla and the other Strozzi were themselves sent into exile. Cosimo's wealth came from banking and related businesses, including his role as papal banker.

Another of the five major Italian powers was Venice. The city in the lagoon was self-consciously different from the mainland; it was also a byword for political stability, ruled by a patrician oligarchy. Other states feared its faceless committees, particularly the Senate.

The threat periodically used by many of these powers against the fifteenth-century popes was that of summoning a General Council, which according to conciliar thought had the power to reform the Church in head and members, as it had notably attempted to do at the Council of Constance. Here, in 1417, Oddone Colonna had been elected as Pope Martin V. His power was carefully circumscribed by the decree Frequens, which obliged him to call further General Councils on a frequent basis.

His successors, however, became increasingly grand in character. Their lofty perception of the papal office inevitably led them into repeated conflicts with the secular powers, who had previously enjoyed considerable control over the Church in their own lands. The long years of papal weakness were now over, and a new era was born.

This would be an appropriate moment to remark on what could be described as a sort of schizophrenia that, in one way or another, affected almost every Renaissance pope. This meant, in practice, that the same man could combine a genuine concern for the welfare of the Church – sometimes allied to personally pious, even mystical, sentiments – with a cynical and worldly estimate of the so-called 'sins of the flesh'. This appears time and again with the popes of this period. The rare case of a total commitment to chastity produced the surprised and delighted official recognition of such a pope as a saint. However sadistic such a pope might be (in the service of the Church that is), the addiction of such a man to chastity (particularly if it was accompanied by excessive mortifications) might well qualify him for official sainthood. Such was the case with Pope Pius V, who had a large amount of people burned to death or tortured in the dungeons of the Inquisition – but wore a hair-shirt and refrained from sex. The pope was duly canonized.

The prerequisite to an appreciation of the popes of the Renaissance is thus an understanding of this pronounced and special form of 'schizophrenia'. There was a kind of neo-pagan tolerance, nay approval, of what in another age had been deemed as licentiousness and depravity. God's creation, in all its sensual, even carnal beauty, was suddenly deserving of praise and, above all, glorification in terms of art. Christ, when seen as Apollo, was the fitting head of a Church viewed with a newly acquired, almost pantheistic, theological appreciation for beauty and goodness in the whole of nature. To be fully human was to ape the divine, within the inadequate limitations of our fallen nature. It was the obverse to what Augustine, 1,000 years earlier, had proposed as a norm for acceptable behaviour, namely the strictest possible sexual continence.

For Augustine, there were various forms of human behaviour that were an inescapable part of man's nature. Most notable, for him, was the making of war. It had gone on since time immemorial and was therefore, according to him, natural to humankind. Thus evolved the theory of the 'just war', whose successful establishment completed a virtual revolution in the Christian overview of right and wrong, and ushered in centuries of mass killing and destruction.

The first Christians had been pacifists. Jesus' mission for them was to bring peace to the world. They recognized each other, as did Freemasons in a later age, by exchanging a secret sign, the 'Sign of Peace'. They refused, on pain of death if necessary, to fight in any war or join any army. However, in the fourth century the Church came under the protection of the Roman Empire, and Christianity became the official religion of the Empire. Pacifism and what we would today call conscientious objection were no longer tolerated. Killing, in prescribed circumstances, was sanctified.

Sex, chiefly under the inspiration of St Augustine in the fourth century, took over as the natural raw material for sin. This became a central point for medieval theological thinking, and was often obsessive, while at the same time the Church became progressively militant in the prosecution of war, including its own 'war' against heretics, infidels and the 'deicide' Jews. This war was approaching its height at the end of the Middle Ages, ushering in the age of crusades, the Inquisition, the 'containment' of Jewry and the elimination of witchcraft. All of these movements, needless to say, were accompanied by terror and death on a large scale. The 'just war' theory, moreover, naturally led to a state of affairs where war was the habitual condition of mankind, becoming in practice more and more extensive, deadly, efficient and profitable.

All of this was accompanied by a different sort of revolution in Church thinking from the late Middle Ages onwards. Except in rare cases, the effort toward heroic virtue in suppressing the sins of flesh was virtually abandoned in favour of more effective ways of making expiation before God for such sins. The sacrament of penance went through various stages of development, as did the official mind of the Church on the subject of the forgiveness of sins in general. While, as always agreed, true contrition for sin merited absolution, logic demanded that God's justice also required some sort of punitive atonement for sins committed. This was required for the guilt that remained even after the sins themselves had been forgiven.

The doctrine of purgatory thus received new impetus, as did that of indulgences. This was based on the principle that a Christian – his sins having been forgiven, thus avoiding hell – must, by certain penances and good works, pay off the 'temporal punishment' still due in God's estimation for past sins. The Church, of course, was the sole (indeed divinely appointed) judge of what was God's estimate of such matters and, by the same token, the sole legitimate dispenser of His mercy, by means of forgiveness and indulgences to replace any public penance.

Thus it was that an efficient method gradually evolved, from the eleventh century onwards, whereby the Church could free its members from the heavy pall of guilt and repression borne throughout the early medieval period due to the sins of flesh to which every human being was subject. Fear of hell dominated these years and many people – Constantine being the most famous example – postponed conversion and/or receiving the sacrament of penance until their deathbeds.

The year 1095, however, was an important turning point. It provided the opportunity for replacing the penances of the early Church, whereby the wearing of sackcloth and ashes or some other public sign of contrition became practically a way of life. In order successfully to launch the First Crusade, Pope Urban II had a brainwave. He promised a remission of all punishment for those who set out to liberate the Holy Land. From that time onwards, such 'indulgences' came to be granted more and more freely. The pope delegated the power to grant them to the bishops and other lower clergy. Indulgences could be limited in time, such as for so many days (a somewhat artificial form of reckoning), or they could be 'plenary', whereby they remitted all temporal punishment due to sin (i.e. punishment to be received in this world or the next – in 'purgatory').

Certain specifically prescribed prayers and good works were necessary to obtain such indulgences. But as the Middle Ages wore on, almsgiving became a central requirement. Indulgences thus became an important and ever increasing source of revenue for the Church. By the time the Renaissance had arrived, funds were pouring in at such a rate as to bring about the grave scandal that eventually occasioned, even if it did not actually cause, the Reformation.

The Church had also, during a similar period, become concerned about another aspect of church finances or, more exactly, a lack of them. In the early Christian centuries, priests had been allowed to marry. But as clerics, particularly bishops, became richer, the authorities grew alarmed when such clerics left their money and possessions to their wives and families. It was thus that celibacy for priests became compulsory. This had originally been decreed in the fourth century, but it fell into disuse. The rule was re-imposed by Pope Gregory VII (Hildebrand) in the eleventh century. Its main motivation was financial but it was possible, by a tangle of somewhat dubious theology, to produce a claim (unsupported in scripture) as to the moral superiority of chastity over marriage and the alleged fact than an unmarried priest, not bound by domestic duties, would be free to give his exclusive attention to his flock.

By the fourteenth and fifteenth centuries, celibacy for the clergy was strictly and universally prescribed – in theory. In practice, things were very different indeed, and the Renaissance saw a veritable explosion of sexual liberation from such an unnatural imposition. This, after all, was an inevitable concomitant of everything that the Renaissance stood for, in terms of artistic expression and of a rebirth of the liberated ideals of antiquity. A formidable type of neo-paganism thus took over. The pure and flat virginal figures of pre-Renaissance art gave way to the flesh and blood images that were conceived by the brilliant painters who now came to the fore. Naturalism took over. Nudity inspired no fear. Inhibitions disappeared. Poets and writers contributed the appropriate accompanying text for such developments.

Chapels and churches were among the principal showplaces for such voluptuous exuberances. Ceilings and walls became covered with vast studies in brilliant colours and a mass of half-naked figures. The familiar faces of emperors and popes could be seen languishing in hell, or tumbling to perdition. The almost abstract Jesus of the 'primitive' period of art gave way to what the Irish poet-playwright Paul Vincent Carroll called 'the royal Christ of the Renaissance'. His mother was no longer depicted as a pale and shrinking, flat-chested virgin, but – in the dramatic three-dimensional revolution of the new art – as a buxom matron breastfeeding her divine Son. The curvaceous and voluptuous models for the Madonnas of the Renaissance were, as often as not, mistresses of the artists.

How did all this, after a century of development, translate itself into the world, for example, of Aeneas Silvius Piccolomini, Pope Pius II? As a typical exemplar of the 'schizophrenia' of which I have spoken, Piccolomini was no foreigner to deep spiritual, as well as more fleshly, longings. As a young man he dreamed of becoming a monk, so fired was his heart with the eloquently mystical sermons and writings of St Bernardine of Siena. This man had a powerful attraction for disciples in every age, including our very own Oscar Wilde in more recent times. But lined up against Aeneas Silvius, the would-be mystic, was Piccolomini, the man of the world with the prolific golden pen. Piccolomini's principal studies took place during the pontificate of Martin V (1417–31) whose chief secretary, Poggio Bracciolini, became his literary model.

It was said of the priests of this time that 'all live in adultery or concubinage or worse'. The latter meant incest and/or sodomy. Buggery was the besetting sin of no less than five of the popes of the Borgia Age (though completely absent in the case of the main Borgia pope, Alexander VI). Bracciolini wrote openly in praise of sodomy, while other writers of the period said that it 'raged like a moral pestilence in the larger towns of Italy'. The custom of some women to attend church with their breasts almost exposed was tolerated, in the hope that men's attentions would be diverted.

Each of the pontiffs here described then, is, spoken of as a man and not as just a pope. Historians of the papacy often fail to describe the various popes as flesh-and-blood individuals, whose characters and private lives inevitably had a very strong, if often unrecognized, influence on the events of their pontificates. 'Serious' writers are suspicious of stories (often scandalous and disagreeable) when they come from sources not deemed to have sufficiently respectable academic weight. Thus many incidents are missed or discounted, to the great loss of the general reader, because of the literary or academic equivalent of political correctness.

The danger of passing on inaccuracies when bringing in such material, as already mentioned, can be avoided or minimized by subjecting all historical material of possibly intrinsic value to the same basic and rigorous tests of credibility. It is thus that, as is hoped and submitted, the Renaissance period in papal history can be made to come more vividly alive, with many incidents included which are not necessarily found elsewhere.

Introduction

Much about the popes in question thus originates from many years of collecting often obscure material, sometimes in the form of little more than one-liners or short paragraphs, but almost all containing little-known points or happenings, without whose retailing the story of these particular popes would be incomplete. Meanwhile, 'mainline' sources are listed in a bibliography that is necessarily extensive, in view of the complexity and controversial nature of the overall subject.

PART I:
POPES OF THE EARLY RENAISSANCE

Chapter 1. POPE NICHOLAS V (1447–55)
'The exaltation of the power of the Holy See'

While the Borgias entered the papal scene with Calixtus III (see Part I, chapter 2), it is Nicholas V who is generally considered to have been the first Renaissance pope. He was also the first pope to see the papacy solidly re-established in Rome, after the continuing schism and turbulent century of exile in France. Nicholas' pontificate lasted from 1447–55. His primary concern was to resurrect and restore a Rome devastated by so long a period of neglect. His eight-year papacy coincided with a period of renewed interest in classical literature and philosophy, the rediscovery of classical principles in art and an explosion of creativity in architecture, painting and sculpture. For this reason, his pontificate must be looked at primarily through his artistic and scholarly achievements. In the world of politics and diplomacy, he was more of a conciliator than an innovator.

Nicholas V was born Tommaso Parentucelli, a doctor's son, on 15 November 1397 in Sarzara, near La Spezia. He augmented the family finances by acting as tutor to rich Florentine families, such as the Strozzi, and established a library for Cosimo de' Medici. This led to his being introduced to leading figures in the city that was the birthplace and centre of the Italian Renaissance. At the University of Bologna his doctorate was in theology, rather than the more usual canon law. Twenty years of service to Bishop Niccolò Albergati of Bologna proved a useful training period for his career in the Church. In 1426 he followed his master to Rome and joined the Curia (the papal court and governing bureaucracy at the Vatican).

Because Bologna was in a state of insurrection, Parentucelli was unable in 1447 to take up his appointment as its bishop. Instead he was made papal legate to the Diet of Frankfurt (meeting princes and other dignitaries of the Holy Roman Empire). For his valuable services in persuading this Diet to recognize Eugenius IV as rightful pope, he had been created a cardinal in December 1446. This achievement was the more notable in that it led to the eventual abandonment of a claim to the papal throne by Felix V, the last Avignon anti-pope (rival claimant to the elected pope). On the death of Eugenius IV, Parentucelli was the compromise candidate for the papal throne. He was duly elected, choosing the name Nicholas in honour of his former master. By the time of his election as Pope Nicholas V in 1447, he had met many of the leading artistic and cultural figures of the day and had become a renowned humanist scholar and bibliophile. It is against this background that Nicholas V has come to be recognized as the first Renaissance pope.

Nicholas V's skills as a conciliator were spotted with delight by his colleagues, for these were skills that the Church urgently needed. His other skills became directed to the restoration of Rome. The effects of the papal schism during the fourteenth and fifteenth centuries, together with the enforced absence of Eugenius IV between 1434 and 1443, had left Rome in a state of ruinous neglect. Animals grazed among the ancient monuments, while dirty, unpaved paths linked the crumbling pilgrimage churches to Constantine's dilapidated basilica of St Peter. Clearly concerned by this state of affairs, Nicholas V embarked on an ambitious scheme of urban renewal, ordering the restoration of early Christian churches, the repair of aqueducts, the paving of streets and the erection of fountains. At least 65 stonemasons are listed in the official Vatican records for this period, many of whom held supervisory roles over an enormous workforce. In addition, architects and artists were attracted to Rome, making it the cultural capital of the West.

The pope's motives for undertaking these projects became evident at the end of his life. In a speech made to the cardinals as he lay on his deathbed, in 1455, he said: '...if the authority of the Holy See were visibly displayed in majestic buildings, imperishable memorials and witnesses seemingly planted by the hand of God himself, belief would grow and strengthen like a tradition from one generation to another and all the world would accept and revere it'.[1]

His attempts to reinstate the authority of the Holy See were greatly assisted by the abdication of the anti-pope Felix V in 1449. Nicholas declared 1450 a Jubilee (the term used to describe a 12-month period, every 25 years, nominated as a Holy Year). As thousands of pilgrims from all over Europe flocked to Rome, the papal finances improved significantly. These were boosted by plenary indulgences issued to all those who confessed, repented of their sins, made the prescribed offering of alms and visited the churches of St Peter, St Paul, St John the Lateran and Sta Maria Maggiore. As the money flowed in – the pope reputedly depositing 100,000 gold florins in the Medici bank alone – Nicholas embarked in earnest on schemes to glorify the Church and to set up the papacy as the leader of western civilization.

One of Nicholas V's first and most significant acts was to establish the papacy at St Peter's and the Vatican, abandoning the former principal papal residence in Rome, St John the Lateran. This latter church and its adjoining palace had long been assigned to the popes in their capacity as bishops of Rome. Writing in a letter probably dating from July 1448, the pope explained the reason for this decision, stressing that St Peter's 'excels in the privilege of special dignity among all the churches of the city and of the world', adding that it was 'the chief and mother church and the seat of our apostolic dignity'.[2]

In order to improve the accommodation at the Vatican Palace, Nicholas V employed the Florentine stonemason, Antonio di Francesco, to build a substantial new wing. The building, three storeys high and one room deep, was subsequently extended with a tower at the western end (added during the papacy of Alexander VI). Various schemes were also undertaken to embellish the papal apartments; the only survivor is the exquisite Chapel of Nicholas V. This tiny cabinet-like room, its ceiling almost twice as high as its width or length, was decorated by the Dominican monk, Fra Angelico, with the help of his assistant Benozzo Gozzoli and a workshop in Rome employing three other painters. The two cycles of frescoes, recording scenes from the lives of St Stephen and St Lawrence, were probably commissioned by the former pope, Eugenius IV, shortly before his death in 1447. Having inherited the project, Nicholas V imposed his own mark on the scheme by having himself painted as the third-century pope and martyr, St Sixtus II, in the ordination scene of St Lawrence. Fra Angelico is believed to have painted three other interiors for Nicholas V, including a private study, the Chapel of the Sacrament and the Chapel of St Peter, the latter being located near or on the site of the Sistine Chapel.

The formidable architectural programme undertaken by Nicholas V included the restoration of 40 early Christian churches in Rome, the erection of numerous fortresses across the papal territories, the repair of the ancient Leonine walls around the Vatican and the construction of the Torre Nova. This enormous tower, built to defend the Vatican and St Peter's, acted as a pendant to Castel S. Angelo, itself the subject of extensive restoration works.

Many of the projects were planned with a view to the Jubilee of 1450. The fifth-century Christian church of S. Stefano Rotondo on the Caelian Hill, for example, housed the tomb of St Stephen and was one of the major pilgrimage sites in Rome. In 1446, this circular building was described by Flavio Biondo as being roofless, with damaged mosaics and cracked marble panels. Nicholas V, having appointed the architect and sculptor Bernardo Rossellino as his *Ingenierie di Palazzo* (palace engineer), gave him the task of restoring and reviving this ancient shrine. Between 1451 and 1453, Rossellino consolidated the church, added a new wooden roof, introduced 44 new windows and decorated the interior with marble doors and altars in a classical style to match the old building. (After his sojourn in Rome, Rossellino returned to Florence, where a conspicuous example of his skill is the lantern surrounding Brunelleschi's dome.)

Nicholas V's enthusiasm for building was not confined solely to the Vatican and the churches of Rome, but extended to the most important secular buildings of the city. At the time of his election the medieval Palazzo del Senatore, used as a government office for the civil administration of Rome, was a long, narrow edifice with three floors, a tower at each end and a ramp leading up to the *piano nobile* (main floor). Within five years, Nicholas V had added three wings on the hill overlooking the Roman Forum, creating a courtyard and adding two towers on the rear wing to match those on the front. The work was carried out by the Lombard stonemason, Beltrame di Martino Varese, and the buildings were adorned with marble windows carved by the Roman sculptor, Paolo Romano.

At the same time, the pope also ordered the construction of the Palazzo dei Conservatori, a new palace erected (at an oblique angle to the Palazzo del Senatore) to house the Council of Rome. It is possible that these extensive construction projects were undertaken in preparation for the visit of Frederick III in 1452, during which he was crowned Holy Roman Emperor by Nicholas V in St Peter's – the last such imperial coronation to take place in Rome. However there is no doubt that the pope also intended these grand secular buildings to impress both citizens and visitors with his authority over the city.

Had he lived longer, Nicholas V would have radically transformed the appearance of the Vatican area. According to his secretary and biographer, the Florentine humanist Giannozzo Manetti, his plans included the construction of three new avenues through the chaotic medieval Borgo district, all culminating in the piazza in front of St Peter's; the addition of a conclave hall, chapels, gardens, fountains and aqueducts to the Vatican Palace; and the total rebuilding of St Peter's itself. Although work began in 1452 on a new apse for the great basilica, known as the 'Rossellino choir', this project was left unfinished on the pope's death in 1455 and was later dismantled *c*.1580.

The multi-talented Leone Battista Alberti – an accomplished musician, painter, playwright, mathematician, scientist, architect and the ultimate exemplar of Renaissance man – is widely believed to have acted as an architectural adviser to Nicholas V in his plans for the urban regeneration of Rome. However there is no documentary evidence to prove this, or indeed to suggest in what ways he might have contributed. What is certain is that he presented the pope with his treatise on architecture, *De re aedificatoria* (*Ten Books On Architecture*) in 1452. This was the first Renaissance work to address classical architecture and ideal town planning.

This publication joined the numerous others accumulated by Nicholas V during his papacy. Nicholas was effectively the founder of the Vatican Library, collecting avariciously and declaring his intention to establish 'for the common convenience of the learned, a library of all books both in Latin and in Greek that is worthy of the dignity of the Pope and the Apostolic See'.[3] By the time of his death in 1455 he had acquired at least 1,200 valuable manuscripts, in addition to precious jewels, gold and silver vessels and rich tapestries with which to adorn papal palaces.

Nicholas V was pre-eminently a man of letters, a bibliophile and a friend of scholars such as Leonardo Bruni and Poggio Bracciolini, both of whom were chancellors and historians of Florence. Bracciolini spent much of his career in papal employment, as did other humanists who needed a day job to support the scholarship for which posterity best remembers them. In a tradition that can be traced back to Petrarch (Francesco Petrarca, 1304–74), Bracciolini was an inveterate seeker of manuscript copies of classical texts. It is in the tradition of manuscript hunters that the scholarly interest of Nicholas may be best understood, with the distinction that he was an active patron of Greek as well as Latin scholars. Petrarch had been frustrated by his ignorance of Greek, and Bracciolini never really mastered it. The Ottoman threat to Constantinople prompted Italian merchants and scholars to buy Greek manuscripts there and sell them in Italy. It later caused Byzantine scholars to seek refuge in Rome, Florence and other centres of learning.

References to a papal library can be traced back to the late thirteenth century, but the collection remained in Avignon when the popes returned to Rome. This provided Nicholas with the challenge of starting a papal library anew, encouraging his fellow bibliophiles to continue their searches for Greek and Latin manuscripts to this end. If they found hitherto unknown texts, the sum of human knowledge would increase. Different copies of the same work were no less useful, for comparison of details and identification of inconsistencies allowed scholars to trace the evolution of the text. In this way Nicholas aimed to centralize knowledge, Christian and otherwise, in Rome (making it *caput mundi* – the centre of the world), just as ecclesiastical power and authority were being unequivocally centralized in the person of the pope.

Two rooms in the Vatican Palace were designated to house the library. Work on the Bibliotheca Graeca was complete by 1455, but further work remained on the Bibliotheca Latina. This was only a small portion of the building work undertaken by Nicholas at the Vatican, where he had a substantial three-storey wing added to provide his principal Roman accommodation. This corresponded to the development of St Peter's, at the expense of the Lateran.

Although papal investment, both of funds and interest in the city of Rome, was insufficient to stave off a plot against Nicholas and his cardinals by a Roman citizen, it was, perhaps, enough to stifle it. In 1448, the Roman patrician Stefano Porcari was exiled to Bologna for alleged participation in riots at the death of Eugenius. In January 1453, Porcari returned to Rome. He conspired to found a Roman republic and to end papal rule. The Vatican was to be set on fire at Epiphany and the pope and cardinals captured. If they resisted, they were to be killed. The hope was that a popular insurrection would ensue. In this, Porcari was following in the tradition of Cola di Rienzo (d. 1354) and others who had attempted to rid Rome of both popes and nobles. The plot was discovered. Porcari and his associates were hanged on 9 January. Ironically Porcari was as inspired by the example of ancient Rome as were the humanist friends and clients of Nicholas.

As death approached, Nicholas V attempted to justify his extensive building schemes and extravagant collecting:

> it is not out of ostentation, or ambition or a vainglorious desire of immortalizing Our Name that We have conceived and commenced all these great works, but for the exaltation of the power of the Holy See throughout Christendom and in order that future popes should no longer be in danger of being driven away, taken prisoner, besieged and otherwise oppressed.[4]

His words were charged with emotion, for the Turks had attacked and taken Constantinople in May 1453, bringing the Muslim army of Mohammed II within striking distance of Christian Europe. The threat that this posed was totally to preoccupy his successor, Calixtus III, thereby virtually bringing to a halt any substantial building projects in Rome over the next three years.

While internal divisions had weakened the Church in the first half of the fifteenth century, political and military divisions between states had destabilized Europe in general. Among these was the renewal of the Anglo-French Hundred Years War by Henry V of England. Cardinal Albergati represented the papacy at a peace conference held at Arras in 1435, designed to settle the differences between England, France and England's wavering ally, Burgundy. The initiative failed. Philip the Good, duke of Burgundy, recognized that Henry's heirs had not inherited the king's skills of military and political leadership, and abandoned his English alliance to throw in his lot with Charles VII of France. The conflict continued until the English were finally driven out of Normandy in 1453.

The aim of Nicholas V, as with the other popes of the period, was to preserve the integrity of the papal territory by playing off the other states against each other. However, his strategy was one of conciliation by instinct and nature, as well as policy.

The first major accord was the 1448 Concordat of Vienna, between the papacy and Emperor Frederick III (reigned 1440–93) who was, strictly speaking, still king of the Romans as he had not yet received the imperial crown.[5] By the terms of the concordat, Nicholas undertook to perform the imperial coronation, in return for which Frederick and the German princes promised to cease their long-standing support for anti-papal General Councils. The way was paved for Frederick's coronation in Rome in 1452.

Closer to home, in 1449 Nicholas restored self-government to the cities of the papal states. Apart from reducing tension in the region, this was designed to free manpower for a potential crusade. Indeed all the peacemaking initiatives of Nicholas can be seen as a means to that end. The need for a united Christian defence against the Ottoman Turks was becoming increasingly pressing with each campaigning season. For the most part, Anatolia (Asia Minor) had been in Ottoman hands throughout the fourteenth century, with pockets of resistance such as Trabzon (Trebizond) incorporated into the Ottoman state in the fifteenth century.

From 1365, Edirne (Adrianople), on the road between Constantinople and Belgrade, was also under Ottoman control, and it was from this base that campaigns in the Balkans were mounted. Constantine's imperial city, his second Rome, was effectively cut off by land but still accessible to the western Christian powers by sea. As the Ottomans advanced closer to Venetian possessions on the Adriatic, the republic suddenly appeared vulnerable, depending for its wealth on the transport of spices and luxury goods from the East. This trade accounted for the creation of the sea empire of Venice. It was something of a personal triumph, and it brought peace to Italy for a quarter of a century.

Nicholas V's skills as a pacifier extended to his dealing with men as individuals. When the anti-pope Felix abdicated in 1449, thus leaving Nicholas in undisputed possession of the papal throne, Nicholas rewarded him with the post of cardinal bishop of St Sabrina and a substantial pension. He was also appointed papal legate to Savoy, where he had once been duke.

Nicholas V was not primarily an administrator; he failed to initiate any programme of reform. His principal ambition and achievement was to bring the intellectual and artistic aspirations of the Renaissance into partnership with the Church.

Chapter 2. POPE CALIXTUS III (1455–58)
'See how the treasure of the Church has been wasted!'

The election to the papacy of Alfonso de Borja as Pope Calixtus III was little more than an accident, yet without it, there might never have been such a phenomenon as the Borgia Age. He was the first of only two Spaniards to occupy the pontifical throne. The legacy of this particular man would not of itself have left us with any reason to link the name Borgia (the Italianized version of Borja) with one of the most colourful periods in the history of the Roman papacy. His short pontificate is remembered chiefly, apart from his obsession with a crusade against the Turks, for its nepotism and the momentous consequences thereof. Among those whom he elevated to the cardinalate were three of his nephews. Two of these received the hat when only in their 20s – one was Rodrigo (son of Borja's sister Isabella), who was to become the infamous Pope Alexander VI. The election of Calixtus may have been an accident, but it was to have fateful consequences.

Only 15 cardinals were present at the conclave that assembled in 1455 to elect a successor to Nicholas V. Even by the standards of the time, this was a barely respectable number to elect the most powerful man in the world (part of the statutory description of him, as then bestowed by the Roman Church, was Supreme Governor of the World). Only 9 of the 15 were real churchmen. The 6 lay cardinals, moreover, had no interest whatever in the things of God. Thus more than a third of those in the conclave would be motivated in their choice of the Vicar of Christ solely by personal or political considerations. As usual the occasion was dominated by two camps – the powerful rival factions of the Orsini and the Colonna. Such factionalism was endemic all over Europe at this time, as was violence and ruthless ambition for power.

Initially one candidate seemed to be advancing rapidly. This was Cardinal Bessarion (with a flowing beard, something no pope had ever worn). But his recent conversion from the schismatic Greek Church soon appeared as a risky attribute. Deadlock set in. This is what contemporary conclavists dreaded. The discomforts, claustrophobic atmosphere, lack of adequate sanitation and general fraying of tempers were not slow to make themselves felt. As one chronicler reported, only the notes which their friends smuggled into the conclave relieved the tedium and frustration.

Another active cardinal was the German, Nicolaus von Kues (in Latin, Cusanus), a philosopher who had argued for the superiority of Councils over popes but switched to the opposite camp and served the papacy so effectively as to negotiate the Concordat of Vienna with Frederick III. Neither he nor his fellow bibliophile Prospero Colonna could command the required two-thirds of the votes in the conclave. Then came inspiration. Why not declare their rivalries temporarily suspended and elect 'one of their own', who could maintain the status quo until, after a few months, a few years (who knew?), they could once more get down to the serious business of fighting each other? The suggestion was adopted with immediate enthusiasm; the very man was in their midst.

This was the pleasantly cynical and, above all, elderly Cardinal Alfonso de Borja, who endeared himself to the assembly by making no secret of his sexually active career or his illegitimate children. In this atmosphere of temporary amnesty Cardinal Orsini emerged as *de facto* spokesman, to whom it was made known that the lay cardinals would brook no further delay and were threatening to abandon the conclave unless Borja became pope. It was instantly agreed that everything must be done to avoid such a scandal. Alfonso de Borja was duly elected. At the age of 77, enfeebled by gout, he could safely be relied upon not to reign for long.

Borja exhibited, however, an unexpected burst of energy upon being elevated and, although his papacy was far from lengthy (just over three years), it was long enough to contain one particular act whose result was to make its mark over Christendom not just for years, not just for centuries, but forever – although based, as will be seen, on myth rather than historical foundation. I refer, of course, to the Borgia ascendancy and legend.

As Calixtus III, Borja was utterly focused upon the need for a crusade. A portrait medallion, commissioned from the sculptor Andrea Guazzalotti in celebration of the naval victory over the Turks off the island of Lesbos in August 1457, reflects this firmness of purpose. Around the papal profile were carved the words: 'I was elected for the annihilation of the enemies of the Faith'. Calixtus III came to this task armed with a Spaniard's keen awareness of those enemies, for *convivienca* (co-existence) between Christians, Muslims and Jews in the Iberian peninsula had long since broken down, and it was only a matter of time before the Christian powers finally annihilated that last outpost of Islam in western Europe, the kingdom of Granada. Calixtus was the subject of a prediction by St Vicent Ferrer about his papal destiny – surely God intended him to achieve great things for beleaguered Christendom?

Although his papacy was brief and his time taken up with other preoccupations, Calixtus had some appreciation for the efforts made by Nicholas V to glorify the buildings of Rome. Contrary to reports from contemporary critics (many of whom were humanists who had lost comfortable sinecures within the Curia as a result of the pope's economies to fund his crusade against the Turks), Calixtus made piecemeal gestures to continue his predecessor's work. He may have scoffed 'See how the treasure of the Church has been wasted!' on walking into the magnificent Vatican Library, but as a scholar he valued its contents and appointed the capable Cosimo de Montserrat as its keeper. While major building projects were cancelled, a modest programme of restoration continued, particularly on early Christian churches in Rome. Furthermore – and surprisingly, in view of their pagan origins – this pious pope imposed a fine of twenty-five florins on anyone caught damaging ancient Roman monuments.

Occasionally, Calixtus commissioned an artist to work for him, as in the case of the altarpiece of *St Anne* by the Spanish painter, Pere Rexach. The right-hand panel of this triptych includes a portrait of Alfonso de Borja, kneeling at the feet of St Ildefonso. Rexach was paid a partial sum of thirty pounds in 1452[1] and, as Alfonso appears in cardinal's robes, the painting must have been completed just before he became pope in 1455. Significantly, the altarpiece was ordered not for his church in Rome, but for the Borja sepulchral chapel in the collegiate church of Játiva. The chapel itself had been commissioned by Isabella, sister of Calixtus and mother of the future Alexander VI – the pope's choice was therefore indicative of his patriotic feelings towards Spain, and his dedication to his family and its roots.

Writing on the appointment of Calixtus III in 1455, the archbishop of Florence noted, 'Calixtus has bound himself by a solemn document – a copy of which I have seen – to devote all his powers, with the advice of the cardinals, to the war against the Turks and the reconquest of Constantinople'.[2] This policy, pursued relentlessly until the pope's death in 1458, had significant implications for culture and the arts in Rome.

Faced with the insurmountable problems of raising support from other European rulers, Calixtus set about accumulating his own funds, with which he hoped to raise an army and build a fleet for a simultaneous land and sea assault on Constantinople. Jewels, table services, church vessels and other precious objects from the papal treasury were sold. On seeing Nicholas V's silver salt cellars, Calixtus gave the order, 'Sell them for the Crusade, earthenware is good enough for me'. Paintings and other works of art acquired by his immediate predecessors were also disposed of, and an atmosphere of Spartan frugality descended upon the Vatican. 'We do not blush to admit that, in furtherance of the immortally glorious task of upholding the defence of the Holy Gospel and the orthodox Faith, an enterprise which we pursue even at the cost of sleepless nights, we have indeed been left with a mere linen mitre.'[3]

Artists and sculptors, formerly employed by Nicholas V on fresco painting and other decorative schemes, were either dismissed or were reassigned to the tasks of painting battle standards and carving cannonballs. For this austere and ascetic man, art served its purpose only if dedicated towards the liberation of Christian Europe from the threat of the Muslims.

Philip the Good of Burgundy was critical of Calixtus' plans. Burgundian nobles (knights of the Golden Fleece) often made extravagant crusading vows but failed to back them up with actions. In 1456 Cardinal Trevisan, a Venetian promoted by Eugenius IV, led a fleet to Naples but King Alfonso failed to produce the ships promised for a combined crusading armada. The Hungarians, led by Janos Hunyadi and inspired by the preaching of St Giovanni Capistrano, stood alone against the Ottomans and famously repelled them at Belgrade (1456). Both Hunyadi and Capistrano died shortly afterwards. Calixtus called for this victory to be followed by united action by the Christian powers, but they remained deaf to his appeals.

The single most important action that Calixtus took in relation to the

Borgia Age was in February 1456, when he appointed his nephew Rodrigo, aged 24, as cardinal. From that time on, Rodrigo Borgia took a central part in the affairs of the Holy See. At first, he was of course too young for the burdens laid upon him, but the manner in which he coped with his responsibilities gives a clue to his later character and accomplishments. We shall examine all of this when discussing his career and the part he played in the election of his four papal predecessors: Pius II, Paul II, Sixtus IV and Innocent VIII. In 1457, Calixtus appointed him vice-chancellor of the Holy See. This placed him in what the newspapers today would call 'pole position' in clerical Rome during the next 35 years – until he became pope himself in 1492.

Rome, at this time, was troubled by internal strife. At the coronation of Calixtus, there was an outbreak of Orsini-Colonna violence as the pope tried to make his way through the city along the traditional route from the Vatican to the Lateran. Amid such tension and hostility, to whom could the pontiff turn for reliable support? Like all the other *quattrocento* popes, he promoted members of his family to significant positions within the Church and the government of the papal states. He was inevitably criticized for so doing. The criticism was all the more pointed because of the xenophobic dimension – to the Italians, Calixtus and his family were Catalan-speaking foreigners.

Of the nine men he raised to the cardinalate, four were from the Iberian peninsula, two of them nephews of Calixtus. Promotion of family interests was an integral part of fifteenth-century European society – men of standing were positively expected to use their position to support those interests. Popes Martin and Eugenius had promoted nephews to the cardinalate, and Nicholas bestowed the honour on his half-brother. The nephew of Eugenius had been made vice-chancellor of the Church, the most senior office below that of pope, so there was already a precedent when Calixtus appointed his *nipote* Rodrigo to that powerful position.

Calixtus accompanied his nepotism by an exaggerated preference for appointing fellow nationals to offices within the Vatican. The papacy now became swamped by a mass of men who were the most hated group of foreigners ever to enter the service of the Holy See. This was a key factor in much that was to follow, and the (all Italian) aggrieved members of the

Vatican establishment did not rest until they had seen off the last of these intruders to whom they gave the contemptuous title 'Catalans'.

Thus Calixtus performed two actions that had lasting and controversial results. He introduced a hated, outside element into an intensely jealous, tightly knit and xenophobic sub-community, and brought about the entry into papal history of a name that has come (quite wrongly) to be more sinister and dreaded than any other – Borgia.

Chapter 3. POPE PIUS II (1458–64)
'He who has never truly felt the flames of love is but a stone, or a beast'

Calixtus died on 6 August 1458. The conclave that assembled to elect his successor fairly sparked with drama. The death of Cardinal Domenico Capranica, the day before the conclave met, almost certainly meant the loss to the Renaissance papacy of an outstanding humanist and potential reformer. As it was, the clutch of cardinals coming together on 13 August was dominated by two formidable figures – Guillaume d'Estouteville, cardinal of Rouen, and Aeneas Silvius Piccolomini, cardinal of Siena.

The latter was easily the foremost personality present. Widely travelled, quick-witted, resourceful, highly literate and a man of the world, he also combined flexibility with an ability to be ruthless when necessary. His French rival had none of these qualities, but was cunning enough to spot that his main chance lay in exploiting the cupidity of his colleagues. He moved in without delay, setting up a series of meetings with the other cardinals in the malodorous area set aside for the latrines.

D'Estouteville promised his Roman palace and the much-prized post of chancellor to the powerful cardinal of Avignon. To Bessarion (who, as we have seen, had been a leading candidate in the previous election) and to the other Greeks, he produced large lump sums, there and then. Seemingly conclusive bargains were swiftly concluded with the Italian cardinals. This did not, however, include Piccolomini. D'Estouteville had last seen him praying in the chapel; perhaps he was deliberately pretending not to know what was going on. This was far from being the case. Piccolomini's own plan was already afoot. He had sent a spy to secrete himself in one of the latrines and to eavesdrop on the conspiracy of his rivals. This may have been Cardinal Calandrini. No one knows, as this part of the scenario was only pieced together from evidence emerging later.

On hearing the report that d'Estouteville had secured the necessary amount of promised votes, Piccolomini sought out Rodrigo Borgia, who said that 'the affair is settled'. But Piccolomini was not to be put off so easily. The first scrutiny (examination of the ballot-papers) had been inconclusive. No one was elected. For the next scrutiny, d'Estouteville was assured of 11 of the 12 votes he needed. The critical vote would be taken immediately after Mass the following morning. The cardinals were silently making their way to pray for 'inspiration', when they found that their way into the chapel was barred. Piccolomini was standing across the threshold. He harangued the astonished conclavists about the disaster that would come from the election of the Frenchman. All the horrors of the Avignon years would return. To Cardinal Calandrini, Piccolomini had already described d'Estouteville as a 'limb of the devil'. This put heart into the timid Calandrini. Another of the cardinals was Colonna, Piccolomini's friend and supporter.

Mass was celebrated, followed by the scrutiny. After the cardinals had, one by one, put their voting slips into the chalice, they were transferred to the altar and counted. Piccolomini and several others made careful notes as the names were called out. D'Estouteville, in announcing the totals, declared that eight votes had gone to Piccolomini, who immediately jumped up and cried, 'Look more carefully!' He knew that he had received nine; d'Estouteville six. And so it proved to be.

A stunned silence followed. Unwilling to believe that an effort had been made to cheat at counting the votes, the cardinals finally agreed to proceed to a decision *per accessum*. This meant that a further scrutiny would give way to the emergence of a consensus, by way of a majority acceding to one or other leading candidate by announcing a change of mind. By this time, d'Estouteville was speechless and half-fainting with emotion. He made no attempt to protest at the new course announced by the dean of the College. (One should, perhaps, mention at this point that we owe so detailed an account of this conclave from the explicit and extensive *Commentaries* of Piccolomini himself, in the third person. He was to be the most literate of popes and was a prolific author, always writing as Aeneas Silvius.)

The silence became more and more tense; soon it was all but unbearable. It was finally broken by the voice of the youthful Rodrigo Borgia who, springing to his feet, exclaimed, 'I accede to the cardinal of Siena!' This not only brought Piccolomini a step nearer to victory, it also had the crucial effect of throwing the whole contest open and apparently turning the tide against d'Estouteville. Two of his supporters hurriedly left the chapel, pleading a call of nature. None followed them and they soon returned. At last, one of the more aged of the conclavists, Cardinal Tebaldo, tottered to his feet and declared, 'I too yield to Siena!'

Tebaldo's accession, however quavering, galvanized the conclave. At that point, in Piccolomini's own words, 'a greater panic filled them all, they lost their voices like men in a house that is shaken by a mysterious earthquake. For Aeneas lacked only one vote, since twelve would make a Pope'. Who would cast the decisive one? The cardinals sat motionless, as if literally petrified, in their stalls. Piccolomini tells us that his penetrating gaze moved slowly around, to remain momentarily fixed unblinkingly upon each face. Finally it came to rest upon the formidable figure of Prospero Colonna, known for the exaggerated feeling he had for his own importance. Could this now be brought to life by a recollection of the prestige that went with being a pope-maker? Piccolomini's intent gaze had 'such a power of concentrated authority' that Colonna slowly began to rise, as if he were an automaton responding to some unspoken but irresistible command. What happened next was utterly amazing.

D'Estouteville and Bessarion, gripped by sudden panic as to what Colonna was about to say, flung themselves upon him to ensure his silence, if necessary by force. When he persisted in his determination to speak:

> they tried to drag him forcibly outside, that even so they might snatch the pontificate from Piccolomini. One on the right, one on the left, they tried to lead him away but Colonna, caring nothing for their insults and foolish words, turned to the other cardinals and cried, 'I too yield to Siena and I make him Pope!'

This shocking scene was immediately followed by an action that could have happened nowhere but at a late medieval papal conclave. Within seconds, the panting, dishevelled cardinals fell apart and prostrated themselves in adoration. Such was the magnetic power of a pope, instantly operative from the moment of his election. Piccolomini, the cultured man of letters, remembered that the hero of the poem *Dido and Aeneas* was called by his creator Virgil, 'Pius Aeneas'. Thus Aeneas Silvius became Pius II.

Piccolomini was, in many ways, the most untypical of all the Renaissance popes, at least as to his early career. This was different from that of a more conventional candidate to the papacy. His service to the Church had long remained that of a layman. Born in 1405, he was not ordained until 1446. He became a cardinal ten years later, only two years before being elected pope. His background yielded an unusual two-fold advantage. His skill and success gained him valuable ecclesiastical approval, while also advancing his status as a man of the world. Both circumstances stood him in the highest stead when most needed. His literary output was immense, making him the most prolific pope not merely of the Renaissance but almost certainly of any other period. Originally seeming destined for an academic life, his subsequent early career, in addition to being an author, involved his acting as a secretary to various influential cardinals and being, above all, a successful diplomat.

From comparatively humble origins in the Tuscan village of Corsignano, with no less than 17 brothers and sisters, his subsequent rise to fame and fortune was spectacular. While not all those elected pope at this time were priests, all, with very few exceptions, were clerics (meaning that they had invariably received at least the minor Orders of the Tonsure and Diaconate). Thus those elected to the papacy while still only 'cardinal-deacons' had to be ordained, both to the priesthood and episcopate, before being crowned, since the pope has to be the bishop of Rome. Piccolomini, on the other hand, had spent most of his life as a layman in the service of the Church. As such, he showed originality and brilliance.

As described in the introduction to this book, Piccolomini simultaneously dreamed of becoming a monk and was a man of the world, with prolific golden pen. His literary inspiration was Poggio Bracciolini, famous for his salacious stories written at his desk in the papal offices. In their printed form, they were published in 26 editions over 25 years. For his master the pope, they became the equivalent of bedtime reading, even though, when the *Index of Forbidden Books* was introduced by Pope Paul IV (1555–59), they were referred to the censors for expurgation.

Piccolomini eagerly absorbed the literature that began circulating, in the form of copies of manuscripts, through the circles in which he moved. Nicholas V had commissioned the poet Francesco Filelfo to write a book of stories described as 'the most nauseous compositions that coarseness and filthy fancy ever spanned'. Nicholas found them an amusing relaxation, and paid Filelfo handsomely for their composition. Piccolomini took to writing in a somewhat similar vein.

Much of his material was based on personal experience. The Church, at this time, was attempting to bring the Hundred Years War between England and France to an end, in favour of France, while stirring up the Scottish King James V into enmity with England. In the latter endeavour, Piccolomini played an important part, visiting Scotland as roving ambassador for the papacy. At this time, he began his *Commentaries* (published as *Secret Memoirs of a Renaissance Pope* in 1988), written in the third person, in which he reports that 'the women there [in Scotland] are fair, charming and easily won'. One of them bore him a son whom he greatly loved. He was heartbroken when the baby died. Moving on to England, he was stranded with his two servants, a guide and a bevy of ladies. Two of the latter, he tells us, took him to a chamber strewn with straw, 'planning to sleep with him if they were asked, as was the custom of the country'. But the future pope resisted their advances, for 'fear it would deter him from keeping a watch against robbers'.

Back in Italy, he fell under the spell of the 'divine' Lucrezia di Algano in Naples. She, however, rejected his advances. He sought solace in work and was made secretary to the man who styled himself Pope Felix V. (The latter was actually, as we have seen, an anti-pope, who putatively occupied the Chair of Peter from 1439 to 1449.) Piccolomini had gone over to the 'conciliarist' faction in the Church, of which Felix became champion, as against the official occupant of the papal throne, Eugenius IV. The conciliarists favoured the wielding of the highest authority in the Church by a General Council rather than the pope alone. Controversy on this subject had raged for nearly a century and was at the centre of the long era of schism (1378–1417). This had only been brought to an end by the resignation of two rival popes and the election of Martin V with conciliar backing. As soon as he had become settled into the papacy, whose possession he owed entirely to the authority of the General Council, he ruled that the Council must be subject to the sole authority of the pope. This contradiction did not go unnoticed, but the will to resist, with the hope now being held out for stability at last, had greatly diminished.

Conciliarism, however, broke out again and Piccolomini was a strong supporter. He owed his elevation to the papacy partly because of the conciliarists. The way that the long-standing dispute was finally solved (by none other than Piccolomini/Pope Pius II) was not unlike the 'solution' imposed by Martin V.

The period of working for Felix V (and conciliarism) was a crucial one for Piccolomini. In early 1442, Felix sent him to Strasbourg. His life and career were about to undergo a radical change, though he did not realize it. He was still a fancy-free layman and, although nearly 40, had lost none of the passion of his youth. On arrival in Strasbourg, he 'grew hot and burned for a woman there'. She was a Breton, named Elizabeth, who was married with a five-year-old daughter. She was charming and vivacious; Aeneas was lonely and lovesick. He fell head over heels in love with her, but their dalliance was necessarily short. Her husband, temporarily away, was soon to return, but not before Elizabeth had conceived a child. Their son was born on 13 November 1442. Aeneas was overjoyed and immediately wrote to his father. He was upset when his father replied disapprovingly, and so wrote back another, much longer letter. This is worth quoting almost in full, as it gives a touching idea of how the mind of Aeneas Silvius worked:

> You write that you do not know whether to be glad or sorry, father, that the Lord has given me a child…but I see only cause for gladness and none for sorrow. For what is sweeter to mankind than to beget in one's own likeness and, as it were, continue one's stock and leave something after one's own death? What on earth is more blessed than to see your children's children? For my part, I am delighted that my seed has borne fruit and that some part of me will survive when I die; and I thank God who has made this woman's child a boy, so that another little Aeneas will play about my father and mother and give to his grandparents the comfort which his father should have supplied. For if my birth was a pleasure to you, who begat me, why should not my son be a joy to me? But perhaps you will say it is my offence you mourn, because I have gotten a child in sin. I do not know what idea you have of me. Certainly you, who are flesh, did not beget a son of stone or iron. You know what a cock you were and I no eunuch, nor to be put in the category of cold-blooded. Nor yet am I a hypocrite who wants to seem better than he is. I firmly confess my error, for I am no holier than David the King, nor wiser than Solomon.

Aeneas moved on to the Diet of Frankfurt, which occasioned his joining the court of the Holy Roman Emperor, Frederick III. The latter was much impressed by his considerable oratorical and literary skills, and honoured him with the coveted position of Imperial Poet Laureate. Aeneas thereupon left the service of the anti-pope Felix and indulged himself in the more 'humanist court of the European Frederick'. He became very friendly with the emperor's colourful chancellor, Caspar Schlick, whose amorous adventures inspired Piccolomini's widely read novella *The Tale of Lucretia and Euraylus*. He also achieved great literary fame for his romantic comedy *Chrysis*, written at about this time. The former piece of writing has been described by some historians as pornographic, and the latter as erotic. Both were, it is true, of a distinctly sensual nature, but they were Piccolomini's last ever writing of this kind. For there occurred, at this time, a dramatic and lasting change in his way of life.

Piccolomini's ordination to the priesthood, which came now, was accompanied by a thorough-going and sincere conversion. He was truly a different man from 1446 onwards. Thereafter, not a hint of scandal was associated with his name. As regards moderation in eating and drinking habits, he had no reason to change his style. His abandonment of an unconcealed attraction for sexual freedom was complete, if not total. (This, as any confessor or professor of moral theology will confirm, is not a contradiction in terms.) He even stopped describing himself as a poet, and all his writings after 1446 were very different in nature. *Chrysis* marked the end of this stage of his literary career.

Some writers have described this poem as erotic. Allowing for latitude in the demands of 'taste', this is not an unfair description of the poem's subject matter. The fact, however, that it was positively his last work of this kind is important. At the same time, it must be noted that *Chrysis*, *The Tale* and other writings, though highly literary and polished, were in no way academic exercises. They were derived from his own experiences.

Piccolomini's very earliest work, the book of love poems, *Cinthia* (1427), was inspired by the object of his first love. Aeneas was an impressionable 21-year-old student at the time, and Angela was a Sienese matron who did not return his love. In the early years, many poems of Aeneas were the expression of sublimated, rather than requited, passion. Some were vicarious,

35

such as his second recorded works *Nymphilexis* (1435), a long (2,000 line) love poem written for a friend in Ferrara in praise of the latter's mistress, Battista. It is worth adding that the general earthiness and most explicit of Piccolomini's romantic writings would, in modern Britain, definitively pass the test demanded in a court of law as to what is not pornographic, or in legal language, obscene. The criterion has been established that if a piece of literature is well written, it will almost certainly escape the accusation of being obscene. Many think this illogical as against the more common-sense proposition that, whereas good and polished writing is likely to conceal the immoral nature of any given material, its disgusting and corrupting character will be fully revealed if it is crudely written. As R.J. Mitchell puts it, *The Tale* 'is incomparably better than the worse anecdotes that passed as *Facetiae* when written by Poggio or Ludovico Carbone or the threadbare *Jests of the Widow Earth* that convulsed several generations of English readers'.[1]

Above all, the early writings of Aeneas show him not only to have been a humanist but also as being supremely human. In dedicating his *Tale* to Caspar Schlick, he wrote,

> do not be ashamed to recollect, if anything of this kind ever
> happened to you, that you too were a man. He who has never truly
> felt the flames of love is but a stone, or a beast. It is no secret that into
> the very marrow-bones of the gods has crept the fiery particle.

The obligation of celibacy thus did not come easily to Piccolomini after his conversion. But he coped with it with pragmatic good sense. Not that the burden of clerical celibacy was particularly onerous at this time. In 1432, the Council of Basel demanded (unsuccessfully) that 'all priests from the highest or lowest rank shall put away their concubines, and whoever within two months of this decree neglects its demands shall be deprived of office, though he be the bishop of Rome'. The then reigning pope had been Eugenius IV, while Piccolomini was a prominent delegate at this Council. Eugenius, too weak to dissolve the Council or declare its pronouncements null, tried to upstage it by calling a rival Council in Florence. This decided that the Council of Basel was composed of 'a beggarly mob, mere vulgar fellows from the lowest dregs of the clergy, apostates, blaspheming rebels, men guilty of sacrilege, jailbirds, men who, without exception, deserve only to be hunted back to the devil whence they came'.

Eugenius was furious that his attempt to dissolve the Council had been ignored, and put a mighty effort into seeing that the Council of Florence (1431–45) succeeded. Its principal accomplishment was the healing of the long-standing rift between the Greek and Latin Churches, but the reunion proved only temporary. Piccolomini, as Pius II, felt strongly that the healthy and natural state of matrimony should not be denied to the clergy. He conceded that matrimony had been denied to priests for some good reasons, but there were much better ones for restoring it. Many priests, he felt, would find salvation easier in the married state than in that of enforced celibacy. This was at a time, it should be added, when many local male parishioners would not accept a curate unless he came with a concubine. They were afraid that otherwise he would debauch their wives.

The difference between the world of Piccolomini during the first two thirds of his life – and his own attitude toward this – and that of the final third is not only immense but complex and puzzling. Though his conversion, on taking Holy Orders, was as genuine as any such thing could have been, it was not taken at face value by various onlookers. So vivid an impression did the sparkling and articulate Piccolomini make on the latter, both as poet and, later, as prelate, that many of them failed to perceive that they were indeed dealing with two different people. In fact, it suited them, mostly disappointed humanists as they were, to fail in this regard. It is a telling sign of the times that Piccolomini was popular among his clerical peers as long as they still saw in him the unregenerate worldly poet; but as soon as he showed signs of wanting to be a worthy pope, serving the interests of the Church, they turned against him. This, in essence, was the origin of the 'bad press' that he continues to receive at the hands of many historians.

While enlightened humanism was needed to revitalize the Church with virtue and compassion, a lurch too far could lead to a new and even more advanced form of neo-paganism. Reform was unquestionably needed, but if it was not undertaken from within the Church, and with great humility, it was feared that it could lead to all-out defection (as actually happened when the Reformation finally burst forth). The humanists hoped to profit by having Piccolomini as a patron. Their ambition in this regard was often tinged with inordinate personal ambition, as well as a desire for the triumph of Renaissance ideals. They were far from satisfied when, after he had become a changed man, he showed himself willing to be a friendly critic but no more.

Piccolomini had for years pleased his erstwhile supporters by his support for the conciliarists, but had made no secret of his overriding aim of organizing a crusade to check the Turkish advance into Europe. He lost no time, after his election, in issuing an eloquent crusade Bull and summoning the Christian rulers to the Congress at Mantua to plan the campaign. (The Bull was issued in October 1458, only two months after he had become pope.)

Almost all the Christian rulers, mustering at Mantua for different reasons, let him down. France would do nothing; Germany was lukewarm. The pope concluded in despair that it was the very conciliarism he had once espoused which had reduced papal influence to such an apparently impotent level. In January 1460 he published a *Bull Execrabilis* condemning, in defiance of his own earlier views, all appeals from the pope to a future Council. He reinforced his change of mind in a second Bull, in April 1463, *In Minoribus Agentis*, in which occur the famous words, '*Aeneam reiscite, Pium suscipite*' ('reject Aeneas, accept Pius').

The words have ceaselessly been exploited to demonstrate that Pope Pius II was a shallow, untrustworthy individual with no realistic claim to greatness. But this judgment is to ignore both the genuine transformation that overtook Pius after 1446, as well as the metamorphosis in international affairs that affected the Church after 1458. It is also, perhaps, a mistake in line with those sometimes made by purveyors of Catholic history who, however painstaking, lack a certain gut feeling for Roman Catholicism when not themselves members of the Church. This may seem like a presumptuous implication that non-Roman Catholic writers are unable to give a fully authentic account of Catholic history. This is in no way true. The fact remains that the seemingly monolithic Roman Church is also a delicate and refined apparatus, suffused with puzzling subtleties and baffling paradoxes.

A member of this Church may spot the significance of apparently minor, but in fact important, attributes that an outsider may never see. Moreover, the insider, by virtue of the candour that accompanies familiarity, is acutely aware of two particular dangers. The first is an exaggeratedly favourable view of the 'one true Church' which is infallible and can do no wrong. The second is the growth of myths wherein the 'whore of Babylon' is seen in a nightmarish light. The myths vary from minor to gross. All are, to an extent, harmful; some are merely ludicrous. In this book, we are concerned with one myth in particular, concerning as it does a period of Catholic history simultaneously productive of some of its most pronounced aberrations, as well as some of its greatest glories. This is what I call the 'Great Borgia Myth' (see Part II). According to myth, the Borgia Age got its bad name almost entirely from one man. In reality, it was the other popes of the time who were equally, if not more, responsible for the notorious reputation earned by the period as a whole. There is no question of trying to whitewash Alexander. That would be impossible; it is also unnecessary.

Quite apart, however, from the major myths of received Roman Catholic history, there are many minor ones that appear as irritants and blemishes. They also require correction. It is perhaps worth adding that one cannot appreciate the Roman Church in all its wonder without looking at it, quite frankly, with 'warts and all'. To view it as perfect and to make clumsy excuses for its faults is to do it a great disservice. It is also an injurious activity that unnecessarily exacerbates the differences between the Christian churches.

Among the minor myths concerning Pius II is the popular assumption that he was spiritually shallow. This is completely negated by reference to his interest in Caterina Benincasa (St Catherine of Siena), while also underestimating the spiritual influence he derived from St Bernardine of Siena. The former was a particularly remarkable woman whose short life – only 33 years – occupied the middle period of the fourteenth century.

During his six-year pontificate, Pius II's literary production, already substantial, was more or less confided to his autobiographical *Commentaries*, themselves crucial to the development of autobiography as a genre. While the *Commentaries* provide a unique and highly quotable insight into the man and the pontificate, they should nevertheless be read with some caution. Pius' vitriolic denunciations of certain French prelates for whoring, drinking and violent behaviour, for example, can be understood in the context of traditional animosity between Frenchmen and Italians, an animosity institutionalized in the Avignon papacy and largely French-inspired conciliarism. Xenophobia also lay behind his criticism of Calixtus III for creating three young cardinals, two of them nephews, whose combined age would have been more appropriate for a prince of the Church. As we have seen, Rodrigo Borgia was in his mid-20s when he was raised to the cardinalate. Pius himself accentuated the trend for creating youthful cardinals by promoting a couple of teenagers to the Sacred College. This he did on the flimsy pretexts that one seemed to be so much older than his years, while the other (a nephew who became Pope Pius III) had been urged upon him by the existing cardinals themselves.

For his six brief years, Pius showed his love for his native Siena by providing it with defence from external foe, as well as internal disputes. In a patriotic act in 1461, he canonized St Catherine of Siena. Additionally, Pius also invested intensively in one small corner of the republic – the remote village of Corsignano.

Thirty miles south of Siena, Corsignano was the birthplace of Pius. He returned there in February 1459. A genuine affection for the place, combined with the desire to leave a lasting memorial of his birth, prompted the pope to embark on an ambitious scheme in which at least 40 buildings were either constructed or restored in the new town, between 1459 and 1464. The chief architect for the project was Bernardo Rossellino who, Pius readily acknowledged, was hated by the Sienese workmen because of his Florentine birth.[2] Corsignano was more than just a thoughtfully proportioned, classically inspired and symmetrically planned new town set amid beautiful Tuscan countryside. Its status was elevated to that of a bishopric and its name was changed to Pienza, in honour of Pius himself. A cathedral and episcopal palace therefore needed to be built from scratch, as well as a papal residence, the Palazzo Piccolomini.[3] Together with the town hall, these were grouped around the central piazza to create a fully integrated whole.

Pius envisaged Pienza as not merely a home from Rome, but a Rome from Rome, an alternative capital (albeit outside the papal states) to which the entire Curia could retreat in the plague-ridden months of late summer and early autumn. Such retreats from Rome were standard practice for all who could afford to move at least a portion of their households out to villas or rural monasteries. Pius planned such *villeggiature* on a grand scale, instructing cardinals such as Rodrigo Borgia and Francesco Gonzaga – the one known to be rich and the other assumed to be so – to build their own palaces in Pienza.

In 1462, Pius returned to survey the rapid progress that had been made in Pienza. The Palazzo Piccolomini is described in rapturous detail in the

Commentaries. A fragment of the whole must suffice here:

> As you enter the palace by the main door, you face a large and lofty peristyle, carried around the square court on monoliths, sixteen feet high and proportionately thick, with bases and capitals skilfully set. There are dining-rooms for winter and summer and the seasons between, chambers fit for kings, and storerooms for various things, both over and under the cellar vaulting. For, when they excavated for the foundations of the palace, they quarried out the very hard rock, to a depth of about sixteen feet and constructed vaulted cellars for wine and oil and other provisions. Certainly a noble larder and one it would be very hard to fill.[4]

By 1462, building costs at Pienza more than doubled Rossellino's original estimate, but Pius' account of this discovery twists it into an opportunity to display humour and generosity when, with irony, he addressed the architect:

> You did well, Bernardo, in lying to us about the expense involved in the work. If you had told the truth, you could never have induced us to spend so much money and neither this splendid palace nor this church, the finest in all Italy, would now be standing. Your deceit has built these glorious structures, which are praised by all except the few who are consumed with envy. We thank you and think you deserve especial honour among all the architects of our time.[5]

He ordered full pay to be given to the architect and, in addition, a present of 100 ducats and a scarlet robe.

In one sense, the pope could afford to be generous, for 1462 was also the year in which alum was discovered at Tolfa, inland from Civitavecchia in the papal states. Alum is a mineral that was used for the fixing of dyes in the cloth industry. Traditionally, supplies of alum had been transported from Asia Minor to western Europe on Genoese ships, but this trade dried up in the mid-fifteenth century, making the Tolfa discovery not only exceptionally timely – miraculous even – but also a money-spinner for the papacy and a lucrative business for the papal bankers. Among the latter, the Medici continued to be pre-eminent. Less than a decade later, Lorenzo de' Medici was involved in an attempt to fix the price of alum mined at Volterra, a town subject to Florence, in order to ensure that the Medici continued to benefit handsomely from the Tolfa enterprise. In 1472 this resulted in a military assault on the small town, which was sacked.

The tranquillity of this glorified villa life should not allow us to be distracted from the problems which pressed upon Pius II, as they did on all of the other Renaissance popes. Their inability to control the vicars, who governed portions of the papal states, was something of a running sore. In Pius' time, the principal irritant in this region was Sigismondo Malatesta, *signore* of Rimini on the Adriatic coast, though Pius compounded the problem by proposing highly unfavourable peace terms to him in 1459. Pius was so determined to humiliate the rebellious Sigismondo that not even excommunication was sufficient punishment. In 1462, he went so far as to 'canonize' him to hell – a unique distinction that has tended to cloud a more balanced appreciation of Malatesta and his iniquities.

Ironically, Pius and Malatesta had a mutual associate in the person of Leone Battista Alberti, who designed the thoroughly classical exterior of S. Francesco – the so-called Tempio Malatestiano – at Rimini, and went on to advise Pius on the transformation of Corsignano. The Venetians generally gave tacit support to Pius' enemies in the early years of his pontificate, and the pope could not have made plainer his attitude towards them:

> Too much intercourse with the Turks has made you the friends of the Mohammedans and you are no more for religion…But what do fish care about law? As among brute beasts, aquatic creatures have the least intelligence, so, among human beings, the Venetians are the least just and the least capable of humanity and naturally, for they live on the sea and pass their lives in the water. To a Venetian, that which is just is what is for the good of the state; that which is pious is what increases the empire.[6]

Compared with the other challenges of Pius' pontificate, Malatesta was, comparatively speaking, something of a little local difficulty. The pope's relations with more powerful rulers deteriorated in proportion to his growing determination to launch a crusade, which they were equally determined to resist. As Pius reflected of himself, 'Among all the purposes he had at heart, none was dearer than that of rousing Christians against the Turks and declaring war against them'.[7] Although Serbia and the Morea (Peloponnese) fell to the Ottomans in 1459, the Christian powers remained indifferent to papal appeals for both unity and a crusade. That indifference was never more obvious than when Pius summoned representatives of the various Christian states to the Congress at Mantua. Painfully thin attendance suggested that it was not just the Venetian republic that was 'no more for religion'. Well versed in conciliar thought and history as he was, Pius feared that failure to heed the papal summons could lead to renewed calls for a General Council. Closing the damp squib that was the Mantuan Congress on 20 January 1460, Pius condemned anti-papal appeals to General Councils.

His primary target was France, where papal power continued to be constrained by the so-called Pragmatic Sanction (of which more later). French hostility to Rome was compounded by papal and Milanese support for Ferrante, king of Naples, when René of Anjou made a bid for the Neapolitan crown in 1460. Ferrante was defeated in battle at Sarno. There were repercussions in and around Rome, where the Colonna, Savelli and Anguillara families revolted and Jacopo Piccinino's men threatened the city in Pius' absence. In 1461 Piccinino retired to the Abruzzi, and Federico da Montefeltro of Urbino forced the Savelli to capitulate. The following year, the citizens of Anjou were defeated by Ferrante and Francesco Sforza, while Federico da Montefeltro quashed Sigismondo Malatesta of Rimini.

Each successive loss of Balkan territory by Christian rulers to the Ottomans inevitably reverberated in Rome, and resulted in ever more urgent but nevertheless unheeded calls for crusading initiatives. One loss had a greater and quite bizarre impact in Rome. The deposed despot of the Morea – a member of the Paleologo dynasty that ruled in Constantinople until 1453 – made his way to Rome, which was an 'open city' for exiles from all quarters. With him he brought the head of the apostle St Andrew, to protect it from the infidels and to reunite it with the relics of Andrew's brother, St Peter. Pius' account of the Roman reception, with which the head was honoured on Palm Sunday 1462, gives the impression of ceremonies unparalleled since the return of the papacy to Rome. He insisted that the cardinals accompany the head on foot, from Sta Maria del Popolo to St Peter's, at least as far as their infirmities would allow:

> It was a fine and impressive sight to see those aged men walking
> through the slippery mud, with palms in their hands and mitres on

their heads, robed in priestly vestments, never lifting their eyes from the ground but praying and invoking the Divine Mercy upon the people. Some who had been reared in luxury and had scarcely been able to go a hundred feet, except on horseback, on that day, weighted down as they were with their sacred robes, easily accomplished two miles through mud and water.[8]

The city route was suitably decorated for such a festive occasion, but the most elaborate decorations of all were those provided by Rodrigo Borgia, the vice-chancellor, for his own palace and all the neighbouring buildings:

> His huge, towering house…was covered with rich and wonderful tapestries, and, besides this, he had raised a lofty canopy, from which were suspended many and various marvels…On the walls were hung many poems recently composed by great geniuses, which set forth in large letters praises of the Divine Apostle and eulogies of Pope Pius.[9]

The by now gout-ridden pope was carried aloft on the *sedia gestatoria* (portable papal throne) into St Peter's basilica. There Cardinal Bessarion stepped forward and made a speech in the person of St Andrew. Pius himself replied as St Peter. East and West were once again reunited in the persons of the two brothers. The spectacle and the speeches were designed to inspire observers with crusading fervour. If it succeeded in doing anything of the kind, the effect was short-lived.

In 1461 the new king of France, Louis XI (reigned 1461–83), sent emissaries to negotiate with Pope Pius. Louis consistently opposed Pius' support for Ferrante against the Angevin claim to Naples, but he nevertheless agreed to revoke the Pragmatic Sanction. This was a measure of the king's strength, not his weakness, for the Pragmatic Sanction had given French nobles powers over appointments to benefices and Louis was determined to destroy noble power and prerogatives. The overarching theme of his reign was the creation of a unified state, at the expense of independent or semi-independent duchies, with power centralized in his hands. By 1463, however, France and the papacy were once more estranged and Louis declined all invitations to participate in a crusade. In 1464 Louis was threatened with excommunication when he expressly told Charles the Bold, then count of Charollais, not to participate in the crusade. Louis was unbowed and responded with the perennial anti-papal threat to summon a General Council. Gallicanism – the assertion of so-called 'Gallican liberties' against Rome, by the Church in France – was once more in the ascendant.

Pius never lost his burning desire to launch a successful crusade against the infidel. The fall of Bosnia to the Ottomans and the execution of its king, in 1463, were the spurs that prompted him to lead this. Whereas the Christian powers had been able to resist his exhortations to 'do as I say', he calculated that they would be impelled to 'do as I do'. The following year he personally 'took the Cross', as generations of crusaders had done before him – although the prospects of inspiring princes and rulers to join him seemed as remote as ever. Preparations were inadequate for a serious military campaign, but this did not deter Pius. In the summer of 1464 he headed eastwards from Rome and got as far as Ancona, the principal port on the Adriatic coast of the papal states, where he waited for the Venetian fleet, led by the Doge, Cristoforo Moro. As the days passed and the fleet failed to appear, Pius, who had been in poor health for some time, grew progressively weaker. Moro and his fleet arrived just in time to honour the passing of the pope, who died at Ancona on 15 August, and whose body was transported back to Rome by cardinals more eager to contest the election than they were to pursue the ill-fated campaign.

The death of Pius was both noble and pathetic. It came in tragic fulfilment of the prophecy contained in his speech, addressed to the cardinals in a secret consistory nearly a year before (23 September 1463):

> We shall imitate Our Lord and Master, Jesus Christ, the blessed shepherd, who did not hesitate to lay down his life for his sheep... We too shall lay down our life for our flock...to help the Christian religion that it be not trampled under foot by the Turks. We shall arm a fleet as great as the resources of the Church permit, we shall go on board ship; old man and broken by infirmities as we are, we shall spread our sails to the winds and be carried to Greece and Asia...We hear your murmurs: If you consider the war so difficult, with what hope do you go on it, when you lack sufficient resources? We are coming to that. War with the Turk threatens us unavoidably. Unless we arm and go against the foe, we believe that our religion is done for. We shall be among the Turks as today we see the despised

race of Jews among the Christians. Unless we make war, we are disgraced...

Our position is that of bankers who have lost their credit; nobody trusts us. The priesthood is a laughing-stock, the very name of cleric is an infamy. They say we live for pleasure, hoard up money, serve ambition, sit on fat mules or pedigree horses, spread out the fringes of our cloaks and go about the city with fat cheeks under our red hats and ample hoods; that we breed dogs for hunting, spend freely upon players and parasites, but nothing in defence of the faith. Nor is it all a lie. Many of the cardinals and other courtiers do all these things and, to speak the truth, the luxury and extravagance of our curia is excessive. Because of this, we are hateful to the people, so much so that, even when we speak the truth, they will not hear us. What, in your opinion, must we do amid such scorn?

...We must turn into paths abandoned long ago. We must find by what methods our forerunners created for us this vast dominion of the Church, and use them. For power is easily retained by those methods which first created it. Abstinence, chastity, innocence, zeal for the faith, religious fervour, contempt for death, desire for martyrdom: these things put the Church of Rome at the head of the whole world...We must go back to those forerunners, who gave their bodies for God's testament. There is nothing we ought not to endure for the preservation of the flocks entrusted to us, even though it means laying down our life...We must die one day and we do not mind where, provided we die well.

There could have been no more trenchant critic of the papacy and of the Church of the day than the pope himself. His desire for reform was genuine. His inability to bring it about was his tragedy.

It is tempting to look back on the pontificate of Pius II as the golden age of the Renaissance papacy. As it happens, the expression 'golden age' was applied to the period corresponding to the pontificates of Julius II and Leo X (see Part III), but was appropriate thereto only in a strictly relative sense. The period in question saw the ascendancy of Michelangelo, Raphael, da Vinci and Bramante. What can, however, be said of Pius II's reign is that, compared to what was to follow, it was truly a blessed and felicitous period.

Chapter 4. POPE PAUL II (1464–71)
'He is surrounded by darkness'

Pius II's successor was the Venetian, Pietro Barbo, who reigned as Pope Paul II. While in physical appearance he was the handsomest of all popes, in his character and habits he was one of the least admirable. He was well aware of his good looks and wanted to assume the papal name of Formosus (Greek for 'handsome'). Apart from anything else, this choice of title would have brought back memories of the only pope ever to have assumed this name. This was the Formosus (891–96) whose fame was due to what happened to him after his death. His body, on the orders of his successor but one, Stephen VI, was exhumed, propped up against the altar in full canonical vestments and subjected to a mock trial. This bizarre episode was known in papal history as the Cadaver Synod.

With his other choice of Marco having being ruled out as too reminiscent of the Venetian war-cry, 'Marco! Marco!', Barbo settled for the name Paul. The name that would have suited him best would have been Narcissus, as he never tired of gazing at himself admiringly in the looking-glass. Indeed he was known to many at the time as 'Pope Narcissus'. He was a voluptuary, who took an excessively sensuous pleasure in beauty in all its forms. Apart from admiring his own features, patrician hands and fine presence, he delighted in peopling his court with beautiful women and graceful youths. When the spirit moved him, he would single out some of the latter, order them to be stripped naked, then racked and tortured. He enjoyed seeing all this being enacted as he lay back amid silk cushions, sipping wine and swallowing grapes and slices of melon, a fruit of which he was particularly fond.

Naturally, details such as these – with no little loss – have not been given pride of place in most of the conventional accounts of his pontificate. He owed his early and rapid preferment to his uncle Gabriel Condelmieri, Pope Eugenius IV, who received him into the ecclesiastical state when he was 14. He had originally been intended for commerce but was persuaded that, in his case, the Church would provide a more lucrative career. He became a cardinal at the age of 23, as bishop of Ceriva, and was also later bishop of Vicenza. In addition, his uncle arranged for him to receive the relatively obscure privilege of becoming a protonotary apostolic of the Roman Church. The power and influence of this particular office was, at that time, considerably greater than most commentators realize. It still exists, but only nominally, and is held by domestic prelates in the highest of the three monsignorial ranks.

His suave and courteous manner enabled him to achieve a reputation for affability and generosity, which his fellow cardinals misunderstood. At the conclave of August 1464, they mistakenly formed the view that, once in office, he could be easily manipulated. Before the conclave, he had signed a 'capitulation' whereby he and the rest of the cardinals swore themselves to an 18-point electoral pact defining the next pope's agenda and calling for a General Council within three years. Other points included fixing the number of cardinals at 24, reforming the Curia and continuing the war against the Turks.

No one was more enthusiastic for such measures than Barbo, his enthusiasm proving all the more persuasive because of his ingratiating demeanour and, human nature being what it is, his urbanity and seductive good looks. He was duly elected on the first ballot. He immediately announced that the electoral pact had provided only guidelines, not mandates, for the coming pontificate. Before the cardinals had recovered from this first shock, he drew up an agreement of his own, making it clear that he intended his rule to be absolute. He summoned the cardinals, one by one, into his chamber, cajoling and/or threatening them to sign the pact. All but one gave in. The spirited Greek Cardinal Bessarion tried to escape but the new pope leaped forward and dragged him back, locking the door and threatening him with excommunication.

The cardinals, though they had capitulated, remained sullen and resentful. Another surprise was in store for them, however – of a different kind. Inordinately vain himself, Pope Paul II shrewdly played upon the vanity of the cardinals by ensuring that they could reflect and share his love of splendour and magnificence. As long as they remained subservient to him, and provided his tall and stately figure could be seen to stand out in every procession, they too were permitted to wear red hats and display purple cloaks and horse-trappings hitherto reserved for the pope alone.

The new pope not only revived the use of the triple crown first worn by Urban V (1362–70), but went a step further. He had a crown specially made for himself, heavier than any previously used. (The excessive weight, it was rumoured, eventually helped to bring about his death.) The magnificent crown was richly encrusted with precious jewels and was valued at 120,000 ducats, three times the hitherto unprecedentedly large amount expended for a similar purpose by his papal uncle.

It may seem that too much is being made of these trivial and outward circumstances. To Pope Paul II, however, they were the very circumstances that mattered most. His eccentricity, morever, combined with his love of opulence, had extremely inconvenient consequences for his officials. He devoted as little time as possible to his papal duties, all of which he carried out only at night. He summoned audiences and other functions at times that suited him, usually in the small hours of the morning. He spent long hours during the day in bed but, owing to chronic asthma, slept only fitfully. He did not particularly mind this, because of his natural indolence and always provided he could retire with a large quantity of precious jewels under his pillow. These he would gaze at and fondle lovingly, sensuously letting them trickle through his shapely fingers. It was only discovered much later that he horded these secretly. At intervals, over the years that followed, caches would be discovered in unexpected places all over the Vatican (and his other, private palace), brimful of gorgeous jewels. He had secreted them away, as an alcoholic might hide bottles of drink.

During his waking hours, he devoted a minimum of time to official duties, having his own original and remarkably effective idea of good government. He treated the citizens of Rome to a more or less perpetual carnival, which he also greatly enjoyed himself. He knew full well that this would please the populace far more than any amount of improvements or good works. That the carnival was clung to with zest for many decades to come showed how right he was. He ensured himself further popularity – and much needed revenue for the papacy later on – by decreeing in April 1470 that, beginning in 1475, there would be a 'Holy Year' every 25 years. He loved festivities of every kind and, following the contempt shown by almost all popes toward the Jews, financed the non-stop entertainment with the help of forced contributions from the ghetto. Such outcasts, after all, could be collectively exploited at will. (An enlightened view of the Jews by the Church has only come about in very recent years, apart, as it happens, from the view taken by Alexander VI.)

Paul II watched the various celebrations from his balcony, either in the Vatican or in the palace he built for himself in the Piazza S. Marco. Having been appointed cardinal priest of the ancient basilica of S. Marco in 1455, he had embarked on the rebuilding and restoration of this church and the construction of the neighbouring palazzo, works that were to continue after his election in 1464. By 1468, the irregularly shaped ninth-century church had been transformed into a symmetrical building, with columns and vaulted aisles. The new coffered ceiling, in blue and gold, was lavishly decorated with Paul II's heraldic crest, incorporating the lion rampant – a symbol reminiscent of the lion of St Mark, the patron saint of Venice, and therefore also appropriate for the church of the Venetian community in Rome.

In addition, a fine new façade of travertine marble was added, providing a two-storey benediction loggia of three bays overlooking the Piazza S. Marco. This architectural embellishment, using prototypes from the ancient classic monuments of Rome, is widely attributed to Giuliano da Maiano, although Alberti may also have been involved in its conception. It is similar to Pius II's four-bay Benediction Loggia at St Peter's (to which Paul II added a second storey of arcades).

The adjoining Palazzo S. Marco, begun in 1455 and completed in 1471, marked a significant development in the palace architecture of Rome. Although it still reflected the militarized elements of earlier papal residences, with rooftop crenellations and the ubiquitous cardinal's tower at one end, this great Renaissance palace, the first of its kind in Rome, was a far cry from the heavily fortified Vatican towers built by Nicholas V.

Following his election, Paul II employed the architect Francesco del Borgo to enlarge his palace still further and, by 1466, he had adopted it as his principal residence. The luxurious and highly decorated interiors of the Palazzo S. Marco were lavishly furnished with the Pope's extensive collections of Flemish tapestries, Byzantine icons, paintings, statues, bronzes, mosaics, coins, medals and innumerable antiques, all of which he collected avariciously. The palace even incorporated its own private foundry, turning out bronze plaquettes. Subsequently renamed the Palazzo Venezia, this vast building was occupied many years later as the headquarters of the Fascist Party and official residence of Mussolini. The magnificent Sala del Mappamondo on the first floor, 70 feet long, 40 feet wide and rising two storeys in height, became an office from which the Duce would emerge onto the central balcony to address the crowds below. Pope Paul II might similarly have emerged to watch the horse races of his carnivals.

Superficial and indolent though he was, Paul II was not unaware of certain measures that needed to be undertaken on behalf of the Church. He gave firm government to the city of Rome and, apart from keeping its citizens contented and entertained, tightened discipline and instituted civic reforms. Unlike most of the popes of his time, he did not engage in simony (the buying and selling of ecclesiastical privileges), and he curtailed certain other forms of abuse, particularly in the sphere of administration. The formal documents for the papal chancery were the concern of the 'abbreviators', who were appointed by the vice-chancellor and held office for life. Paul II reorganized them into a new and smaller college, limiting their number to 70 and restricting the vice-chancellor's nominations to 12. This had the double effect of controlling a source of corruption in the papal court and reducing the influence of the vice-chancellor, who happened to be Cardinal Borgia (later Alexander VI).

Although Paul II's dilettantism and clumsy Latin earned him the disdain of intellectuals, he was easily their match in the battle of wits. They did not carry their convictions so far as to refuse his lavish gifts of silver and gold. Meanwhile, spurred on by his love for objects of physical beauty, he was an avid collector of works of art and he installed the first printing press in Rome. Furthermore, Paul II believed in the active restoration of Rome, motivated – as was Nicholas V – by a desire to promote the power of the papacy and emphasize the splendour of the Christian capital. He not only continued the work of his predecessors on the rebuilding of early churches, including St John the Lateran and Sta Maria Maggiore, but also instigated restoration work on the Pantheon, the ancient pagan arches of Titus and Septimus Severus, and the classical statues of Marcus Aurelius and Alexander and his horse Bucephalus.

Simultaneously, contemporary sculptors such as Bartolomeo Bellano and Mino da Fiesole were frequently commissioned by Paul II. The former produced a life-size statue of the pope, which was completed in 1467 and erected outside the cathedral in Perugia. Even in death, extravagance and vain display prevailed. Paul II's tomb, paid for by his nephew, Marco Barbo, and carved by Mino da Fiesole and Giovanni Dalmata, was the largest and most elaborate fifteenth-century tomb in Rome. It formed the shape of a magnificent triumphal arch, with the marble effigy of the pope lying recumbent on a sarcophagus, and was richly decorated with carved reliefs. It did not survive the subsequent rebuilding of St Peter's, although fragments still exist in the Vatican Grottoes and in the Louvre in Paris.

Paul II's curtailment, as mentioned above, of the excessive numbers and privileges of the 'abbreviators' involved the closing of the Roman Academy in 1468. As the Academy was an elitist enclave of various (more or less genuine) literary figures, this act has been cited by some commentators as proof of his philistinism and spite against scholars. However, the allegation is an example of a not uncommon mistake made by historians of the Renaissance papacy. Worthless as he was in most respects, Paul was not acting out of pure pique, or through philistinism, in abolishing the Academy. What was once an authentic assembly of scholars and antiquaries (attracted to the Stoic teacher, Pomponius Lectus) had deteriorated into a pretentious and affected association, gaining its members chiefly from the ranks of the unemployed former abbreviators.

The whole incident produced one of the few occasions when one is almost tempted to feel some admiration for Paul II. One of the Academy's faculty members, Bartolomeo Platina, made a public condemnation of Paul's predecessor, Pius II, accusing him of being a tyrant. Apart from his occasional impetuous indiscretions, this was the last thing he was. Unfortunately, Paul overreacted. He had Platina thrown into the dungeons of Castel S. Angelo to do penance. When Platina protested, the pope ordered him to be tortured. He also had Pomponius Lectus imprisoned as an accomplice. The prisoners now employed a different strategy and promised 'to celebrate in prose and verse to the name of Paul', if he would set them free. At this point, Paul appears to have lost any real interest in the affair. He concluded that the two Stoic philosophers were merely silly and shallow.

Accordingly he ordered their release, but ultimately with unhappy results for himself. Platina was an historian, and he took his revenge on Paul by giving an extremely unfavourable account of him in his *Lives of the Popes*. He refers to him as 'a great enemy and despiser of human learning, branding those for heretics that gave their minds to it'. The whole affair was a sad example of one of this pope's most fatal weaknesses. Though potentially domineering and overbearing, he was often too lazy to act with consistency. While not afraid to strike, he did not always go for the kill. His instincts about the Academy were quite correct, and his disapproval of its neo-pagan ideas and its attacks on the Church, by using the weapons of buffoonery, may even have been a demonstration of a latent realization of his duties as 'Vicar of Christ'.

His reputation in history, at any rate, owes much to his treatment at the hands of Platina, despite no lack of appropriate material with which to paint an unfavourable picture. As for the Academy and Platina, their fortunes revived under Sixtus IV (see Part I, chapter 5), by which time the Church was suffering from different and far worse troubles.

Paul II tried unsuccessfully to mount a crusade against the Turks. The Christian ruler who might most appropriately have led such a crusade, the king of Bohemia, was suspected of being a Hussite. Paul excommunicated him in 1466 and even singled him out as the deserving object of a crusade.

In 1471 Pope Paul II died, aged only 54. Several Roman versions exist as to the cause of death. One is that, on donning his weighty tiara on one final occasion, he died of apoplexy. Some say he was strangled at dead of night. Most accounts say he expired after gorging an excessive amount of the melons that he so enjoyed. These, however, are typical fantasies of the Borgia Age. What almost certainly happened was that, after an immoderate feasting on melons, he expired from the excessive effect of being sodomized by one of his favourite boys.

Apart from such encounters, he did not care for intimate intercourse of any kind; even his three nephews were not especially favoured. Impartiality and superficial kindness were his chief social characteristics. He hated to refuse petitions and therefore gave few audiences. Above all, he dreaded condemning criminals to death. And yet he could be severe on occasion, as when he would suddenly turn upon an impostor with an accusation of untruthfulness. 'He is surrounded by darkness' was one verdict, and the knowledge that he was not loved saddened him for, as he said himself, 'a little wormwood can pollute a hive of honey'. The best that can be said of his pontificate was that it contained no initiative with lasting evil effects for the Church and the world. This is more than can be said of the reigns of his two immediate successors.

Chapter 5. POPE SIXTUS IV (1471–84)

'He lowered the moral tone of Europe'

The dominating desire of Sixtus IV, successor to Paul II, was to obtain for his family a leading position in Italy. Other popes had engaged in simony – some out of family loyalty, others from political considerations – but under him it became the chief influence in papal policy. Under him, moreover, the worst defects of the Renaissance papacy were glaringly revealed for the first time. Its vices were now seen to have outstripped its virtues (as appearing under Pius II), and the new pontiff's own development provides a striking example of the corrupting influence of office. Paradoxically, however, this pontificate saw the achievement of some of the most glorious artistic accomplishments of the Renaissance period.

Francesco della Rovere, the son of poor parents at Savona, entered the Franciscan Order at an early age. As a teacher at various Italian universities, he was highly esteemed by Cardinal Bessarion and other serious churchmen for his learning, skill in controversy and apparent zeal for reform. In 1467, aged 53, he was general of his Order and cardinal of S. Pietro in Vincoli. So unimpeachable a record fully justified his election. Nevertheless, such expectations as he had aroused were belied from the start. It was as though the purely secular tastes and ambitions so long pent up within the churchman suddenly burst out with uncontrollable force. The keynotes of his pontificate were lavish grandeur in Rome and unscrupulous political initiatives in the rest of Italy.

The extent of his nepotism scandalized even the least sensitive of his contemporaries. Of his six young nephews, two – Giuliano della Rovere (later Pope Julius II) and Pietro Riario – were immediately made cardinals, and a third, Girolamo Basso, was similarly promoted a few years later. A shower of offices and favours descended on other members of his family.

Pope Sixtus IV has had a mixed reception from historians. Verdicts vary from his being damned with faint praise, to being denounced as a 'bountiful benefactor toward whores'. He did, however, achieve some creditable accomplishments. From his own point of view, there is no doubt that he wished to be seen as a saintly and religious man, a benefactor and leader of the people, and a true Renaissance prince. Nowhere are these combined spiritual and temporal aims more clearly defined than in the reconstruction and revival of the Hospital of Santo Spirito, in which Sixtus IV took an intense personal interest. This project, undertaken between 1473 and 1482, was undoubtedly his most significant contribution to the public secular buildings of Rome.

Situated on the Borgo Santo Spirito, one of the three main routes from the Ponte S. Angelo to the Vatican, it still functions to this day as a hospital. It was originally founded between 1198 and 1201 by Pope Innocent III, a papal predecessor revered by Sixtus IV. The initial purpose of the institution was to provide a haven for the foundlings and orphans of Rome. In undertaking its radical reconstruction, Sixtus IV not only maintained this function but also dramatically added to the hospital's facilities, in an attempt to improve the provision of healthcare for both Roman citizens and visiting pilgrims. By the time the major building work had been completed, in the summer of 1476, the Hospital of Santo Spirito had become the largest building in the area, rivalling even old St Peter's.

The earliest surviving inventory of the hospital, taken in 1536, lists a cloistered courtyard for abandoned infants and their wet nurses, flanked by a dormitory accommodating 14 female and 5 male foundlings. In addition, there were 65 beds in the Corsia Sistina, this being a vast infirmary for the indigent sick; a further 30 beds for wounded patients in the 'Hospidaletto'; and new living quarters for the staff. Innovatively, Sixtus IV also ordered the construction of a separate courtyard for noble patients, with accommodation for their servants on the ground floor and spacious airy chambers above for the sick. Writing in 1581, a century after the completion of the building, Gregory Martin described the sumptuous luxury of the facilities for the rich:

> Also fairer chambers above with their galleries for gentlemen...
> There may come gentlemen and gentlemen's servants, who, in their owne lodgings, neither should nor could be so conveniently attended.[1]

In providing such an institution for all classes of Roman society, many of them known for their turbulent opposition to papal authority in the past, Sixtus IV no doubt hoped to foster support and obedience. Certainly he left the beneficiaries of his charitable works in no doubt as to who had instigated this massive social project by commissioning local workshops of artists to embellish the main infirmary and its chapel with an imaginative scheme of fresco decoration. This cycle of painting is clearly indicative of how the pope wished others to see him, and also demonstrates what he must have considered to be among his greatest achievements. Following the initial image entitled *Innocent III Orders the Construction of the Hospital*, a series of biographical scenes from the life of Sixtus IV include *Sixtus IV Visits the Old Hospital*, *The Reconstruction of the Old Hospital*, and *Sixtus IV Founds the Vatican Library*. There are also numerous views depicting the pope receiving foreign rulers and, as if to emphasize his spiritual as well as temporal authority, the cycle culminates in the extraordinary *Entry of Sixtus IV Into Paradise*.

In addition to expanding the city's hospital accommodation, Sixtus IV is also credited with the transformation of Rome from a medieval to a Renaissance city. As the first pope to make a substantial impact on this urban environment since Nicholas V, his building projects were surpassed in Renaissance times only by those of his nephew, Julius II. Old streets were widened and paved, and new roadways were opened up such as the Borgo S. Angelo, a straight avenue leading from the Castel S. Angelo to the Vatican. Other improvements designed to facilitate the progress of pilgrims to St Peter's included the construction of the Ponte Sisto to relieve the crowds crossing the Tiber via the Ponte S. Angelo during the Jubilee year of 1475. The parapet of the bridge bears an inscription inviting all those crossing it to pray for its creator: 'You who pass by here offer a prayer to God so that Sixtus IV, excellent Pontifex Maximus, may be healthy and for long so preserved. Any of you, whoever you are, to whom this request is made, be healthy too'.

The role of Sixtus IV as the people's artistic benefactor was epitomized by his decision, in 1471, to move an important collection of antique sculptures from the papal church of St John the Lateran to Nicholas V's Palazzo dei Conservatori on the Capitol. The group included the famous Etruscan bronze of the she-wolf, associated with Romulus and Remus, dating from the fifth century BC, and the colossal head of Constantine II from a fourth-century statue – both of which are still housed in the Capitoline Museums. The pope's intention, as stated on an inscription erected at the time, was to 'restore' these classical relics, 'in his immense benignity', to the people of Rome. It was an important gesture, for it suggests an early attempt to create the first public museum in the city.

Church architecture in Rome also benefited from the pope's munificence. The Augustinian church of Sta Maria del Popolo was rebuilt between 1472 and 1480, to the designs of Baccio Pontelli and Andrea Bregno. This was one of the earliest Renaissance churches in the city, and was subsequently used as the burial place for the della Rovere family. The church of Sta Maria della Pace, built on the orders of Sixtus IV between 1478 and 1483 in honour of the Blessed Virgin, commemorated the end of the war with Florence.

Just four months after his election in August 1471, Sixtus IV began the conversion of two large rooms on the ground floor of Nicholas V's wing at the Vatican. Following on the efforts of his predecessor, the pope announced his intention to install the Bibliotheca Graeca and the Bibliotheca Latina in these chambers, describing this plan – in remarkably similar terms to those of the original founder – as being: '…for the enhancing of the Church militant, for the increase of the Catholic faith and for the convenience and honour of the learned and studious'.[2]

The Vatican Library and archives having thus been established and opened for the first time to scholars, Sixtus IV appointed the humanist, Bartolomeo Platina (formerly tortured under Paul II), as his librarian. In order to commemorate both the appointment and the inauguration of the Library, the pope commissioned a fresco from Melozzo de Forlì in 1477. Originally painted on the northern wall of the Bibliotheca Latina, the painting shows Sixtus IV on his throne with Platina kneeling in front of him. The pope is also surrounded by four of his nephews: Giovanni della Rovere, prefect of Rome; Girolamo Riario, the future governor of Forlì; Cardinal Giuliano della Rovere, later Pope Julius II; and Raffaele Riario, protonotary apostolic. The fresco was transferred to canvas in the nineteenth century and moved to the Vatican Pinacoteca, where it has remained on display since 1833.

In his favour, it has been pointed out that Sixtus IV revived much of Rome's former glory, founded the Sistine choir, built the Sistine Chapel and established the Vatican Archive. But as already mentioned, he also practised nepotism on a blatant and lavish scale. He established the Spanish Inquisition and annulled the decrees of the reformist Council of Constance (1414–18). He was, as examined later in this chapter, also personally involved in a murderous conspiracy. All of this helped to prepare the way for the Reformation.

His attitude toward Venice and the Venetians is a comparatively minor matter, but it throws an interesting light on his character. Is it possible that the odious personality of his Venetian predecessor had something to do with this? The most powerful weapons in the hands of popes, at this period, were ultimately 'spiritual' ones and Sixtus IV promised a plenary indulgence to anyone who killed a Venetian. His hatred of the powerful republic was, in fact, a symptom of his maniacal make-up. Time and again, he anathematized and excommunicated Venetian citizens, but he freely resorted to more material methods as well. He threatened to seize any Venetian ecclesiastics found outside the domains of the republic and to sell them as slaves to the Turks.

Sixtus IV was in constant need of money to supply his insatiable family, to wage war against his neighbours and, importantly, for his own debauches. To help pay for his war against the Turks he built a noble *lunapar* (brothel) in Rome, for both sexes. It was estimated that the courtesans of Rome paid him, 'every week a Julio of gold, which made an annual revenue of 26,000 ducats'. He showed, in fact, great ingenuity in the matter of raising money. He increased taxes, including the one on priests who kept mistresses, and found a new source of income by selling rich men privileges to 'solace certain matrons, in the absence of their husbands'.

He himself was bisexual, while also engaging in incest. He had several 'nephews', or illegitimate sons, whom he made cardinals. Two of his beautiful young nephews – Pietro Riario (reliably believed to be Sixtus' son by his own sister) and Giuliano della Rovere – were also 'the instruments of his infamous pleasure'. While Giuliano went on to become Pope Julius II, Riario's life was cut short, through 'succumbing to his dissipations'. He was charming and witty, however, and Sixtus made him fabulously wealthy by plundering the papal treasury. According to one anonymous, but often quoted, chronicler of the age, 'the family of the Cardinal of St Lucia, having presented to him a request that it should be permitted to commit sodomy during the three hot months of the year – June, July and August – the pope wrote on the bottom of the petition, "Let it be done, as requested".'

One of the best known and most notorious incidents of his pontificate was the so-called Pazzi conspiracy. After the death of Pietro Riario, his place was taken in the pope's affections by his brother Girolamo – who dragged Sixtus into a plot directed against Lorenzo and Giuliano de' Medici. At this time, Lorenzo was the most influential of Italian potentates, and was also behind most of the plotting which was then endemic throughout the peninsula. The Pazzi conspiracy was part of a complicated web of mutual antagonism.

Florence played a dominant role in the Italy of this period. The most illustrious humanists and artistic authors of the Italian Renaissance were Florentines, at least to begin with. The leading family in Florence was that of the mighty Medici, and the failure of the Pazzi conspiracy is the highest testimony to the popularity of that great but tyrannical house. The conspiracy took place in 1478; for its immediate causes, we must go back two years.

The Medici and Pope Sixtus IV were natural enemies. This was for quite different reasons than the pope's hatred of Venice (based as it was on a largely irrational and purely personal prejudice). His quarrel with the Medici was of a more practical nature. It was down-to-earth, devious and deadly. Sixtus IV purchased Imola, the most important town in the Romagna, for Girolamo Riario – to the disadvantage of Florence, which had been on the point of acquiring the territory itself. The purchase involved internal rivalries within Florence, after Lorenzo de' Medici, as its powerful ruler, had put difficulties in the pope's way. The purchase was accordingly financed by the banking house of the Pazzi, bitter rivals of the Medici. Thus the Medici lost the valued position of papal receivers.

Meanwhile, in 1476 the murder of Galeazzo Maria Sforza, in Milan, had produced a wave of admiration for the ethics of political assassination. Girolamo Riario, fearing for his future in the event of the death of his uncle the pope, hatched a plot for the assassination of Lorenzo and Giuliano de' Medici, with the help of the archbishop of Florence. Historians favourable to Sixtus claim that, though the pope unquestionably desired the overthrow of the Medici, he could not, and did not, countenance assassination. What actually happened?

The chosen assassin was a man named Montesecco, who had an interview with the pope, while Girolamo attempted to extract from him the promise of a pardon for the murder before it was even committed. Sixtus, however, was too wily for him. His answer to his favourite was, 'You are a beast!', but Girolamo knew, from the way in which these words were uttered, that his uncle was being disingenuous. The pope's next words were very significant, supplying Girolamo (and the pope, for that matter) with a convenient alibi before the tribune of history. 'I tell you', he said, 'I do not want any man's death, but a change of government'. Girolamo immediately knew what the pope really meant, and the criminal preparations went ahead.

Girolamo sent his brother Raffaele to Florence to organize the assassination. During a solemn Mass in Florence cathedral, at the very moment the archbishop of Florence – who, of course, knew of the plot – was raising the host, the conspirators stabbed Giuliano de' Medici with their poniards. Lorenzo defended himself courageously and succeeded, though wounded, in reaching the sacristy. Meanwhile the congregation turned on the conspirators, disarmed them and later hanged them naked in the church windows. This started a pointless war between the papacy and Florence, which plunged the whole of Italy into a bloodbath.

Sixtus is, of course, best known for the creation of the Sistine Chapel, built between 1477 and 1481 as an imposing chamber in which the pontiff and the 200 clerics of the papal chapel could meet and worship, and as an appropriately grand setting for papal elections. It also became the home of the Sistine choir, which was founded at this time. Once the building work was complete, Sixtus IV summoned some of the greatest painters of the day to decorate this vast room, now the main chapel of the Vatican Palace. The group included Pietro Perugino (who is believed to have supervised the project), Sandro Botticelli, Domenico Ghirlandaio, Cosimo Rosselli and Luca Signorelli. Their work on the chapel walls was undertaken between 1481 and 1483. The 28 niches between the high windows were filled with portraits of the popes of the first three centuries after St Peter. Below these are frescoes depicting scenes from the lives of Jesus and Moses, on opposite sides of the chapel.

These fresco cycles were carefully planned to incorporate the contemporary papal symbolism of Sixtus IV, by reflecting both the struggles he faced and his determination to impose the authority of the papacy. Botticelli's *Punishment of the Rebels* in the Moses cycle also alluded to those who were demanding conciliar reform of the papacy and to the Florentine princes who had recently fought against the pope. The citing of Moses and Jesus, in the particular guise of religious leaders and dispensers of law, was also intended to emphasize the importance of the pope as their appointed successor. Perugino's *Christ Giving the Keys to Peter* thus underlines what Sixtus IV would have felt was his God-given authority. In this scene, Christ hands the golden key of spiritual authority directly into Peter's hands, with the base-metal key of temporal authority hanging below it, thus representing the pope's temporal power. This he hoped and expected to hold with the help of the compliant monarchs of Christendom.

Sixtus, however, left another, more sanguinary legacy. In 1478 he issued a papal Bull sanctioning a new inquisition in Castile. Later it spread to the whole country. It became known as the Spanish Inquisition. Some historians have tried to portray this action by Sixtus in a favourable light, by claiming that he sent a message in which he stressed the need for moderation and the necessity of freedom from domination by political parties. The latter objective is given for the appointment of the Dominican Thomas de Torquemada as Grand Inquisitor. In fact, as Reinhard Heydrich was to the Nazi Gestapo, so was Thomas de Torquemada to the Italian Renaissance.

The decision to unleash upon the world what was to become a monstrous terror was made in reply to the supposed need to investigate the credentials of newly baptized Jews and Muslims, after most of Spain had been re-conquered from the Moors. Within three years, Torquemada had burned 2,000 Muslims in Andalusia alone; within a decade, he had condemned hundreds of thousands of men, women and children to rot in dungeons across Spain. He also had 114,000 people tortured to death, including 10,200 who were burned alive simply because their conversion to Christianity was under suspicion. (Such accuracy in citing actual numbers is possible because of the exactitude of the records kept by the self-righteous officials who authorized the deaths. The same curious phenomenon occurred in the course of the Nazi Holocaust against the Jews.)

In Henry Charles Lea's classic *History of the Inquisition of Spain*, there is a description of a typical case. A pregnant young woman was accused of being a 'crypto-Jewess'. She had her baby in jail before being brought before the Tribunal of Toledo. The witnesses against her were two workmen who lodged in her house. They said she did not eat pork and changed her underclothes on a Saturday. For reporting this to the Inquisition, the men were awarded with three years' indulgence.

The girl's name was Elvira del Campo. She vigorously protested her innocence. She was, she affirmed, a Christian. Her father was a Christian, but it seems that her mother had some Jewish ancestry. From the age of 11 she had taken against pork, which made her sick. Her mother had taught her to change her underclothes every Saturday, a habit which had no religious significance. The Tribunal, however, warned her that she would be tortured if she did not tell the truth, but she had nothing to add to her denial. She was stripped naked and her arms bound. The cord was twisted until she screamed that they were breaking her arms. On the sixteenth turn, it snapped.

Next, she was tied down on a table with sharpened bars running across it. The ropes tying her down here progressively tightened until, in desperation, she finally cried out that she had broken the law. She was then asked, 'What law?' She could not think of any of God's laws that she had broken, so a piece of cloth was rammed down her throat with a rod and the water torture began. She was unable to speak when this was over, so the torture was suspended for four days, during which time she was kept in solitary confinement.

When the next session commenced, she could do no more than beg for her nakedness to be covered, before she broke down completely. Eventually she admitted that she was Jewish and begged for mercy. The judges granted her pleas, to the extent of stopping the torture, but they confiscated her property and sentenced her to a further three years in jail. After six months she was released, but she had gone insane. There is no further record of her or her child. Unfortunately, this was far from being an isolated case. It is typical of thousands that could be cited.

The Spanish Inquisition, authorized by Sixtus IV, lasted for over three centuries. As the years passed, its methods became more efficient, and thus crueler. Its victims came to be counted by the hundreds of thousands. In 1808, when Napoleon invaded Spain, his hardened troops had their stomachs turned by some of the sights they discovered. It was akin to what Allied troops found in concentration camps as they penetrated into Germany and occupied Poland at the close of the Second World War. Underneath a Dominican monastery in Madrid, the French troops found torture chambers full of prisoners, all naked and mostly insane. They evacuated the dungeons and blew up the monastery. The Inquisition in Spain was officially suppressed in 1813. However, it continued its work for another 20 years.

Sixtus IV died in 1484. His death prompted the creation of one of the most exquisite pieces of fifteenth-century Italian sculpture, commissioned by the pope's nephew, Giuliano della Rovere. The Florentine sculptor and goldsmith, Antonio Pollaiolo, produced a magnificent bronze tomb, which was completed in 1493 and remains to this day in the grottoes of St Peter's. The recumbent figure of the pope lies on a bed of intricately carved cushions and drapes, raised on a base, adorned with the seven Liberal Arts and the art of Perspective, the three Theological Virtues and the four Cardinal Virtues. Its symbolism epitomizes how the pope thought of himself – as a religious leader and Renaissance prince – but it is hardly in accord with the views of others. As one commentator put it, he 'embodied the utmost possible concentration of human wickedness'. The nineteenth-century historian Bishop Creighton said, by way of masterly understatement, 'He lowered the moral tone of Europe'. The severity of his behaviour as instigator of the Spanish Inquisition alone would justify this assessment. But there was another factor.

Few pontificates illustrate more graphically the overriding paradox of the Renaissance as it affected the papacy. This was in producing examples of unparalleled artistic and architectural beauty, alongside some of the basest acts of depravity and cruelty in the annals of history.

Chapter 6. POPE INNOCENT VIII (1484–92)
'The Pope is full of greed, cowardice and baseness'

While Sixtus IV can be remembered for instituting a reign of terror that plagued the civilized world for the next three centuries, his successor can be remembered for something even worse. He sanctioned the persecution of witchcraft with a papal Bull which, because of its horrific consequences, was arguably the most evil official document ever signed by any sovereign or leader in history. (Nothing Alexander VI did approached this in terms of ultimate wickedness.)

The conclave whereby Giovanni Battista Cibo became Innocent VIII was a hotbed of intrigue. The scheming eye of Giuliano della Rovere – the future Pope Julius II – fell on this lackadaisical Genovese son of a Roman senator as someone whom he could easily manipulate. He temporarily buried his latent hostility toward Rodrigo Borgia in order to secure his co-operation in electing Cibo. The latter also had the support of Lorenzo de' Medici, who was anxious to exact his revenge for the plot against his life and to re-establish the influence of the Medici at the heart of the papacy. This objective, as will be seen, was achieved with permanently tragic consequences for the Church and for the world.

Both della Rovere and Borgia meant one day to be pope. Yet each knew his time had not yet come. Borgia was undeterred by Cibo's being an intimate friend of della Rovere; he was also a special favourite of his own. He may even have considered that victory for Cibo would lull della Rovere into a state of false security and lead him to overplay his hand during the ensuring pontificate. Such a supposition would not have been not entirely incorrect.

The night before the first scrutiny in the conclave was to take place, Borgia and della Rovere as temporary allies met secretly, disguised in their servants' clothes. Having agreed on Cibo, the next step was to purchase the undecided votes. Accordingly they went round, from cell to cell, awakening the cardinals with the news that the pope was made. Having given them signed promises of lavish grants and benefices, Cibo was duly elected. What kind of pope did he become? This had much to do with contemporary attitudes toward the sexes.

The Church has always been strongly male-dominated and anti-feminist. This took a particularly ugly form in the late Middle Ages. A woman was expected to know her place, whether as wife, spinster or nun. If she showed some special skill, tried to educate herself or, worst of all, presumed to achieve the same sort of things as a man, she came under immediate suspicion. Was she a sorcerer? Probably. There was no other rational explanation, especially since the ancient religion, with its mysterious rites and midnight incantations, had never disappeared. Many were still attracted to its pagan ceremonies.

Innocent VIII, in the midst of his own dissipations, became convinced that Christianity was being threatened by witchcraft. He was urged on by Heinrich Krammer and James Sprenger, two savagely misogynistic Dominicans. They were obsessed by what they saw all around them as the fruits of witchcraft, and composed a handbook that became the authoritative work on the subject. It was entitled *Malleus Maleficarum* (*The Witches' Hammer*), and Innocent was its most enthusiastic reader. He announced that he was going to give the handbook, crammed though it was with grotesque and ludicrous allegations and examples, his blessing and guarantee of official status. He composed a papal Bull, which appeared as the preface to the *Malleus*. The Bull was entitled *Summis Desiderantes* and was dated 5 December 1484.

The Bull ordered the Inquisition in Germany to proceed with the utmost severity against supposed witches. The pope personally gave supreme authority as inquisitors to Krammer and Sprenger, who were particularly interested in copulation with Satan. According to Sprenger, this practice was far from uncommon. 'A woman is carnal lust personified,' he wrote. 'If a woman cannot get a man, she will consort with the devil himself'. Sprenger was well known for his aversion to women, as evidenced by his remark, 'I would rather have a lion or dragon loose in my house than a woman'.

In his Bull, the pope wrote:

> Man and women straying from the Catholic faith have abandoned themselves to devils, *incubi* and *succubi* [male and female demons who have sex with living people while they are asleep] and, by

incantations, spells, conjurations and other accursed offences, have slain infants in their mothers' wombs, as also the offspring of cattle have blasted the produce of the earth…They hinder men from performing the sexual act and husbands cannot know their wives, nor wives their husbands.

How much of the Bull was written by Krammer and/or Sprenger is not known for certain, but it is clear that they took a major part in its composition. Sex, as already noted, had long been a supreme source of sin in the eyes of the Church; the sins of the flesh, however, in everyday life, had come to be accepted as inevitable and most appropriately dealt with by way of absolution and indulgence. In the face of phenomena that churchmen could not fully understand, they began to detect the devil at work on all sides and to devise means for combating this. Such means were themselves deeply infected with suppressed sexual desires, often of a perverted kind.

Sprenger, apart from his obsessive disgust for women, showed closely detailed concern with the male organ. His interest, he would have us believe, was occasioned exclusively by theological motives. 'The power of the devil lies in the privy parts of men,' he wrote. And these parts must be protected, especially by Dominicans. The *Malleus* reports a story related by a Dominican Father:

> When I was hearing confessions one day, a young man came to me and, in the course of his confession, woefully said that he had lost his member. Being astonished at this, and not being willing to give it credence easily…I obtained proof of it when I saw nothing on the young man's removing his clothes and showing the place. Then, using the wisest counsel, I asked him whether he had suspected anyone of having so bewitched him. And the young man said that he did suspect someone but that she was absent and living in Worms. Then I said, 'I advise you to go to her, as soon as possible, and try your utmost to soften her with gentle words and promises'. And he did so. For he came back after a few days and thanked me, saying that he was whole and had recovered everything. And I believed his words, but again proved them by the evidence of my own eyes.

For men to lose their penises, apparently, was not uncommon during the papacy of Innocent VIII, according to the *Malleus*:

> Witches...collect male organs in great numbers, as many as 20 or
> 30 members together, and put them in a bird's nest, or shut them
> up in a box, where they move themselves, like living members, and
> eat oats and corn...It is all done by devil's work and illusion...For a
> certain man tells me that, when he lost his member, he approached
> a known witch to ask her to restore it to him. She told the afflicted
> man to climb a certain tree and take that which he liked out of a nest
> in which there were several members. And when he tried to take a
> big one, the witch said, 'You must not take that, because it belongs
> to the parish priest'.

An unhealthy obsession with sex played a strong part in the Church's preoccupation with witchcraft. The young Dominican and Franciscan friars, who were charged with extracting confessions and with driving the devil from the bodies of their victims, derived considerable sexual satisfaction from their labours. Without violating their vows of celibacy, they could justify the sexual excitement they felt while flogging nubile naked women with the comforting thought that they were doing God's work. That the pope, by encouraging such activity, was driving the papacy to a new low in religious atrocity was no concern of theirs.

The appalling state of affairs that Innocent brought about was no passing phenomenon. It inaugurated centuries of persecution by the Inquisition in central Europe, which rivalled the worst excesses of Hitler and Stalin.

No one knows how many women were arrested, on rumour and hearsay alone, and sent for investigation without any recourse to legal protection. Over the next 300 years, hundreds of thousands – there may even have been millions – of women (and some men) disappeared in the middle of the night, never to return from what has earned the name of 'God's gulag'. The women were dragged into dungeons, stripped naked, shaved clean of all their body and head hair, before they were tortured and mutilated until they confessed whatever the morbid friars wanted them to say. The survivors of the ordeal were summarily hanged or burned to death, whether they confessed or not.

When Granada, the last Moorish stronghold in Spain, fell in 1492 Innocent was overjoyed. He urged the Grand Inquisitor, still Torquemada, to intensify the purge of Moors and Jews. Those who would not convert were swept clear of Spain, resulting in what the author Peter de Rosa described as 'a wave of emigration not matched until the 1930s, in Nazi Germany'.

With Innocent's blessing, the two witch-finders, Krammer and Sprenger, travelled the land, leaving behind them a trail of blood and fire. The usual methods employed by the inquisitors, however – of stripping, flogging, racking and thumb screwing – were not considered 'real torture'. To get some idea of this, one must consult the highly revealing *Tariff of Torture*, drawn up by the archbishop of Cologne. He hit upon the ingenious device of making the families of the victims of the witch-hunt pay for the tortures inflicted. He carefully listed the scale of fees involved. These included separate charges for squeezing thumbs, toes and legs in vices. To have a victim's tongue cut out, for example, and have red-hot lead poured into her mouth, was five times as expensive as a straightforward whipping. What happened to those who did not pay is not recorded, but the *Tariff* proved indirectly to be very useful to the torturers. It provided a strong incentive to every accused witch to confess her devilish sorcery before she bankrupted her relations. She was promised a reward, moreover, if she confessed straight away – namely the privilege of being strangled before being burned.

Krammer and Sprenger had a marked preference, in extorting confessions, for stories of orgies and black masses. The *Malleus* instructed all would-be witch-finders to promise their victims a minor penance and then burn them. Another favoured stratagem was to hold out the promise of pardon to a suspected witch if she gave the names of other witches, and then get another inquisitor to condemn her.

Pope Innocent VIII was too idle to pursue a consistent policy in most matters. Conventional histories of the popes, especially Catholic histories, have blandly ascribed this to the fact that he was amenable and easy-going. The gist of the matter is that, in general, Innocent was content to drift with the tide. Trivulzio, the famous soldier, is quoted as saying: 'The Pope is full of greed, cowardice and baseness, like a common knave; were there not men about him who inspired him with some spirit, he would crawl away like a rabbit, and grovel like any dastard'.[1]

At first, the pope left all affairs to della Rovere. Later he became a virtual puppet of the Medici, and appointed Lorenzo's 14-year-old son, Giovanni, as cardinal. This was the latter's first step toward becoming pope (as the homosexual Leo X, who precipitated the Reformation). Innocent was homosexual himself; to be more exact, bisexual, as he fathered several illegitimate children, including his worthless son, Franceschetto, whom he gave in marriage to the daughter of Lorenzo de' Medici. He thus cemented a convenient and opportunistic alliance.

He slept almost continuously, waking to gorge himself on gargantuan meals. That he did not drink heavily has enabled respectful historians to describe him as 'abstemious'. He grew grossly fat and increasingly inert, being able, toward the end of his life, to take for nourishment no more than a few drops of milk from the breast of a young woman. When he seemed to be dying, an attempt to save his life was made by sacrificing the lives of three healthy young men to provide a blood transfusion. (Ironically, this attempt was made by a Jewish doctor.) The young men supplying the blood were paid one ducat each. Having died in the process and, with the onset of rigor mortis, the coins had to be prised from their clenched fists.

There was, it is true, another side to Innocent's nature. David R. Coffin cites a letter written by a Florentine musician living in Rome, dated 17 August 1490.[2] The musician records that he had been summoned the day before to play his viol outside the bedroom of the pope, who was, at the time, suffering from one of the fevers thought likely to kill him. Late on, he had been called into the pontiff's room where he encountered the pope's daughter, Teodorina, nursing her sick father. That this meeting took place at the height of summer suggests that the musician may have visited Innocent VIII in the Villa Belvedere. It also confirms that the pope used music to alleviate his physical suffering.

If Innocent VIII was indeed amenable, easy-going, idle and constantly under the personal supervision of Giuliano della Rovere, there is also no doubt that he suffered from chronic ill-health throughout his papacy. On at least three occasions, in 1485, 1486 and 1490, the pope's condition became so serious that rumours abounded in Rome of his imminent demise. It may have been the first of these serious illnesses that prompted him to embark on the construction of the Villa Belvedere, the first Renaissance villa in Rome and undoubtedly his most significant contribution to the Vatican Palace.

Built between 1485 and 1487, the Villa Belvedere was perched on the escarpment of Monte S. Egidio, on a site north of St Peter's and the Vatican Palace.[3] It afforded magnificent views towards Monte Mario and overlooked the meadows known as the Prati, which then extended as far as the banks of the Tiber. The Roman chronicler and historian, Stefano Infessura, recorded the construction of the expensive new building in his diary, noting that Pope Innocent VIII had '…built in the vineyard, beside the papal palace, a palace which is called from its view, the Belvedere, and is well known to have cost 60,000 ducats for its construction'.[4]

It seems likely that this edifice was originally intended only as a large, airy, open loggia and terrace, situated at the edge of the Vatican gardens to provide a private and peaceful place of relaxation during the hot Roman summers. However, almost immediately, Innocent VIII instituted a second round of building works, in order to convert the Belvedere into a small but habitable villa. A service wing was added at the southeast corner, and internal walls and fireplaces were inserted to create a small suite of papal apartments, together with a chapel and sacristy.

It would appear that the pope, when considering the placing of his new residence, was strongly influenced by the ancient treatise, *De Architectura*. Written by Vitruvius around 30 BC, and first published in Rome in about AD 1486, it stipulated that villas should be sited on hills to provide a good view, and that they should be orientated towards the northeast to avoid the stifling summer heat. Furthermore, the former papal architect and adviser Leone Battista Alberti, who had himself derived much from the writings of Vitruvius, had particularly stressed the importance of such a location for health reasons: 'Doctors advise that we should enjoy the freest and purest air that we can; and, it cannot be denied, a villa situated high in seclusion will offer this'.[5]

The Villa Belvedere must have seemed the ideal spot for a man in frequent need of rest and recuperation – a place of retreat, a place where Innocent VIII could reside in peace, removed from the squabbles of the Vatican court and the pressures of the outside world.

The vaulted loggia of the pope's new villa, based on the ruins of Late Antique imperial villas in Rome, was completed in about 1487. Shortly afterwards the Perugian painter, Pinturicchio, was commissioned to decorate its walls and ceiling along with his assistant, Pier Matteo d'Amelia, and a team of minor decorative artists. The scheme, like the building itself, took its inspiration from the writings of Vitruvius and Alberti, the former having stipulated that: '…in covered promenades [the ancients] used for ornament the varieties of landscape gardening, finding subjects in the characteristics of particular places; for they paint harbours, headlands, shores, rivers, springs, straits, temples, groves, hills, cattle, shepherds'.[6] To emulate this, Pinturicchio divided the south wall of the loggia with painted pilasters, to match the open arcades of the north wall. The spaces between each set of pilasters were then covered with landscape views, now only fragmentary, but vividly described by Giorgio Vasari in the middle of the sixteenth century: Pinturicchio 'depicted Rome, Milan, Genoa, Florence, Venice and Naples in the Flemish style, something which was rarely employed until that time and which was very pleasing.'[7]

By pointing out the innovative nature of this decoration, Vasari had identified an important point. The illusory architectural pilasters and the landscapes of the Villa Belvedere – painted as if they were views beyond the walls of the room – represented an early and significant antiquarian revival of similar schemes of decoration used in the Roman villas of antiquity.

In June 1488 Andrea Mantegna, court painter to Francesco Gonzaga of Mantua, arrived in Rome with a letter from his patron, giving him leave of absence to work at the Vatican. Innocent VIII, recognizing Mantegna as one of the most accomplished Italian painters of his day, had been attempting to persuade him to come to Rome since his election as pope. The artist was immediately set to work on the decoration of the chapel and sacristy at the west end of the new Villa Belvedere. Although his frescoes and an altarpiece depicting the baptism of Christ were subsequently destroyed, various written accounts have survived that indicate how the rooms were decorated. Two eighteenth-century guidebooks to the Vatican, written by Agostino Taja and G.B. Chattard,[8] describe the sacristy as being adorned with illusionary pilasters separating the walls into compartments, each of which contained the painted depiction of an open cupboard holding the paraphernalia of a sacristy, including chalices and mitres. Giorgio Vasari, writing about 60 years after Mantegna had completed his task, praised the quality of the work and the vivid realism, particularly in the altarpiece fresco in the chapel:

> Andrea worked on every detail with such love and precision that
> the vault and walls seem more like illumination in manuscripts than
> paintings, and the largest figures in the work are over the altar,
> which he did, like the other parts, in fresco; while St John the Baptist
> is baptizing Christ, people standing around him are removing their

clothes and making signs that they wish to be baptized. Among the figures, there is a man who wishes to pull off a stocking clinging to his leg with the sweat and who, crossing one leg over the other, pulls it off inside-out with such a violent effort that both pain and discomfort clearly appear in the expression on his face: this ingenious detail amazed everyone who saw it in those days.[9]

Music was clearly an important theme in the decoration of the Villa Belvedere. In the main loggia, the lunettes above the landscape panels hold pairs of putti playing drums, harps, lutes, pipes and trumpets, interspersed with the arms of Innocent VIII. Likewise, the vaulted and coffered ceiling of the Room of the Prophets – the chamber linking the loggia with the papal apartments – was adorned with female figures playing musical instruments, while the smaller loggetta, alongside the pope's bedroom, was decorated with a choir of singing male figures in addition to its landscapes and hunting scenes.

Music had long been considered beneficial for the sick. However, Innocent VIII would undoubtedly have been influenced by the advice of Gabriele Zerbi, a professor of medicine at the University of Rome. In 1489 Zerbi published a treatise on old age, entitled *Gerontocomia*, in which he claimed that 'music is the most powerful of the arts, and harmony has the admirable virtue of lessening the pains of human souls and of making them pleasant'.[10] The treatise was dedicated to Innocent VIII and, the following year, the pope increased the professor's salary from 150 florins to 250 florins.

Just two months before his death in July 1492, Innocent VIII received the Holy Lance (legendarily used to pierce the side of Christ) from the Turkish Sultan during a magnificent ceremony enacted in Rome on 31 May. The event marked the high point of his pontificate and was duly commemorated in the creation of his tomb, carved in bronze by Antonio Pollaiolo between 1493 and 1497. This monument, one of the few to be moved to the nave of the new St Peter's, is unusual in that it incorporates two figures of the deceased. A huge seated figure of Innocent VIII, his right hand raised in blessing, displays a replica of the Holy Lance in his left hand. Below this (although originally above, prior to its transferral from the old St Peter's) lies the recumbent figure of the dead pope.

After the pontificate of Innocent VIII was to come that of Alexander VI, for so long – quite wrongly – considered the worst pope in history.

PART II:
POPE ALEXANDER VI
(1492–1503)

Chapter 1. THE ELECTION OF RODRIGO BORGIA

'I am the Pope, the Pontiff, the Vicar of Christ!'

As Richard III is to English history, so is Alexander VI to that of the papacy. In each case, the posthumously constructed image of a late fifteenth-century figure has become so compelling as to obscure the reality of his life. The blackening process began, respectively, with Henry Tudor's victory at Bosworth in 1485 and with Giuliano della Rovere's election as Julius II in 1503. The Tudor propaganda campaign was designed to shore up Henry VII's tenuous claim to the English throne. Julius II, on the other hand, was motivated by little more than revenge against the Borgia family, whose control of Rome and the papacy drove him into exile for a decade. In the case of Alexander, and of the Borgia in general, a number of other elements came into play; each of these will be examined in turn.

Rodrigo Borgias became Pope Alexander VI in 1492. The eminent Florentine historian, Francesco Guicciardini (1483–1540), has given us a striking portrait of the Italy of 1490, just prior to Alexander's accession:

> It is obvious that ever since the Roman Empire, more than a thousand years ago…Italy had never enjoyed such prosperity or known so favourable a situation as that in which it found itself so securely at rest, in the year of our Christian salvation 1490 and the years immediately before and after. The greatest peace and tranquillity reigned everywhere; the land under cultivation no less in the most mountainous and arid regions than in the most fertile plains and areas; dominated by no power other than her own, not only did Italy abound in inhabitants, merchandise and riches, but she was also highly renowned for the magnificence of many princes, for the splendour of so many most noble and beautiful cities, as the seat and majesty of religion, and flourishing with men most skilful in the administration of public affairs and most nobly talented in

all disciplines and distinguished and industrious in all the arts. Nor was Italy lacking in military glory according to the standards of that time, and adorned with so many gifts that she deservedly held a celebrated name and reputation among all the nations. [1]

This celebrated passage of Guicciardini's has greatly influenced appreciation of the period. However, a few critical points may be worth making. In 1490 Guicciardini was seven years old; his portrait of 'tranquillity… peace and quietness' was not a contemporary observation. Instead, it was written with the hindsight of middle-age, a time when childhood summers so easily become golden. Guicciardini himself admits to professional bias: 'And yet the position I have served under several popes has obliged me *to desire their greatness for my own self-interest…*'[2] So were the years surrounding 1490 truly a golden age? Italy was a nation divided into hostile states, with all too temporary alliances. It was a place where the papal vicars, that is, the local 'bosses' in the papal system, owed more allegiance to themselves than the Church. It was a place of warring families, such as the Orsini and the Colonna. And it was a place where murderous brigands lay in wait for unsuspecting travellers.

However dubious the status of 1490 as a golden age, certainly great turbulence was to come in the years ahead. Wave upon wave of French, Spanish, imperial and Swiss armies would descend from the Alps or arrive from across the sea to use Italy as their battlefield. Rome itself would be sacked. The first such invasion came in 1494 – thus, early sixteenth-century writers, reflecting upon the recent history of the Italian states, fixed upon 1494 as the start of their calamities. With an all too convenient neatness, this was shortly after Alexander VI's accession to the papacy. It has been seductively easy to damn him by association, without asking the pertinent questions, 'How would *you*, as Pope, have responded to invasion?' and, 'Would your response have been any better than his?'

The conclave of 1492 was contested by two clearly defined parties: one backed by Ferrante of Naples, the other by Milan, which was then ruled by Ludovico Sforza. Ludovico was popularly known as 'il Moro', from his emblem of the mulberry. He ruled in the name of his nephew, Duke Gian Galeazzo.

Ludovico's brother, Ascanio Maria Sforza, had established himself as one of Rome's most significant power brokers. (His first taste of Curial politics had been the previous conclave, in 1484, having been a cardinal for just five months.) But in 1492, at 47, he was still considered rather too young to be elected to an office from which it was well nigh impossible to be deposed. Furthermore, his status as Ludovico's brother (his 'man in the Vatican') effectively put him out of contention. To concentrate power to such a degree would be highly dangerous, not just for the papacy but for all of Italy.

In the course of the first three scrutinies, the frontrunner of the 'Milanese' interest was – ironically enough – the Neapolitan noble, Cardinal Oliviero Carafa, who had reached the eminently electable age of 62. With Carafa out of favour in Naples and Ferrante's son, Giovanni d'Aragona, having died in 1485, the 'Neapolitan' candidature was assumed by Giuliano della Rovere, on account of his proven Colonna allegiance and anti-Milanese record. He was, however, only two years Ascanio's elder, again severely limiting his chances of election. As Cardinals Colonna and Savelli belonged to the Neapolitan grouping, Orsini and Conti automatically sided with the Milanese.

Venetian sympathies were with any member of della Rovere's party who stood a reasonable chance of defeating the Milanese bloc, though it would appear that the pope's most active involvement was to secure admittance to the conclave of the patriarch of Venice, Maffeo Gerardi, who had never resided in Rome. This was achieved with a minimum of fuss because it was neatly matched by the admission of another hitherto unheralded cardinal, Federico da Sanseverino, a Sforza protégé. Sanseverino's promotion in 1489 had been a sign of Innocent's gratitude to the young man's father, the *condottiere* (professional soldier), Roberto da Sanseverino. The Venetians Giovanni Michiel and Giovanni Battista Zen were then aged 48 and 50 respectively, and proved popular with voters in the 'Neapolitan' faction, but Venice made no effort to secure victory for either of them. The memory of a Venetian pontiff, Paul II, uncle to Michiel and Zen, was evidently still fresh.

After decades of lobbying for one Medicean candidate or another, the remaining major Italian power, Florence, finally had its own tame cardinal in the person of Giovanni de' Medici. As things worked out, the latter was torn between loyalty to Ascanio Sforza, to whom he owed the red hat and in whose interest his maternal kinsman Cardinal Giovanni Battista Orsini was aligned, and a Florentine desire to keep on good terms with Ferrante, in the light of which Giovanni's brother Piero, the new head of family, urged him to side with Giuliano della Rovere. Giovanni formed a trio of independents, with Sanseverino and the Genoese Antoniotto Pallavicini, all of whom divided their votes between members of the two factions.

Few cardinals changed their votes between the first and second scrutinies. The third scrutiny witnessed a polarization around the figures of Carafa for 'Milan' and Michiel for 'Naples'. Each of them received 10 votes but stood little chance of persuading the opposition cardinals to break ranks. Only Rodrigo Borgia received support from members of both factions and from two of the independent trio in all three scrutinies. Born in 1431, he was of a similar age to Carafa. A compromise candidate was required, and Borgia's voting figures made him the most obvious choice. This, rather than any pre-planning by Ascanio Sforza, made it possible for Borgia to emerge as unanimous victor in the fourth scrutiny on 11 August 1492. *Even Giuliano della Rovere voted for him.*

Some of the earliest accusations of impropriety on Alexander VI's part emerged in connection with this conclave. The charge was simony, which was specifically forbidden when the practice of electing popes by means of conclaves was regularized. Alexander was neither the first nor the last pope to attract such accusations; his predecessors and successors, Sixtus IV, Innocent VIII, Julius II and Leo X also incurred the charge. It seems unlikely that fifteenth-century power brokers, vying for near-absolute control of the most powerful organization in the world, would be greatly troubled by the moral niceties of simony; nevertheless, suspicion is one thing and proof is quite another. And these were supremely worldly men, well used to covering their tracks and employing what we now term 'plausible deniability' for morally dubious actions.

Whether simony was (or was not) employed in this, as in other Renaissance papal elections, it seems unlikely that the outcome of any such papal election could be crudely determined by a simple 'simony factor'. Papal elections were notoriously difficult to rig. Acknowledging such difficulty, the contemporary Roman proverb sagely noted, 'He who goes into a conclave as pope, comes out as cardinal'. As we have seen earlier (e.g. Pope Pius II), the outcomes of conclaves could be singularly messy businesses.

CHAPTER I. The Election of Rodrigo Borgia

Cardinal Rodrigo Borgia had played a key part in deciding the outcomes of the four previous conclaves. He must have been a master of the rules of the game, and probably willing to employ every weapon in a very well-stocked arsenal. As second-in-command to the previous five popes, he would have had supreme inside knowledge of the scandals and 'hot buttons' of his fellow cardinals. He would have known (perhaps literally, in some cases) 'where the bodies were buried'. Thus, to ascribe the outcome of his election simply to simony smacks both of sour grapes and of a determined lack of appreciation of his vast political skills. At 61 he well knew that, in all likelihood, this was his last chance. And he seized it.

'Evidence' for the simony charge included a colourful story from Infessura,[3] about four mules loaded with silver being sent from Borgia's palace to that of Ascanio Sforza. The private property of any cardinal elected pope was considered fair game, to be looted by the public. So it makes sense that the four mule-loads of silver might be both a bribe and a sensible reallocation of soon-to-be pillaged property – apart from the fact that the mules were going in the wrong direction. At the time of this alleged incident, Sforza was a candidate and Borgia was not. This inconvenience of timing has conveniently been ignored by many subsequent commentators. Of course, one may posit that Borgia had the outcome 'in the bag' all along, but this is to descend into the realms of conspiracy theory where desired outcomes are always under complete control. The most sophisticated political players always know (to their undoubted chagrin) that desired outcomes remain stubbornly outside their complete control. Borgia would have been no exception.

Apart from ignoring the timing, a second disruptive factor in the Infessura saga is this: Infessura cites the tale as rumour. Using such expressions as 'it is said', 'we hear' and 'everybody thinks' conveniently absolves the 'historian' from personal moral responsibility as to the veracity (or otherwise) of his claim. Then along come later commentators who conveniently erase the 'on dit'. Rumour slides into 'fact'. Certainly, by the nineteenth century, this particular accusation had become a matter of fact rather than rumour, with the moralizing historian, Ludwig von Pastor, declaring that electoral deadlock was broken by Borgia employing the 'rankest simony', promising bishoprics and senior offices in return for votes.

Infessura continues to have a problem with his timing when he tells us that

81

Cardinal Gherardo, having sold his vote to Borgia, was thereby disgraced and stripped of his benefices on his return to Venice. Unfortunately for Infessura, and even more unfortunately for Gherardo himself, the poor man died at Terni and never managed to return to Venice.

Leaving aside such inconvenient problems of timing, if Borgia had merely resorted to simony to gain a unanimous result, he must have had very deep pockets indeed. While in no way poor, Borgia had already pawned his benefices to raise money. Now he was mysteriously able to buy Giorgio Costa, the immensely rich cardinal of Lisbon, and a Colonna, an Orsini, a Sforza and a Medici (Giovanni de' Medici, son of Lorenzo the Magnificent, later Leo X). Buying just these five of his twenty fellow cardinals would have bankrupted Borgia many times over. Many of Alexander's critics in the centuries after his death have remained blithely unconcerned about such practical matters. The very word 'simony' has a spuriously convenient neatness to it. Contemporary rumour had it that France had apportioned 200,000 ducats and Genoa 100,000 ducats to secure a result for della Rovere. If so, clearly this was a complete waste of money. It would appear that the simony business was both complex and uncertain.

More recent historians have radically modified the simony charge by pointing out the inevitability of Borgia's multiple bishoprics, together with the vice-chancellorship, being redistributed. The new pope actually presided over a reasonably equitable division of the spoils. Ascanio was the new vice-chancellor of the Church. On 31 August, the bishoprics were reallocated. Within the Sacred College, Alexander's title had been cardinal-bishop of Porto. That now went to Michiel, who was replaced at Palestrina by Girolamo Basso della Rovere. In the kingdom of Aragon, Cardinal Savelli received the bishopric of Mallorca, Orsini that of Cartagena, and Pamplona in the kingdom of Navarre was given to Pallavicini. Ascanio had entertained Hungarian ambitions for a few years, so was well satisfied with the see of Eger (Erlau) in that kingdom. In the papal states, the spoils included the commendatory abbacy of the wealthy Benedictine monastery of Subiaco, northeast of Rome, and the castellanships of certain fortresses.

Historians have argued for centuries about this particular papal election. It may well be that every dirty trick in the book was employed. But, if one stands back apace and adopts a strictly rational approach, it seems obvious that to elect Sforza or della Rovere was simply too risky in terms of concentration of power. As previously noted, electing Sforza meant giving too much power to Ludovico il Moro and Milan. And, after two important legations to France, della Rovere was perceived as the French candidate in 1492. In terms of power political considerations, the new orthodoxy is that della Rovere was ultimately the beneficiary of Francophobia on the part of the overwhelmingly Italian conclave. The lessons of Avignon were still fresh in the minds of many. To elect a possible pawn to the French superpower would have been an even more dangerous move than that of risking a Sforza hegemony. Borgia was the only heavyweight candidate left. A second-rate compromise candidate, it is true, could have been elected – but the previous incumbents had scarcely been sterling successes.

Whatever the deliberations, any rational cardinal would have recognized that the papacy needed a strong, capable figure with a proven track record. Flawed though he undoubtedly was, that person was Borgia. Was their decision a wise one? The French affair of 1494 (see Part II, chaper 3), not two years after the election, surely demonstrated that their decision was indeed a wise one. Of course all decisions, however wise near the time, can have far-reaching and unintended consequences; the election of Alexander was to be no exception.

Ultimately della Rovere had voted for Alexander. Ultimately, in fact, *all* of his fellow cardinals had done so. As Alexander later wrote, '...by the will of God, whose designs are unfathomable, they [the cardinals] elected me on 11 August unanimously...'[4] But in a letter to Ascanio Sforza, some two years later, he sadly refers to della Rovere:

> Whereas he might have hoped much from us, because of the dear memory of his uncle, our predecessor Sixtus IV, yet after having with great magnanimity given us his vote and the votes of his friends in the conclave, he later grew angry, and this precisely because he saw that you had penetrated very deep into our affection.[5]

Many years before, towards the end of his life, Pope Sixtus had walked along the shore at Porto, in the company of his nephew, Giuliano della Rovere and his friend and second-in-command, Rodrigo Borgia. In a mood of mutual affection, perhaps even brotherhood, how could any of these three have known how the deadly rivalry between della Rovere and Borgia would resonate across the centuries?

Alexander had resoundingly won the race for the papacy; but what manner of man was he? It has been claimed that, when he found himself chosen, he cried with exuberance, 'I am the Pope, the Pontiff, the Vicar of Christ!'[6] He could not wait to don his papal vestments. His enthusiasm was entirely unconcealed. Aeneas Silvius and Pius X shed tears of sorrow upon their respective elections. Conversely, Alexander anticipated the cry of Leo X, son of Lorenzo the Magnificent, 'God has given me the papacy and I am going to make the most of it!' Exuberance aside, the new pope had an unrivalled track record of competence in dealing with church affairs. He was the right age, 'about 60, which is the age, as Aristotle says, when men are wisest'. 'His health is excellent, and he endures all fatigue marvellously. He is very eloquent in speech, and has a natural, graceful manner which never forsakes him.' And, crucially perhaps, he also 'knew how to handle money matters very well'.[7]

At news of Alexander's election to the papacy, the city of Rome went into rejoicing mood. One onlooker noted, 'Mark Anthony himself was not received so magnificently by Cleopatra'. Nor was the applause merely local: 'Everywhere and especially in Rome, people were seized with a lively emotion, as if God had chosen this prince as the instrument of His special designs'.[8]

Jason del Maino, a contemporary commentator and habitué of papal circles, warmly congratulated the cardinals on making such a wise choice. Addressing the pope himself, he declared:

> You have nothing to learn from others during your pontificate. Against you alone no accusation of ignorance can be made. You know the needs of the Holy See and of religion, you know what a Roman pontiff must do, what is permitted to him and what is useful. In your great wisdom, you have no need of any man's counsel. Consult yourself alone, obey yourself, follow your inclinations, take yourself for a model...you will never fall into error if you rely upon your own judgement.[9]

Coronation Day, 26 August, was sullen and stifling with heat. All Rome emerged for what turned out to be one of the greatest ceremonies ever seen. Cardinals, nobles and diplomats thronged the streets. Artillery salvoes thundered across the city, delighting the new pope. The Borgia arms, a bull on a golden ground, was prominently displayed. Cheering crowds pressed against the triumphal procession, from St Peter's to the Lateran – where even Alexander's fabled constitution deserted him. He fainted in the heat. Two cardinals helped him into the basilica. At the altar, seated in his papal chair, he fainted again. As one witness noted, 'it forcibly reminded me of the instability of all human things'. Indeed, Alexander's entire papacy would prove compelling evidence for such instability.

According to the Borgia myth, Alexander began as Rodrigo Llansol or Lanzol, a vicious Spanish bandit who reinvented himself by changing his name to Borgia and entered the Church at the behest of his uncle, Pope Calixtus III. The less exciting truth is that Alexander was born Rodrigo Borgia, of minor Spanish nobility. He clearly owed his rise in the Church and his election as cardinal to the blatant favouritism of his uncle Calixtus. Such was the nepotism of the age. What most distinguished Alexander from many another such recipient of gifts was his superb ability. When asked who was the most illustrious of popes, Sixtus V is said to have replied, 'St Peter, Alexander and ourselves'. Urban VIII gave as his answer, 'St Peter, St Sylvester, Alexander and me'.

By the time of his election to the papacy, Borgia had been vice-chancellor (effectively second-in-command) to five popes of very different personalities, who all held him in the highest professional esteem. He was entrusted with delicate missions. Benefices were showered upon him. Pius II had approvingly noted, 'Rodrigo Borgia is now in charge of the chancellery; he is young in age assuredly, but he is old in judgment'.[10] His reputation, at this stage, was excellent. It was only later that it became sullied by calumnies.

Years later, a 1486 Bull of Innocent VIII expands this theme:

> Innocent, Bishop, servant of the servants of God, to his venerable brother Rodrigo, bishop of Porto and vice-chancellor of the Holy Roman Church...while you have been clad in the splendour of cardinalitial dignity, you have served the Church of Rome under the pontiffs of happy memory Calixtus III, Pius II, Paul II, Sixtus IV our predecessor, and also ourself, for almost 30 years. During this time you have aided us to bear the responsibilities of the Church, bending your shoulders in constant labour with unvarying diligence,

assisting the Church with your exceptional prudence, your subtle intellect, your prompt judgement, your faithfulness to your sworn word, your long experience, and all the other virtues to be seen in you. Not once have you ceased to be useful to us.[11]

Borgia's tenure as vice-chancellor was marked by almost unerring competence. He possessed sound administrative skills and excellent judgement. This was no mere self-publicist, scaling the greasy pole of politics. Borgia had the political acumen of a modern-day power broker, combined with the managerial ability of a multi-national chief executive. At the four previous papal elections, he had played the roles of power broker and king-maker. He was no 'wild card' candidate. Conversely, his vast track record seemed to make him the ultimate safe pair of hands. If Guicciardini chooses to mark 1490 as a golden age for Italy, it is salutary to recall that the then Cardinal Borgia had been second-in-command of the Church for almost 35 years. If there is credit to be had for Guicciardini's fabled paradise, does not Cardinal Borgia share in this credit? Certainly it is facile to blame Alexander for the tumult into which Italy was plunged so quickly after his coronation.

Racism was undoubtedly a factor in the election of 1492. Francophobia worked against della Rovere. As we have seen, there was a strong Spanish presence in Italy, whether more specifically in the Spanish college at the University of Bologna, or more generally in the Neapolitan kingdom of Alfonso the Magnanimous and his successor in Naples, Ferdinand I (Ferrante). It was not simply that the western Mediterranean, including the cities of Naples and Rome, was the domain of Aragonese merchants. Rather, when viewed from Aragon, Naples was seen as part of a greater Aragonese commonwealth.

The most direct means by which King Ferdinand of Aragon was able to exert influence in Naples was through the person of his sister, Ferrante's second wife. Seen in this context, the papal election of Rodrigo Borgia – born in the kingdom of Aragon and Catalan-speaking, but long resident in Italy – was much more logical than the election of a French or French-backed pope would have been. The Avignon 'captivity' had not been forgotten.

There was also a darker side to the racism at this time. Although the Italian peninsula lacked unity, being a mere collection of city states, it nevertheless regarded itself as the possessor of a superior civilization. France was feared. Germany was barely tolerated. But Spain was detested as the last European country to have been civilized by the Rome of antiquity. Not only was Alexander Spanish; like his uncle, Calixtus, he was a Catalan, a particularly hated breed in Rome. A commentator at the time wrote that:

> The Spaniards claim to be Goths and so they are, apart from a very small number of cultivated and moral people. The greater part are certainly uncultivated and desire to remain so; they have no aspiration for learning; they feel no need either of refinement of manners or improvement of life. The young people are not educated to this end but, on the contrary, are degraded; for instead of sending them, as is done in the rest of Europe, to be prepared for life by people of nobler condition, they are kept with their own inferiors, who teach them all the ways of evil. Among them it is a virtue to know how to deceive and to rob one's neighbour with skill and cunning. They are pompous and sensitive to affront; barbarians, and like all barbarians, lustful; old and young sing beneath their mistresses' windows.[12]

Certainly Alexander had not been kept with 'inferiors'. By 1492, he had lived in Rome for more than 40 years. He was steeped in the Italian culture of the Curia, and thoroughly *au fait* with Italian politics at the highest level. Yet with close associates, he still spoke Catalan. During his papacy, he was to elevate 19 Spaniards to the cardinalate. He surrounded himself with Spanish advisers. Calixtus III, the former professor at the University of Lerida and president of the Sacred College of Naples, was derided as 'the Barbarian Pope'. Similarly, Alexander, for all the pomp and glory of his coronation, would be similarly scorned as 'the Marrano Pope'.[13] (Marranos were converted Spanish Jews, often accused of retaining Jewish sympathies.)

In 1460, more than 30 years before his election to the papacy, Pope Pius II had sent the young Cardinal Borgia a stinging reprimand on the subject of sexual morality:

> We have learned that your Worthiness, forgetful of the high office with which you are invested, was present from the 17th to the 22nd hour, four days ago, in the gardens of Giovanni de Bichi, where there

were several women of Siena, women wholly given over to worldly
vanities. Your companion was one of your colleagues [Cardinal
d'Estouteville], whose years, if not the dignity of the office, ought
to have reminded him of his duty. We have heard that the dance
was indulged in, in all wantonness; none of the allurements of
love was lacking, and you conducted yourself in a wholly worldly
manner. Shame forbids mention of what took place, for not only
the things themselves but their very names are unworthy of your
rank. In order that your lust might be all the more unrestrained,
the husbands, fathers, brothers, kinsmen of the young girls were not
invited; you and a few servants were the leaders and inspirers of this
orgy. It is said that nothing is now talked of in Siena but your vanity,
which is the subject of universal ridicule. Certain is it that here at
the baths, your name is on everyone's tongue. Our displeasure is
beyond words.[14]

Borgia replied immediately to the pope. His answer to the charges was
contained in a letter that significantly was destroyed when his reputation
was later being blackened. Three days after the first letter, Pius sent a second
one, much less assertive and more forgiving in tone. But Bartolomeo Bonatti,
the Mantuan envoy, having been denied admittance to the aforesaid event
(a christening), had nevertheless secretly observed it and noted, 'By God, if
the children born within the year arrive dressed like their fathers, many will
appear as priests and cardinals'.[15] Bonatti spent that Sienese summer, 'in the
company of the most triumphant cardinal and the most beautiful woman
that ever was'. The 'most beautiful woman' was the courtesan, Nachine.
The cardinal was Borgia, earlier described by Gaspare da Verona as:
'…handsome; with a most cheerful countenance and genial bearing. He is
gifted with a honeyed and choice eloquence. Beautiful women are attracted to
love him and are excited by him in a quite remarkable way, more powerfully
than iron is attracted by a magnet'.[16]

At the time of his election to the papacy, Alexander was no longer a
handsome youth but a powerfully featured man who had achieved more
than double the life expectancy (less than 30, in fifteenth-century Italy).
He retained a keen interest in the pursuits of the flesh. His mistress, Giulia
Farnese, at 18, was not so very much older than his 12-year-old daughter,

Lucrezia. Even more scandalously, they all lived in the same house, presided over by Adriana de Mila, mother of Giulia's cuckolded husband, Orsino Orsini.

In Alexander, it is clear, we have a multi-faceted individual of great complexity. He is the arch political fixer, who scrambles into his papal vestments with childish delight. He is culturally Italian, yet uses guttural Catalan with his confidants. His excellent managerial ability confirms his right to be the chief executive of the oldest and best-established organization in the world. And yet he is an unabashed sensualist, with a scandalous private life. Closer to our own time, perhaps only world figures such as President Kennedy or Chairman Mao offer any kind of parallel. As with Kennedy, in pursuit of ultimate power Alexander would run the gamut from good to evil, morality to amorality. And yet, like Julius Caesar, his memory would be selectively interpreted:

> The evil that men do lives after them.
> The good is oft interred with their bones.
> So let it be with Caesar...[17]

As chief servant of the Church, how did the new pope stand? As vice-chancellor for successive popes, over previous decades, he had long enough to devise his political philosophy. One episode, dating from his early years, may well have been pivotal. Shortly after his appointment as a cardinal, his uncle, Pope Calixtus III, had made him papal vicar in the March of Ancona. In a conspiracy that was typical of the age, a nobleman of Ascoli had assassinated Giovanni Sforza, the tyrant of the town. Lauding his crime as a victory for the people, he promptly assumed the mantle of tyrant himself before being ousted by another conspiracy. In a defensive move (and probably so that he could buy time for further conspiracies), he seized the papal fortress, which purported to guard the area yet was seemingly incapable of guarding itself.

Arriving in Ascoli, the newly appointed Cardinal Borgia identified two victims in this unsavoury episode – the papacy and the people. The rightful authority of the papacy was being flouted, while the people were suffering, sometimes with their own blood. The situation was intolerable. He therefore ordered the papal forces to launch an attack upon the fortress, which duly fell. The tyrant was captured and sent to Rome.

Although this particular episode had a fortunate ending, it highlighted the Church's difficulty in governing its territories, especially when confronted with unscrupulous tyrants. Pursuing a divide and rule policy of encouraging these tyrants to fight each other was the policy of a canny organization, yet one lacking essential power. Employing papal vicars to control Church territories (poachers turned gamekeepers?) was little better, as there was never any guarantee that the gamekeepers would stop poaching. Indeed despotism and extortion of the Church's subjects by these papal vicars seems to have been the order of the day.

As second-in-command to pope after pope, Cardinal Borgia may well have felt that a change of policy was needed. Certainly, after his election as Alexander VI, there was a decisive change of policy. It was radical in its simplicity. In Rome, the pope must govern in his own right, not as the consort of powerful families. Consequently, their power must be reduced. Beyond Rome, the pope must have power to govern the papal states. As intermediaries, papal vicars were, at best, necessary evils; at worst, they were uncontrollable tyrants. For too long, they had been allowed to run amok, practising their evil trades of extortion towards their subjects and treachery to the papacy. Their power must be curtailed. High-minded crusades to distant lands were much less important than the establishment of centralized papal control in the dominions of the Church. Alexander the Spaniard, 'the Marrano Pope', would thus transform the political system of a country that was not his own.

Alexander's policy of centralized papal control ran counter to the desires of the kings of France and Spain, who viewed the ruins of the Holy Roman Empire as fit territory for their own dynastic ambitions. And it ran counter to the wiles of Venice, Florence and Naples. All were potential enemies.

Nepotism aside, Alexander was nothing if not even-handed. (And the blood ties of nepotism, however unfavourably we may view them over 500 years later, may have been a practical precaution.) But, as principal servant of the Church, he was prepared to go against the desires of kingdoms, states, vicars and nobles. He was also prepared to attack the laxity of the lower classes, feudally clinging to this or that protector. The practical affairs of Rome would be far better administered. Wrongdoing would be punished with the full force of the law. (There had been 220 murders in Rome alone, in the short time between Innocent's last illness and the coronation of Alexander.) A commission for prison inspection was created. The mercenaries who flocked to the capital to sell their unsavoury services to the highest bidders were summarily expelled. Each Tuesday, the new pope would make himself personally available to hear complaints and petitions.

As without, so within. Alexander instigated a reign of austerity for the papal household. Expenditure was limited to some 20 to 30 ducats per day. Only one dish was permitted at dinner. Alexander's parsimony in culinary matters resulted in other cardinals (and his sons Cesare and Juan) avoiding invitations to his dinner table in favour of extravagant banquets elsewhere. Many years later, this culinary avoidance would be twisted into the legend that people feared to dine with Alexander lest they be poisoned – an unintended consequence of a regime of austere living. His staple diet was fish (mostly sardines), bread, cheese, fruit and rough red wine. This fact is very rarely mentioned.

Politically, Alexander was prepared to go much further, radically further. As he memorably put it, '…the town which gave Law to the world, should be prepared to give laws to itself'.[18] The *Reformationes Alexandri VI* addressed the administration of the state, the rights of citizens and criminal justice. But, rather than reforming the constitution of Rome, crucially he gave Romans the right to reform and modify it themselves. Henceforth such a constitution would lie outside the aegis of the Holy See.

This enlightened political thought was 400 years ahead of its time. Years later, when Alexander's tyrannical son, Cesare, brought such 'modern' government to the Romagna, the political experiment was judged a great success – apart from those with inevitable vested interests who found their hegemonies nullified. The name 'Borgia' is not immediately recognizable as being synonymous with good government. And yet Alexander's government of Rome and Cesare's government of the Romagna are resoundingly to their credit.

With so many powerful vested interests imperilled, it was inevitable that some would fight back viciously. And, of course, the scandals of Alexander's private life provided ready ammunition. He, together with his children Cesare and Lucrezia, would be conveniently arranged in a public relations triptych as the apotheosis of evil, as the Borgia myth. But all of this was still to come...

Chapter 2. THE FIRST YEAR AS POPE

'The one thing a Pope can do for his relations is to provide them with goods while he is still alive'

By the time of his elevation from cardinal to pope, Alexander had seven illegitimate children – four sons and three daughters. The first three children, Pedro Luis, Isabella and Girolama, born to unknown mothers, are of minor historical importance. But the next four children, Cesare, Juan, Lucrezia and Jofré – all born to the Roman Vanozza Catanei – came to be key players in Alexander's dynastic game. Two of them, Cesare and Lucrezia, captured the imaginations of admirers and detractors alike over the next 500 years.

Alexander wasted no time in putting the credo of Lorenzo's letter into practice. As mentioned in the previous chapter, five days after the coronation the bishopric of Valencia was reallocated. It had been held by Alexander since 1458, and was now given to his 17-year-old son, Cesare. At 10 years short of the required age for episcopal office, having cure of souls was simply not an option for Cesare, but he could receive the temporal income from what, after three generations, had effectively become a Borgia family inheritance. Alexander's dynasticism was perfectly consistent with behaviour among the non-clerical elite of his era. Thanks to his lead as pope, it became increasingly so among dynasties of clerics.

As Alexander's second son, Cesare was destined for a clerical career. Being of illegitimate birth Cesare required a dispensation, which Sixtus had provided in 1480. Many sons of priests obtained such dispensations in this period, but sons of cardinals – and popes – were something of a novelty. In the secular sphere, Ferrante of Naples was living proof that the bastard sons of laymen in the age of the Borgias were not necessarily at a disadvantage. The same could be said of Leonello and Borso d'Este, who ruled Ferrara prior to their legitimately born brother, Ercole. Innumerable cases could be cited of a nobleman's legitimate and illegitimate children being brought up together. Some historians have argued that Cesare was born in Spain and was not Rodrigo's son at all, but the emotional bond between them definitely seems to have been that of father and son.[1] Likewise Cesare displayed care and concern for his mother, Vanozza Catanei. His upbringing was that of a noble, who was made a protonotary apostolic at the age of seven as well as a canon of Valencia and archdeacon of Jativa (all of them within his father's Valencian bishopric). His early career thus followed the pattern of the late Giovanni d'Aragona, Ferrante's son and another juvenile bishop, who had been accompanied by Rodrigo when he first arrived at the great Benedictine abbey of Monte Cassino to assume the empty but lucrative office of commendatory abbot. Cesare's noble birth was further confirmed by his early education, for he studied with private tutors, Paolo Pompilio and Giovanni Vera. Both were Catalans, but are known by the Italian forms of their names.

Cesare's academic progress can be distinguished from that of boys of the urban 'middling' sort in this period, who followed lessons in rudimentary literacy with the study of exceedingly practical mathematics at abacus school. A small proportion of boys, including Cesare, went on to study Latin grammar in private schools, as a prelude to university study and careers in the higher professions. Cesare's university studies began when he went to Perugia at the age of 14, the same age at which his exact contemporary, Giovanni de' Medici, began his studies at Pisa. After two years Cesare transferred to Pisa, to continue the study of civil and canon law, intended as a prelude to an illustrious ecclesiastical career. In 1491 he received his first bishopric, that of Pamplona, capital of the Pyrenean kingdom of Navarre. Cesare remained in Pisa for a short while after his father's papal election, but duly emerged as the most fiery and forceful of the Borgia dynasty, with a reputation for ruthless cruelty which matched Rodrigo's weakness for women.

Jofré, the fourth of Rodrigo's children by Vanozza Catanei, was also in Holy Orders and similarly loaded with benefices at the disposal of his father, including the archdeaconry of Valencia. As we have seen, by 1492 it had become standard practice for popes to appoint their *nipoti* to the Sacred College, and Alexander lost no time in doing precisely that. His own sons were too young to be useful as cardinals, so he appointed Giovanni Borgia-Lanzol (the son of his sister Juana), as archbishop of Monreale in Ferdinand of Aragon's Sicilian kingdom. He was instantly cultivated as a powerful figure, in the tradition of Pietro Riario, but became more marginal after the promotion of Cesare to the cardinalate in 1493.

As previously noted, contemporary life expectancy was below 30. In spite of the advantages of their birth, three of the children of Rodrigo conformed to that statistic. The first and second dukes of Gandia, Pedro Luis and Juan, died at age 26 and 21 respectively. As the first-born of an Aragonese noble, Pedro Luis was sent to Spain to cultivate the king of Aragon. He took part in the campaign to conquer the Muslim kingdom of Granada, and secured royal favour in the shape of the duchy of Gandia and betrothal to the king's cousin, María Enríquez. When he died in Rome, in 1488, he bequeathed his duchy to Juan. Rodrigo's second son by Vanozza Catanei inherited not only the duchy but also María Enríquez and the responsibility of acting as the Borgia intermediary with King Ferdinand. Juan seems to have displayed little to recommend him as a diplomat or, indeed, in any other respect.

As Juan's case illustrates, the social elite was exempted by wealth from the more general rule that men in this period could not afford to marry until they were aged 30 or more. On average, girls of less than elite birth married at 18. The nobility of Rodrigo's daughters was confirmed by the fact that the eldest, Isabella and Girolama, were probably 16 and 14 respectively at the time of their marriages in 1483. Girolama and her husband, Gian Andrea Cesarini, died the same year. Isabella lived until 1541. Through her daughter, Giulia, she was the great-great-grandmother of Pope Innocent X (reigned 1644–55), the pontiff immortalized by the paintings of Velazquez.

Rodrigo's daughter Lucrezia was the third major player in the Borgia legend, after Alexander VI and Cesare. She was born in 1480, in the *rocca* (fortress) at Subiaco, where her father often spent the hot summer months in his capacity as commendatory abbot of St Clemente. She was initially brought up by her mother. Her education, which included the study of poetry, Latin and Greek, distinguished her from the vast majority of her female contemporaries, few of whom were instructed in the ancient languages. In due course, she moved to the household of her father's cousin, Adriana de Mila. As has been noted, Adriana was stepmother to Orsino Orsini, the cuckolded husband of Alexander's mistress, Giulia Farnese – who also shared the same palace of Sta Maria in Portico. This was a gift from Cardinal Zeno. It had a private door into St Peter's. Alexander merely had to stroll across the basilica to visit his daughter *and* his mistress.

It was not unusual for girls of a certain social standing to make such a move (albeit rarely to such a famous address), possibly to learn 'finishing' skills and graces. When Pedro Luis died in 1488 he left young Lucrezia a sizeable dowry of 10,000 ducats, making her an attractive marriage proposition, notwithstanding her illegitimate birth. She had been betrothed to two noblemen even before the conclave of 1492.

It would be instructive to dwell, for a moment, on the marital history of Vanozza Catanei, the woman who provided Rodrigo with something approaching the stability of family life. The non-noble status of this native Roman was underlined by the fact that she did not contract the first of her three marriages until she was 30. This was in 1474, the year in which she first became pregnant by Cardinal Rodrigo. Cesare was therefore born while Vanozza was married to an elderly lawyer, reminding one of stock plots about younger wives deceiving older husbands. Niccolò Machiavelli's play, *Mandragola*, is a classic of this sort. Juan, and possibly Lucrezia, were born between marriages, and Jofré was born after Vanozza's second marriage. Although she married a third time, Vanozza's story provides excellent proof of the financial advantages of (multiple) widowhood, for she was able to gain a respectable income from property ownership, the money from which she put into charitable causes. Her relationship with the future pope ended before 1486, and another woman duly took her place.

In 1489 Adriana de Mila's stepson, Orsino Orsini, had married the young and beautiful Giulia Farnese, from one of the less prominent Roman baronial families. It may have been at her wedding that she first encountered Cardinal Rodrigo Borgia. She was easily young enough to be his daughter and soon became his mistress, a role she continued to occupy after his papal election. This was an unparalleled situation and did much, when it became known, to weaken Alexander's personal authority. In an *avviso* (handbill) printed in 1494, Giulia was identified as the 'Bride of Christ'. The cuckolding of Orsino Orsini also weakened Alexander politically, fuelling the animosity between him and the Orsini clan from the outset of the pontificate. Giulia had one daughter, Laura Orsini, and there was inevitable speculation that Rodrigo was the father. This can be countered by the fact that Pope Julius II

96

sanctioned Laura's marriage to his nephew, Niccolò, in 1505, so presumably he had no grounds for suspicion about her parentage.

The first diplomatic crisis of Alexander's pontificate – the Cibo castles affair – was small fry in comparison to events from 1494 onwards, and created the impression that the pope overreacted. Within days of the conclave, Innocent VIII's son, Franceschetto Cibo, sold his castles at Anguillara and Cerveteri for 40,000 ducats to Virginio Orsini, commander of the armies of King Ferrante of Naples. This transaction was what we would now term a 'distress sale'. Cibo was terrified that these castles would be disbursed as part of Innocent's estate. The castles were strategically positioned: Anguillara overlooked the via Cassia and the via Clodia, while Cerveteri overlooked the via Aurelia. Anguillara was particularly close to Virginio's stronghold at Bracciano, and thereby reinforced Orsini control of the region north of Rome. The deal was negotiated by Giuliano della Rovere and took place in his palace. Piero de' Medici, who was related to both Franceschetto and Orsini, supported it, as did Orsini's boss, Ferrante.

As a power manoeuvre, the sale of the Cibo castles had unfortunate implications for Alexander. Sale of papal property without papal consent directly contravened papal authority. It was also illegal. Della Rovere's role smacked of treachery, while its relative lack of concealment showed arrogance, bordering on contempt. (By this action, Alexander must have regarded della Rovere's true colours as irrevocably nailed to the mast.) Naples and Florence were directly interfering in the affairs of the papal states and moving towards a power bloc, threatening to the papacy and to Milan. Increased Orsini power in the Roman Campagna was similarly directly threatening to the papacy, while any imbalance in the near-omnipresent Orsini/Colonna power struggle was disturbing, to say the least.

Alexander was alarmed. Only days into his papacy, the gloves were already off. He mounted a legal attack, declaring the sale null and void. He allocated troops for a military attack, if need be. He mounted a political attack, quickly creating the League of St Mark, an anti-Neapolitan alliance between the papacy, Milan and Venice. And, finally, he mounted a diplomatic attack, promptly dispatching anti-Orsini appeals to the various

European powers, particularly France. Herein lay the origins of perceptions that he was dangerously dependent on France – even to the extent of being responsible for the French 'intervention' of 1494 (see Part II, chapter 3). There is no reputable evidence for this latter assertion.

King Ferrante of Naples, realizing that he was being comprehensively outmanoeuvred, tried a different tack. Knowing Alexander's weakness for family advancement, he proposed a marriage between Sancia, his granddaughter (daughter of the duke of Calabria) and Alexander's son Jofré. Alongside this, he suggested that Alexander enter into a political alliance with Naples, although he was cunning enough to make no suggestion that Alexander abandon the alliances with Milan and Venice. But Alexander knew well that any alliance with Naples would inevitably nullify alliances with Milan and Venice, and that the papacy would be reduced to a satellite of Naples. Unsurprisingly, he refused both propositions.

By legal, military, political and diplomatic means, Alexander had thwarted Ferrante in his ambitions. Outwitted on all sides, one weapon alone was left to the disgruntled king. He realized that a discredited pope is a politically weakened pope. And the chosen weapon with which to discredit Alexander was calumny. On 7 June 1493 he thereby wrote to his relatives, King Ferdinand and Queen Isabella of Spain. This letter is the first known attack of its kind on Alexander, the precursor to what would ultimately turn into a flood of invective. With supreme irony, it was composed by one of the most immoral and discredited men of the age.

The letter stated that Alexander had attempted to bribe both the Orsini and Colonna families, in a plot to remove Ferrante's *condottieri* (professional soldiers). Bizarrely, it stated that Alexander had asked Orsini to stand firm on the Cibo castles deal. It attested that Alexander intended to appoint 13 cardinals, at a minimum of 20,000 ducats per cardinal, as a money-making ruse. It also stated that Alexander was offering the kingdom of Naples to the duke of Lorraine and considering an alliance with the Turks to attack Naples from the south. Alexander's sole motivation was to advance his children by any means possible. Ferrante claimed that he, not Alexander, had advocated a legal enquiry into the sale of the Cibo castles. And he further claimed that not only had Alexander refused this enquiry, but he had countered with a matrimonial alliance.

So much for Ferrante's arguments. The tone of his broadside is worth noting, as it set a precedent for many later attacks on Alexander:

> The Pope has no respect for the Holy Chair and leads such a life that people turn away in horror. By fair means or foul, he seeks nothing but the aggrandizement of his children. What he wants is war, and has persecuted me without cease since the first day of his pontificate. There are more soldiers than priests in Rome. The Pope desires war and rapine, and his cousins, the Sforzas, drive him on, seeking to tyrannize over the papacy and make Rome a Milanese camp.[2]

Ferdinand and Isabella were alarmed that a Spanish king of Naples and a Spanish pope should be in such a condition of enmity. Their ambassador, Diego Lopez de Haro, was duly dispatched to Rome to ask Alexander to stop his preparations for war and to make peace with Ferrante and Orsini. Alexander assured de Haro of his desire for a settlement; but he would not change his demand for a legal enquiry and judgement. As Ferrante had insisted that the demand for a legal inquiry had come from *him*, he was nicely hoisted by his own petard. Accordingly, he wrote to Ferdinand and Isabella, thanking them for their intervention. The nimbleness of Alexander's negotiating skills had made a fool of him.

Ferdinand and Isabella were scarcely disinterested parties. True, the matter of Orsini's few castles, no matter how strategic, was of little import to them. But they had their own agenda, and a dark one at that. It concerned the Spanish Jews who had converted to Christianity, the Marranos. Some conversions were genuine; others undoubtedly arose out of self-interest and fear of persecution. They comprised an ethic group within society, a group of different origin, race and, possibly, true faith. (Though they prayed to Christ in public, did they yet pray to their own god in private?) In Spain, during the reign of the previous king, Henry IV, the Marranos had acquired great power. They had risen to positions of importance in commerce, finance (both public and private), government, the court and the clergy. Thus, they controlled finance and the civil service, while exercising considerable influence over the Church in Spain.

Spanish patriots were concerned that the true loyalty of the Marranos was not to Spain, but to themselves. In an atmosphere horribly reminiscent of Nazi Germany in the 1930s, resentment festered on a grand scale. Inevitably it erupted into outright persecution, aided and abetted by the sinister forces of the Inquisition. As with Nazi Germany, the reason why the State did not make a protective intervention was precisely because the State was the prime instigator. In any case, the State was effectively Ferdinand and Isabella, who wanted all the money they could get their hands on for a vigorous programme of national reconstruction. In the courts, the Jews were deprived of their assets. In murky ghettoes and in the dungeons of the Inquisition, they were deprived of their lives.

The situation in Rome was vastly different. The Jews in Italy, it is true, also comprised a distinct ethnic group within society. But, like the Protestant population in the Republic of Ireland in the twentieth century, those in this group were neither powerful nor aggressive. There was no need to fear or resent them. There was a tradition of separatism, but there was also a tradition of tolerance. And, for a Renaissance pope, Alexander was unusually tolerant. He viewed the Jews as fellow human beings who were simply mistaken in practising a religion not wholly supported by true doctrine. At his coronation, he replied to their formal homage in terms which were cordial yet intellectually honest in terms of his values and those of the Church:

> Hebrews, we admire and respect your Holy Law since it was given your ancestors by the most High God through the hands of Moses; but we are opposed to the false observance and interpretation you have of it, because the Apostolic Faith teaches that the Redeemer whom you await in vain has already come, and that he is our Lord Jesus Christ, who with the Father and the Holy Spirit is the Everlasting God.[3]

Ferdinand and Isabella were, however, hell-bent on persecuting the Jews in Spain. With an arrogance matched only by their inhumanity, they demanded that Alexander also persecute the Jews in Rome, especially those who had fled from Spain. That, not the Cibo castles, was the true mission of Diego Lopez de Haro. Alexander heard out de Haro with impeccable courtesy. He assured him of his high regard for the Spanish rulers and of his love for his birthplace, Spain. But he pointed out that the Jews posed no threat to Rome. And he absolutely refused to persecute them. All of this was couched in temperate language and was the epitome of reasoned argument.

Ironically, this negotiating 'smoothness', as some called it, on the part of Alexander helped to inspire the legend of his Machiavellian personality. But the sober reality was that his arguments were invariably reasoned, fair and humane. As with Ferrante, de Haro and his sponsors Ferdinand and Isabella were intellectually outclassed by Alexander. Allegations of trickery were more sour grapes. Alexander could have persecuted the Jews with impunity. He could have stolen their money, while currying favour with the Spanish superpower. But he chose not to.

The persecution of the Jews was the covert part of de Haro's mission. Alexander's opposition, however pleasantly couched, was unrelenting. He fully agreed with the overt part of de Haro's mission, the requested settlement with Virginio Orsini and King Ferrante. As it happened, this settlement was entirely overtaken by events when King Charles VIII of France, as inheritor of the house of Anjou, began citing his prior right to the state of Naples. Charles started to raise an army to enforce his claim, in no uncertain manner. Ferrante was now looking at a nightmare scenario. But Alexander also was greatly perturbed. Bad enough to have the troublesome state of Naples south of Rome; far worse to have the infinitely greater superpower of France at his back. An invasion by Charles was a threat both to Naples and to the papacy. In face of a mutual enemy, Ferrante and Alexander hastily compromised.

Interestingly enough though, Alexander still had his way with the Cibo castles, insisting that the contract of sale was legally void. He proposed that a new sale be made – from the Holy See to Virginio Orsini. Orsini would pay 40,000 ducats to the papal treasury, not Cibo. It may well be that Alexander secured a commitment from Orsini to pass on these castles to his son for, several months later, Orsini did just that. Alexander emerged from these negotiations having won a judicial victory, kept the Cibo castles from passing to Naples, appropriated the full sale price for the papacy and, perhaps most importantly of all, reinforced, in no uncertain terms, his authority and that of the Church. He also prevented the conflict getting out of hand. Certainly, wars have been fought over far less.

On the face of it, appealing to other countries on a purely domestic matter seems an overreaction. But was the Cibo castles affair a purely domestic matter – or was it an attempt by Ferrante and della Rovere politically to castrate Alexander just days into his pontificate? If, as seems highly likely, it was the latter, then Alexander's willingness to redefine the problem as his authority on trial and to raise the ante from the domestic to the international is compelling evidence of his ability to play at political brinksmanship – and win.

However pragmatic the alliance with Naples, the mores of the age demanded that such alliances should be sealed by marriage. Ferrante proposed a marriage between his daughter, Lucrezia, and Alexander's son, Cesare; this would mean Cesare's abandoning his clerical state. Alexander vetoed it in no uncertain terms. The alternative was an agreed marriage between his son Jofré and Sancia, the illegitimate daughter of Alfonso of Calabria and granddaughter of Ferrante.

Thus was the Cibo castles affair resolved but it left one notable casualty – Cardinal Giuliano della Rovere. He had approved the Cibo/Orsini contract, in his own palace, without Alexander's knowledge. By approving this secret and illegal sale of Church property he had, in effect, committed treason. By acting as Ferrante's adviser during Alexander's negotiations, he had been counsellor to the opposition in an action against the papacy. No greater treachery could be envisaged. Alexander denounced him in full consistory (that is, in front of all the cardinals).

During the conflict, della Rovere had retreated to the fortress of Ostia, where he was bishop. Situated at the mouth of the Tiber, with strategic control of all shipping to and from Rome, it was admirably poised for a blockade to work in tandem with an attack on the city by Ferrante. As it happened, no such attack ever came. A chastened della Rovere returned to Rome, to be magnanimously pardoned by Alexander.

Della Rovere had been made cardinal by his uncle, Pope Sixtus IV. A fiery character, he was forced to behave himself with Sixtus, the possessor of an even more fiery temper. But, as controller of the Vatican, he specialized in causing grief to the much more temperate Innocent VIII. Now, with Alexander VI occupying the chair that might have been his, he was faced with a truly authoritative figure, however temperate in language and manner. Not long after being pardoned by Alexander, he fled to France to encourage preparations against none other a figure than Ferrante, his erstwhile client. He was truly a man of wayward passions and shifting loyalties.

The alliance with Naples was sealed by the proposed marriage between Jofré and Sancia. The anti-Neaolitan League of St Mark was sealed by another marriage, this time between Alexander's daughter Lucrezia and Giovanni Sforza, Lord of Pesaro, cousin to Ludovico and a papal vicar of the Romagna. Giovanni was a widower of 26; Lucrezia was a mere 12 years old. They were married on 12 June 1493, the first time that a pope's daughter had been married at the Vatican. A splendid affair, reminiscent of Alexander's coronation the previous year, it demonstrated the new pope's policy of seamlessly aligning his dynastic interests with those of the Church. Alexander presided, with his stunning mistress, Giulia Farnese, little more than five years older than the bride.

Lucrezia's wedding banquet has been cited as an orgy. Boccaccio, the Mantuan envoy, mentions a sermon, a comedy, the distribution of presents and a ball, at which ladies danced with one another. His closing phrase reads: 'Thus passed the evening: if well or ill, I leave Your Excellency to judge'. This seemingly suggestive phrase was, in fact, common to the diplomatic language of the time. The 'orgy' seems to have been more fiction than fact.

Alexander kept the newly marrieds close by him, and thereby under his control. For the following year, Lucrezia and Giovanni remained in Rome. With this marriage, Alexander sealed the League of St Mark. He brought a significant papal vicar to heel. And he secured Giovanni's military skills for periodic service with the papal army.

Perhaps the final word on the Cibo castles affair should belong to the Milanese envoy who wrote:

> Does this look like a pope who has lost his head? As far as I can see, just the contrary is the case. He has negotiated a League which made the King of Naples groan; he has contrived to marry his daughter to a Sforza who, besides his pension from Milan, has a yearly income of 12,000 ducats; he has humbled Virginio Orsini and obliged him to pay; and he has brought King Ferrante into a family connection with himself. Does this look like a man whose intellect is decaying? Alexander intends to enjoy his power in peace and quietude.[4]

Assuredly, Alexander fully intended to use his power. But, as events transpired, it would not be in peace. And it would not be in quietude.

While the Cibo castles affair had brought Alexander into conflict with Ferdinand and Isabella of Spain, in conjunction with the Marrano subtext, Alexander remained 'the Spaniard in the papacy' and the rulers of Spain had need of his intervention on another matter. This was vastly more important than Cibo's castles. It was ultimately immeasurably more significant to Spanish power than the persecution of the Jews, or even the Spanish Inquisition itself. And this time, Alexander was able to intervene in a way that was to benefit Spain, while markedly adding to the international authority of the papacy.

Throughout most of the fifteenth century, Portuguese mariners had enjoyed a monopoly on exploration down the coast of Africa. The impetus came in 1415, when Ceuta, on the North African coast, was captured by a Portuguese army, among whom was the prince who has come to be known as Henry the Navigator (Infante Dom Henrique). It was he who sponsored the first Portuguese voyages along Africa's Atlantic coast. By 1444, these expeditions had reached as far as the Senegal river. In 1455, and in conformity with the powers granted him in the discredited Donation of Constantine, Nicholas V had granted the exclusive right to explore the region and exploit its trading potential to subjects of the king of Portugal. The valuable oceanic route to the Indies spices was duly opened up when Bartolomeu Dias rounded the Cape of Good Hope in 1488.

Meanwhile, the Genoese adventurer Columbus failed to win Portuguese support for his plan to reach those same Indies by sailing westwards across an over-optimistically narrow Atlantic. Flush with victory at Granada, in January 1492, Ferdinand and Isabella granted him permission to sail in their name. During the first of his four transatlantic voyages, he rather panicked at the realization he had discovered a 'new' world, broke with the Portuguese tradition of seeking nothing more aggressive than trade, and planted the flag of Castile in the islands of the Caribbean.

When Columbus returned to Spain in March 1493, the monarchs found themselves landed with a distant empire. Legal clarification was required. The pope was the only person assumed to have the authority to dispose of Atlantic islands. Alexander's Bull *Inter caetera* determined the hemispheres of Portuguese and Spanish exploration, with a line drawn on the globe from pole to pole, 100 leagues to the west of the Azores and Cape Verde Islands. Portuguese interests were confined to the eastern side; Spanish interests to the west. After Portuguese protests against the decision of the Spanish pontiff, the line was moved further westwards by the treaty of Tordesillas

(7 June 1494), thereby making it possible for Pedro Alvares Cabral to claim Brazil for Portugal in 1500. A portion of the first gold brought from America was used for the decoration of roof timbers in the basilica of Sta Maria Maggiore, in the city of Rome.

Alexander had made his intervention at the behest of Spain. He had made his original judgement seemingly in favour of Spain. Might a more equitable division of the spoils have had the result that Portugal, not Spain, became a European superpower? Might there have been a Portuguese Armada instead of a Spanish one?

At a stroke, Alexander had increased the status of the papacy, involved the Church in the opening up of the New World, and gained valuable political capital with the Spanish superpower. Inevitably, the Spanish political capital that accrued was used to facilitate a third dynastic marriage, this time between Alexander's son Juan, duke of Gandia, and María Enríquez. In August, the 17-year-old Juan left for Spain, laden with riches and good advice from Alexander. By November, however, he was receiving letters from both Alexander and Cesare rebuking him for antagonizing the Spanish court by his disrespect for his adopted family. Not least was the charge that he was too busy spending time in brothels to consummate his marriage. In addition to his predilection for *belles de nuit*, Juan was also gambling heavily and engaging in what we would now term 'loutish behaviour' (such as killing dogs and cats for fun). He was a singularly unpleasant fellow, by all accounts. Nevertheless, he remained his father's favourite. The pregnancy of María Enríquez proved to Alexander that the marriage had, thankfully, been consummated, however belatedly and half-heartedly. (Ironically, Juan's emotional coldness to his arranged bride would be paralleled, years later, by that of Alfonso d'Este, the third husband of his sister Lucrezia, in a similarly arranged marriage.)

Alexander always took great care to preserve good relations with Spain. Over the 11 years of his pontificate, he created 43 cardinals, none of whom was Portuguese. His critics chose to see only Spaniards raised to the sacred purple, whose holders then numbered 18. What contemporaries and later commentators alike overlooked was that Alexander's promotions came closer to conciliar ideals of geographical representation in the Sacred College than any since those of Eugenius IV, in 1439. At no time was this more apparent than in September 1493, when he raised six Italians, two Spaniards, two Frenchmen, an Englishman and a Pole.

It must be remembered, moreover, that not all such appointees were resident at the Curia, with the consequence that 'working' cardinals were as predominantly Italian as before. Among the Italians, there was a variety of Renaissance types: the scholarly Giovanni Antonio di Sangiorgio; Giulia Farnese's brother, Alessandro (mockingly known to all and sundry as 'the petticoat cardinal'), who went on to become Pope Paul III; the avid Venetian collector of books and antiquities, Domenico Grimani, and Ippolito d'Este, archbishop at seven and prince of the Church at fourteen. Ippolito was the son of Ercole d'Este, duke of Ferrara and his wife, Eleonora d'Aragona, who had been feted in Rome in 1473. He gained a military and literary reputation, but had no obvious interest in the Church or inclination towards the celibate clerical life.

What the Spaniards lost in numbers on this occasion, they made up for in strength of character. The teenage Cesare Borgia was as ill-suited to the cloth as Ippolito d'Este, a trait he made little attempt to disguise. Bernardin Lopez de Carvajal was a Castilian and no friend of the Borgias. His ascent of the ecclesiastical ladder was due to the patronage of Ferdinand and Isabella, for whom he was ambassador at the Curia. In 1492, Carvajal masterminded the Castilian celebrations in Rome, after the fall of Granada, an event that inspired him for the remainder of his life. His world view was that exhibited in the writings of Columbus, in which Spaniards (and Portuguese) had a divine mission to conquer the Holy Land, whether by land or sea, install Ferdinand as king of Jerusalem and thus usher in the Last Days. It was Carvajal who delivered the pre-conclave address, in 1492, in which he impressed upon the electors the urgency of ecclesiastical reform. His disappointment contributed to his split with Alexander, early in the pontificate. The Frenchmen promoted in 1493 included Jean Villiers de la Grolaie, now best known as the patron of Michelangelo's *Pietà* in St Peter's basilica. During his own days as a cardinal Alexander had been criticized for excessive cultivation of secular princes – a trend we can see in his decision to send red hats to the son of the Polish king and to Archbishop John Morton of Canterbury (to whom Henry VII was grateful for securing the papal indulgence for his marriage to Elizabeth of York).

The years 1492–94 saw the beginnings of the most significant artistic commission of this pontificate, namely the decoration of the Appartamento Borgia by the Umbrian painter Bernardino di Betto (known as Pinturicchio), and his assistants. Although Pinturicchio had been involved in the Sistine Chapel decoration in the early 1480s, he was favoured more by Alexander than by any other pope, and also received a pension from Cesare Borgia. The apartments had been built by Nicholas V, but were left undecorated at his death. Alexander resolved to remedy this at the beginning of his pontificate, the rooms offering a splendid opportunity to make his mark as soon as possible. The decoration of the six principal rooms provide a useful lesson in the Renaissance ability to mesh Christian and pagan traditions, with little or no apparent difficulty.[5]

The decorative scheme in the first room is devoted to the 12 sibyls and 12 prophets, representing the Gentile and Jewish Churches respectively, who foretold the coming of the Messiah. It was in this room that Cesare allegedly had his brother-in-law, Alfonso, duke of Bisceglie, murdered in 1500 and where Cesare himself was imprisoned by Pope Julius II in 1503. In lunettes in the second room are figures of the Apostles holding lines from the Creed; these frescoes are attributed to Pier Matteo d'Amelia. The third room is a celebration of the kind of formal education experienced by Alexander, Cesare and all of their more educated contemporaries: the *trivium* (grammar, dialectic, rhetoric) and the *quadrivium* (geometry, arithmetic, astrology, music), which together comprised the seven liberal arts. The decoration of this room has been attributed to Antonio da Viterbo.

Devoted to the saints, the fourth room was painted by Pinturicchio himself and is regarded as his masterpiece. The saints in question include the Virgin Mary, to whom Alexander had a strong devotion, Paul the Hermit and Anthony Abbot, Sebastian, Susanna and Barbara.[6] The room also contains a depiction of the legend of Iris, Osiris and the bull-god Apis, in a clear reference to the heraldic bull of the Borgia family. Greatest attention has been devoted to the depiction of St Catherine of Alexandria disputing with the Emperor Maximian, various commentators having supposed that the saint with the long golden hair and richly embroidered gown must be a portrait of Lucrezia and, by the same token, that the bearded warrior Maximian, on his elaborate bull-embellished throne, must be a portrayal of Cesare. The only portrait to which Lucrezia's name can be attached with any certainty is that shown on a medal made after her third marriage to Alfonso d'Este, in which her hair happens to be arranged in what could be interpreted as a more prosaic version of the Pinturicchio fantasy. In the absence of firm evidence there is, however, no reason to suppose that Pinturicchio took the young woman as his model, nor that Bartolomeo Veneto did so in later years.[7] Portraits of Cesare display a greater consistency than do those which might be of Lucrezia, though again there can be no firm guarantee that Pinturicchio's Maximian is anything other than a warrior type.

We are on much safer ground in the fifth room of the Appartamento Borgia – that of the mysteries of the Christian faith – for here Alexander himself is shown in a bejewelled cope, kneeling in adoration before the risen Christ. This Resurrection scene takes its place as the greatest of the mysteries, between the Annunciation, the Nativity and the Adoration of the Magi, and the Ascension, Pentecost and the Assumption of Our Lady. Apart from this portrait, numerous depictions of Alexander survive in various media. On medals, he can be seen in profile or breaking open the Holy Door at the beginning of the Jubilee of 1500. These extremely portable images in turn inspired the creation of panel portraits and manuscript illuminations, including the sumptuously decorated Christmas missal (c.1500) in the Vatican Library.[8] Another example is provided by Hieronymus Bosch, who painted his satire on human folly, *The Haywain*, towards the end of Alexander's pontificate. Among the press of foolish people, it included the pope, the emperor and the king of France. The papal profile clearly resembles those on Alexander's portrait medals.[9]

For a pontiff so reviled in print after his death, Alexander was peculiarly well served by painters, whose posthumous images of him are rather more flattering than those produced during his lifetime. One case in point is Albrecht Dürer's *Madonna of the Rosary*, in which the infant Christ presents the kneeling Alexander with a crown of roses, as the Virgin Mary places a similar wreath on the head of the Emperor Maximilian. The Augsburg banker Jakob Fugger, Dürer himself and other personalities of the period can be identified in this altarpiece, which was made for S. Bartolomeo di Rialto, Venice, in 1506.[10] Some two decades later, Titian also included Alexander in an even more overtly Venetian work: *Bishop Jacopo Pesaro presented to St Peter by Pope Alexander VI*.[11] As a Venetian and as commander of a papal fleet, Pesaro had been a unifying figure in a papal-Venetian league whose combined forces scored a victory over the Turks at S. Maura on 30 August 1502. Titian alludes to the victory by including galleys in the background and a victor's laurel on top of Pesaro's banner, which includes the Borgia arms very prominently.

The rooms of the Sibyls and the Creed are located within the Torre Borgia, a defensive structure which once delineated the northwest corner of the Vatican Palace but has since lost its martial character by being surrounded by later building projects. If the Appartamento Borgia served to connect Alexander with Nicholas V, the most architecturally ambitious of the fifteenth-century popes, his completion of the benediction loggia at St Peter's marked him out as an heir of Pius II. The loggia was designed to play a significant part in the great Jubilee of 1500, and other Roman building projects of the 1490s were clearly intended to be completed in time for the Holy Year. Renovations undertaken at St John the Lateran in 1493 can be seen in that context. Like Sixtus IV in the early 1470s, Alexander was concerned to ease the flow of pilgrim traffic in the city and, to that end, cut a swathe through the densely packed buildings between Castel S. Angelo and St Peter's to create the Alessandrina or Borgo Nuovo in 1499. Thus, in terms of urban planning, Alexander can be placed firmly in the tradition of Nicholas V – as can that of the via Recta to Julius II and the via Giulia, and the similarly straight streets laid out for the Medici popes, to Leo X and Clement VII. From the 1930s the via della Conciliazione obliterated the via Alessandrina, though its route can nevertheless be traced along the northern edge of the great Fascist thoroughfare.

Alexander had confounded his enemies in the affair of the Cibo castles. He had refused, point blank, to bow to the Spanish dictate for persecution of Jews. He had formed a strategic alliance with Ferrante of Naples and sealed it with an arranged marriage. He had formed a counter alliance, the League of St Mark, and sealed it with another marriage. He had adjudicated on the geographical division of the New World. He had aligned himself with the Spanish superpower by the favourability of his judgement and strengthened this alignment with a third marriage. In Rome, on behalf of the Vatican, he had commissioned Renaissance masterpieces, thus adding greatly to the status of the Church.

But, however adroitly he had managed to wield influence with opposing political interests, he well knew that his problems were not ending. In truth, they were merely beginning. The whole of Europe was bracing itself for a power struggle, where the Vatican was highly unlikely to emerge victorious. And Alexander's nemesis, the treacherous Cardinal Giuliano della Rovere, having dramatically switched sides, was preparing to be as treasonous to his country as he had been to the Church.

Alexander has been criticized for cultivating secular princes. But, as with the Marrano dictate from the Spanish rulers, he was unafraid to go against their interests, if need be. Barely two years into his papacy, his political acumen, negotiating powers and moral courage would be tested to their utmost. In the balance would hang control of Italy, Rome and the very status of the papacy itself. Failure would not be a viable option.

Chapter 3. SCHEMES, SCANDALS, FANATICISM AND INVASION

'...arrayed in a black doublet edged with gold brocade, belted in the Spanish fashion with sword and dagger...Spanish boots and a velvet biretta'

In 1493 the only significant secular ruler to die was Emperor Frederick III, leaving Maximilian I as head of the house of Habsburg, king of the Romans, and *de facto* emperor. 1494, by contrast, witnessed the deaths of Ferrante, king of Naples since 1458, and Gian Galeazzo Sforza, the sidelined duke of Milan. Ludovico il Moro added the ducal title to the authority he already held. Before the year was out, Piero de' Medici was exiled, ending 60 years of Medicean control in Florence. Those facts alone suggest the end of an era, but they fail to take account of the connecting thread provided by the French Charles VIII's invasion of the peninsula. This came about as a consequence of the extinction of the ducal house of Anjou and the reversion to Charles of its claim to the Neapolitan kingdom.

During the regency of Charles' elder sister, Anne de Beaujeau, a campaign had begun to reduce the independent duchy of Brittany to French subjection. François II, the Breton duke, died in 1488, leaving the duchy to his 12-year-old daughter. In an effort to maintain Breton independence, this spirited girl consented to a proxy marriage with Maximilian of Habsburg. However, encouraged by his sister, the 18-year-old Charles marched into Brittany and compelled the young heiress to marry him, in 1491. By the terms of that marriage, Brittany remained independent, under the rule of its duchess who was also queen of France (Anne's regency having ended that same year).

In military terms, the Breton campaign was effectively a dress rehearsal for an intended invasion of Italy, in 1494 – a rehearsal denied to the Italian states. The French army possessed the same crucial advantage as had the

Spanish army in the recent successful Granada war; they had cannon with masonry-penetrating iron cannonballs. Hitherto, high city walls had provided reasonable defence against attackers with scaling ladders; now they fell away when pierced by increasingly heavy and increasingly accurate cannonballs.

City walls aside, the first step was to determine whether Alexander's resolve would crumble when politically tested. Peron de Basche was duly despatched to Rome to demand the investiture of Charles. Alexander easily flummoxed him by nimbly sidestepping the decision. He simply declared that Charles' claims should be transferred from the political sphere to the judicial. They would be examined, and judged, by a tribunal of the Holy See. Recourse to arms was ruled out. Thus Basche was getting a stern message that invasion would certainly result in Alexander's refusing an investiture on behalf of Charles. Faced with calm, implacable logic, Basche did what all bullies do; he blustered and resorted to threats. A General Council would be called; Alexander would be deposed. Unfortunately for him, Alexander did not respond well to such threats; the unhappy fellow returned to France empty-handed. Alexander had decisively won the first round.

Several months later, Charles sent another envoy, Guillaume Briconnet, the newly appointed bishop of St Malo. He was more reasonable, but Alexander kept to his policy. As with the Cibo castles affair, Alexander wished to resort to legal inquiry and legal judgement, not browbeating and crude political threats. He was thus promoting reason, not force, either physical or verbal. But he was also buying time.

Alexander's skills at diplomacy, Ferrante's skills at deception and their joint influence at the Spanish court might have been enough to keep the French threat in stalemate. Certainly Ferrante would have fought like a tiger to retain control of Naples. But his death in 1494 – 'sine cruce, sine luce, sine Deo' (crossless, lightless, Godless) – deprived Alexander of a key ally, however fickle and self-serving. Worse, it brought matters to an abrupt head. Ferrante's heir, Alfonso II, demanded that Alexander recognize *his* right to the throne. Recognition and investiture would irrevocably commit Alexander to the cause of Naples. And Alexander, like so many of his age, was a man who liked to play both sides and steer well clear of irrevocable commitment.

What to do? Alexander already had his policy, but he must have reviewed it and questioned it one more time. Certainly a Borgia dynasty would flourish better under the protection of France than any temporary ally such as Naples. But French dominion of Naples would surely give them control over all of Italy. And this would lead the papacy straight back to another Avignon, another unthinkable 'Babylonian captivity'. Faced with what was best for his family and what was best for the papacy, Alexander made a decisive choice. He did what was best for the papacy. He agreed to the recognition and investiture of Alfonso.

Typically, however, Alexander still hedged his bets, driving a hard bargain for his children. Cesare received benefices. Neapolitan principalities were granted to Juan and Jofré. Juan was also offered 33,000 ducats per year as a *condottiere* in the Neapolitan army, even though he was living in Spain. The date of the arranged marriage between Jofré and Alfonso's daughter, Sancia, was brought forward.

Alfonso was duly crowned in Naples on Ascension Day, 8 May 1494, in what was very much a Borgia family affair. Alexander's nephew, Cardinal Juan Borgia-Lanzol, crowned him. His brother, Galceran Borgia-Lanzol, was a standard bearer for Jofré. Jofré (who married Sancia three days later) carried the crown. Again, Alexander was aligning dynastic and papal interests. But the omens were unpropitious. It was the day of the full moon, so chosen by a superstitious Alfonso. Burchard, the papal master of ceremonies, wrote that Alfonso's orb was attached to his hand by silk cords and a chain. If it fell, disaster would follow. No more fitting metaphor could have been devised.

Alfonso's investiture meant that there was no going back. Events were now set on a collision course. For Charles, his coveted prize was being snatched away from him. The College of Cardinals was split. Alexander had lost his old ally, Ascanio Sforza, who viewed the Neapolitan alliance as anti-Milanese. Della Rovere was in France, urging a Church Council which would depose Alexander on the convenient pretext of his supposedly simonical election.

In the opposing camp, Alexander had the bare bones of a papal army; clearly it could mount no feasible defence against the French one. The loyalty of cities within the papal states was not to be counted on. Even a desperate attempt to gain money from the Sultan Bayezid, a crusade target of Charles, was fruitless. As a contemporary official in the Curia noted, Alexander's only real ally was the unfortunate Alfonso. In July, the two of them met at

Vicovaro. Ferrantino, Alfonso's son, would take their joint forces into the Romagna to defend the Lombardy border. Meanwhile Federigo of Aragon, Alfonso's brother, would mount a naval attack on Genoa.

As if matters were not bad enough, Alexander was vexed with a domestic crisis. Lucrezia's husband, Giovanni Sforza, was hopelessly compromised – by being a *condottiere* of Milan by birth and a *condottiere* of Naples by marriage. Alexander, weighed down by much greater burdens, brusquely told him to please himself as to which side he fought for. Understandably Giovanni wanted to support the Sforzas; but he also wanted to retain control of Pesaro, a papal fief. The luckless fellow wrote to his cousin, Ludovico il Moro, with profuse protestations of Sforza loyalty. With, one must suppose, unintentional humour, he claimed that he would have eaten the straw of his mattress rather than become a papal *condottiere*, had he known where this would lead. Certainly Pesaro seemed a safer place for him than Rome. Alexander was always reluctant to let his children out of his sight. But, in this case, an outbreak of plague in Rome swayed him. He gave Lucrezia permission to leave the city for two months. On 31 May, Giovanni and Lucrezia departed. With them were Alexander's mistress, Giulia Farnese; her chaperone, Adriana de Mila; and a retinue of maids-in-waiting. Overseeing all was Francesco Gacet, Alexander's confidential agent. His instructions were to have everyone back in Rome by the end of July.

Free of fearful, plague-ridden Rome and away from the stern influence of Alexander, Lucrezia and Giulia were set to party. Giulia was still only 19, Lucrezia a mere 14. Dressed in the height of fashion, 'as if we had despoiled Florence of brocade', they threw themselves into a frenetic social life, a frivolous pursuit of pleasure. Frequent letters to Alexander did a questionable job of reassuring him. Lucrezia wrote: 'We hear that things are going badly in Rome and I implore your Holiness to leave, but if that is not practical, to take the greatest care'. Giulia somewhat archly noted, 'As your Holiness, upon whom all my well-being and happiness depends, is not here, it is impossible for me to enjoy these pleasures, because, where my treasure is there, my heart is also'. The ladies were in no hurry to return. Nor was Giovanni, still morally compromised, a member of the Neapolitan army and, shamefully, now also a spy for the Sforza clan.

In July, Giulia received news that her eldest brother was dying. She insisted upon going to him. Gacet and de Mila hurried her through the mountains, to the Farnese family home at Capodimonte. Giulia's unfortunate husband, Orsino Orsini, made a surprise arrival at Bassanello, only 30 miles away, ignoring his military role in a desperate bid to recover his wife. On hearing this unwelcome news Alexander became irate, commanding Giulia to avoid her husband and return to Rome. When she didn't return, Alexander, in his role on this occasion of spurned lover, unleashed a stream of invective against the 'thankless and treacherous Giulia', her brother, Cardinal Alessandro Farnese, and against the unreliable chaperone, Adriana de Mila, who had 'finally laid bare the malignity and evil of her soul'. Threatening Giulia with excommunication was an act of papal rage spilling over into, again no doubt unintentional, comedy.

The French army crossed the Alps on 2 September 1494. Sweeping southwards, they intercepted Lucrezia and Giulia on the via Cassia. The captured ladies were chivalrously escorted to Montefiascone and a ransom of 3,000 ducats was promptly paid by Alexander. Still escorted by the French, they were brought to the gate of Rome on 1 December. Alexander met them in person, 'arrayed in a black doublet edged with gold brocade, belted in the Spanish fashion with sword and dagger; he wore also Spanish boots and a velvet biretta'. On the edge of ruin, Alexander cut a swashbuckling figure; doubtless the young ladies were impressed. That night, Giulia slept in Alexander's palace...

As Alexander predicted, the French had come both by land and sea. The land army brought what we would now term 'culture shock' to the Italians. In the world of the Italian Renaissance, war, as much else, had been transmuted to art and commerce. The *condottieri* aimed at elegant military solutions, usually involving capture of territory and prisoners for ransom. They were great strategists, master tacticians, supremely knowledgeable about theories of fortifications and artillery. But they were not skilled, experienced practitioners of military butchery. Guicciardini noted that, before this climactic year of 1494, battles, however protracted, were relatively bloodless and artillery bombardment 'was managed with such want of skill that it caused little hurt'. But the mercenary Swiss infantry were well disciplined and merciless. And the 'diabolical rather than human instrument' of iron firing cannonballs struck terror into opponents.

The results were predictable. The unnerved Italians were psychologically defeated. The invasion became a triumphal procession. Children waved banners with the French arms. At Asti, Charles met with the deadly trio of conspirators, Ludovico il Moro, Ercole d'Este and Giuliano della Rovere, united all in their pursuit of Alexander.

However, a complication struck when Charles fell ill with smallpox at Asti and the army was delayed. The Neapolitans had calculated that Charles would head south, through the Romagna; consequently they sent their armies northeastwards. Instead, the French took the westerly route, entering Florentine territory at Sarzana, whose garrison rapidly capitulated. Fearful of the fabled might of French artillery, the commanders of fortress after fortress surrendered without a fight. Little did they know that most of the artillery was still being transported southwards by sea. They allowed themselves to be beaten, not by insuperable odds, but merely by the spectre of perceived threat.

In emulation of his father's mission to Naples in 1480, Piero de' Medici attempted to pull off a feat of heroic diplomacy. Instead, he succeeded in handing over Florentine's principal port, Pisa, together with Livorno and the other coastal fortresses, to the invaders. The history of Franco-Florentine banking and commercial relations made friendship with Charles look reasonable, in spite of the loss of face. The Medici bank was already a shadow of its former self, and it now collapsed completely amid the political turmoil of 1494. Piero and his kinsmen were promptly exiled for bringing such disgrace upon Florence. (Piero died in 1503, but the family regrouped under the leadership of Cardinal Giovanni, in Rome.)

The sudden absence of the Medici was a tremendous shock to the Florentine political elite. No one active in politics could remember the years before 1434 and the beginning of Medicean dominance. No other networks existed in 1494 to do as the Medici themselves had done in 1434, when they assumed the dominant role previously held by factions headed by Maso degli Albizzi. It was in this context that Florentines looked for someone else to guide them; that someone was Savonarola.

Girolamo Savonarola (1452–98) was the grandson of a famous Paduan physician, Michele Savonarola, employed by the Este of Ferrara. He was born at Ferrara. After a sudden conversion experience, he entered the Dominican monastery of S. Domenico at Bologna in 1475, and rapidly attained fame as a preacher and theologian. Unlike the Benedictine monks with their vow of stability, Dominican friars moved from friary to friary, city to city.

Between 1482 and 1485, Savonarola gained his first experience at the church of S. Marco, Florence, which had benefited in material terms from the patronage of Cosimo de' Medici and his successors and, in artistic and spiritual terms, from the 45 frescoes painted in and around the friars' cells by Fra Angelico. It was virtually a Medici dwelling; so much so that it was at the request of Lorenzo that Savonarola was recalled there, in 1490. The following year, he was elected prior. Until 1494, Savonarola was very much a footnote in Florentine history, even though he presided over a flourishing institution which attracted many young patrician men to the Dominican life. It was only the extraordinary circumstances of 1494 that brought him out of his convent and into the attention of contemporaries and of posterity.

In December 1494, Savonarola preached a series of powerful sermons on the reform of the Florentine constitution and, doubtless, did so in an accent that betrayed his Ferrarese origins and the fact that he was a foreigner in Florence. (Hitherto he had confined himself to preaching on the spiritual and social themes that were the friars' conventional subject matter.) In his preaching, Savonarola presented Charles as the instrument of God's vengeance on sinful Florence. Both God and king would need to be placated. Political and economic crisis demanded reform of the structures and practice of Florentine government. In a tradition stretching back to Aristotle, he explained how systems of government are determined by climate. Thus, in hot regions, where men are 'more faint-hearted...because they are less full-blooded', they naturally lend themselves to rule by monarchs. In the cold regions of the north, where 'blood is abundant but intelligence scarce', monarchy is also the most appropriate form of government. In Italy's middle region, he continued, 'there is an abundance of both blood and intelligence', where popular, republican government comes naturally; the people would not stand for being bridled by a monarch. Flattering his audience, he added that nowhere did popular government come more naturally than in Florence.[1]

Curiously for a Ferrarese, whose state was periodically threatened by

Venetian armies, Savonarola recommended the adoption of an essentially Venetian constitution (albeit without a doge-like figure to provide continuity as life chairman of the various senior councils and committees of government). According to the political thought of the Renaissance era, Venetian government embodied the Aristotelian ideal mix of monarchy (in the person of the Doge), aristocracy (the Senate) and democracy (the Great Council/Maggior Consiglio). Modern notions of democracy were alien to this system, the Maggior Consiglio consisting of adult non-clerical males from patrician families. This acted as a pool from which men were selected to assume more specialized roles, whether in Venice, in the government of its mainland and sea empires, or as ambassadors.

Such was Savonarola's impact that the equivalent of a Senate and a Maggior Consiglio were soon created. The principal object of the exercise was to increase the number of people taking part in government, after Medicean narrowing of the political class. 3,000 men sat in the Florentine Great Council. This was the highest level of participation that the republic ever achieved in its entire history. The downside of this outburst of democracy was that it put power and responsibility into the hands of politically inexperienced shopkeepers, who could quite clearly be distinguished from the patrician merchants who held public office in Venice.

While Savonarola continued to make his apocalyptical utterances, the French advance continued unabated. It was matched with a naval victory against a Neapolitan fleet, off Rapallo. Back in September, Ascanio Sforza had instigated a Colonna revolt; the port of Ostia was seized and the French flag fluttered above it. Rome was vulnerable to naval attack. As if on cue, French ships appeared at the mouth of the Tiber. Cardinal Francesco Todeschini-Piccolomini (the future Pope Pius III) was sent by Alexander to negotiate with Charles. However, the Neapolitan marriage of his brother Antonio suggested he was less than impartial. Giuliano della Rovere persuaded Charles not to see him. Inside the city walls, Alexander had his erstwhile king-maker, Ascanio Sforza, and the other pro-French cardinals arrested.

The end came with a typical piece of Italian Renaissance treachery. Virginio Orsini swapped allegiances and gave the massive castle of Bracciano to the French. The defence of Rome was now hopeless. On Christmas Day 1494, Alexander ordered Ferrantino to withdraw his troops to Naples. He considered fleeing to Naples himself, but decided against it. He therefore instructed the city fathers to surrender to Charles, and retreated to Castel S. Angelo. On 31 December, the invading French army marched into Rome through the Porta del Popolo. In Alexander's bitter words: 'The French came in with wooden spears and found they had nothing to do but the quartermaster's work of marking the doors with chalk'.

Castel S. Angelo was Alexander's last remaining defensive position. Although Nicholas V had added circular corner towers to the fortress, improved artillery meant that further developments had to be undertaken in the 1490s. (Ironically, Giuliano della Rovere had set the standard with his castello at nearby Ostia, built in the 1480s, with lower, thicker walls designed to withstand attack from siege artillery.) In the course of the Italian Wars, engineers had developed the earth-filled angled bastion of Castel S. Angelo in such a way as to ensure that it would not collapse under enemy fire and that no section of wall was left unprotected by covering fire. Architects served as military engineers, such as Leonardo da Vinci at Piombino and Michelangelo Buonarroti at Civitavecchia. Alexander's chief engineer at Castel S. Angelo was the Florentine Antonio da Sangallo the elder, who had already worked for the then Cardinal Borgia to reinforce the fortifications at Nepi, north of Rome, and went on to fortify nearby Città Castellana, strategically placed on the via Flaminia. Houses were demolished around Castel S. Angelo so that the outer earthworks could be extended, and there was even a plan for diverting the Tiber in order to strengthen the defences on all four sides. After improvement, the fortress was thought to have sufficient storage space to withstand a siege of up to three years.

While Alexander took refuge in Castel S. Angelo, Charles, the triumphant invader, installed himself at the Palazzo S. Marco (now Palazzo Venezia) in the centre of Rome. Alexander was abandoned by his allies and surrounded by his enemies, who held near-absolute military power. A lesser man would have buckled. A later pope, Leo X, upon coming under threat by another king, still some distance from Rome, cravenly implored, 'We shall see what the most Christian King will do, we shall place ourselves in his hands and shall ask him for mercy'. But Alexander was made of sterner stuff. Now only the very last recourse was left to him. Clearly his enemies could not be defeated by military means. But they might yet be defeated by psychological means. In Alexander, they were to encounter a subtle strategist, a nimble psychologist supremely capable of leading a negotiation masterclass.

Rome was in the grip of the French. Their cannons were pointed at Castel S. Angelo. Alexander began his psychological warfare by spreading a rumour that, at the first cannon shot, he would present himself for all to see, on the castle walls, wearing his pontifical vestments and holding the Sacred Host in his hands. As an exercise in political brinksmanship, this was spectacularly effective. The cannons stood silent, impotent. Alexander had effortlessly won this round. But he was keenly aware that he would have to win *every* round if his papacy was to survive.

The French army had entered Rome to cries of '*Viva Francia!*' But invading armies very quickly wear out their welcome. The French army, like many such armies before and after, behaved in a barbaric fashion. Rape, violence and assassination were rife. Food quickly ran short. Houses of 'people who mattered' were unwisely ransacked, including the palace of Vanozza Catanai, Alexander's former lover and the father of four of his cherished children. In horrible contrast to Alexander's religious toleration, Jews were brutally strangled. Romans were hanged on the Campo dei Fiori. The ugly and boorish Charles VIII conspicuously lacked the social graces of Roman high society. Fearful of being poisoned by his hosts, every morsel of food, every goblet of wine had to be tasted in his presence; only then was it deemed fit for his gluttonous consumption.

With each passing day of January 1495, the Roman love affair with the French invaders cooled. As with so many climactic meetings in history, the outcome would ultimately be decided by personalities – the 64-year-old pope versus the young king and his retinue of advisers.

Of Charles, Zaccaria Contarini had written:

> His Majesty the King of France is 22 years of age; he is small and ill-made, ugly of countenance, with large, colourless eyes; he is short-sighted; his nose is aquiline and both longer and thicker than is natural; he has lips likewise thick, always hanging open; his hands twitch with spasmodic movements very ugly to see, and his speech comes hesitantly. My opinion may be erroneous, but it seems to me certain that physically and morally he does not amount to a great deal.[2]

Earlier, the astute Ludovico il Moro had sagely noted:

> This King of France is young and of poor judgement; he is not
> advised as he ought to be. His advisors are in two groups: the
> one...and the other...absolutely opposed in all things to the first.
> In their determination to overcome each other, they have no care
> for the interests of the Kingdom. And each group is concerned
> with gaining money, with no care for anything else. All of them
> together would not make half of one competent man...When one,
> giving his attention to the matter for an instant, came to a decision
> and ordered that certain instructions be given, there was instantly
> another to cancel what the first had done. The King is haughty and
> ambitious beyond all imagining, and he has esteem for no one...[3]

Giuliano della Rovere and the French cardinals urged Charles to depose
Alexander and call a General Council to elect a successor – a breathtaking
act of treachery. Unsurprisingly, Alexander's cardinal emissaries espoused
an opposing view. Charles had come to Italy to receive the investiture of
Naples. Might this not be better progressed through an understanding with
a pope, already *in situ* and with generally accepted authority?

With consummate understatement, Philippe de Commines commented,
'The King was young and his surroundings did not fit him for so great a work
as the reform of the Church.'[4] Charles was impatient to get on to Naples.
Alexander was equally impatient to get him out of Rome. On 10 January,
part of the wall of the supposedly impregnable Castel S. Angelo had collapsed
of its own accord. (So much for the ability to withstand a three-year siege.)
The Colonna were terrified that 'their' city and their power were collapsing
into ruin. Even Cardinals Sforza and della Rovere, both candidates for the
papacy, began to lose their nerve, fearing that calling for a General Council
might cost them their very lives.

With supreme irony, della Rovere himself warned Charles of a popular
uprising. Everybody wanted a way out of the impasse. Everybody wanted a
deal.

Terms were agreed five days later, on 15 January. The French army
could proceed uncontested across the papal states. Alexander's son, Cesare
Borgia, would accompany them as papal legate – in reality, a euphemism for

hostage. The French would also receive custody of the Turkish Prince Jem, a papal prisoner since 1489.

A few words must be said of Jem a popular, exotic, yet ultimately tragic figure. He was the son of Sultan Mahomet II. On the death of his father, he fought against his brother, Sultan Bayezid II. Defeated in battle, he sought protection from the Knights of Rhodes, who gave him their sworn word to protect him. But the sworn word of these Christian gentlemen proved utterly worthless. Sultan Bayezid, now ensconced as the Turkish ruler, bribed the venal Knights to imprison Jem, for 40,000 ducats per year. Shamefully they accepted, and European rulers shamelessly fought over him. The king of France had sent him to Pope Innocent VIII, who passed him on to Alexander. Now Charles VIII wanted him back.

Jem had been a popular figure with Romans in general and the Borgias in particular, regularly going riding with Alexander's sons. However, self-interest overruled sentiment. Alexander, struggling desperately for outside support, once more tried to solicit aid from the Turks. And he used the prospect of handing Jem over to the French as a lever. Unfortunately, when his emissary, Bocciardo, was captured with incriminating evidence, his enemies achieved an unexpected propaganda coup. Jem's value as a negotiating pawn dropped accordingly and including him in the deal was adjudged a small price indeed to get the French out of Rome.

For their part, the French agreed that Alexander could keep Castel S. Angelo. The keys of Rome would be handed back. Charles promised obedience and loyalty to Alexander as the true pope. To keep the peace, there would be an amnesty for Churchmen who had defected to France. And certain castles and cities would have French governors. Crucially, however, there was neither mention of Neapolitan investiture, nor ecclesiastical reform. Alexander was getting rid of the French, while sidestepping their initial demands. He was giving away surprisingly little of lasting value.

Alexander and Charles met the very next day, on 16 January 1495. In what we would now term a 'charm offensive', Alexander won over the heart and mind of the gauche king, effortlessly conveying an impression of affability laced with innate superiority. As the Mantuan envoy noted, Alexander 'gratifies the French in every way; favours of all sorts are bestowed on them'. But when the awkward question of the investiture of Naples was raised, Alexander wriggled out of it by citing a need for 'closer examination'.

On 17 January Alexander said Mass in front of a huge crowd, including 20,000 soldiers in the great square of St Peter's. Charles himself acted as server. Alexander might be forgiven for heaving a great sigh of relief.

On 27 January the French left Rome, to the heartfelt joy of those who had cheered their entrance only a month previously. Charles must have felt that, with his new-found friend Alexander, he was leaving behind an ally. He would have done well to heed the grim maxim, which resonates across the centuries. 'Put not your trust in princes.' For, in truth, this prince of the Church had outwitted him.

Charles marched off to Naples, leaving a half-secured Italy behind him. Despite Spanish equivocation, Alexander well knew that King Ferdinand and Queen Isabella could never tolerate an imbalance of power due to permanent French control, either of the papacy or of Naples. In Velletri, the Spanish ambassadors caught up with Charles. They delivered stern protests against the occupation of papal towns, the treatment of the pope and the advance upon Naples. Antonio de Fonseca, one of the envoys, declared that any attack upon Naples against the will of its suzerain, the pope, would constitute a flagrant breach of papal authority. Charles made stuttering attempts to justify himself. Quite reasonably, he pointed out that Alexander had, of his own volition, made an agreement with him. Somewhat ineffectually, he claimed that, after conquering Naples, he would have its ownership judged by the pope, whose decision he was fully prepared to accept. But crucially, with touching honesty yet abysmal political judgement, he finished by pointing out that he had simply come too far to go back and any further discussion of the matter was pointless.

With his last statement, Charles had played straight into de Fonseca's hands; his *fait accompli* set the French position firmly outside the law. In front of Charles, de Fonseca held up the treaty of Barcelona, between Spain and France. He ripped it into pieces and threw them on the floor. Before God, he said, Ferdinand and Isabella were released from the tenets of the treaty! De Fonseca's arguments were the same as those employed by Alexander. It was as though the invisible hand of Alexander was dictating de Fonseca's approach, to harass Charles psychologically while eroding his moral authority.

The campaign of attrition against Charles continued unabated. Shortly afterwards, Cesare Borgia, the papal legate cum hostage, disguised himself as a lowly groom, eloped from the French camp and escaped from the town. Publicly Alexander condemned Cesar's escape, sending the bishop of Nepi to Charles with the most profuse of apologies. And Charles sent Philippe de Bresse to Rome in protest against this breach of the agreement. But no amount of diplomatic niceties could disguise the stark fact that Cesare was gone, never to return.

With Naples firmly fixed in his mind, Charles continued his advance. As before, terror propaganda, the legend of French prowess and brutality, decimated resistance. As the French approached Naples, King Alfonso abdicated in favour of his son, Fernando II, known as Ferrantino, and fled to Sicily where his cousin, Ferdinand of Aragon, was king. Ferrantino soon followed. The Aragonese kings of Naples were relative newcomers, to whom the native nobility had no particular allegiance and against whom they had rebelled in the 1480s. At the end of February, the French arrived at Naples. The weather was mild; spring flowers were peeping through the warm soil. As with his arrival at Rome, Charles entered the city to rapturous applause. One commentator noted, 'In the short space of a few weeks, the French conquered, as by a miracle, a whole kingdom, almost without striking a blow'.

Charles had achieved his objective – and yet already his luck was turning. Cesare's defection, while humiliating, could be dismissed as an irritant. But the loss of his second hostage was far worse. The unfortunate Prince Jem was ill-prepared for the rigours of an army on the march. Before Capua, almost within sight of Naples, he contracted a fever. He struggled forward, towards Naples, on horseback. But, barely a month after being entrusted to Charles' custody, he died.

Inevitably perhaps, Alexander has been accused – quite wrongly – of having had Jem poisoned. The assassination of Julius Caesar was a case study in how the questionable benefits of 'wet work' and 'termination with extreme prejudice' could be utterly negated by moral outrage from an aggrieved populace. (Undoubtedly Machiavelli, as with our contemporary politicians, would have regarded such negation as due to poor public relations.) But, since Caesar, assassination has either been public, attributable and an overt instrument of terror (the Sicarii, the Assassins of Alamut, the Mafia, ETA,

IRA, al-Qaeda) or it has been covert with 'plausible deniability' (e.g. the assassinations secretly commissioned by many 'civilized' nations, in our own time).

It is relevant at this point that we observe the convenient emergence (for the myth-makers) of the mysterious *cantarella*, a whitish powder with a delayed action, a supposedly proven Renaissance poison. For the Borgias, deniability would have been paramount. But 500 years later, *cantarella* seems a mythical archetype, akin to the 'delayed death touch' that reputedly killed Bruce Lee. And, alas for conspiracy theorists, there is no evidence whatsoever to link Alexander with Jem's death. Motive? Certainly Jem's death weakened Charles' position. But already Alexander was making good progress towards weakening it far more. And, if Sultan Bayezid offered a bribe for the killing of his brother, there is no sign that such a bribe was ever collected. Jem's untimely death seems entirely attributable to natural causes. One hopes that his spirit, freed at last from the machinations of avaricious power mongers, found solace in the hereafter.

Charles would have done well to heed the maxim later succinctly expressed by Santayana, 'Those who do not learn from history are condemned to repeat it'. His army's sojourn in Rome had begun well and rapidly gone sour. The same thing happened in Naples. The defeated Neapolitans were treated with contempt. In an act of overweening folly and tactlessness, Charles placed the crown of Naples on his own head in the cathedral. The profuse applause was entirely self-serving. The writer, Giovanni Pontano, who had hitherto praised Ferrante, now derided him, lauding Charles instead. Such traitors make singularly unreliable allies.

Having assumed the crown of Naples, Charles gave himself over to the pursuits of the flesh as the place cast its sultry spell over him. Meanwhile his retinue asset-stripped everything in sight. And finally, belatedly, not only Italy but the whole of Europe woke up to the perils of the French adventure. Alexander proved annoyingly unbribable, steadfastly refusing an investiture despite Charles' offer of 150,000 ducats as a down payment and an annual tribute of another 40,000. (This point is not stressed in pro-myth accounts.)

Meanwhile, the crown, so recently placed there, sat shakily upon the king's head. Ludovico il Moro, having hastened the French arrival, now schemed for their departure, fearing an old French claim to Milan. Venice was concerned about the imbalance of power in Italy and its unwelcome implications for sea routes in the Mediterranean. Spain could not afford a European imbalance of power, with the French seizure of Naples and consequent threat to Sicily – where Gonsalvo de Córdoba, the great Spanish general, was promptly sent.

The so-called Holy League, comprising Milan, Venice, Spain, the papacy and the Emperor Maximilian came into being on 31 March 1495. The only notable absentee was Florence, which adhered to its French alliance. As we have seen, Florence was then at the height of its Savonarolan moral revolution. It was also in economic turmoil, the Pisan revolt having deprived it of its principal port. This suited Venetian and Milanese mercantile interests. Maximilian, who was not the most reliable of allies in any circumstances, offered to crush the Pisans in return for coronation by the pope. As Savonarola was the most public advocate of the Franco-Florentine alliance, Alexander saw that the Dominican's authority had to be destroyed. Savonarola refused a papal summons to Rome. Alexander retaliated by forbidding him from preaching.

Ostensibly the Holy League was brought into being to fight the Turks. Its true aim was the defence of Italy, the papacy and the Holy Roman Empire. And it was a marriage of convenience. On Palm Sunday, Pope Alexander, so recently Charles' amiable friend, ordered the solemn proclamation of the League through the papal territories. There was a fit of public celebration across the land – except that now, those who had cheered for Charles were cheering against him. Charles was to learn a harsh lesson indeed; gaining a crown and keeping it require very different qualities.

The formation of the Holy League meant that the lines of communication between France and its army were threatened. Clearly, if Charles remained in Naples, sooner or later he would be trapped. Accordingly, he split his army in two; one half remained, the other began a slow retreat to the Alps. Twenty thousand mule loads of plundered Neapolitan treasures slowed their progress. Rome, which had seen the French depart not three months previously, now trembled at their return. A contemporary noted, 'People are in terror. Rome has never been so entirely cleared of silver and valuables. Not one of the cardinals has enough plate left to serve six persons. The very houses are being dismantled'.[5]

Anybody with any sense got out of Rome as fast as they could, taking their valuables with them. One such refugee was Alexander himself, who fled to Orvieto, with most of the cardinals. Cardinal Pallivicini was deputized to greet Charles in Rome and minimize the expected damage from the retreating French army. As it happened, this time around, the French were relatively disciplined. Perhaps they feared retribution.

Charles was most anxious for an audience with Alexander. Frustratingly, the investiture of Naples remained as elusive as ever. And yet, if he could somehow prise Alexander from the Holy League, all might not be lost. But Alexander was equally anxious not to see Charles. Charles headed towards Orvieto. Alexander decamped to Perugia – beyond the scope of the French army. In the north of Italy, the forces of Milan and Venice were forming. Charles awoke to his terrible folly. An audience with the canny Alexander was impossible. The investiture was a failed dream. Italy, which had once welcomed him to its bosom, had viciously turned against him. As a conqueror, he was a sham. As a reformer, he was an abject failure. With delicious irony and typical Italian duplicity, Savonarola, who had once preached the glories of Charles, now, with equal vehemence, denounced the French king.

By now, Italy could have meant only one thing to Charles – escape. The approaching Alps were his refuge. At the Taro, his progress was blocked by the forces of the Holy League. At Fornovo, near Parma, on 6 July 1495 his weary army was forced to fight a far greater force. The battle was fierce. Both sides claimed victory, but the sober reality is that only the poor tactics of the opposition saved Charles from being taken prisoner. Both armies were composed of mixed nationalities. The French forces also numbered Italians, Swiss and Germans, but the forces of the Holy League were heavily dependent upon mercenaries. And, at Fornovo, these mercenaries were more concerned with looting the royal convoy than pressing home their military advantage. One consequence of this encounter was that, in later years, Machiavelli lobbied for the creation of a citizen militia. He realized that the security of the Italian states could never be safely entrusted to gold-hungry mercenaries. And, in *Il principe*, he repeated Alexander's argument that unity between the Italian states was a pressing need, if the disaster and humiliation of 1494 was not to be repeated.

In a papal Bull of August 1495, Alexander dedicated stern words 'to our very dear son in Jesus Christ, Charles, most Christian King of the French'. The French army must cease and desist. In effect, Alexander delivered a public relations coup with the French queen, the French cardinals, the French nobles and the Parlement of France. As with the Vietnam war, the effect was to hamstring the military by criticism 'back home', from their own side.

Charles scuttled across the Alps to safety, leaving behind his sword, his helmet, his gold seal and a 'black book' of portraits of his amours. Conversely, Alexander returned to Rome in triumph. Gonsalvo de Córdoba won back Naples and King Ferrantino returned to his kingdom. The Aragonese dynasty was rapidly restored. Some of the French army escaped by ship; but many others were mercilessly cut down, in hopeless fealty to their king's foolish dream.

Keenly aware that the danger persisted, Alexander continued to mastermind opposition to the French. He threatened the Swiss allies with religious sanctions. He urged Spain to war. And he urged Maximilian to fight. He was driven by two overriding aims – the maintenance of the Holy League and the independence of Italy.

In truth, the Holy League, that cynical marriage of convenience, began to unravel almost immediately. As we have seen, Ludovico il Moro, having welcomed Charles into Italy, later turned against him. But he showed little resistance as the retreating French army passed through Milanese territory, his commitment to the Holy League being distinctly half-hearted. Now, in a breathtaking display of duplicity, he made a second volte-face and re-established relations with Charles. Naples, once out of immediate danger, would, of course, go its own way. Venice, an uncertain ally at the best of times, was itself a cabal of opposing interests. Tellingly, Ludovico remarked, 'Each of these [Venetian] lords knows more than I, but not all of them together'. Sadly Maximilian showed that even emperors may be rendered politically impotent by vassals who produce neither money for battle nor men to fight.

However many the faults of Charles VIII, nobody could possibly doubt either his physical or moral courage. But his abrupt exit was more of a French self-defeat than an Italian triumph. Guicciardini chooses to regard 1494 as an *annus horribilis* in Italian history and undoubtedly he is right.

The Italians had shown themselves to be Byzantine in their amorality, changing sides with dizzying alacrity. Treason and treachery were their watchwords. Italy was a country hopelessly divided and thereby utterly compromised. The Holy League, however worthy an aspiration, proved, in practice, to be made of straw. Despite the best efforts of Alexander, any proper show of unity was a pipe dream. Where one army had come, another would follow... and another. The history of Italy would be soaked in blood.

But all this was to come. For the present, that inveterate plotter, Giuliano della Rovere, and the invader, Charles VIII, had both been soundly thwarted by Alexander. A day of reckoning with Savonarola, the fickle friar, was surely not far away. Della Rovere would, of course, continue with his machinations; nothing less was to be expected. But Charles, who once must have seemed almost unbeatable with his control of so much of Italy and of Rome, had been given a sound lesson in negotiation. Alexander, reduced to a refugee in Castel S. Angelo, could reasonably have been expected to capitulate; indeed, a lesser pope would almost certainly have done so. (And what then would have happened to the papacy – a return to Avignon?) Alexander persuaded Charles to vacate Rome, while giving away virtually nothing of lasting value.

And Alexander himself? When it mattered most, he would not be bribed. When it mattered most, he would not be compromised. For once, he laid aside the cause of Borgia advancement. To claim that he was, in some arcane manner, responsible for the French invasion, is spurious. To claim that he was not the most instrumental factor in its swift dispatch is incorrect. As principal servant of the Church and thereby entrusted with its stewardship, Alexander's behaviour, in those terrible days of 1494 and 1495, is to his everlasting credit. However golden the fabled time of 1490 was for the likes of Guicciardini, the reality is that, only five years later, the papacy, Rome, and much of Italy might have fallen under permanent French control. That this did not happen is almost entirely due to Alexander's supreme competence.

One way to appreciate the true scale of Alexander's achievement is this – imagine that, after Dunkirk, Hitler had invaded England in 1940, had actually conquered London, and had then been persuaded by Churchill to remove himself and his army to whence he had come. Flawed a man as he undoubtedly was, Pope Alexander VI showed immense courage and near superhuman competence in dealing with the barbarian within his gate. For this, he deserves the enduring thanks of generations of Romans, Italians and Catholics. In their darkest hour, he did not desert them.

Chapter 4. A FOUL MURDER AND A LIVE BURNING

'I must have seen more than 100 bodies thrown into the Tiber'

Oh Italy! Trouble after trouble shall overwhelm you; troubles of war after famine, pestilence after war. There shall be rumour upon rumour: barbarians on this side, barbarians on that. The law of the priesthood shall perish and priests shall be stripped of their place. Princes shall wear hair-cloth, the people be crushed by tribulation. All men will lose courage and, as they have judged, so shall they themselves be judged.[1]

Thus cried Girolamo Savonarola. The French had departed, leaving a deadly legacy of syphilis in Naples. The troubled year of 1495 came to an end with titanic floods. The Tiber's banks burst; parts of Rome were a full 3 metres under water. Houses were washed away, people drowned in their dozens, hundreds of livestock perished. The flourmills, by the river, were put out of action, so cutting the bread supply. Physical and financial hardship abounded. Perhaps the crowning symbolism came when Alexander's cardinals, coming out of a consistory, were almost washed away to their doom. Only an undignified scramble on to the bridge of S. Angelo saved their hides. Even normally level-headed men spoke of God's terminal judgement on the Italians. Superstition was rife. Savonarola had cited Charles VIII as God's scourge on Italian sinners. Florentines imagined that only the Svengali-like influence of Savonarola over Charles had saved them. Now the rabble-rousing friar was threatening such precarious stability as still existed.

Talleyrand, the great French power broker of the Napoleonic era, astutely noted, 'War is diplomacy by other means'. Conversely, one might suggest that diplomacy is war by other means. By mere words, Alexander had defeated an entire army. By mere words, he had stymied the ambitions of the French king. So he was uniquely positioned to appreciate the potentially lethal power of words.

In Florence, the preaching of Savonarola had instituted what would now be termed a 'cultural revolution'. This involved not merely reforms of the constitution and of taxation, but a social crusade against lax morals and for spiritual regeneration. The friar's nineteenth-century biographer, Pasquale Villari, provides us with a striking summary of this revolution, conveniently omitting any sign of dissent:

> The aspect of the city was completely changed. The women threw aside their jewels and finery, dressed plainly, bore themselves demurely; licentious young Florentines were transformed, as by magic, into sober, religious men; pious hymns took the place of Lorenzo's Carnival songs. The townsfolk passed their leisure hours seated quietly in their shops, reading either the Bible or Savonarola's works. All prayed frequently, flocked to the churches, and gave largely to the poor. Most wonderful of all, bankers and tradesmen were impelled by scruples of conscience to restore ill-gotten gains, amounting to many thousand florins. All men were wonderstruck by this singular and almost miraculous change...[2]

Throughout history, cultural revolutions have rarely had lasting benefits. Whatever the true nature and likely longevity of 'this singular and almost miraculous change', to a concerned pope, one thing was certain: Savonarola was an ongoing threat to the stability of Italy. As the French invasion had shown, he had the propensity to use words in a highly inflammatory manner. In short, he was a 'loose cannon'. He must be stopped.

Alexander's initial attempts at conciliation had been fruitless. Raising the ante, a papal brief was sent to the Franciscans at S. Croce, the rivals to Savonarola's Dominicans at S. Marco, in which the pontiff condemned 'a certain Fra Girolamo' as 'a seeker after novelty and a disseminator of false doctrines'.[3] Alexander also sought to end Savonarola's authority by ordering S. Marco to return to the obedience of the Dominican Lombard Congregation, from which it had lately gained independence. The friar promptly responded, defending his teaching. Examination of his sermons reveals that their content was perfectly orthodox.

What was certainly not orthodox was Savonarola's claim that he had a private hot-line to God, who whispered in his ear alone and gave cast-iron guarantees. Thus continued the good friar: 'As we have received from Him [God] His infallible promise, we guarantee the accomplishment of this with the most perfect certitude...' Even the infidel Turks would be converted to Christendom, because 'He [God] has had the goodness to reveal it to me...'[4]

Alexander remained unconvinced by the existence of a hot-line from God to Savonarola or, indeed, anyone else. In mid-October 1495, a further letter had ordered Savonarola to stop preaching altogether, in private, as well as public. Alexander sternly rebuked him:

> In your pronouncements, you predict the future and affirm that all you say comes from the eternal light and as an inspiration of the Holy Spirit, whereby you lead simple men away from the road of salvation and from obedience to the Holy Roman Church. You ought to have preached unity and peace, instead of these things which the populace calls prophecies and divinations. You should further consider that the conditions of the period do not permit the proclamation of such doctrines, for if, by their own nature, they are liable to cause discord, even if complete peace were reigning, how much more are they bound to do so, at a moment when there are already so many rancours and factions. [5]

And yet Alexander was still prepared to offer an olive branch of forgiveness, inviting Savonarola to come to Rome, 'where we shall receive you with a father's heart'. But this Savonarola rejected. Alexander tried further conciliation in the shape of a cardinal's hat, the highest honour he could bestow. (The pope's wisdom over this offer must be doubted.) By the winter of 1495–96, there seemed to be no further option but to leave the preacher to destroy himself. Alexander well knew that, by coming into conflict with Savonarola, he was also coming into conflict with Florence. Thus it was possible for the ardent Savonarolans in senior ranks of the Florentine government to obtain papal permission for the friar to be their Lenten preacher, in 1496. These sermons proved to be among the most forceful he ever preached.

Savonarola was one headache for Alexander. But he had many others. From the beginning of his pontificate he realized that the great families of

Rome and Italy, the papal vicars and the other Italian states all constituted ongoing threats to the papacy. The invasion of Charles VIII had amply demonstrated that any of them were prepared to switch allegiance at any time. A so-called defender of the papacy might, for political expedience and by diplomatic sleight of hand, become an aggressor. Such aggressors must be punished. They must be rendered impotent. The remainder of Alexander's papacy would be devoted to this unrelenting struggle.

The struggle quickly gathered momentum. During the French invasion, both the Colonna and the Orsini had defected. The Colonna had been reconciled (temporarily). But the Orsini remained in the service of the French. Virginio Orsini, the puppet of Naples in the Cibo castles affair, had later switched sides against Naples and subsequently become a prisoner of the Neapolitans when the remnants of the French forces surrendered. Alexander tried to reason with the Orsini. That they, like Savonarola, were heedless of reason is not an indictment of Alexander's powers of persuasion but rather an indicator of the heightened temper of the times. But, when the Orsini did not listen to reason, Alexander excommunicated them.

Meanwhile Alexander's son Juan, duke of Gandia, linked up with Gonsalvo de Córdoba to attack the French garrison at Ostia. Italian cannon and Spanish infantry breached its defences. Gandia returned to Rome like a conquering Caesar. As ever, his doting father indulged him. De Córdoba, a military man outstripped by a popinjay, was mortally insulted. On Palm Sunday, he refused to take the palm from Alexander's hand. He left his place in St Peter's and sulked on a bench near the altar steps.

De Córdoba was not the only man of stature in Rome to look on, horrified, as the spoiled Borgia children ran amok. Alexander had his brood back with him. Jofré had discovered a taste for extravagance (his 73 personal servants were an affront to Alexander's parsimony). Meanwhile his wife Sancia transformed herself into a Roman society hostess – as did her sister-in-law, Lucrezia. The two trendsetters combined to make the Vatican a temple of high fashion. Burchard, the ever-disapproving master of ceremonies, thought their conduct a disgrace. Sancia was what we would nowadays term a 'wild child'. Over the winter, tales of her immorality were rife. It was even whispered that both Borgia brothers, Juan (Gandia) and Cesare, vied for the sexual favours of their sister-in-law. Incest would become forever associated with the Borgia name – as, indeed, would poison.

So much for Sancia and the extravagant but luckless Jofré. Giovanni Sforza, the hapless husband of Lucrezia, was faring little better. Their marriage was one of cynical political convenience – now dangerously outdated. Once Alexander had switched allies from Milan to Naples, only the combined Holy League made any arrangement with the Sforzas credible. But the Holy League, another marriage of cynical political convenience, was quickly breaking up. By 1496, Milanese involvement had slackened and Giovanni Sforza had lost his political value to the Borgias. Any military relevance was dubious. His performance in the anti-Orsini campaign was nondescript. He was also suspected of spying for his relatives, the Sforzas. Alexander regarded him with deep suspicion.

Understandably, Giovanni felt safer in Pesaro than in Rome. But Lucrezia was bored with the provincialism of Pesaro. When, after the 1496 summer season in Rome she refused to return there, Giovanni must have known that his days were numbered. The Mantuan envoy dryly noted, 'The lord of Pesaro seems to be sheltering something under his roof that others do not suspect'. A blazing row with his brother-in-law, the overweening duke of Gandia, made matters even worse.

On Good Friday 1497, Giovanni fled to Pesaro. A message to Lucrezia asked her to join him. Another message to the Milanese envoy claimed that his abrupt exit was due to 'dissatisfaction with the Pope'. The Milanese envoy dismissed this rationale, bluntly informing his master, Ludovico il Moro, that the real reason for Giovanni's flight was Lucrezia's 'lack of modesty, which had already put the lord of Pesaro into great discontent'. The anti-Borgia gutter press produced numerous salacious tales, including an incestuous relationship between Lucrezia and Alexander, who supposedly wanted a divorce to keep her all to himself. Thus originated one of the many imaginary elements of the great Borgia myth.

Giovanni had fled, but divorce proceedings quickly followed him. Giovanni stood to lose not only his wife Lucrezia, but also her money and even Pesaro, which he held in fief from Alexander. The papal emissary duly arrived with a cruel ultimatum – dissolution of the marriage, either through invalidity or non-consummation. As the former would never stand up in court, a helpless Giovanni was left with the latter. In vain, he protested to his Sforza relatives that the marriage had been consummated more than 1,000 times. In tacit acknowledgement of his political impotence, they blithely ignored him. The only remaining course left to him was a humiliating public statement of his sexual impotence.

Lucrezia wisely absented herself from the fray, seeking refuge in the Dominican convent of S. Sisto. Opinion as to her motives was divided. One commentator noted, 'Some say Madonna Lucrezia will turn nun, while others say things I cannot entrust to a letter'. But Lucrezia's continued absence became an embarrassment for Alexander, who sternly sent the sheriff of Rome to pluck her from the convent. Alas, the luckless sheriff met his match in a formidable abbess, who promptly sent him packing. Lucrezia remained within the protection of the convent walls. At 17, she had been married for three years. Collaborating with the non-consummation stratagem might well involve her in a highly embarrassing inspection by a midwife to ascertain whether she was *virgo intacta*...

Meanwhile Giovanni was boxed in by formidable people. The carrot of 31,000 ducats, pertaining to Lucrezia's dowry, was advanced to him. And the stick of the withdrawal of Milanese protection of Pesaro was broken over his back. He bitterly wrote, 'If his Holiness wishes to establish his own kind of justice, I cannot gainsay him'. In November 1497, he duly 'admitted' his impotence. His marriage had ended even more cynically than it had begun. He was a laughing stock in the eyes of the world. Any prospect of happiness for Lucrezia and himself had been wantonly sacrificed on the altar of Borgia dynasticism.

Alexander may well have fretted at Lucrezia's prolonged sojourn at the convent. His actions, at this time, did him no favours in the eyes of posterity. His favourite son, Juan, duke of Gandia, was in Rome to console him. Alexander showered material goods on Gandia, who came first in his affections. His other children were next in line for largesse, followed by his Spanish cronies, including another intake of Spanish cardinals. The aggrieved Romans protested against this cabal of Spaniards. The Colonna had not been paid for their part in the Orsini campaign, while the Orsini bitterly resented the price of the return of their castles. Ironically the duke of Urbino languished in the Orsini prison at Soriano until he found the means to raise his own ransom. Urbino does not appear to have been an employee of Alexander; even if he had been, such employers were not usually responsible for paying ransom for captured *condottieri*. But, in this instance, Alexander's shabby financial parsimony seems like meanness of spirit. Certainly it contrasts poorly with the extravagant remuneration given to other pro-Borgia types, particularly the many who had never risked their own skins in battle.

The abuse of the honours system continued unabated. In May 1497, Cardinal Borgia-Lanzol was made legate of Perugia. In June 1497, Cardinal Cesare Borgia received the honour of crowning King Federigo as king of Naples. In the same month, Alexander called a secret consistory to give the papal cities of Benevento and Terracina to Gandia and his heirs in perpetuity. Amongst the cardinals, only Piccolomini had the courage to speak out against the loss to Church and Christendom. Outside the consistory, no less a power than King Ferdinand of Spain echoed Piccolomini's fervent protest against this blatant asset-stripping.

But Gandia was fated never to acquire these papal cities. On the evening of 14 June 1497, with his brother Cesare Borgia and his cousin, Cardinal Juan Borgia-Lanzol the elder, Gandia went to dine with his mother, Vanozza Catanei, in a vineyard by S. Pietro in Vincoli. The banquet was to celebrate Cesare's imminent departure to crown King Federigo in Naples. Afterwards the three of them, together with their servants, rode back on their mules towards the Vatican. At Ponte S. Angelo, Gandia excused himself and made to take his departure, presumably intent upon some amorous rendezvous. The other two, fearful of his safety, advised him to take more servants. But Gandia rode off with only two people: a groom and a mysterious masked man who had been with them earlier. The masked man mounted the mule behind him.

Subsequently it appears that Gandia told the groom to go to the Vatican, collect his light armour and meet him at the Piazza Giudea. But Gandia never met the groom, although one account places him in this neighbourhood at around midnight, after an engagement with a notorious courtesan, Madonna Damiata.

By the next morning, Gandia had not returned. Doubtless he was sleeping off the previous night's pleasure. By afternoon however, Alexander was badly worried. He ordered a complete search of Rome. Instantly the city was paralysed by terror. Was this a coup against the Borgias? Shops and dwellings were locked up, thereby frustrating the search. People hid in the sanctuary of familiar places, trying to ignore what might be happening out on the streets. Soon Gandia's groom was discovered, badly wounded and near incapable of speech. Then his mule was found. Ominously, the harness showed signs of struggle.

On the next morning, 16 June, the searchers made a breakthrough. A Slav boatman, who slept in his barge at the Ripetta, admitted that around midnight on the evening in question he had seen a man on a white horse, with four other men on foot, approach the river bank. Thrown across the horse's back was a body, which had been hurled into the refuse-strewn water. The rider told the others to throw stones at the dead person's cloak, to weigh it down. When the Slav was quizzed why he had not mentioned this before, his reply was revealing, but in the wrong way: 'In the course of my life, I must have seen more than 100 bodies thrown into the Tiber from that spot, and I never heard of anyone troubling his head about even one of them'.

However, this body was different – very different. The river was dragged and a corpse was soon recovered from it, near a garden owned by Ascanio Sforza. It was Gandia. He was fully dressed. His money was in his purse and his dagger was in his belt. But his head, body and legs were gouged with multiple wounds and his throat was cut. Blatantly, robbery was not a motive. To judge from the severity of the wounds, hatred was. In the vocabulary of a later age, Gandia's life had been 'terminated with extreme prejudice'. He was a mere 20 years old, already hopelessly besotted by many kinds of depravities.

His father was shattered. Burchard records, 'When Alexander heard that the duke had been murdered and his body thrown like carrion into the Tiber, he was perfectly overcome; he shut himself in his room, overwhelmed with grief and wept bitterly'.[6] The body of Gandia, the latest casualty in the Borgia saga, was taken to S. Angelo where it was cleaned, robed and laid out in state. That very same night, it was escorted by 120 torchbearers to the church of Sta Maria del Popolo, where it was buried. Not a light showed in the Castel S. Angelo. But, amid the keening of the mourners, from a window high above Alexander could be heard, agonizingly calling out his dead son's name, again and again.

Who killed Gandia? His body had been in the water for two days and provided no clues. The groom died of his injuries without managing any coherent communication. But the list of suspects was full to overflowing. Gandia had made powerful enemies, both in Spain and in Rome. Giovanni Sforza had motive. Urbino had motive. Gonsalvo de Córdoba had motive. Cardinal Ascanio Sforza, near whose garden his body was found, had motive. A few days earlier, Sforza and Gandia had been involved in a vehement row over the killing of a servant of Gandia's and the subsequent execution of some of Sforza's retinue. Yet it seems unlikely that such a canny creature as Sforza should have had Gandia murdered on his very doorstep. Certainly Alexander seemed to think so, for he absolved Sforza from any suspicion. But, to be on the safe side, Sforza promptly fled the Vatican.

Who, then, did kill Gandia? The Orsini? The Colonna? Count Antonio Maria della Mirandola? The latter's daughter had supposedly been ravished by Gandia and his house was near the fateful part of the river where the body had been found. Even Jofré, Alexander's own son, may have had motive, as a cuckold bent upon revenge. (Earlier, as we have seen, both Gandia and Cesare had been romantically linked by the media with their sister-in-law, Sancia.) There was a seemingly endless stream of people with motive. The multiple lacerations pointed at a personal, rather than professional, assassination although, of course, this may have been a deliberate ruse to throw investigators off the scent. To the horrified Romans, it seemed that only one thing was clear; the perpetrator had *denti lunghi* – a long arm for vengeance.

One name not immediately mentioned as a suspect in Gandia's murder was that of his brother, Cesare. Some months later, the first rumour appeared in a report from the ambassador of Ferrara to Duke Ercole. 'I have again heard it said that the cause of the Duke of Gandia's death was the cardinal, his brother'.[7] Unfortunately this is yet another example of the '*on dit*' school of reporting, absolving the narrator from either responsibility or any need for evidence. The charge was amplified, both in Venice and in Ferrara, where Giovanni Sforza and the exiled Orsini nobles had taken refuge. Much, if not all of this amplification was anti-Borgia propaganda. And, when Cesare seemed to have murdered Lucrezia's second husband, three years later, it was felt that a man who could kill his brother-in-law could and did kill his own brother.

Alexander's suspicion seems to have rested longest upon the Orsini. But no guilty party was ever found. There was no trial, no conviction. And, after a while, enquiry subsided. It was as though Alexander had stopped looking for the guilty party. Over 500 years later, it seems impossible that we will ever know who killed Gandia. A large part of history credits Cesare with the killing but this is 'history' written well after the event, neatly fitting into the obsessive Borgia legend – but with not a shred of evidence. Ranke states: 'He had his brother, the duke of Gandia, cast into the river; he had his brother-in-law killed, the son of the duke of Calabria, the handsomest young man ever seen in Rome; and further he had Vitellozzo [Vitelli] killed, the most valiant man of the time'.[8]

Was Cesare capable of the murder? Undoubtedly. His later record attests to a marked capacity for duplicity and violence. But being capable of murder and committing a particular murder are two very different things. Did Cesare have motive? He may well have been sharing the sexual favours of their sister-in-law with Gandia. So there is a possible motive of sexual jealousy. Nine years earlier, when their older half-brother, Pedro Luis died, the duchy of Gandia had gone to Juan. Gandia was marked out for a secular career, whereas Cesare seems to have been the ecclesiastical 'back-up'. Certainly Cesare received an ample supply of the Borgia spoils – but Juan was showered with them. Above all, perhaps, it was Gandia, not Cesare, who was the apple of their father's eye. If Cesare was to become 'first among equals', as he subsequently did, it could only come about through the removal of Gandia.

In a celebrated passage by Arthur Conan Doyle, the eminent detective Sherlock Holmes refers to a dog that, in a particular situation, should have barked but did not. Alexander, the man who fought so hard over the Cibo castles, who outfaced the king of France and his conquering army, was seemingly content to find no guilty party for the murder of his favourite son. This simply lacks credibility. That Cesare, moreover – a man later acknowledged as 'terrible in revenge' – would have allowed such an incident to go unpunished, is bizarre. Put bluntly, it beggars belief.

So we are left with the dark, fearful suspicion that Cesare was indeed responsible for the murder of his brother, Gandia. A wiser perpetrator would have contracted the murder from a far distance, taking infinite care to be 'plausibly deniable'. And Cesare may have orchestrated Gandia's murder via some other malcontent with a grudge against the overbearing playboy. But Cesare's nature seems to have been remarkably 'hands on'. The lacerations on Gandia's body speak of emotional, as well as physical violence. Both types of violence seem to have inhabited Cesare's soul.

If Cesare murdered his brother, did he stop to think of Alexander's suspicions falling upon him? Or did he merely consider that, having presented Alexander with a *fait accompli*, his future was assured? From that point onwards, did their relationship change? Did Alexander, the horrified father, become psychologically in thrall to his son, who clearly feared neither God nor man?

Whoever was responsible and whatever duplicity surrounded Gandia's murder, one thing was agreed upon by everyone – Alexander was riven with grief. It is said that he touched neither food nor water for three days. Five days after the murder, at a consistory with every cardinal in Rome (except the errant Ascanio Sforza) and every important ambassador in attendance, Alexander sorrowfully declared:

> The blow that is fallen upon us is the heaviest that we could possibly have sustained. We loved the duke of Gandia more than anyone else in the world. We would have given seven tiaras to be able to recall him to life. God has done this in punishment for our sins. We, on our part, are resolved to mend our own life and to reform the Church.[9]

Alexander lost no time in striving to do just this. The first thing he did was to keep his children at a distance. Lucrezia was already sheltering in the Dominican convent, and Cesare had to depart for Naples to crown Federigo as king. But Jofré and Sancia were removed to Squillace. And the pope let it be known that henceforth he would not be subject to the whims of his progeny.

A commission was created from six of the more spiritually inclined cardinals, 'the best and most God-fearing'. Their mission was top-down reform of the Church, beginning with Alexander himself. Work soon started. A startled Florentine envoy noted, 'The reform commission sits every morning in the papal palace'. By the end of July, only six weeks after Gandia's murder, a draft Bull of Reformation had been created. Simony was outlawed. The pope might not transfer Church property to the secular realm. Dealings between popes and secular princes would be scrutinized. Cardinals would be created from all nations, in accordance with their respective sizes. No cardinal should possess more than one bishopric or receive more than 6,000 ducats a year from benefices. A cardinal's household might not exceed 80 persons, nor should there be more than 30 horses. Jugglers, comedians, conjurers, troubadours, singers and musicians must remain outside the cardinal's palaces. Boys must not be employed as valets or grooms of the chamber. Cardinals were not allowed to hunt, nor attend tournaments, pagan dramas or carnivals. They must live simply. Holy Scriptures should be read during meals, at which there must be no more than one boiled and one roast meat. Finally, to cap such unostentatious lives, their funerals should not cost more than 1,500 ducats apiece.

So much for the reform of cardinals. The draft Bull continued to address corruption, all the way down through the various layers of Church administration. Offices might not be sold. Bribes might not be accepted. Children might not make religious vows. Existing vows by children were deemed invalid. Priests might not have concubines. Rules were made for the collection of tithes and Church taxes. A prescribed fee was set for each Church transaction. Abbeys and convents must put their houses in order. In Rome, wharf dues were forbidden; even the city's grain supply would be regulated.

After 35 years experience as vice-chancellor, none of these reforms would have come as a shock to Alexander. But the vehicle of change was fatally flawed. However admirable the reforms, they could only be implemented by the very people who stood to lose most. Corrupt cardinals and bishops would never support reform of their own corruption. The no less corrupt Church administrators were busy lining their pockets. The clergy were living slothful existences, with little regard to the members of the Church whom they supposedly served. True and lasting reform of the Church could only come about from a General Council. And, however much the commissioners argued for it, this would have been impossible at that time. Even della Rovere later explained why. As Pope Julius II, he bluntly stated,

'The Council has been long postponed since the time of Pope Alexander because of the calamities which then afflicted Italy and still afflict it'.

However much Alexander genuinely desired a spiritual cleansing of the Church, he could not afford to let the power of the papacy become compromised by increased power among the cardinals. (Would he have so nimbly outwitted Charles VIII if every sideswerve had to go to committee?) Neither could Alexander allow the Church to be questioned as a political entity at a time when he was desperately fighting for its independence. Sadly, for a Church which needed reform, the draft Bull never became more than a draft. And, tragically for a well-meaning Alexander, failure to reform the Church was followed by a corresponding failure to mend his own life.

Ironically, in contempt of any such spirit of reform, Cesare had wasted no time in propositioning King Federigo for material goods, while speculatively eyeing up his daughter, Carlotta. A commentator wryly noted, 'It would not be surprising if the poor King was driven into the arms of the Turks to escape from his tormentor'. Seemingly Alexander tried to keep an emotional distance between Cesare and himself on the latter's return to Rome. But his resistance crumbled. Inexorably, Cesare began to take the place of Gandia in his father's affections and dynastic hopes. He asked the pope to arrange his release from the cardinalate to become a free agent in the secular world. While Alexander began discreetly arranging this, he gave Cesare benefices worth another 12,000 ducats per year. So much for reform! In contempt of the proposed hunting prohibition, pope and cardinal chased game together. In September 1497, not two months after the appearance of the draft Bull, the Venetian envoy wrote, 'I will make no comment on these matters but it is certain that this Pope permits himself things that are unexampled and unpardonable'.

By the end of 1497, Lucrezia was free of her first husband, the unfortunate Giovanni Sforza. But she was not free of the charge of incest, which he had made. Rumours buzzed around Rome. And, early in 1498, these rumours were augmented by further tales of her pregnancy. A young Spaniard, Pedro Calderon (known as Perotto), had acted as her go-between while in the convent. In February, Burchard noted that Perotto's body had been found in the Tiber, 'where he did not fall of his own volition'.[10] Not a week later it was elsewhere reported that 'a young woman of the retinue of Madonna Lucrezia was also found drowned in the river. The reasons for this are not known'. It seems that the Tiber was filling with bodies from the Borgia retinue! Soon afterwards, another account bluntly stated, 'It is reported from Rome that the daughter of the Pope gave birth to a child'.

Did Lucrezia have incestuous relations? Did she have a bastard child? The duke of Gandia's name was cited. His own murder fed the conspiracy theories of the time. Cesare's name was cited. And Perotto's name was cited. According to the Borgia myth, Perotto did indeed have carnal relations with Lucrezia. Cesare vowed to avenge this affront. But it was not so much an affront to family honour as it was to the possessiveness of Cesare, who also, some whispered, enjoyed his sister's favours. Dagger in hand, it was said, Cesare chased Perotto through the ante-rooms of the pope. Stumbling into the aged Alexander, Perotto was caught by Cesare, who plunged his dagger repeatedly into the wretched, quivering body. Perotto's blood spurted upwards, drenching Alexander's face and the papal robes he wore...[11]

It's a great story – but one wholly unsupported by fact. Burchard says simply that Perotto's body was found in the Tiber 'where he did not fall of his own volition'. There is no mention of chases through Alexander's ante-rooms, of waving daggers, of blood-spattered robes. If such a drama actually happened, would Burchard not know about it? If he knew about it, was he too frightened to say? The problem with the '*on dit*' school of reportage is the lack of burden of either responsibility or proof. Because anybody can say anything, they do. And the inconvenience of fact must never be allowed to get in the way of a good story.

Certainly, if Lucrezia had an illegitimate child at this time, it is most surprising that there is no further mention of the fact. The Borgias had a record of acknowledging and taking good care of all of their children, whether legitimate or not. But inevitably, Lucrezia's name was further blackened. On the subject of possible marriage with his son, the Prince of Salerno scoffed, 'Do you think I would receive into my family a woman who, as everyone knows, has slept with both her brothers?' But, if this woman was not deemed good enough for Salerno, elsewhere she did not lack admirers and suitors for her hand. Alexander began to ponder another dynastic marriage for Lucrezia – and one for Cesare.

CHAPTER 4. A Foul Murder and a Live Burning

Meanwhile the Savonarola problem continued unabated. 1497 had come to an end with the friar celebrating Mass at Christmas and announcing his intention to resume preaching, which he did during the early months of 1498. Vanities were again burned in the pre-Lenten season. Alexander threatened Florence with interdiction. In the eyes of the pope, the friar was becoming more trouble than he was worth. From one of the Franciscan friars of S. Croce came a bizarre proposal that was sure to bring matters to a crisis – Savonarola could prove the truth of his teachings by accepting an ordeal by fire. If he entered the fire, he would burn, unless saved by a miracle; if he refused, the people would cease to put their faith in him.

After an unexplained postponement, the trial by fire was arranged for 7 April. A Dominican and a Franciscan champion were each required to pass through the flames in the Piazza della Signoria. Savonarola sensed it was a trap, and thus it proved to be. Delay followed upon delay. There was a riot in the Piazza, a sudden storm and the suspicious disappearance of the Franciscan champion inside the Palazzo della Signoria. After many tense hours, the authorities finally declared that the ordeal would not take place after all. This, of course, was exactly what Savonarola wanted.

During the next couple of days, S. Marco was attacked and stormed. The prior and two other friars were arrested and imprisoned. During his imprisonment and trial, Savonarola was deserted by many of his followers. With the secular and ecclesiastical authorities united in their desire to be rid of him, and with the aid of torture, the heresy charges were easily 'proved'. On 23 May 1498, the fires were finally lit in the Piazza for the execution of the three friars. Afterwards Savonarola's ashes were thrown into the Arno to prevent their becoming treasured relics to those *piagnoni* who remained loyal to the end.

However much Alexander might have wished to avoid such a grisly ending, he had long ago realized that the only conceivable solution was to let Savonarola destroy himself. And this is exactly what happened. A threat to the instability of Italy and the papacy was no more. Yet again, Alexander had outmanoeuvred another dangerous opponent. Yet again, he had won time to strengthen the papacy. But now, six years into his reign, he must have been wondering if policy would always be overtaken by a lurch into the next crisis. Back at his coronation, a witness had grimly noted that 'it forcibly reminded me of the instability of all human things'. The bodies were piling up. Savonarola, the deluded mystic, was no more. The beloved duke of Gandia was no more. And a third, entirely unexpected death would soon plunge Alexander's papacy into its next crisis.

Chapter 5. MURDER IN THE VATICAN

'There are, in the Vatican, so many cases of hatred'

As Ferrante's death in 1494 had triggered a diplomatic and military chain reaction, so did that of Charles VIII in April 1498. He was not yet 30. Although he had been ill for a few days, the end came after he hit his head on a low doorway leading to the dry moat at Amboise. His attendants did not dare move him from the moat, where he lay for nine hours before expiring. As Philippe de Commines reflected, 'And so this great and powerful King died, and in such a miserable place, where he possessed so many magnificent houses'.[1]

All four of the king's children by Anne of Brittany had died in infancy. Charles was succeeded by his brother-in-law and distant cousin, Louis, duke of Orléans – whose paternal grandmother was Valentina Visconti, daughter of Giangaleazzo Visconti, duke of Milan. Thus Louis inherited a claim to the duchy of Milan, as Charles VIII had to the kingdom of Naples. Each claim was entirely independent of the other, but advanced by French kings just four or five years apart.

Louis had several motives for cultivating Alexander. Most immediately, he needed to secure both the annulment of his marriage to Louis XI's daughter, Jeanne, and a dispensation to allow him to marry his predecessor's widow, Anne of Brittany, or risk loss of the recently acquired duchy. A dispensation would be needed because Louis' aunt was also the grandmother of Anne of Brittany.

The marriage between Louis of Orléans and Jeanne de France had initially been proposed within days of her birth in 1464, and took place in 1476. The young bride was unnaturally short of stature, misshapen of body and far from fair of face, but she was possessed of a gentle soul and caring nature. Louis objected to the marriage in the strongest possible terms, but he was forced into it by Jeanne's father, Louis XI. It was a problem that had festered for over two decades and came to an abrupt head as soon as the duke of Orléans became king of France. Both parties presented their cases before a tribunal, the king arguing that the marriage had not been consummated, while Jeanne maintained that it had but refused to compromise her royal dignity by submitting to a physical examination.

Callously, the king made application to Alexander to be released from a 'cripple, afflicted with scrofula, repellent in person and mind'. At the same time his counsellor, Georges d'Amboise, coveted a cardinal's hat. And Louis had need of a third favour, both sinister and menacing; another Italian invasion would be greatly aided by the cultivation of allies in the peninsula.

For Alexander it was a case of, 'The king is dead, long live the king!' He was presented with a new king of France and a new agenda. Now there was a claim on Milan, as well as Naples. Spain would be an unreliable ally. King Ferdinand looked coldly at a scandal-prone papacy; his cousin, the duchess of Gandia (Juan's embittered widow), filled his ears with complaints about the Borgias. Naples was more or less a Spanish dependency. And, most ominously, Gonsalvo de Córdoba and his Spanish troops remained on Italian soil. Alexander would have to tread very warily indeed with Louis…

Meanwhile, the Holy League was falling into abeyance. Venice was not averse to the destruction of Milan as an independent state, especially at a time when there was a renewal of military action between the republic and the Ottomans. With Savonarola as the public voice of the Franco-Florentine alliance now dead, there was little likelihood that Florence would back a French invasion. When Alexander sent envoys to France in July, the official purpose was to seek support for a crusade as another Jubilee year approached, but the covert reason was to seek to limit possible French intervention in Italy in support for the Florentine recovery of Pisa. In effect, Florence could be left out of the political power equation between 1498 and 1502, as the republic's government lapsed into chaos.

The papacy lacked the military resources of Spain, France or Venice; its armies were invariably hastily recruited. In 1498 it so happened that the Orsini and Colonna, from whom the papacy's military commanders were so often drawn, were temporarily in league with each other, against the pope. As a cardinal, Rodrigo Borgia had cultivated many of the princes of western Christendom. This stood him in good stead when, as pope, he was obliged to balance the ambitions of so many hostile and potentially hostile states.

Alexander's short-term expedient was, as ever, by way of alliances sealed with dynastic marriages. Don Alfonso of Bisceglie, the brother of Jofré Borgia's wife, Sancia, was the illegitimate son of Alfonso II and the nephew of King Federigo of Naples. Alfonso the elder was termed by one commentator, 'the cruellest, most vicious and lowest of men'. But Alfonso the younger, the possessor of vast estates and a gentle youth of striking good looks, was deemed a suitable second husband for Lucrezia. Chillingly, he was reminded by one contemporary writer of the fate that had befallen poor Giovanni Sforza and, indeed, a previous engagement of Lucrezia's which Giovanni had usurped: 'The other husbands are not dead, Alfonso, they live. Two have been cheated of their hopes, and your punishment awaits you. It will profit you nothing to take your name from Parthenope, or to be of royal stock. You, too, will fall'. In June 1498 Lucrezia and Alfonso were married. Her dowry was 41,000 ducats. But there was a condition that she would not have to go to Naples during Alexander's lifetime. Her second marriage again took place in the Vatican, but was devoid of the pomp and circumstance of the first.

At 67 (and half-way through his papacy), Alexander remained in robust health. But he could not live forever and, despite all his efforts at nepotism, the Borgia succession was sickly. His son, Pedro Luis, the first duke of Gandia, had died without heir. Juan, the murdered second duke of Gandia had left a son – but his mother, María Enríquez, ensured that access to the child and his inheritance was closed. Alexander bitterly lamented that this child was 'closer to the King of Spain than to us'. The youngest son, Jofré, prince of Squillace, was the runt of the litter. Alexander had no confidence in him and placed few responsibilities upon him. If the Borgia family was to have a future, let alone a dynasty, it must come about through Cesare. And, to do this, Cesare must leave the priesthood.

During the first half of 1498, Cesare had rarely worn his cardinal's robes. Sometimes he would dress as a French courtier, sometimes as a *condottiere*, sometimes as a hunter, occasionally even in oriental garb. It was as though, almost like a child, he was dressing up in order to test the various roles that might be open to him outside the Church. Finally, only two months after Lucrezia's wedding, in August 1498, Cesare came before a consistory where he renounced his cardinal's robes forever. The cowed cardinals gave unanimous agreement but, ironically and impertinently, the Spanish ambassador protested. Alexander matched irony with irony, in a devastating riposte. Cesare's leaving of the priesthood was necessary for the good of his soul!

Renouncing the cardinalate meant the loss of 35,000 ducats a year in benefices. But, on the very day when these Church riches were renounced, the French envoy arrived in Rome with arrangements for secular riches, courtesy of Louis. By a dazzling sleight of hand, the former cardinal of Valencia was no more. In his place stood the new duke of Valence, knight of the Order of St Michael. Cesare was to have a guaranteed income of 20,000 gold francs per year and another 20,000 gold francs as a personal allowance. The Borgia alliance with Naples would be further sealed with a second marriage between Cesare and Princess Carlotta; this would have the full support of Louis. And, once Louis had conquered Milan, Cesare would receive the town of Asti.

Thus Cesare, duke now and cardinal no more, emerged triumphantly from the shadow of his brother, the murdered duke of Gandia. In Italy, he was known as the duke of Valentinois, popularly abbreviated as 'il Valentino'. He would go to France to repay Louis in kind. The French king would, at last, have his divorce. His adviser Georges d'Amboise would receive his cardinal's hat (which might, or might not be necessary for *his* spiritual welfare). The promise of the gift of Asti presupposed a papal blessing for a French invasion of Italy and conquest of Milan. And there was an implied caveat that, in focusing upon Milan, the French would, albeit temporarily, ignore Naples. The mutual interests of Louis, of the papacy and of Borgia dynasticism were well intermingled. Alexander wrote thus to King Louis, 'We are sending your Majesty our heart, that is to say our beloved son, the duc de Valentino, who is to us the dearest of all'. Alexander was also delivering the *coup de grâce* to the Holy League. And he was unleashing forces of unrest in Italy which would have far-reaching consequences.

In 1498, the 23-year-old Cesare was a prince among men, a handsome, dashing figure of restless intellect, proficient alike on the hunting field and in the boudoir. He was his father's son – and more. His proud spirit bowed to no obstacle. Ever conscious that his father's papacy might soon end, he knew well that he had little time and much to achieve. The next five years would witness his meteoric rise and equally meteoric fall. Few men in history make such an impact in a mere five years as to be remembered 500 years later. And even fewer have names that become synonyms of infamy. Cesare Borgia is one.

In October, he began the journey from Rome with a display of treasure that made his fellow citizens gasp. Fifty mules and two hundred servants carried it. Alexander had provided 200,000 ducats, cynically extorted from penitents commuting their sentences. Chests were filled with jewels. Prize horses were shod with silver. A commode with a golden bowl was covered with a golden cloth. Cesare was dressed in the height of fashion, his black plumed biretta an ironic acknowledgement of his years as a cardinal. From a window in the Vatican, his father watched his departure with, no doubt, mixed emotions of sadness and pride.

Cesare and his retinue arrived by ship at Marseilles and proceeded across France at a stately pace. The papal solution to the French king's marital problems must not be seen to arrive with indecent haste. At Avignon, he was welcomed by none other than Giuliano della Rovere, his father's erstwhile arch-enemy, now astonishingly forgiven once again by Alexander. Cesare and della Rovere dined together in splendour, tarnished only by the pain of syphilis, from which both were suffering. Cesare continued his triumphal diplomatic procession, to the amazement and disdain of the French nobility, who viewed the magnificence of a pope's bastard son as the vain display of a parvenu. Louis was reputed to have secretly watched Cesare's arrival at Chinon, littered with rubies and diamonds, his boots and horse's tail covered with pearls. The French king is said to have acidly commented upon 'the vainglory and foolish bombast of this duke of Valentinois'.

When Cesare and Louis formally met, they feasted, talked, whored and got down to the serious business of negotiation. This process lasted throughout the winter of 1498 to 1499, with proposition and counter-proposition. Unsurprisingly, the divorce commission decided in favour of Louis. By now, as it was common knowledge that Cesare possessed the required dispensation, he had to hand it over. With elements of farce, the sad travesty of marriage between Louis and Jeanne came to an end. Jeanne was made duchess of Berry and devoted the rest of her life to religion. Her Order of the Annonciade was approved by Alexander in 1501, four years before her death. Miracles were duly attributed to the intervention of this long-suffering princess, who was beatified in 1742 and canonized in 1950. Although the case of this royal annulment may have superficial similarities to that which convulsed the English political elite in the 1520s, the parallel was not sufficiently great for it to be cited in the debate about Henry VIII's first marriage.

Louis' divorce was only one part of the equation. Georges d'Amboise was made cardinal, but failed to secure his second objective as papal legate in France. Back in Italy, Alexander played a guessing game with Naples and Milan, nimbly balancing their benefits to him against corresponding French benefits. Cesare, the man of action (as would shortly be revealed) wearied of the deliberately prolonged negotiations in France. But Alexander, the consummate deal-maker, played Naples and Milan against France to secure the maximum advantage with the minimum risk of fallout.

In the end, the wishes of a lady tilted the delicate balance of negotiation. Just three weeks after the tribunal decided in favour of King Louis, he married Anne at Nantes. Princess Carlotta of Naples was among the bride's attendants. She made clear her opposition to the proposal that she might be a suitable wife for Cesare. The door to Naples finally closed and the door to France swung open.

Ironically for Cesare the Lothario, a niece of Louis XII also turned him down. But, in May 1499, Louis finally decided upon a marriage between Cesare and his cousin, Charlotte d'Albret, sister of the king of Navarre. The wedding took place immediately. The morning afterwards, a horseman left for the Vatican with a dispatch stating that the marriage had been consummated. Cesare had given Charlotte 'eight marks of his virility'. But Cesare's enemies at the French court had a different account. Their story was that a laxative had been swapped for an aphrodisiac. When the syphilitic Cesare had quaffed the wrong mixture, the resulting effects had been comical and embarrassing.

Be that as it may, Charlotte was soon pregnant. Their daughter Luisa was born the following year, by which time Cesare was back in Italy. She never saw her father. Cesare evidently had no further use for Charlotte, who sought solace with the ex-queen's religious community at Bourges. Truly women were ill-used by the likes of Louis and Cesare. Perhaps only with his mother

Vanozza and his sister Lucrezia was Cesare capable of genuine affection to women. His greatest passions were reserved for war and conquest.

But Cesare's marriage had a more sinister aspect. The marriage contract between Louis and himself noted that 'the duc de Valentinois, his house, his friends and allies would render great and noble services to the French crown, particularly with regard to the conquest of Naples and Milan'. In return, Louis promised military assistance to Cesare to realize his own, as yet undisclosed, ambitions in Italy. Many Italians had doubted Alexander's motives for Cesare's visit to France. Now their worst fears were realized. Incredibly, Alexander, who had routed one French army from Italy, was now plotting the arrival of another. Cardinal Sforza protested bitterly. Alexander curtly dismissed him with the cutting remark that his own brother, Ludovico il Moro, had first invited the French army into Italy. Soon afterwards, the Spanish ambassador stormed out after a savage altercation with Alexander. Lucrezia's beloved husband, Alfonso, fled, like his predecessor Giovanni Sforza, on a fast horse. Again, like Giovanni, he wrote, begging his six months pregnant bride to join him. The letter was intercepted by papal soldiers; Alexander was taking no chances. He almost met his match, though, in Alfonso's spirited sister, Sancia. When he ordered her back to Naples, she refused to go. Finally she was forced to leave Rome under duress. Alexander would not allow her money for the journey, regrettably showing how spiteful he could sometimes be.

However disastrous the effect upon his children's marriages, Alexander simply could not allow them to join their partners in Naples, where they would certainly be taken hostage. With characteristic ingenuity he made Lucrezia the governor of Spoleto, a papal fief; the useless Jofré accompanied her to this safe place.

In September 1499 the French army invaded northern Italy. As before, city after city surrendered or was taken. Resistance was futile. Ludovico il Moro, the doyen of treachery and traitor to Italy, fled for his life. With typical Renaissance double-dealing, the castellan of Milan made a private deal with the invading French. On 6 October King Louis entered Milan to tumultuous applause. By his side, rode Cesare. He had returned to Italy to usher in a new era of war and treachery.

By October, Cesare was already free of his obligation to Louis and could call in the favour. He received an army of 1,800 cavalry and 4,000 infantry for a conquest of the Romagna. Back in July, Alexander had prepared the legal and moral ground by excommunicating the vicars. Non-payment of their annual *census* provided a convenient excuse. The real reason was their independence of the papacy and worrying dependence upon external powers. From the beginning of his pontificate, Alexander had yearned to bring these papal vicars to heel. Now, seven years later, with a French army commanded by a son who was no longer a cardinal, the task could finally begin.

In November Cesare arrived in the papal states, intent upon capturing the cities of Forlì and Imola, ruled by Caterina Sforza, niece of Ludovico il Moro. Ludovico's flight had left her position perilously exposed. And, as the single Romagna ruler who had kept her independence from Venice, it was cynically viewed that her downfall would cause no reaction from Venice. Caterina was well aware of her danger and had been assiduously fortifying her fortresses against attack. Obviously she could only personally take charge of the defence of one of them. And therein lay her downfall. However much she might strengthen bricks and mortar, relying upon human loyalty was a very different matter. In fifteenth-century Italy, loyalty was as fickle as the wind. Caterina was feared, not loved. To die for her held little appeal for either citizens or soldiers, all of whom were well aware of the previous consequences of resistance to the French.

In the event, Caterina took personal command of Forlì and delegated command of Imola to two Romagnol *condottieri*, one in charge of the fortress, the other in charge of the town. When Cesare's advance guard arrived (ironically under the command of another Romagnol professional soldier), the gates of the town obediently swung open. Would the fortress prove to be of sterner stuff? A local carpenter revealed to Cesare a weak spot in the fortress wall. Cannon were moved into position and bombardment began. In a face-saving exercise, the commander agreed to a negotiated surrender if outside help did not arrive within three days. Accordingly, three days later Cesare received the formal surrender. The former commander, Dionigi Naldi, promptly took service under Cesare. He brought with him highly valuable infantry expertise, together with equally valuable local connections for recruiting Romagnol infantry. These would prove to be cornerstones of Cesare's later campaigns in the Romagna.

On 25 February 1500, a triumphant Cesare returned to Rome, amid scenes of characteristic Borgia splendour. Caterina Sforza, his prisoner, accompanied him, proud and unflinching in adversity, resembling 'another Zenobia, bound in golden chains'. Cesare's retinue moved through Rome, in stately procession to the Vatican, while church bells pealed and the cannon of S. Angelo thundered across the city. In the Vatican Alexander, weeping and laughing all at once, lovingly embraced him. Cesare, the coming man, had finally arrived. A markedly different fate awaited Caterina, whose constant attempts at escape were foiled and who stubbornly refused to revoke her rights to Forlì and Imola. She was placed in the grim fortress of Castel S. Angelo.

1500 was Jubilee year in Rome. 200,000 pilgrims thronged St Peter's Square for the pope's Easter blessing. Alexander, the effective administrator, had improved the infrastructure of the city and its surroundings. Pilgrims to Rome meant money flooding into the city and the Church. With coffers swollen with pilgrims' money and with a general Christian enthusiasm for the Jubilee, the time seemed ripe to bring up the subject of another crusade, especially as Venice was once again being threatened by the Turks. A secret consistory was assembled to produce a plan for a crusade. Emissaries were sent out to the great European states to solicit support and raise funds. The profits from the papal alum mines at Tolfa were earmarked for the war chest. And on 1 July a Bull was issued, calling for another crusade.

The upshot of all of these endeavours was a great deal of money raised, a great deal of discussion, but not much action. A league was formed between the Church, Hungary and Venice and a combined fleet was brought into being. However, motives may have been mixed. The more that the Venetians were harrowed by the Turks, the less able they were to prohibit the conquest of the Romagna. There is no suggestion that Alexander in any way abetted the Turks; but the fact remains that their presence, though a threat to Christendom, was, at that moment, a benefit to him.

France and Spain were too intent upon carving up Naples between themselves to have very much enthusiasm for a crusade. The Treaty of Granada, signed in November 1500, had tacitly acknowledged that, as neither nation was likely to secure Naples for itself, it would be better for the spoils to be divided. King Federigo's desperate attempts to solicit Turkish support were, ironically, used to discredit him and his Aragonese dynasty.

Alexander fully colluded in this Neapolitan break-up. There was probably nothing he could have done to stop it. And he doubtless reasoned that it was better to have two superpowers, rather than one, occupying Naples. One such power would be a formidable threat to the papacy. With two, there was always the possibility of divide and rule...

Alexander's seeming volte-face on Naples coincided with an unsavoury incident that happened in August 1500. The dynastic marriages between Lucrezia and Alfonso, and Jofré and Sancia, had been rendered redundant by Alexander's alliance with France. Thenceforth both Alfonso and Sancia were embarrassments in Rome. As we have seen, Lucrezia was packed off to be governor of Spoleto, taking Jofré with her. When she was eventually reconciled with Alfonso, his situation remained a difficult one. On the evening of 15 July, after a visit to Alexander who was ill at the time, Alfonso was set upon on the very steps of St Peter's by a gang of armed ruffians. They stabbed him in the head, in the right arm and in the leg. Two passers-by bravely intervened, beating off the ruffians and dragging Alfonso back into the Vatican for safety. Lucrezia and Sancia rushed to nurse him. Initially he refused medical help, swearing that he could not afford to trust anyone in Rome. Finally he managed to get word to his relative, Federigo of Naples, who promptly sent his own doctor.

Much public speculation ensued as to the motives and identity of the attackers. Certainly Alfonso's marriage with Lucrezia had become a political redundancy; but that is not to say that the Borgias actively wished his death. And to attempt an assassination on Alfonso's way from Alexander's sick-bed seemed worthy of an unaccustomed degree of crudity and callousness. Popular opinion was more inclined to place bets on the Orsini, for two reasons: Alfonso was a good friend of the Colonna, to whose castle he had fled in the previous year, and Lucrezia, as an arm of the Borgias, was encroaching upon Orsini estates. But was it the Orsini? Rome was the world capital of intrigue, conspiracy and assassination. The Florentine envoy sagely wrote: 'There are, in the Vatican, so many causes of hatred, both old and new, so much envy and jealousy, both public and private, that scandals will always arise'.

During the following month, Alfonso seemed to be recovering, aided by Lucrezia and Sancia. By Alexander's orders his rooms were closely guarded, and his food was tasted for poison. Cesare demanded ever more stringent security measures. And yet Cesare…could his own brother-in-law have been behind the attack? Cesare's reply to the implied accusation is said (*'on dit'*!) to have been equivocal, to say the least, 'I did not wound the Duke, but if I had, it would have been no more than he deserved'. Furthermore it was reported that Cesare had visited Alfonso and threatened that 'what was not done at noon may be done by nightfall'. It was claimed that Alfonso became ever more convinced that Cesare was indeed behind the attack and that Lucrezia, Sancia and Alexander were at their wit's end, horribly convinced of impending disaster.

At this point, accounts diverge. One school of thought is that Alfonso had a relapse and simply died of his wounds. But a very different version has become woven into the history of the Borgias. The Venetian ambassador, Capello, recounted that on 18 August Alfonso had seen Cesare walking in the garden below him, and shot at him with his cross-bow. The arrow missed. Shortly afterwards, Cesare's lieutenant, Michele Corella (known as Don Michelotto), is said to have forced his way into the Vatican with armed men, claiming that Cesare had instructed him to find the person who had shot the arrow. Forcing the ladies from the room, Don Michelotto is said to have strangled Alfonso.

His body was buried, without ceremony, the same day in the church of Sta Maria delle Febbre. He was a mere 19. Burchard's account runs thus: 'The physician of the dead prince and a certain hunchback were brought to S. Angelo. They were examined by the inquisitors but soon released, since the man who had done this thing was well known, but went unpunished'. A week later, Alexander is said to have confided to Capello that Alfonso had made an attempt on Cesare's life. The implication was that this attempt justified his murder. Tellingly, the envoy wrote that even Alexander seemed afraid of Cesare. Was denial of wrongdoing behind the banishing of his own daughter to the grim fortress of Nepi? As Capello further noted, 'Madonna Lucrezia was formerly in favour with the Pope but now he does not love her and has sent her to Nepi'. She termed herself *La Infelicissima* and went into mourning in that dark place, comforted only by her baby son, Rodrigo, whose very name can only have reminded her of her father and the terrible misfortune that his machinations had caused. Back in Rome, Cesare revelled in his triumph. 'This duke, if he lives,' wrote the astute Capello, 'will be one of the first captains of Italy'. With the hindsight of history, we view Capello's verdict and marvel at its prescience.

Certainly Cesare's reputation as an assassin did him great political damage. If he assassinated his very brother-in-law, if his soldiers turned surrendered towns like Forlì into 'a glimpse through the gates of hell', then how could any sane person do business with him? Looking more closely, the first attack on Alfonso seems to have been bungled in a way that was quite uncharacteristic of the highly competent Cesare. And why wait another month to finish off the job? It seems far more likely that the first attack was made by person or persons unknown. Did the second, fatal attack stem from Cesare's provoked rage for Alfonso's cross-bow shot at him? If true this does not, in any way, excuse Cesare. But it fits the portrait of a proud, passionate and, indeed, violent man, not some deranged psychopath or demon from the underworld.

However, Alexander's lack of response to poor Alfonso's death constitutes another moral compromise that made it ever easier for his enemies to traduce him. One way or the other, Alexander, the man whose motto might have been, 'what is good for the papacy is good for the Borgias', was being brought down by his family. His beloved son, Gandia, had been killed, either by enemies inspired by his feckless character, or by his own brother, Cesare. Cesare, the prince among men, had supposedly behaved little better than a common murderer with Alfonso. All his life, in countless debates, Alexander had appealed to the rational, the judicial. Should he have brought his own son to trial? Was he denying justice to a murder in the very rooms of the Vatican? Morally, Alexander was making a most fateful choice. By throwing in his lot with Cesare (whether guilty or not), he must have known there was no going back. Certainly, as a compassionate man, he would have privately suffered agonizingly for Lucrezia at Nepi mourning Alfonso, the lost love of her life.

Undaunted by any of this, Cesare now returned to the job that had been left unfinished by the defection of the French army – the subjugation of the Romagna. Alexander, the arch-diplomat, secured the acquiescence of neighbouring Venice by promising more Venetian cardinals and aid against the Turks. With Venice 'onside', the next requirement was a war chest to buy and keep an army solely devoted to Borgia interests. In September 1500, 12 new cardinals were created (thereby further weakening the power of the other cardinals). Cesare, the former cardinal, lavishly entertained them at a banquet where they paid dearly for their supper. On average, each cardinal brought 10,000 ducats with him. Cesare's war chest duly swelled by another 120,000 ducats.

Meanwhile Alexander, the most financially astute of popes, devised ever more novel methods of fund-raising. For 25,000 ducats, King Ladislaus of Hungary was allowed to free himself of an unwanted wife. Two Portuguese kings, who had died excommunicated, were subsequently granted absolution upon production of the necessary fees. Even ordinary people could pay their way out of purgatory or the prospect of it; Mass, confession and contrition were no longer invariably required. Alexander was the first pope to assert that indulgences were sufficient to relieve souls from purgatory. And he was the most successful pope to date at converting spiritual intervention into hard cash. As with diplomacy and negotiation, Alexander could have given lessons on fund-raising to the political incumbents of twenty-first-century Washington.

Money buys military prowess. Diplomacy can rob enemies of political allies. For their conquest of the Romagna, Alexander and Cesare had prepared most carefully on the financial, military and diplomatic front. In August, the final steps of preparation were taken. Alexander excommunicated Manfredi of Faenza, Malatesta of Rimini and his former son-in-law, the wretched Giovanni Sforza of Pesaro. By promising his support to the French in the division of Naples, Alexander had ensured that they would add to Cesare's force. But crucially, this time the French would not comprise Cesare's main army; they would augment it. Now Cesare had his own mercenary army to gain territory and his own administrators to keep it. On the last day of September, he proudly displayed his troops to an admiring Alexander, in front of St Peter's. A few days later, they left for the Romagna.

The first objective was Pesaro, where he had previously been thwarted. On the way there, news arrived that the citizens of Pesaro had exiled Giovanni Sforza, who promptly fled to Venice. By the end of October, Cesare had entered Pesaro. The lesson of Imola had been well learned; this time, Cesare's army was disciplined with the helpless citizens.

Among the ambassadors who accompanied Cesare on his campaign in the Romagna was Pandolfo Collenuccio, who acted as the eyes and ears of Ercole d'Este of Ferrara. In a postscript to a lengthy report, dated at Pesaro on 29 October, he shed some light on Cesare's rather Iberian attitude towards time, as well as on his character:

> The duke's daily life is as follows: he goes to bed at three, four or five o'clock in the morning…Immediately on getting up, he sits down to the table and, while there and afterwards, he attends to his business affairs. He is considered brave, strong and generous, and it is said he lays great store by straightforward men. He is terrible in revenge – so many tell me. A man of strong good sense, and thirsting for greatness and fame, he seems more eager to seize States than to keep and administer them.[2]

So much for Pesaro. Rimini quickly surrendered also, and Pandolfo Malatesta joined Giovanni Sforza as an exile in Venice. But the third city of Faenza, under the leadership of Astorre Manfredi, successfully held out against Cesare. Autumn drifted into winter. The army found itself short of supplies and was riven by dissent. Cesare retreated to Cesena and made it the administrative capital of his newly created Romagnol state. He spent the winter of 1500–01 in Cesena and proved to be a more effective ruler than Collenuccio had anticipated. Thus refreshed, in the spring he returned to the bombardment of Faenza, which duly surrendered in April. The terms of surrender included safe conduct for Manfredi. But had Astorre Manfredi, the young and popular papal vicar, been allowed to go free, he would have become a focus for resistance to Borgia rule. As with Caterina Sforza at Forlì, Manfredi became a prisoner of Cesare. Ironically, on the very day in June 1501 that Caterina was released from S. Angelo (through French diplomatic intervention), the unfortunate Manfredi went into it. In June 1502, his strangled corpse was dragged from the Tiber. Once again, Cesare's assassin, Don Michelotto, had struck. All Italy was shocked by this murder, following upon those of Alfonso and Gandia. The moral was stark: cross Cesare Borgia and you will pay with your life.

In June 1501 Cesare, now also duke of Romagna, returned to Rome to be greeted once more by his adoring father, Alexander, 'as though he had conquered the lands of the infidel and not the devoted subjects of the Holy See'. Alexander issued a Bull agreeing to the Treaty of Granada, which France and Spain had already secretly signed. Louis would become king of Naples, while Ferdinand would become grand duke over Apulia and Calabria; both would hold their territories in fief from the Church. Alexander blessed the French troops as they left Rome with Cesare's mercenaries. City after city was destroyed. Colonna *condottieri* defended the city of Capua, which was sacked by the French forces. At Capua, Burchard estimated, 6,000 citizens were killed, including females and clerics: 'Whatever women they found they treated without mercy, cruelly raping the girls or taking them as booty'. One rumour has it that 40 of the most beautiful women were reserved for Cesare; but this rumour relies upon a single source – Guicciardini, writing an anti-Borgia treatise well after the event from the safety of Florence. Naples itself surrendered on 4 August 1501. King Federigo could offer no further resistance to the dismemberment of his kingdom. He surrendered and went into exile in France. His son, the duke of Calabria, was less fortunate – he spent the next 38 years in Spanish prisons. Between 1501 and 1503, therefore, Louis was ruler of at least part of Naples, to add to the duchy of Milan (which he ruled from 1500 to 1512).

The fall of Naples meant the fall of the Colonna, its ally, and the owners of the territories ravaged *en route*. Burchard relates that, in the summer of 1501, Alexander left Rome to inspect properties in the Campagna confiscated from the Colonna, Savelli and d'Estouteville families. He left the 20-year-old Lucrezia in charge at the Vatican, bastard daughter as she was of a disgraced pope, and a woman with a scarlet reputation, whether deserved or not. No more convincing proof was needed of Alexander's secular approach to the administration of the papacy. Many were outraged. And yet, with consummate irony, Lucrezia, like Cesare and Alexander, proved an excellent administrator. Her chief adviser was Cardinal Jorge da Costa, who happened also to be her godfather.

So swift was the Neapolitan collapse that Cesare was back in Rome by mid-September. As the most notorious and strictly non-ceremonial passage of Burchard's diary relates, the pope's son, all too evidently, had time on his hands:

> On Sunday evening, 30 October, Don Cesare Borgia gave a supper
> in his apartments in the apostolic palace, with 50 decent prostitutes

or courtesans in attendance, who, after the meal, danced with the servants and others there, first fully dressed and then naked. Following the supper too, lampstands holding lighted candles were placed on the floor and chestnuts strewn about, which the prostitutes, naked and on their hands and knees, had to pick up as they crawled in and out amongst the lampstands. The Pope, Don Cesare and Donna Lucrezia were all present to watch. Finally, prizes were offered – silken doublets, pairs of shoes, hats and other garments – for those men who were most successful with the prostitutes. This performance was carried out in the Sala Reale and those who attended said that, in fact, the prizes were presented to those who won the contest.[4]

From this account, it appears that the women in question were likely to have been prostitutes of the more common sort, rather than the high-class and highly cultured courtesans who emerged in the later sixteenth century and went on to host salons and have their poetry published. With its resident population of male clerics and equally large transient population, whether lay or clerical, Rome provided ample employment for prostitutes. Indeed Rome and Venice were the prostitution capitals of Italy in the Renaissance period. As for the episode with the chestnuts, it must be treated with considerable caution, for Burchard was not an eyewitness to the event and there is no knowing how the story was elaborated and embellished before it reached him. Be that as it may, this account was grist to the rumour machine that would shortly engulf the Borgias, now approaching the apogee of their triumph.

Chapter 6. A MAN 'TERRIBLE IN REVENGE'
'The dead of night covered all things'

In terms of relations between Alexander and secular princes, the latter part of the year 1501 was dominated by negotiations for a marriage between Lucrezia and Alfonso d'Este, the already widowed heir to the duchy of Ferrara. The Este were papal vicars on a different scale to those Cesare had just destroyed. They were secure, well-established Italian princes. Marriage for Lucrezia into the house of Este was a social triumph on a grand scale. Another advantage to Alexander lay in Ferrara being traditionally anti-Venetian, which was useful in curbing any Romagnol ambitions retained by the republic. For his part, Ercole d'Este, Alfonso's father, worried about Cesare's recent campaign and sought good relations with the Borgias in the hope of retaining the state he had ruled since 1471.

Ercole d'Este was determined to make Alexander pay dearly for Lucrezia's marriage. He demanded 100,000 ducats as dowry, as well as the permanent right to be freed of the annual *census* which he owed as a papal vicar. Both conditions were seriously damaging to the finances of the papacy. Alexander's dynastic ambitions would undermine the economic stability of the Church. The proxy wedding was celebrated on 30 December. Heedless of cost, Alexander turned it into a lavish spectacle, involving all of Rome. It was yet another public relations demonstration of relentless Borgia power. A week later, Lucrezia left Rome for Ferrara. She never returned. At just 21 years of age, she was embarking on her third and final marriage.

As with the progress of her mother-in-law, Eleonora d'Aragona, in 1473, Lucrezia's journey to Ferrara occasioned spectacular pageants in all the cities she visited en route. Cardinal Francesco Borgia and a host of Roman nobles accompanied her, as did more than 700 courtiers and servants of all types. It was a continuation of the Borgia public relations offensive, a blatant demonstration of seemingly unstoppable power. Each city vied with the one before to pay homage to Lucrezia – although some of the cheering citizens must have privately shuddered at the dread thought of her brother, Cesare.

Alfonso d'Este met his bride for the first time on 31 January 1502. Her formal entry into Ferrara followed, three days later. So splendid was the reception that Lucrezia considered it the highpoint of her already eventful life. The poet Ludovico Ariosto, an Este servant from 1501, was among those who presented literary greetings. A host of foreign ambassadors were present, but priority was given to the French envoy whose master, Louis XII, was protector of both the Este and the Borgia. Although he overestimated her age by three years, the Ferrarese chronicler, Bernardino Zambotto recorded the favourable impression made by Lucrezia on her arrival:

> The bride is 24 years of age; she has a beautiful countenance, sparkling and animated eyes; a slender figure; she is keen and intelligent, joyous and human, and possesses good reasoning powers. She pleased the people so greatly that they are perfectly satisfied with her, and they look to her Majesty for protection and good government. They are truly delighted, for they think that the city will greatly profit through her, especially as the Pope will refuse her nothing, as is shown by the portion he gave her, and by presenting Don Alfonso with certain cities.[1]

The wedding festivities occupied the pre-Lenten carnival period and provided one of the greatest expressions of Ferrarese Renaissance court culture. Reflecting the personal enthusiasm of Ercole d'Este, five plays by Plautus were presented between 3 and 8 February, complete with incidental music and dancing. For the more martial types, such as the bridegroom Alfonso, there was a tourney. For all onlookers, there was the spectacle of seeing a constellation of Italy's ruling elite gathered for the celebration.

Elisabetta Gonzaga had accompanied Lucrezia from Urbino. Also present was the groom's sister, Isabella d'Este, wife of Gian Francesco II Gonzaga of Mantua since 1490 and every bit her father's daughter in the matter of the cultural patronage for which she is now best remembered. The Este had also been connected to the Sforza of Milan by two dynastic marriages, but this bond was loosened by the deaths of Alfonso's first wife, Anna Sforza, and Ludovico il Moro's wife, Beatrice d'Este, in 1497.

Meanwhile, back in Rome, in the spring of 1502 Cesare was growing restless. The relationship with his father was altered; now it was as if he had some arcane power over Alexander. To superstitious Romans, their pope seemed possessed by a succubus. The Borgias were surely in league with the devil. How else could their good fortune persist? Enemies raged; the rumour machine went into overdrive. Typical was this comment: 'These are the days of the Antichrist. The bestiality and savagery of Nero and Caligula are surpassed. Rodrigo Borgia is an abyss of vice, a subverter of all justice, human or divine'.

With his many critics, Alexander was as tolerant as he had originally been with the Marranos, with Savonarola, even with della Rovere himself. His tolerance would be unusual in our time; in his era, with the power to condemn detractors to the dungeons, it seems no less than amazing. Alexander was a consummate master of public relations where the papacy/Borgia dynasty was concerned. Diplomatic initiatives would pave the way for military interventions; public spectacles such as Lucrezia's wedding and journey to Ferrara would dazzle the populace and condition them to Borgia superiority. But, where his personal reputation was concerned, Alexander made absolutely no move to shield himself. You could say what you liked about him. People did.

This curious dichotomy between managing the corporate image while ignoring the personal image is a vital strand of Alexander's paradoxical character. This is a pope, secular to the point of abandonment, who is oddly conservative and protective of the Church. This is a penny-pinching financial manager, who will nevertheless blow the budget on yet another lavish spectacle for the citizens of Rome, half of whom are hopelessly terrified of him. This is a sybarite whose table, as already mentioned, is so unappetizing that no one will eat with him because ('on dit'), 'they will be poisoned'. Alexander's carelessness of his personal image (his refusal to defend himself, his endless tolerance of bitter invective) was probably a mistake and a very bad one at that. He, above all people, could have disarmed his critics by his rhetoric. He, above all people, could have greased palms and had very different messages fluttering among the gossipmongers of Rome. But he did not. In Santayana's famous dictum, already quoted, 'Those who do not learn from history are condemned to repeat it'. Later politicians, with an eye to posterity, would do well to take the lesson of Alexander VI to heart and hammer their desired public image into the public image. For the last 20 years of his life, Winston

Churchill did exactly that. Was he right to do so? Undoubtedly. By contrast, Alexander's supreme indifference towards the management of his public image has contributed towards his later portrayal as a monster.

But, if Alexander was magnanimous, Cesare was not. This was a man 'terrible in revenge'. As Alexander told the envoy of Ferrara:

> The duke is a good-hearted man, but he cannot bear an injury. I have often told him that Rome is a free city, that everyone has a right to say what he pleases. Many things are said of me, but I take no notice. The duke replies, 'It may be that Romans can publish slanders, but I will teach them to repent'.

Cesare filled Rome with his spies. Punishment was ruthless. 'He takes one man's goods, another man's life, a third he drives into exile, a fourth he condemns to the gallows, a fifth he throws from his house for the sake of some Spanish heretic.' It was said that a masked man in the Borgo, denouncing Cesare, was seized and that his hand and his tongue were cut off and fastened to each other. Even the protection of the illustrious might prove no protection whatsoever against a vengeful Cesare. The author of a critical pamphlet, a protégé of the mighty Venetian ambassador, was nevertheless strangled. His body was flung into the Tiber, to join the host of other abandoned bodies floating in those refuse-strewn waters. In words that resonate across the centuries, Egidio of Viterbo wrote tellingly of these times:

> The dead of night covered all things. Besides domestic tragedies, never were sedition and bloodshed more widespread in the states of the Church; never were bandits more numerous, never more wickedness in the city; never were informers and assassins more used. Men were safe neither in their rooms, nor their houses, nor their castles. The laws of God and man were as nothing. Gold, violence and lust ruled undisputed.[2]

In the year of 1502, Italy was in a state of utter disarray, ripe for plucking by the Borgias. The French occupation of Naples gave them need of the papacy. Venice was struggling with the Turkish challenge. Ferrara was sealed with the alliance of Lucrezia's marriage. Florence and Siena, riven by internal dissent, were lining themselves up as soft targets. In February, Cesare took Alexander and six of his cardinals to show off his base camp at Piombino; its fortifications had been built by none other than Leonardo da Vinci. They also visited Civitavecchia, Corneto and Elba. On the sea voyage back from Elba, Alexander's galley was beset by a terrible storm. The cardinals wept and wailed in despair. Even the sailors were in mortal dread. Throughout, Alexander sat praying in the bows, enduring the storm with perfect equanimity. Once, many years before, his life had been threatened by another storm; then, his behaviour had been exactly the same. It was as though he was contemptuous of death – or, at the very least, untroubled by it. Alexander was a strange, paradoxical, hopelessly compromised man. But there is never any doubting his courage.

Alexander's intention had always been to decimate the papal vicars. By now, they were a distinctly endangered species. Guidobaldo da Montefeltro remained in Urbino, Francesco Maria della Rovere was in the Adriatic coastal town of Senigallia, and Giulio Cesare Varano was further south in Camerino. Cesare bought the artillery train of the former king of Naples, via hefty withdrawals from the papal treasury. Some of his former *condottieri* came back to join him. New people were brought in. By June, Cesare's army of Italian and Spanish mercenaries had swollen to 6,000 infantry and 2,000 cavalry.

On 5 June Alexander excommunicated Giulio Cesare Varano on an old charge of murdering his brother together with a newer one of shielding Church rebels. Alexander and Cesare were once more playing their Church/State trick, rendering their targets politically impotent before striking mercilessly.

It was assumed that Cesare's first aim would be the capture of Camerino. However, on 6 June the Romans learned that there had been an anti-Florentine revolt in Arezzo, which, most ominously, had been taken by Vitellozzo Vitelli, a captain of Cesare's army. Was this evidence that the Borgias were getting ready to attack Florence? They vehemently protested their innocence. Vitelli's brother had been executed by Florence; he had good reason to hate this state. But was he simply acting on his own behalf? It seemed distinctly unlikely, especially given his closeness to Cesare...

On the one hand, Alexander ordered Guidobaldo da Montefeltro to send reinforcements to Vitelli; on the other hand, Cesare subsequently ordered Vitelli to withdraw, much to his disgust. Both Borgias continued to protest that Vitelli had acted entirely of his own accord. By now, all of Italy was agog at the Borgia guessing game. What were they up to? Whose neck would be next on the block?

Alexander was enthralled at his son's quick capture of Urbino and, subsequently, Camerino, where the citizens opened the gates to avoid a sack. 'He could not contain his joy at the news but he must get up from his chair and go to the window, and there have the letter from his duke of Valentinois read aloud.' Florence, clearly startled at Cesare's *coup d'état*, sent the bishop of Volterra to discover Cesare's next target. The bishop was accompanied by a man whose name has become a synonym for cold-blooded political amorality. In Cesare, this man saw the apotheosis of such a philosophy.

> This lord is truly splendid and magnificent, and in war there is no enterprise so great that it does not appear small to him; in the pursuit of glory and lands he never rests nor recognizes fatigue or danger. He arrives in one place before it is known that he has left another; he is popular with his soldiers and he has collected the best men in Italy; these things make him victorious and formidable, particularly when added to perpetual good fortune.[3]

Thus wrote Niccolò Machiavelli about Cesare Borgia. Machiavelli could hardly have been more impressed by Cesare's audacious actions in this campaign, interpreting them as the marks of a genuine leader who dictated events and was not a victim of them. But, with the sobriety of hindsight, we may well feel that Machiavelli was seduced by a 'halo effect' of first acquaintance with so striking a figure as Cesare. True, Cesare was victorious, formidable and seemingly all conquering. But 'perpetual good fortune' is a notoriously fickle lady with her favours. The greatest figures in history are often those most harshly tested in adversity. And Cesare, a godlike 27-year-old, was well-nigh untested in adversity.

As a 'hands-on' leader of men, Cesare could be inspired. But, as the employer of *condottieri*, he was becoming a bad risk. Cesare's commanders wondered about their future security; after all, they were smaller fry than the duke of Urbino. These mercenaries were lords of estates and townships in their own right. They were little fish, which Cesare was using to decimate bigger fish. When would their turn come? 'They were afraid that the dragon was preparing to swallow them one by one'. Such fear inspired treacherous plotting against Cesare.

The cynicism and amorality of Cesare's opportunism with Urbino provoked horrified alarm in a land already suffused with cynicism and amorality. Who could curb Cesare's excesses? Certainly not his doting father. Louis XII, already angry about Vitelli's capture of Arezzo, was becoming plagued by complaints from dispossessed vicars. He tersely told Cesare to cease and desist.

Cesare confounded his enemies by slipping across to Milan to meet Louis face-to-face (hence Machiavelli's 'He arrives in one place before it is known that he has left another'). Alexander was terrified that Cesare would be seized. But Cesare's charm offensive worked perfectly. Louis was entirely won over by Cesare's personal touch. And Cesare humbly apologized for Vitelli in Arezzo. Typically, each had ulterior motives. Louis well knew that trouble with Spain was brewing in Naples, and he wanted Cesare's army on his side and not on the other. So Cesare, much to the chagrin of his enemies at the French court, was treated with great honour. He was offered the added enticement of French troops to take the formerly French-protected city of Bologna. Truly, this was an era of political expediency.

Back in Rome, Alexander worried about French kings in general and this one in particular. He was scathing of those who begged Louis to intervene in Italy:

> Those idiot cardinals [Giuliano della Rovere, Ascanio Sforza and Raffaele Riario] who surround the King of France have described Italy to him as a paradise, yet he has found hell here. We very much hope to see them discredited with the King, for the reward of the dishonest is always the hatred of those who begin by favouring them.[4]

After almost a month with Louis, Cesare returned to Camerino as covertly and speedily as he had left it. Lucrezia, one of probably the only two women he cared about, was seriously ill in Ferrara. Cesare broke his journey to be with her for a mere two hours. Little did either of them know what divergent and harsh futures awaited them.

No matter how rapidly he moved, even Cesare could not be omnipresent throughout his new domains. Moreover, for a Borgia state to stand any chance of survival after the deaths of its founders, there needed to be a dynasty. Cesare's sole legitimate child was his daughter, Luisa; Louis had earlier agreed to an arranged marriage between Luisa and Federigo Gonzago, the heir to the duke of Mantua. At this juncture, the most enigmatic of the Borgias appeared on the public scene – Giovanni, known as the *Infans Romanus*. In September 1502, Alexander travelled to Camerino to install the child as its duke. Giovanni was assumed to be Cesare's illegitimate son, as confirmed by a Bull of 1501. The Camerino appointment was regarded as natural for the son of such a father. What was not made public was a second Bull (also of 1501), which named Giovanni as Alexander's son. Even greater mystery surrounded the identity of his mother, so much so that a rumour circulated that he was Lucrezia's child. The Bulls were evidently designed to scotch this rumour.

In common with Lucrezia's son Rodrigo, young Giovanni was spirited away to Naples in 1503, but unlike Rodrigo he later went to live with her at the Ferrarese court. In Ferrara, there was no speculation that he was anything other than the duchess' half-brother. (When the male line of the Varano family died out in 1527, Giovanni made a legal challenge to regain the duchy of Camerino, but it failed completely.)

A Bull of Leo X reveals the existence of another Giovanni for whom papal parentage was claimed. According to the Bull, this boy was born in 1503 and Alexander was his father. Nothing further can be said about his birth, with any certainty. He had an unremarkable clerical career, and became abbot of Cicciano di Nola.

The Borgia winning formula of sealed alliances, papal excommunications, military victories, gained territories, sound administration and yet more sealed alliances was working perfectly. But for how long? Cesare's absence at the French court had given anti-Borgia conspirators (such as the Orsini), deposed vicars and his anxious *condottieri* another month to plot against him. When Cesare announced Bologna as the next target, he sparked outright revolt. Giovanni Bentivoglio of Bologna, a proud *condottiere* turned into a Borgia target, provided Cesare's rebels with a ready-made leader. As many of these same rebels had sworn not to attack Bologna in the previous year, they used this as a convenient excuse.

At meetings in Todi in September and in Magione in October, the conspirators formed themselves into an anti-Borgia alliance, the so-called Diet of Magione. But they made odd bedfellows, each of them out for themselves, their hatred and fear of the Borgias the only common denominator. Cesare would soon mockingly term them 'the Diet of failures'. Along with Giovanni

Bentivoglio of Bologna, Gianpaolo Baglione from Perugia, Vitellozzo Vitelli from Città di Castello and Oliverotto da Fermo felt themselves to be possible targets. (Vitelli had been an Orsini associate in 1496–47 and, like the Orsini, had no depth of loyalty to the Borgia.) Montefeltro was present to argue the case of the dispossessed vicars. Pandolfo Petrucci, lord of Siena, was regarded as the mastermind. The Orsini were making full use of the political astuteness of Cardinal Giovanni Battista Orsini, who was lobbying Louis and the French. His kinsman, Paolo Orsini, also in the conspiracy, was mockingly known by his soldiers as 'Madonna Paolo' for his effeminacy. Francesco, duke of Gravina, an Orsini who had once tried to wed Lucrezia, perhaps deserved better company.

Between them, they had control of most of Cesare's army. Had they showed an ounce of his talent, they would surely have destroyed him. But they were a group, not a team and, worse, they acted as though they did not believe in themselves. Indecision and delay were their watchwords; potential support was thereby alienated. Florence feared Cesare – but it also feared Vitelli and the Orsini, who supported the Medici. It was loath to become committed until the conspirators had a track record of success. Venice was embroiled in war with the Turks. Anti-Borgia propaganda was whispered in the ear of Louis, but, for the moment, Cesare's charm offensive ensured the French king's support.

If the conspirators were to move against Cesare, they must do it on their own. In October, Paolo Orsini seized Urbino. Camerino too fell to the conspirators. Baglione and Vitelli, advancing towards Urbino, defeated a contingent of Spanish troops at Calmazzo. Yet, at the same time, the Orsini were attempting to cut a deal with Alexander in Rome. The conspirators were not only conspiring against the Borgias. They were also conspiring amongst themselves. Both conspiracies would cost them dear.

Cesare withdrew his loyal troops from the environs of Urbino and Camerino. He reformed his forces, brought in new *condottieri*, hired fresh Gascon and Swiss mercenaries and enlisted the help of the Romagnol militia. On 7 October Machiavelli arrived in Imola, in his role as Florentine envoy. Soon afterwards, he sent the following missive back to his political masters:

> As regards the situation here, the state of this lord, since I arrived
> here, has been held together by good fortune; of which the chief cause

has been the firm conviction held here that the King of France will help him with men, and the Pope with money; and another thing which has been helpful to him is the delay of his enemies in closing in on him. Now I judge that it is too late to do him much harm because he has provided all the important cities with garrisons, and has provisioned all the fortresses.[5]

Fascinated as he was by Cesare, Machiavelli's judgement convinced Florence that backing the *condottieri* amounted to joining the losing side. And the king of France was indeed sending men to Cesare; he too had decided which side was going to win. The Diet of Magione, indecisive in strength, proved gutless in adversity. Cesare was right to name them 'the Diet of failures'. Conspiring amongst themselves to the end, they vied with each other in being the first to come over to Cesare and betray their former comrades. By the end of October, Paolo Orsini, Petrucci and Bentivoglio had made overtures to Cesare while, back in Rome, Cardinal Orsini was making similar overtures to Alexander. Cesare inexorably strengthened his military position and sardonically watched his enemies rush to destroy themselves.

And yet the surrender terms were remarkably generous. Urbino and Camerino must be returned to Borgia rule. But the *condottieri* would receive an amnesty, although each one of them would have to give a son to Cesare as hostage to their good faith. Paolo Orsini took Cesare's terms back to his fellow conspirators; all of them accepted except Baglione of Perugia, who distrusted Cesare's mercy. With Bentivoglio of Bologna, a separate treaty was drawn up – his position was confirmed but he must serve with Cesare as *condottiere*. Thus did Cesare separate the leader from the pack.

Cesare's apparent magnanimity was viewed by more doubting political eyes than those of 'the Diet of failures'. 'I fail to understand how such injury can be expected to find forgiveness',[6] was Machiavelli's sceptical verdict. And Giustinian, the Venetian ambassador in Rome, echoed this sentiment:

> The nature of the duke is not to pardon those who have injured him nor leave the vendetta to others; he has threatened those who have offended him and in particular Oliverotto, whom the duke has sworn to hang with his own hands, if he can get him into his clutches.[7]

Be that as it may, Cesare reoccupied Urbino and Camerino and prepared to capture Senigallia, with his new yet redundant allies, the vanquished *condottieri*. On 30 December the town surrendered without a shot being fired. The following day Cesare invited the *condottieri* there, while the bulk of their armies remained outside the walls. Cesare and the *condottieri* entered Senigallia; the gates closed behind them. They continued to the palace. Cesare was the very soul of affability to these men who had betrayed him. Suddenly, soldiers moved into place and seized them. Vitelli, da Fermo, Orsini and Gravina were taken; Petrucci was the only one to escape. Orsini and Gravina (another member of the Orsini) became pawns in the overall Borgia/Orsini war – albeit pawns under a probable death sentence. Vitelli and da Fermo had no such usefulness. As judge and jury, Cesare wasted no time in exacting his revenge. The two of them were seated back-to-back and strangled. Da Fermo cried bitterly. Vitelli, that brave soldier, begged to be allowed absolution from the pope, the father of his murderer.

On whose side was the treachery at Senigallia? Inevitably history accords Cesare with having acted with snake-like cunning. Yet Cesare's letters written from Senigallia, within a day of this event, tell a different story. He asserts, to Alexander and to Isabella Gonzaga amongst others, that his erstwhile allies turned conspirators, who had revolted, 'turning our arms against ourselves', were engaged in a fresh conspiracy at Senigallia. They were:

> pretending that they had come with few men, when in fact they brought all the soldiers they had been able to collect, with whom and with the aid and agreement of the captain of the enemy fortress, they combined to do against our person that which, forewarned of the affair, we have done against them.

In other words, his actions were a necessary pre-emptive strike and they were fair game. It was Cesare's considered view that 'the world must be happy and content, especially Italy, which sees thus suppressed and extinguished the public and calamitous pest from which its populace suffered'.[8]

What is the truth about the conspiracy of Senigallia? It is, perhaps, yet another tantalizing puzzle about the Borgias, in which we will never be certain that we know the true answer. Whichever version one accepts, no-one can doubt Cesare's coolness and courage. These *condottieri* were both seasoned soldiers and seasoned traitors; violence was their stock in trade.

Cesare was surrounded by them. The merest slip on his part, or on the part of his associates, and he would have been the first to die. Of the Magione conspirators it seems that only Baglione had read Cesare correctly, as had the more astute Machiavelli and Giustinian. And as had Alexander himself ('The duke is a good-hearted man, but he cannot bear an injury.'). There was no clemency, no forgiveness, no mercy from Cesare. This was the man who, as already mentioned, reputedly had another man's tongue and hand cut off and nailed together for using mere words against him. Did the fools of Magione imagine that Cesare would pardon them? With command of most of his army, they had their chance to finish him. And they bungled it.

Thus passed the last day of 1502. The following day Cesare and his henchmen left for Perugia, from which Baglione promptly fled. As Cesare carried on into Tuscany, the Sienese government took the precaution of expelling Pandolfo Petrucci, which averted a bloody revenge. In an attempt to vanquish Orsini power once and for all, the Borgias made a two-pronged initiative. Cesare had Paolo and Gravina disposed of in Tuscany. In Rome, when Alexander learned of the coup at Senigallia, he ordered a mass arrest of the Orsini and their supporters. Of all those who had dared to express their distrust of the Borgia, the Orsini were the ones whom Alexander had most firmly in his sights. He had never forgotten the Cibo castles crisis at the very outset of his pontificate. On 3 January 1503, Cardinal Orsini, the head of the family, was arrested. An elderly, blind man, he did not survive long in the depths of Castel S. Angelo. Heedless of protests from other cardinals, Orsini's assets were seized. Giulio Orsini escaped to his castle at Ceri, some 10 miles from Rome, and mounted a counter-attack. The alum mines at Tolfa were destroyed, thus seriously weakening revenue to the papacy/Borgia war chest. Young Jofré was forced to run to his father for safety. Alexander had the Vatican barricaded, and strongly advised his cardinals to do likewise.

The Orsini regrouped under Giulio Orsini at Ceri and Virginio Orsini's son, Giangiordano, at Bracciano. Alexander took a serious view of the threat. He tersely ordered Cesare to abandon his military adventures in favour of a return to protect Rome and stamp out the Orsini. When Cesare vacillated, it is rumoured that Alexander threatened to excommunicate him. Curiously, as Cesare made his way towards Rome, he rejected the opportunity to attack Bracciano. Was it because the mighty fortress had proved impregnable in

1487, or because both Cesare and Giangiordano were knights of the French Order of St Michael and therefore bound not to fight one another? Petrucci returned to Siena, as soon as Cesare's back was turned.

In March Cesare returned to the fray, bombarding Ceri with 6,000 cannonballs. In April, it was forced to surrender. Giulio Orsini received exile in France rather than the death normally meted out to Cesare's vanquished enemies. Alexander came to Ceri to witness the wanton destruction of the castle. Not long afterwards, the mighty Bracciano also surrendered. Louis XII, Giangiordano's former protector, turned arbitrator, influenced him to follow Giulio's example of exile in France. 'These things make him victorious and formidable, particularly when added to perpetual good fortune.' Thus did Machiavelli judge Cesare. And it was true. The mightiest of castles had fallen to him. Seasoned *condottieri* trembled at his approach. He was master of the papal states. Only the power of France in Italy checked his dynastic ambitions. On 11 January 1503, one commentator, Priuli, had written of Cesare in his journal: 'Some wish to make him King of Italy, others wish to make him an Emperor, because he succeeds in such wise that no-one could have the courage to refuse him anything whatever'.[9]

Alexander played a waiting game throughout the winter of 1502 to 1503, seeing whether Spain or France would gain the upper hand in Naples. The utility of the French alliance was evidently in serious doubt. In the meantime, the pope sought an agreement with Venice, but it was a short-lived scheme.

On 28 April came the event that determined which of the invading powers was the more attractive papal ally. Gonsalvo de Córdoba scored a decisive victory over the French, at Cerignola in Apulia. The Treaty of Granada was dead, and the way was clear for Ferdinand of Aragon to assume control of the entire southern kingdom. He ruled it through a sequence of governors. At the same time, it became clear that Venice was increasingly hostile to the creation of a Borgia state in the Romagna. It was not coincidental that two important Orsini *condottieri*, the count of Pitigliano and Bartolomeo d'Alviano, were then employed by Venice. A north-south split appeared reasonable; France and Venice, on one hand, Spain and the papacy, on the other. Alexander gave de Córdoba permission to enlist mercenaries in Rome.

Cesare was once again getting ready for war and conquest. But first, he needed money. The Borgia fund-raising machine swung into action. A new cycle of brutal extortion of Jews and Marranos began. (How disillusioning to see the extent to which Alexander's former tolerance had disappeared.) In March, a consistory decreed that 80 new places would be created in the Curia. Each new place would bring in another 760 ducats. 'I leave it to your highness to count the profit to the Pope', the Venetian envoy acidly reported to his masters. Cesare, the former cardinal who had left the Church 'for the good of his soul' personally supervised these activities. What was good for the Borgias was good for the Church…

In April, Cardinal Michiel was poisoned and died in agony. ('More wealth for the Borgias', furtively whispered onlookers.) Bishop Santa Croce, an Orsini sympathizer, was executed and his assets seized. Nine new cardinals were named by Alexander on 31 May – the last such creation of his pontificate. Appropriately enough, five of them were Spaniards, bringing the grand total of Spanish cardinals to 16. The remainder comprised three Italians and an Austrian, Melchior von Meckau. The French cause was not entirely neglected, for it seems that the Florentine Francesco Soderini owed his promotion in part to the favour of Louis XII and to Cesare Borgia. Soderini had been Florentine ambassador at the king's court in 1501–02, and again from November 1502 until promotion to the Sacred College. His brother had become the republic's new *gonfaloniere a vita* in September 1502.

New talent in the Sacred College? Giustinian, the Venetian envoy, did not think so. His verdict was scathing: 'all have paid handsomely for their elevation – 20,000 ducats and more – so that something between 120,000 and 130,000 ducats has been collected. Add to this the 64,000 from the sale of offices plus what Cardinal Michiel left behind, and we have a fine sum.'[10]

In the hot summer of 1503, Cesare was casting a covetous eye upon Tuscany as the next target. Alexander was busy persuading the Emperor Maximilian to grant Cesare Siena, Pisa and Lucca. So much had been accomplished. The papal vicars were destroyed. The *condottieri* had been culled. Great families, such as the Orsini, were ground under the Borgia heel. The Borgia machine was surely unstoppable. The summer was a mere respite, a breathing space between one bout of victories and the next. And yet, a mere three months after his appointment, the rising star Cardinal Soderini arrived in Rome. His presence was required in the conclave – to elect a new pope.

Chapter 7. THE END OF ALEXANDER'S REIGN
'He bought the papacy with his soul'

In the summer of 1503, Rome was even hotter than usual. The proximity of the marshes, combined with lack of hygiene in the city, gave rise to epidemics. On 7 July Francesco Fortucci, a Florentine employed in Rome, wrote thus: 'Here are many sick with fever, and people are dying in great numbers'. Several days later, he repeated the message: 'Many people are dying of fever and there are some cases of plague, it is said'. On 22 July he begged to be allowed to quit Rome, arguing that he was so terrified that he could not work competently. Fortucci's superior, ambassador Alessandro Cracci, had died of fever only two weeks previously. Antonio Zeno, who took over from Fortucci, was already seriously ill.

In August, the situation grew worse. Zeno reported that, with the terrible heat and the number of people going down with fever, Rome was in crisis. Understandably, Alexander was greatly perturbed; worse, he seemed depressed. 'Many people are dying; we should give a little more attention', he rebuked the politicians with whom he was working. Normally in August the political elite left Rome to escape the heat and plague. But this was no time for papal government to be in recess. A French army was marching south to do battle in Naples. Cesare's army was encamped in a line stretching from Rome to Perugia. If Cesare left imminently for the Romagna, he would avoid an obligation to help the French.

On 5 August, Cesare and Alexander dined with the newly appointed Cardinal Adriano Castellesi at his country vineyard at Monte Mario, a short distance from the Vatican. It may well have been a farewell supper for Cesare. The same day, Cardinal Borgia-Lanzol the elder died of fever. Sound administration had been the backbone of Borgia policy, and Borgia-Lanzol had done an excellent job. But in the previous few years, through a sedentary lifestyle, he had allowed himself to become obese. Two days later, Alexander watched the funeral of Borgia-Lanzol from afar and gloomily remarked, 'It is a bad month for fat people'. Was he also referring to himself? When an owl swooped in through the window, he whispered, 'An omen. A bad omen...'

During the following week, many people observed Alexander's unwonted depression. So many had died – enemies, friends, children. And now yet another French army marched on Naples. Soon there would be more bloodshed, more deaths. Where would it all end? 11 August was the anniversary of Alexander's accession to the papacy. And Alexander had always possessed a child-like love of celebrations. With what exuberance he had first scrambled into his papal vestments! But now, 11 years later to the day, he was gloomy and preoccupied.

On 12 August, a full week after the supper with Cardinal Castellesi, Alexander and Cesare both succumbed to fever. Alexander was bled. The fever seemed to abate and Alexander was able to sit up and watch his carers play a game of cards. But on 14 August the fever returned with a vengeance. In a desperate attempt at remedy, the 72-year-old Alexander was bled again. (Cesare was also still fighting the fever, but was aided by a stern constitution and all the vitality of youth.)

On Friday 18 August Alexander, surrounded by five of his cardinals, made his last confession and received holy communion. Later, his confessor gave him extreme unction. At around six o'clock, he finally lost consciousness. Shortly afterwards, Rodrigo Borgia, Pope Alexander VI, died.

Inevitably rumour had it that Alexander and Cesare were poisoned; it was supposed to have happened at the meal with Cardinal Castellesi. Borgia myth has it that Alexander and Cesare were arch-poisoners. If the biter was bitten, then was this not a triumph of natural justice? Yet, not content with this pleasing symmetry, the rumour machine insisted that Alexander and Cesare went to poison Castellesi, but were poisoned themselves. This conspiracy raises symmetry to the level of elegance.

How were they poisoned? Accounts vary. One story says that Cesare had sent specially prepared wine to Castellesi's house. But through some mishap, it got into the hands of a servant 'not in the know'. Cesare was delayed in arriving at Castellesi's. A thirsty Alexander arrived first, and quaffed the deadly potion. Cesare arrived afterwards and followed suit. It's a great story, worthy of Hollywood – the Borgias destroyed by their own evil. But it's a story that stands up poorly to level scrutiny.

As ever with the Borgias, the principal motive ascribed to their actions was money. So Castellesi was to be murdered for his money. The only problem here is that Castellesi seems to have been relatively poor; so much for motive. As for modus operandi, was Cesare (and Alexander, for that matter) such a consummate bungler? Servants not in the know, wine not recognizable – this is the stuff of farce. Compare Cesare's ice-cool competence at Senigallia. Many labels might be attached to Cesare; bungler is not one of them.

Cesare and Alexander fell ill a full week after the meal with Castellesi. Once more, we are back in the realm of the deadly *cantarella*, a 'delayed death touch', which kills after a convenient time has elapsed. But where is this *cantarella*? If it existed, surely it would have attracted the attentions of the intellectually curious, such as Machiavelli and Leonardo da Vinci. 500 years later, can it be made now? Has it ever been made? It does not seem to figure greatly in the conspiracy theories of the twentieth and twenty-first centuries.

And lastly, just for the sake of argument, let us imagine that Cesare and Alexander did, indeed, go to Castellesi's house to poison him. A week passes. Cesare still has no idea that the servant has slipped up and the wine has been drunk in the wrong order. But, a week later, when Castellesi is well and Alexander and Cesare both succumb to fever, they both must know, with horror, what has happened. Both know with certainty that Alexander is for the grave, and only youth can possibly save Cesare. During Alexander's brief respite, on 13 August, he would hardly have been seen watching his cardinals play cards. Alexander, or Cesare, or both, would have desperately been plotting events after Alexander's death, knowing full well what was going to happen. That they did not do this indicates that they did not know any such thing. The only possible alternative is that they were stupid. And stupid is not a word that could reasonably be applied to Alexander or Cesare.

As ever, we will never know the truth of what happened, but the likelihood of Borgia self-poisoning sits poorly with any sort of critical analysis. It seems likely that the pope's fatal illness cannot be attributed to any deficiency in Castellesi's hospitality – nevertheless he considered it prudent to leave Rome, and did not return for nearly two decades.

On the subject of poisoning cardinals, it is interesting to note that whereas 27 cardinals died during Alexander's 11-year papacy, 36 died during the next but one papacy of Julius H (della Rovere). As eliminators of unwanted rivals,

Alexander and Cesare seem to have been markedly inferior to della Rovere, if the poison theory is taken seriously. In reality, such increased numbers of deaths may be better attributed to additional numbers of cardinals rather than to murderous popes. On the subject of popes' deaths, it is instructive to recall that all of the five popes who preceded Alexander died in July/August, the time of greatest heat and greatest danger of ill-health or plague. The solution was to get out of Rome. As has been noted, this was not a viable solution for Alexander in the summer of 1503. Far too much was at stake. As vice-chancellor to all of these five popes, Alexander well knew the dangers of a Roman summer. But he stayed at his desk and did his work as best he could. Sadly, it was to cost him his life.

There are two histories of the Borgias. There is the real history of what actually happened. And there is the imaginary history, the Borgia myth, the 'public image' of the Borgias. In 1968 Professor Michael Mallett crucially noted that this latter image, 'however distorted it is, may be of more historical significance than the real, often more complex situation'.[1]

Burchard's graphic account of the immediate afterlife of Alexander, or at least of his mortal remains, can be said to mark the transition between the reality of Alexander's papacy and the distortions of the black legend that rapidly evolved around the Borgia name. It twists perfectly natural phenomena into tales of the macabre, and is wholly in keeping with Burchard's morbid preoccupation with witchcraft and diabolism:

> ...the complexion of the dead man became increasingly foul and black. Already, by four o'clock on that afternoon, when I saw the corpse again, its face had changed to the colour of mulberry or the blackest cloth and it was covered in blue-black spots. The nose was swollen, the mouth distended where the tongue was doubled over, and the lips seemed to fill everything. The appearance of the face then was far more horrifying than anything that had ever been seen or reported before. Later, after five o'clock, the body was carried to the chapel of Santa Maria della Febbre and placed in its coffin, next to the wall, in a corner by the altar. Six labourers or porters, making blasphemous jokes about the Pope, or in contempt of his corpse, together with two master carpenters, performed this task. The carpenters made the coffin too narrow and short, and so they

placed the Pope's mitre at his side, rolled his body up in an old carpet, and pummelled and pushed it into the coffin with their fists. No wax tapers or lights were used, and no priests or any other persons attended to his body.[2]

In spite of his long residence in Rome, it can be argued that Burchard shared a wider Germanic tendency to perceive diabolic interventions in human affairs, and it is from him that we first hear of devils seen around Alexander's tomb.[3] It was a tendency not confined to Germans, and stories soon circulated that Alexander had made a pact with the devil, stories that became ever more elaborate and were often inconsistent in their details. Followers of Savonarola were among those who propagated the legend, developing the friar's assertion that Alexander was no Christian, but rather a Marrano. Anti-Semitism was a standard feature of contemporary popular preaching, sometimes involving accusations of the ritual murder of Christian children by Jews.

One of the earliest examples of the diabolic pact story is contained in a letter from Gian Francesco Gonzaga, marquis of Mantua, to his wife, written less than a month after the Borgia pope's death:

> When [Alexander] was ill, he began to Hiyaspeak. His words were these: 'I will come, you are right, wait a little'. From this, those who knew his secret understood that, after the death of Innocent [VIII], while in the conclave, he bought the papacy with his soul and, among other points, it was agreed that he should hold it for 12 years…there are others who affirm having seen seven devils around him at the moment of his death; at once, his body began to boil and his mouth to foam, like a cauldron on a fire.[4]

Two years after writing this account, Gonzaga was surprised by Alexander's posthumous popularity in Rome. Nevertheless, the damage had been done. The story entered literary tradition with the *Commentaria* (1506) of Raffaele Maffei, written to please Alexander's arch-enemy, Julius II. Come the Reformation, Maffei was duly read by Protestant authors such as the ex-Carmelite turned Protestant exile, John Bale. Bale saw the development of the papacy as 'a plaine way to Antichrist'. The pope is not the Vicar of Christ; he is the Vicar of Satan. Alexander VI is 'a very riotous tyrant', who owes the papacy to 'his league with the devil' and reduces Rome to 'a slaughterhouse'.

Through Bale, Alexander's alleged pact with the devil was picked up by other English writers and became a commonplace of anti-Catholic propaganda. It reached the stage in the form of *The devils charter, containing the life and death of Pope Alexander the Sixt* (1607), a riot of sadistic cruelty by the prolific poet, Barnabe Barnes. Barnes also used an English translation of Guicciardini's *Storia d'Italia* (1534), which applied a new moral code to Alexander's pontificate. Italy too produced a crop of Protestant authors who found markets for their version of events in Lutheran and Calvinist countries of northern Europe, which, in turn, produced their own variations on the theme. In 1599, the German Lutheran, Georg Rudolf Widman, made Alexander's pact with the devil part of the Faust legend. The following year, another Lutheran, Johann Wolf, published on the same subject. For Wolf, 'the Pope [any Pope] is a devil'. Specifically, he states that:

> As cardinal, Alexander spent his whole life working to become Pope. So that he might achieve this aim more easily, he addressed himself to black magic…promising obedience to the devil…It was decided that Satan would appear to him as a protonotary. When [Alexander] asked how long he would be Pope, [the devil] replied in such a way that Alexander thought he had been promised 18 years – in fact he reigned for only 11 years and eight days.[5]

When Alexander fell ill, he sent for his book of magic. However Satan was already sitting on the papal throne, robed in papal vestments!

Moving on into the modern period, the Borgias became as much a focus for anti-clericalism as for anti-Catholicism. Italians were not necessarily any more enamoured of the pre-Reformation Church than were north European Protestants. Indeed, it has been claimed that southern Europeans – meaning essentially Italians and Spaniards – have been more interested in the Borgias as figures in church and politics, while the northern Europeans, with their less precise knowledge of Rome and the other territories concerned, developed a greater interest in the *supposed* characters of Alexander, Cesare, Vanozza and Lucrezia.[6]

For the Borgias as political figures in European literature the focus switches from Alexander to Cesare, and the saga begins with Machiavelli's assessment of the latter's career. During his mission of October 1502 to January 1503 the Florentine envoy witnessed Cesare at the height of his unscrupulous powers,

Plate 1: Aeneas Silvius Piccolomini (later Pius II) receives his cardinal's hat from Pope Calixtus III. Fifteenth-century fresco by Bernardino Betti (called Pinturicchio). © The Art Archive / Piccolomini Library Siena / Dagli Orti

Plate 2: The assembly of the clergy with Pope Sixtus IV. Detail from *The Triumph of Saint Thomas Aquinas* (1471) by Benozzo Gozzoli. © The Art Archive / Musée du Louvre Paris / Dagli Orti

Plate 3: Pope Alexander VI. Detail from *Madonna dei Racommandati* (*c.*1500) by Cola da Roma. © The Art Archive / Museo Diocesano Orta / Dagli Orti

Plate 4: Pope Julius II orders the building of the Vatican and St Peter's. From a ceiling painting (1827) by Emile Jean Horace Vernet. © The Art Archive / Musée du Louvre Paris / Dagli Orti (A)

Plate 5: *The School of Athens* (1509–11). Fresco by Raphael, Stanze della Segnatura, Vatican. © The Art Archive / Vatican Museum Rome

Plate 6 (*left*): The pope acts as a moneychanger with the sale of indulgences and religious dispensations (1521). Satirical woodcut by Lucas Cranach the Elder. © The Art Archive

Plate 7: Portrait of Pope Leo X, with Cardinal Giulio de' Medici and Luigi de Rossi. Painted by Raphael, *c*.1517. © The Art Archive / Galleria degli Uffizi Florence / Dagli Orti (A)

Plate 8 (*left*): King Henry VIII and Pope Clement. Cartoon from a sixteenth-century broadsheet. © The Art Archive

Plate 9: Pope Paul III (Alessandro Farnese). Detail from the fresco *Pontificate of Pope Paul III* (1553–63) by Francesco del Rossi (called Il Cecchino or Il Salviati). © The Art Archive / Palazzo Farnese Rome / Dagli Orti

Plate 10: *The Last Judgement* (1536–41). Fresco by Michelangelo, Sistine Chapel. © The Art Archive

Plate 11: Pope Pius V concludes the Holy Alliance against the Turks in 1571.
Sixteenth-century painting from the Sienese school. © The Art Archive / Sienese State
Archives / Dagli Orti (A)

and was unashamedly impressed. While states and dynasties buckled at the very approach of foreign armies, Machiavelli regarded Cesare as the ablest Italian military commander around and, consequently, Italy's best hope for uniting against and expelling the invaders. If the ruthlessness he displayed at Senigallia was the price to be paid, then the end justified the means.

Machiavelli's international reputation and that of the Borgias became intertwined only after the posthumous publication of *Il principe* in 1532. Written in 1513, it was dedicated to Lorenzo de' Medici, duke of Urbino, son of Piero and nephew of the reigning pope, Leo X. It was through the marriage of Lorenzo's daughter, Caterina (in French, Catherine de Medicis) to the future Henri II, and her subsequent influence as queen and queen dowager of France, that the reputation of that slim book and its author spread. Her reputation among French Protestants reached its nadir in the wake of the St Bartholomew's Day massacre of 1572. One consequence was the publication of the *Discours d'etat contra Machiavel* (abbreviated to the *Anti-Machiavel* in English) by the Huguenot exile, Innocent Gentillet, in 1576. The Florentine queen and the Florentine political commentator stood or fell together. Both appeared on the English stage in works by Marlowe. *The massacre at Paris* conflates the events of the French Wars of Religion, while 'Machevil' declares 'I count religion but a childish toy' in the prologue to *The Jew of Malta* (*c*.1590). Anti-Catholic propaganda in English drama brings us back to Barnabe Barnes and *The devils' charter*. More specifically, it brings us back to the character of Cesare Borgia. In Barnes' version, he is the epitome of sadistic cruelty, who reaches his lowest ebb by killing his own brother, the duke of Gandia.

The blood continued to flow in nineteenth-century historical romances about the Borgias, of which Emma Robinson's three-volume *Caesar Borgia* (1846) provides a notable example. By that date, though, some authors displayed a sneaking admiration for Cesare. In his *Poemes Saturnies* (1866), Paul Verlaine was inspired by a portrait of Cesare – handsome, noble, powerful but terrible. The rehabilitation of Cesare by nineteenth-century Italians, meanwhile, had a clear contemporary purpose. After three-and-a-half centuries of foreign invasions and occupations, Machiavelli's exhortation to unite and liberate Italy was finally heeded in the unification process known as the Risorgimento. Cesare Borgia could be cast as a proto-Risorgimento figure, attempting to rid the peninsula from the blight of multiple states and petty princelings, and presenting a picture of Italian military achievement in the process. An example of this sub-genre is Pietro Cossa's play, *Il Borgia*, staged in Turin in 1881.

The third literary tradition inspired by the Borgia concerns their private lives and centres on the women of the family, Vanozza and Lucrezia. Again the trail leads back to the diarist, Burchard, who reproduces the text of an anonymous letter accusing Lucrezia of having incestuous relations with both her father and Cesare. Alexander himself dismissed the letter with an ironic laugh, but enemies of the Borgias seized on it as invaluable 'evidence' to discredit them all at a stroke. The Borgias happened to be more closely knit than some other papal families; it was a gift for mischief-makers.

The impact of such anonymous accusations was effectively cancelled by Lucrezia's subsequent career in Ferrara and the protection of marriage with an illustrious lord. Her last meeting with Cesare had been because of her serious illness after the birth of a stillborn child, just seven months after her arrival in Ferrara. Cesare had been to Milan to meet Louis XII and changed his plans in order to visit Lucrezia. (This was the frantic period in which Cesare's military captains conspired against him; two hours was all he could spare at Lucrezia's bedside.) She nevertheless rallied and moved to her favourite Ferrarese convent, Corpus Domini, to recuperate.

When Alexander died in August 1503, Lucrezia did not yet enjoy the security of being the mother of the Este heir, for her eldest surviving son by Alfonso was not born until 1508. She feared a backlash against her, but had already acquired enough of a reputation for charitable works and as the focus of Ferrara's vibrant court culture, to render that fear unfounded. Her popularity among the people of Ferrara never waned. Among those who offered her condolences on the loss of her father was the Venetian poet, Pietro Bembo:

> I called upon your Majesty yesterday, partly for the purpose of telling you how great was my grief on account of your loss, and partly to endeavour to console you, and to urge you to compose yourself, for I knew that you were suffering a measureless sorrow. I was able to do neither the one nor the other; for, as soon as I saw you in that dark room, in your black gown, lying weeping, I was so overcome by

my feelings that I stood still, unable to speak, not knowing what to say. Instead of giving sympathy, I myself was in need of it, therefore I departed, completely overcome by the sad sight, mumbling and speechless, as you noticed or might have noticed.[7]

Bembo was a relative newcomer to Ferrara, but he was already familiar with the life of a court presided over by a woman. Court culture was alien to his native Venice, but not to the Veneto, where the Venetian patrician, Caterina Cornaro (or Corner), was given the lordship of the hill town of Asolo in compensation for the loss of Cyprus, of which she had been queen. It was at Asolo that Bembo set his *Gli Asolani* (*c.*1497), a dialogue on love, containing numerous lyrics through which he expressed his own love for Maria Savorgnan. By the time it was printed, in 1505, Bembo had forged a close friendship with Lucrezia – who became duchess of Ferrara that year, when Alfonso succeeded his father, Ercole. It was to Lucrezia that *Gli Asolani* was dedicated.

Bembo provided Lucrezia with a degree of cultural sophistication which Alfonso could not match, and their relationship can be traced through a sequence of love letters (including nine from Lucrezia to the poet, seven of them in Italian and two in Spanish). In 1506 Bembo moved to Urbino, where Elisabetta Gonzaga presided over the court of her husband, Guidobaldo da Montefeltro. Our image of Bembo tends to be mediated by Baldassare Castiglione, the Mantuan diplomat and courtier who idealized the court of Urbino in *Il Cortegiano* (published 1528) and presented the Venetian as the great advocate of Platonic love. His correspondence with Lucrezia was certainly written in that vein, and it should not be assumed that they were lovers in the non-Platonic sense.

An inventory of Lucrezia's books, made around the time of her marriage, reveals perfectly conventional literary interests, for they were mostly devotional works. Like her letters to Bembo, some of these were in Italian and others in Spanish. During her 17 years in Ferrara, her reputation for piety and good works increased with the passage of time, creating something of a parallel with her mother, Vanozza, who observed her daughter's career with some pride, albeit from a distance.

At the same time, Bembo was merely the first of her literary admirers, for it was natural that Ferrarese men of letters should dedicate their works to the young duchess. Among these was Ariosto who, in his masterpiece *Orlando furioso* (1516), placed her portrait in the temple to women. Ariosto continued the epic story of Charlemagne's paladins where Matteo Maria Boiardo had left off his epic *Orlando innamorato* (1483, 1495), which provides a notable reminder that fifteenth-century Ferrarese court culture was particularly distinguished by an enthusiasm for chivalry. This included not merely the 'matter of France' – Charlemagne and the paladins – but also the 'matter of England', for Dukes Leonello and Borso were named after two of the knights of the Round Table, Sir Lionel and Sir Bors. It was Borso who built the Palazzo Schifanoia ('*sans-souci*') in Ferrara and had its principal room, the Sala dei Mesi, decorated with frescoes.

Ferrara's court culture reached yet greater heights under Duke Ercole, who extended the city by building the so-called Herculean Addition and promoted the careers of writers and artists through the sort of collaborative projects that only courts could sponsor. The first Ferrarese printing press had begun operation in 1471, attracted by the thriving university which boasted as many as 45 professors by 1474. Among the most venerable of their number, for both learning and sheer longevity, was Niccolò Leoniceno, who was born in Vicenza but acquired his reputation as professor of medicine at Ferrara. In 1497 he published *De morbo gallico* ('On the French disease'). Whether syphilis really was brought into Italy by French troops or by Spanish soldiers who had acquired it (indirectly?) from sailors returning from Columbus' early transatlantic expeditions, it certainly seemed to be a new phenomenon in the peninsula. Less interest has been taken in another work by Leoniceno, *De dipsade et pluribus aliis serpentibus*, on poisonous snakes (Bologna, 1518, but written earlier). This he dedicated to Lucrezia, as duchess of Ferrara, a connection that 'may have contributed to her reputation as a connoisseur of poisons'.[8] It is a reputation that does not bear scrutiny and appears to have developed after her death.

In 1505 Lucrezia gave birth to her first child by Alfonso, a son named Alessandro, after the late pope, but he died at the age of just two months. A second Alessandro was born in 1514 and died, aged two. Four of Alfonso and Lucrezia's children survived infancy: Ercole (1508–59), who succeeded his father and became Duke Ercole II in 1534; Cardinal Ippolito II (1509–72), creator of the famous water gardens at the Villa d'Este at Tivoli, to the east of Rome; Eleonora (1515–75), who went on to become abbess of the Ferrarese convent of Corpus Domini; and Francesco (1515–78) who became marquis of Massalombarda. The duchess also took responsibility for Cesare's illegitimate children, Camilla and Girolamo. The former entered the religious life, took the name Lucrezia, and became abbess of the Ferrarese convent of S. Bernardino. She died in 1573. Girolamo married twice and fathered two daughters, but little else is known of his life except that he committed at least one murder.

Lucrezia herself died on 24 June 1519, eight days after giving birth to a stillborn child. With death near, she had written to the Medici pope, Leo X, for his blessing:

> Most Holy Father and Honoured Master: With all respect, I kiss your Holiness's feet and commend myself in all humility to your holy mercy. Having suffered for more than two months, early on the morning of the 14th of the present, as it pleased God, I gave birth to a daughter, and hoped then to find relief from my sufferings, but I did not, and shall be compelled to pay my debt to nature. So great is the favour which our merciful Creator has shown me, that I approach the end of my life with pleasure, knowing that, in a few hours, after receiving for the last time all the holy sacraments of the Church, I shall be released. Having arrived at this moment, I desire as a Christian, although I am a sinner, to ask your Holiness, in your mercy, to give me all possible spiritual consolation and your Holiness's blessing for my soul. Therefore I offer myself to you in all humility and commend my husband and my children, all of whom are your servants, to your Holiness's mercy.
>
> In Ferrara, June 22nd, 1519, at the fourteenth hour.
>
> Your Holiness's humble servant,
>
> Lucrezia d'Este[9]

She was duly buried in the convent of Corpus Domini, where Alfonso was also interred after 15 years of widowhood. Until the 1570s, her children survived as guarantors of her reputation in Ferrara.

Interest in Lucrezia subsided until the nineteenth century, but Vanozza emerged as a key figure in a book of 1655 by Tomaso Tomasi, one of the Italians who sought their fortunes in France during the minority of Louis XIV, when Cardinal Mazarin (originally Giulio Mazzarini) was first minister. In his *Vita di Duca Valentino*, Tomasi tried to exonerate Alexander by attributing all his problems to Vanozza, depicted as an Eve-like original sinner who manipulated her lover by means of witchcraft. Tomasi's intention was to find favour with the hierarchy of the Church by transferring the blame to Vanozza, even if it meant seriously exaggerating her role and her influence in the process. Tomasi's text soon fell into the hands of an Italian convert to Calvinism, Gregorio Leti. He had no use for Tomasi's Catholic apologetics, but spied a neat parallel between Alexander VI in the clutches of Vanozza Catanei and Louis XIV in thrall to his mistresses, Mesdames de Maintenon and de Montespan. His Baroque romance, *Vita di Cesare Borgia detto il duca Valentino*, was published in Geneva in 1670.

The revival of interest in Lucrezia began with Victor Hugo's play, *Lucrece Borgia* (1831), which he set in Ferrara at the end of her life. Hugo let nothing stand in the way of a good yarn, which, in this case, included assassination, adultery and incest, spanning three generations of the Borgia family. In 1838, the last of the indirect line of the Borgias – Don Mariano Tellez-Giron y Beaufort Spontin Pimentel, prince of Squillace, duke of Osuna and Gandia – met Disraeli in Paris. Of Mariano, Disraeli recorded:

> He is a great dandy and looks like Philip II...When he was last in Paris, he attended a representation of Victor Hugo's *Lucrece Borgia*. She says in one of the scenes 'great crimes are in our blood', and all his friends looked at him with an expression of fear. 'But the blood has degenerated', he said, 'for I have committed only weaknesses'.[10]

A charming story of this effete, urbane fellow, the last of the Spanish Borgias! Cesare would have sneered at him with contempt. But Alexander, with his tolerance of human frailty and his perennial sense of fun, would have laughed heartily.

The nineteenth-century historian Ferdinand Gregorovius later dismissed Hugo's play as a 'grotesque aberration of poetry', but it had sufficient popular appeal to cause the composer, Gaetano Donizetti to turn it into a two-act opera, *Lucrezia Borgia*, in 1833. When this was produced in Paris, in 1840, Hugo raised objections, so it was withdrawn from performance and rewritten as *La rinegata*, with the action moved to a Turkish location.

Fantasies and poetic inventions multiplied, an example from the later nineteenth century being the novel *Angela Borgia* (1891), by the Swiss author

Conrad Ferdinand Meyer. Dark and light, vice and virtue are juxtaposed in the characters of the amoral seductress Lucrezia and her cousin Angela, who is ready to sacrifice herself for the man she loves. Meyer's Lucrezia also committed incest with her brother, a point that commentators have raised in connection with Meyer's own domestic circumstances; he lived with his sister for many years and, after his marriage, in a *ménage à trois*.

Lucrezia made papal history an attractive subject for nineteenth-century painters. In *The Borgia family* (1851), Dante Gabriel Rossetti endeavoured to encapsulate the entire black legend on a single canvas, Alexander leering over the shoulder of the lute-playing Lucrezia, while Cesare's pent-up violence is expressed in the act of beating time on a wine glass. Less menacing is Giuseppe Boschetto's painting *Lucrezia Borgia governatore della Chiesa* (nineteenth century), where the little Lucrezia sits on a large papal throne, head bowed over the letter in her hand, while a red-robed cardinal – presumably intended to be Jorge da Costa – sits nearby, poring over further papers. She is presented as something of an anomaly, but the viewer is possibly not intended to be shocked. Gaetano Previati, on the other hand, did not aim for subtlety in *Il sacco di Capua* (1890), depicting an alleged violent episode in 1501. Cesare Borgia and his captains sit in a gloomily lit chamber, as the women of Capua are taken prisoner and paraded naked before them.

As long as historians were unable to gain access to the relevant archival sources, poets and novelists had free rein and the public believed their fanciful version of historical events. The Vatican Archive – the Archivo Segreto Vaticano – remained closed to scholars, as regards this period, until the latter years of the nineteenth century. The transition from poetry to archival research can be found in the life of the German historian, Ferdinand Gregorovius, who arrived in Rome in 1852 as a 'late-romantic' poet, inspired by the Italian travels of Goethe and the example of the German Nazarene painters resident in the city. By 1871 he had completed his *History of the City of Rome in the Middle Ages* but, before he left Rome, he discovered a volume of documents produced by the fifteenth-century Roman notary, Camillo Benimbeni, a collection that included many pieces of relevance to the history of the Borgia. Further research took him to Modena, where the Este archives are housed, and to the Gonzaga archive in Mantua. The Vatican remained out of bounds. The result was his biography of Lucrezia, published in Germany, in 1874. (The above works are mentioned here as deserving of slightly more descriptive comment than is normally practical in a bibliography.)

Equally remarkable as history and as literature is the *Chronicles of the House of Borgia* (1901), written by Frederick Rolfe, 'Baron Corvo'. It exhibits a fund of arcane knowledge, including details of various types of poison known in the Renaissance period, but is not free of unscholarly indulgence, as in: 'This year also died the 12-toed, chin-tufted, excommunicated little Christian King, Charles VIII of France, and was succeeded by his cousin, Louis XII, a thin man with a fat neck and lip and an Ethiopic nose and exquisite attire.'

Back in the mainstream, Gregorovius has been succeeded by generations of Borgia historians and biographers, reacting against the crude popular image of blood, poison and incest. Their research has acquitted Alexander, Cesare, Lucrezia and their kin from some of the more sensational accusations made against them since the sixteenth century. Still to come, however, was a further, definitive exposure of the great Borgia myth.

Chapter 8. THE MYTH AND THE MAN
'He died in August 1503 and was buried in Hell'

When we speak of 'the age of the Borgia', we are not merely looking at a time between two dates; we are conjuring up a particular image of government and social behaviour. The success of the myth has ensured that we associate the word 'Borgia' with poison, with incest, with utter amorality. For the Church it implies simony, nepotism and a surrender of the spiritual to the secular at its very worst. We do not think of St Francis Borgia, who gave such unstinting service to the Jesuits. Instead, we think of Lucrezia, the alleged whore of Babylon; of Cesare, the prince of darkness; and of Alexander, the anti-Christ, who 'bought the papacy with his soul'.

'The Borgia Myth' might well have been the name of an early historical crime novel – a novel to enthral the world for all of 500 years. It is only in the last century that its veracity has been seriously called into question. Considerable damage had been done meanwhile, both to history and to the reputations of the Borgias. The myth is one of the greatest stories of all time – but myth it unquestionably is, rather than truth.

The Borgias were people of their time, not ours, although there are Shakespearean themes of comedy and tragedy which run through all times. The Borgias had their share of such themes; sadly, for them, more tragic than comic. It would be invidious to treat them as saints (although Lucrezia showed increasing saintliness towards the end of her life). But to treat them merely as arch-sinners shows a disrespect for historical accuracy, bordering upon outright contempt.

Much of the important evidence, both for and against the integrity of the Borgias, has already been mentioned. Lest the sheer volume of evidence drown the narrative, we have been forced to be selective. Nevertheless, it may be appropriate to review a few key pieces of evidence, inasmuch as they have given rise to the myth. Hence this special chapter summarizing the main arguments of Orestes Ferrara.

Alexander VI was born Rodrigo de Borja, Italianized as Borgia. The historian Platina called him Rodrigo Lanzol. Pope Calixtus III did have a nephew called Lanzol – but it was a different nephew. Nevertheless, the confusion has been perpetuated by many later writers in order to deny Borgia's noble ancestors. In a document discovered in 1924, in the archives of Valencia, it is quite clear that Rodrigo's father, well before his son's birth, held the name of Borja and not Lanzol.[1]

One document of seminal influence to later historians was somewhat verbosely entitled: 'Life of don Rodrigo Borgia, later Pope Alexander VI, and of Cesar Borgia and his brothers, sons of the said Pontiff, with Memoirs of the most secret events that took place during this pontificate, the whole drawn from manuscripts in the Vatican Library'.[2] The account has Borgia's father alive many years after his death, and has the young Rodrigo as a bandit in Spain, when he was actually serving the Church. It subsequently has him both as a lawyer and a soldier in Spain, besides being a page to King Alfonso V. Somehow he lives in Spain for 28 years, despite a well-documented life in Rome. It also places Vanozza Catanai in Spain, with Borgia as the lover of her and her two daughters, simultaneously. It has Calixtus III dying while Borgia was still in Spain, and it has the subsequent conclave electing Innocent VIII (with no mention of the intervening reigns of Pius II, Paul II and Sixtus IV). These gross historical errors form the base for a farrago of poisonings, assassinations and incest.

Another calumny[3] states that Rodrigo, at the age of 12, in response to a verbal insult killed another boy of the same age but a lower social class. This supposed attack was ferocious; the young Borgia is claimed to have stabbed his victim repeatedly in the pit of his stomach, trying to find the place where it would hurt most. Neither Borgia's father nor the law, it is stated, made any attempt to punish him. In fact, it would have been impossible for Borgia's father to punish him, as he died when Borgia was only 10 years old. This tragic tale was prefaced with the usual 'It is said', thus absolving the narrator from any obligation to be accurate. Inevitably, with the passing of time, such rumour became accepted fact.

With regard to the young Borgia's having acted as a professional soldier in Spain, he affirmed on different occasions, in stark contrast to Pope Julius II, that he had no knowledge of military affairs. There is no evidence that

CHAPTER 8. The Myth and the Man

he ever brought his piercing intelligence to bear on the many military campaigns during his reign – which would be incredible if he possessed personal experience as a Spanish *condottiere*.

Part of the Borgia myth has a rough, ignorant Rodrigo Borgia coming to Spain only after the coronation of Calixtus in 1455. However a Bull of Pope Nicholas V in 1449 authorized Rodrigo Borgia, canon of Valencia, to live outside the places from which his benefices came. A discourse of Jason del Maino gives added evidence that young Borgia left Spain in 1449. Instead of being some rough Spanish bandit, Borgia studied law at the university of Bologna – as is documented by contemporary notes. Borgia certainly put his legal studies to good effect. Again and again in his reign as Alexander VI, he advocates the resolution of conflicts by calm and independent legal arbitration, rather than by verbal or physical force. Sadly, a document attesting to his legal studies at Bologna has the scurrilous comment scribbled on it, at a much later period of Borgia vilification: 'He died in August 1503, and was buried in Hell'.[4]

In a secret consistory, at the beginning of his reign, Calixtus named three new cardinals – Rodrigo Borgia, Luis Juan del Mila and Don Jaime of Portugal – *in petto*. This meant that the appointments would only be made public at a later date. The secrecy of the consistory and the *in petto* nominations have been taken as evidence that the other cardinals resisted these nominations and only acquiesced in hopes that the pope would die before anything was made public. It is also claimed that Calixtus made a public announcement of these nominations in the month of September, when the effects of the summer heat – lack of hygiene and plague – kept the opposition cardinals out of Rome. In direct opposition to this speculation, in the Bull making Rodrigo Borgia a cardinal, the pope affirms that this was a unanimous decision from all the cardinals present and there was but a single absentee, the cardinal of Ostia. The signatures of all participants are at the end of the document.[5] While *in petto* nominations were unusual, for various reasons of convenience they have been used at many other times, before and since.

As evidence of Borgia's immorality, a letter of Cardinal Ammanati Piccolomini[6] accuses him of having secured the election of Sixtus IV by intrigue, of being vain and malignant and of having spent the Church's money in a futile mission to Spain. It further accuses Cardinal Borgia of using missions such as this as a way of accumulating wealth to buy his papacy at a later date. The truth appears to be the exact opposite. Borgia's missions abroad were extremely expensive; to accomplish them, Borgia had to raise a great deal of money. In the case of the Spanish mission, he had to pawn all his benefices – auctioning them to the highest bidder for three years. It was difficult to find a moneylender prepared to take the risk. The benefices might be lost, either by the death of the holder or by the whim of the pope. Thus, Pope Sixtus IV had to issue a special Bull authorizing the loan and stating that Borgia's benefices, if they passed to another for any reason whatever, should not yield the new owner the right to receive the income until the money loaned upon them had been completely repaid. Cardinal Piccolomini reported that the election of Sixtus IV was accomplished by the wire-pulling and bribery of Cardinal Borgia. In fact, Borgia opposed his election at every ballot and only went over to the opposing side when there was a clear majority.

Some words referring to the Cardinals Piccolomini and Borgia have been taken as evidence that they were both deeply dissipated. But the letter, contained in the document *Cardinalis Papiensis Epistolae et Commentarii*, published first in Milan, then in Frankfurt, makes clear that the key expression 'changed way of life' referred to a change of relations between the two men. Unfortunately, Cardinal Piccolomini seems to have been a singularly unreliable character witness, changing his opinions according to his own situation. Referring to Borgia's Spanish mission, he had elsewhere written, 'everybody wants to see you [Borgia] here [Rome] and considers your presence necessary that you may exercise your predominating influence...' On one occasion, he accused Borgia of not wanting to have anything to do with him because Borgia wanted to cultivate the friendship only of the great. Yet, on another occasion, alluding to former quarrels, he asked Borgia to forget the past and resume their erstwhile friendship.[7]

The truth seems to be that, to this extent, Cardinal Piccolomini's own character was enigmatic. As an impractical person, he made enemies in Rome. Yet, as an extremely sensitive person, he made himself even more enemies over trifles. He insulted and ridiculed Cardinal Bessarion, who was regarded, then and later, as a saint. The invective upon Bessarion was not taken seriously; the invective upon Borgia was. When Borgia had been selected for a delicate political mission to the court of Spain, Cardinal Piccolomini was the only person to object. It seems probable that Piccolomini wanted to be sent himself; given his personality, he would have been a most unsuitable choice. How much better it might have been if he had studied the qualities of his more gifted colleague, instead of succumbing to invective.

In fact, there seems to have been remarkably little criticism of Rodrigo Borgia before he emerged from the conclave as Pope Alexander VI. As we have seen, Borgia had been the vice-chancellor to five successive popes. He was no 'wild card' candidate. Conversely, he was the most familiar of known quantities in Rome and Italy. So much of the criticism of Borgia's earlier life came not at the time but decades later. Any fair-minded person could not help but wonder – how much of the criticism is due to political expediency and downright envy?

The enmity between della Rovere and Alexander seems to have begun in 1492, and not before. The election of Alexander was a rude blow to della Rovere's ambition. As a man of savage temper, he was wont to take umbrage at any setback – as is amply demonstrated during his reign as Pope Julius II. Despite being favourably treated by Alexander, as we have seen, within days of the conclave he was plotting with Virginio Orsini and King Ferrante of Naples against the papacy. In effect, he was engaging in treason. His subsequent exhortations at the French court to invade Italy and depose the pope were also highly treasonous. Plainly, della Rovere's word against Alexander is the word of a traitor.

It is ironic, given Alexander's exemplary conduct during the French invasion of 1494, that he has been accused of encouraging it. The sole proof of this accusation is a papal Bull in which he authorizes the French army passage through the papal states. The date of this Bull is 1 February 1494, at a time when Alexander had been in negotiation with the king of Naples. On the face of it, this appears proof of a most puzzling duplicity. But the Bull is dated according to the Florentine mode, in the old style – in the modern calendar, the date would be 1 February 1495, for the old style year began on 25 March, in honour of the Feast of the Annunciation. And so it is that Alexander's Bull does not date from the period when he was negotiating with Naples. Instead, it dates from a period when the

French had been in Rome and when, consequently, the authorization of free passage dealt not with their entering the Church's territories but with their leaving them.[8]

The first documented assertion that Cesare killed the duke of Gandia is contained in a dispatch sent to Duke Ercole from Venice by Alberto della Pigna, ambassador of Ferrara: 'I have again heard it said that the cause of the duke of Gandia's death was the cardinal, his brother'. Della Pigna had heard this at Venice, far from Rome. He sent it on to Ferrara, also in Venice, where the rumour had not yet been heard.[9] In support of this communication, della Pigna claims that the widow of the duke of Gandia had Cesare arrested in Spain in 1504, in order to avenge the murder of her husband. As we will see, Cesare's arrest and subsequent incarceration were a political manoeuvre, inspired by King Ferdinand of Spain and designed to impress Pope Julius II. There is no evidence of a sister-in-law's revenge being any part of the motivation.

In response to the claim that Cesare killed the duke of Gandia for his kingdom, as we have seen, Cesare did not inherit this kingdom. The dukedom of Gandia, together with other possessions in Rome and Spain, passed to the son of the murdered duke and not to his brother. Thus this claim fails any scrutiny whatsoever. If Cesare killed Gandia, it was certainly not for the latter's money.

Sometimes 'historical' accounts of what happened have become rolled together into omnibus editions. Apropos of the Perotto murder, in a letter from a certain Poggio, secretary of Bentivoglio, lord of Bologna, to Ercole d'Este, it is said that Perotto died not in the Vatican but in prison. Thus, there are three conflicting versions of the same story. Burchard says that Perotto died in the Tiber, while Poggio asserts that Perotto died in prison. The scurrilous *Letter to Silvio Savelli* (of which more later) states that he died in the Vatican. Faced with these three conflicting versions, later historians have rolled them all into one. The omnibus version has Perotto arrested, first placed in prison and then taken to the Vatican, where he was murdered in Alexander's arms. Perotto is then flung into the Tiber, and is finally fished out by the very authorities who had been responsible for flinging him into it.[10]

As we have seen, on the death of his son Alexander was moved towards reform of his private life and of the Church. While Alexander's private life would be unimaginable for a pope in our time, it was not so very unusual for a pope in his time. Certainly, while he was invariably ready to use his political influence for the advancement of the Borgias, he never thus used the higher interests of the Church or its states. He took his stewardship of the Church much more seriously than has been credited by many commentators.

Reform of the Church in the reign of Alexander was, however desirable, quite simply an impossible dream. The historian De Roo has discovered information gathered by the commission and resulting proposals, all preserved in the Vatican, in two special volumes, one of 346 pages, the other of 132 pages.[11] Cardinal Carafa, one of the most active members of the commission, proposed four papal Bulls, addressing specific issues. As the investigation proceeded, the goals envisaged grew larger. The cardinals were forced to abandon the idea of reform by papal action alone. A General Council would be required.

A General Council, at that time, was a political impossibility. The Church was ruled, politically as well as spiritually, as an absolute monarchy. This was a situation that had come about gradually, from various causes. As we have seen, during Alexander's reign the papacy was not long removed from the Avignon captivity. From the time of Nicholas V, the papacy had struggled to build itself up as an international power, 'punching above its weight' with the French and Spanish superpowers. It had no comparable revenues and no comparable armies. Even in Rome, families such as the Colonna and the Orsini continually threatened it. The other states of Italy, such as Venice, Florence, Milan and Naples, were questionable allies at best, deadly foes at worst. The papal territories were still ruled by papal vicars, ruthless middlemen and *condottieri* with little loyalty to the Church. The Turks were a constant threat, as was invasion by France. In short, the papacy was surrounded by enemies, both within and without Italy. Always there was the possibility that the papacy would become a satrap of Spain or France – as could so easily have happened during the 1494 invasion.

For Alexander and for his successors, the summoning of a General Council was a move as dangerous as it was radical. It would be naïve to assume that spiritual reform could somehow take place without political reform. And political reform, however desirable *per se*, would weaken the papacy as an international power and increase the likelihood of it being taken over by one European country or another. Voltaire memorably remarked, 'Liberty has no relevance in a city under siege'. During the reign of Alexander, the papacy was continually under siege. Any challenge to the undisputed power of the pope was tantamount to going from a monarchy to a republic while in a state of war. However laudable in theory, it would undoubtedly be a path to political ruin. Alexander was far too politically astute to make this mistake. The first attempt at reform of the Church – the Council of Trent – needed several more decades to come about. Sadly, it also needed Martin Luther as a catalyst.

It must also be said that some of the documents produced in the propaganda war against the Borgias are of questionable provenance. For example, with Stefano Infessura, there exists no original text of his journal.[12] It is not only that some manuscripts are in Latin, others in Italian, still others in dialect. There are huge differences between different copies. It is evident that his work has been altered and rewritten to order. For instance, some copies favour the Colonna, others the Orsini. While it is all too clear what the contradictory copyists say in their vilification of Alexander, it is simply impossible to know what Infessura himself actually said.

Elsewhere, we have the '*on dit*' approach to history, where calumny becomes rumour, and then fact. As we have seen, so much of this calumny was originally prefaced by 'it is said', 'we hear', 'everybody thinks', thereby absolving the narrators from any responsibility for accuracy.

One account has Alexander fathering not one but many children in Spain, at times when he was not even in the country. We have seen the Infessura account of Cardinal Gherardo selling his vote at the conclave to the then Cardinal Borgia and being disgraced upon his return to Venice; a place the poor man never reached, because he died at Terni.[13] A rumour that Vanozza Catanei kept houses of ill repute in Rome is uncorroborated and sits oddly with her respected position in Roman society. At her death in 1518, she was given a funeral worthy of a cardinal; Pope Leo X was represented by his chamberlain.[14]

For the times he lived in, Alexander's tolerance of criticism, both fair and foul, was quite amazing. He criticized Cesare for refusing to demonstrate the same tolerance. Much of the invective against Alexander has been inspired by the (typically) anonymous *Letter to Silvio Savelli*, affected to be addressed to one Savelli, an exile in Germany. Alexander laughed heartily when he read the letter, which seemed to him simply absurd. Later he allowed Savelli to return to Rome, and it is even probable that he protected him.[15]

The myth of Borgia poisoning has never been verified. 500 years later, the mysterious *cantarella* has still not been identified. Many of the allegedly poisoned cardinals were not Alexander's enemies but, instead, his friends; conversely, many of his enemies outlived him. As we have seen, twenty-seven cardinals died during Alexander's eleven-year papacy. Thirty-six cardinals died during the nine-year papacy of Julius. Thus, whereas, on average, just over two cardinals died for each year of Alexander's papacy, four cardinals died for each year of Julius' papacy, almost twice as many. Yet Alexander is regarded as a poisoner, whereas Julius is not. Surely this judgement is perverse.

A huge impetus towards the blackening of Alexander's reputation was, as stressed elsewhere, inspired by his deadly enemy, Cardinal della Rovere, when he became Pope Julius II. Former servants and staff at the Vatican were tortured to obtain 'confessions', which would never be accepted today. Della Rovere, like Cesare Borgia, had the most amazing mixture of good and bad qualities. Sadly, where Alexander was concerned, he allowed a political opponent who repeatedly bested him to become an object of hatred. His intolerance of Alexander contrasts markedly with Alexander's tolerance of him. Certainly the 'black propaganda' put out by Julius is a shameful blot on his own papacy.

Unfortunately, the death of Julius did not bring a retraction of the calumnies against Alexander. As we will see, sadly for the Church, it merely led to a stream of incompetent popes. Thus the lies against Alexander were never retracted. They were allowed to continue, unabated. Further, if Alexander were to be held up as a kind of 'hate object', other incompetent occupants of the papacy might deflect some of the wrath of the Roman mob. Both the Reformation and the Counter-Reformation had even greater need of one man who could be the personification of evil. That man became Alexander. Machiavelli, the Florentine patriot, was viewed as the personification of amorality, a theorist in an age that had abandoned God. The Borgias were seen as the prime activists of this age. Thus, the names of Machiavelli and Borgia became indissolubly linked – to the lasting detriment of both.

The story of Pope Alexander VI, it can be said, is one of Shakespearean tragedy. Here is a man who leaves his Spanish homeland for the power centre of Rome. Over decades, he serves his apprenticeship as vice-chancellor to five consecutive popes. Pius II notes, 'Rodrigo Borgia is now in charge of the chancellery; he is young in age assuredly, but he is old in judgment'. Innocent VIII writes, 'Not once have you ceased to be useful to us'. Cardinal Rodrigo Borgia is the most competent senior churchman of his time. He has managerial talents comparable to the chairman of the greatest multinational of our own time. Always he covets the greatest prize in the Church. Finally, he wins it. He first scrambles into his vestments with delight, crying, 'I am the Pope, the Pontiff, the Vicar of Christ!'

Immediately he sets out his agenda of good government – of the citizens of Rome, of the papal states, ultimately for all of Italy. But to do this, he must go against the vested interests of the great Roman families, the papal vicars, the *condottieri*, the citizen states of Italy. Always he must ensure that the papacy extends itself mightily when dealing with the French and Spanish superpowers. Always he must avoid the papacy's becoming caught, like a nut in a nutcracker, between hostile powers.

Not two years into his papacy, the country is invaded. The French take control of much of Italy and nearly all of Rome. By the power of words and with great moral courage, Alexander persuades them to leave. In so doing, he saves the papacy from becoming a French satellite, from a return to Avignon. If this was the single achievement of Alexander's papacy, he would merit our undying respect.

'The one thing a Pope can do for his relations is to provide them with goods while he is still alive'. Alexander does a Herculean job of aligning dynasty with papacy. Much of the time, his motto might have been, 'What is good for the papacy is also good for the Borgias'. And yet fate runs amok. His son Juan is wanton; his son Jofré is worthless. When Juan, his favourite child, is callously murdered, Alexander is riven by grief. His grief impels him to reform of the Church. But a necessary General Council is a political impossibility. Consequently, the reforms never happen. And, with Gandia gone, Alexander enters a dangerously symbiotic relationship with his son Cesare, an aspirant Italian Alexander the Great.

CHAPTER 8. The Myth and the Man

From then on, Alexander the policymaker and Cesare the man of action become a dream team. The great Roman families are crushed. The papal vicars are decimated. The citizen states are outfaced. The *condottieri* are vanquished. Through sword and cannonball, tyranny dies and responsible government arrives in the papal states. Order comes out of chaos. In contrast with the lacklustre previous papacies, Alexander achieves so very much more.

But something goes horribly awry. Alexander, the protector of the Marranos, descends to extortion. Alexander, the loving father, sees his daughter Lucrezia's happiness destroyed with the wanton death of Alfonso, her second husband. Alexander, the indulgent parent, finds Cesare, the wild card of Italian politics, becoming ever more uncontrollable. Cesare's achievements come too easily. He is too favoured by good fortune. And it allows him to be capricious, wilful. He sleeps all day long, ignoring the affairs of state, mortally insulting would-be allies. Alexander's wistful refrain, 'What will happen to him after our death?' is the cry of every parent for every child.[16] But Alexander's sad reflection, 'I do not know if he will be able to keep what he has acquired' is horribly prescient.

Yet he soldiers on. With consummate irony, this most secular of popes constantly strives to do what is best for the Church. However prone to the delights of the flesh, this is a man with a stern and unrelenting sense of duty when it matters most.

Finally he dies – in harness, working to the very end, striving to avert yet another impending crisis. With his death, his dynasty collapses like a pack of cards. His reputation and those of his children are savaged. The Borgias achieve their place in history as denizens of evil. There is not a shred of hard evidence to support the myth of incest (and with Lucrezia, the daughter he so loved). As for stories of murder and poison – it was strange how his worst enemies were unscathed. 'I could easily have had vice chancellor Sforza and Cardinal della Rovere killed. But I did not wish to harm anyone, and pardoned 14 traitorous nobles, in league with France'.[17]

Alexander was entrusted with the sacred stewardship of the Church; he served it well. Would that he had been less tolerant of the personal attacks upon himself. The vilification, which he treated good-humouredly, was used as source material for so much further calumny throughout the succeeding centuries. It has done his reputation terrible and lasting harm.

The Renaissance was a time of grandeur, peopled by men and women of greatness. But it was also a time of great turbulence and huge excess. Alexander's pontificate coincided with the period of greatest fermentation of the whole Renaissance. It was a time of monstrous upheaval. Somebody had to be blamed for all this upheaval, this turbulence, this excess. Alexander, already vilified by the hatred of his arch-enemy, Giuliano della Rovere, has become a hate object throughout all of history. He, together with his children Cesare and Lucrezia, have been neatly arranged into a public relations triptych, the apotheosis of evil. But it is a myth – fiction, not fact. It is the world's first and most long-lasting historical 'soap', with demons and monsters to keep us convulsed with terror in the dead of night.

It is essential to bear in mind at every stage – as well as by way of summary – the insistence by Professor Michael Mallett on the vital effect of the hatred of Julius II on Alexander VI's reputation: 'It was this hatred which led the same Julius to torture confessions of crimes, supposedly committed at the command of the Borgias, out of Alexander's servants, and to eradicate as far as possible every evidence of Borgia achievement.'[18]

PART III:

POPES OF THE HIGH RENAISSANCE AND COUNTER-REFORMATION

Prologue

Although the height of Borgia power passed with the death of Alexander VI in 1503, the family saga can be profitably followed further into the sixteenth century, especially if it is interwoven with the political and ecclesiastical history of the time. This avoids the historical distortion of viewing the principal Borgia figures as little more than a trio of larger-than-life characters who cavorted in the Vatican around the year 1500.

It is also deceptively simple to label the Borgia as 'Renaissance' figures without appreciating the dynasty as part of an historical continuum. This section of the book therefore explores what can be called a continuing Borgia Age, from the death of Alexander to that of his great-grandson, Francisco de Borja (known in English as St Francis Borgia) in 1572. The death of St Francis occurred within a matter of weeks of that of the last of the popes we are here considering, Pius V.

Something has already been related of the life of Lucrezia, following her marriage to Alfonso d'Este and her move to Ferrara in 1502. If the marital history of her son and grandchildren is traced, it illustrates both the impact of the Italian Wars on the Italian states and the formation of an aristocratic elite from families that had risen to prominence through election to the papacy. Thus Alfonso and Lucrezia's son, Duke Ercole II, married Renée de France, second daughter of Louis XII. She had initially been intended as a prospective bride for Charles of Ghent (the future Emperor Charles V), but only because Charles' grandfather, Ferdinand of Aragon, eyed Naples and Milan as a potential dowry. After her father's death, Renée's value in the marriage market declined and Louis' successor, François I, substituted his own infant daughter as Charles' prospective bride. By 1517 Renée's name was being put forward as a possible bride for the son of the margrave of Brandenburg but, by 1522–23, the 12-year-old was being offered as both bride and bribe to the duke of Bourbon, 20 years her senior. In 1528, she finally reached the altar with Ercole d'Este, who also received Modena and Reggio into the bargain. The illegitimate Este line came to an end with the eldest

205

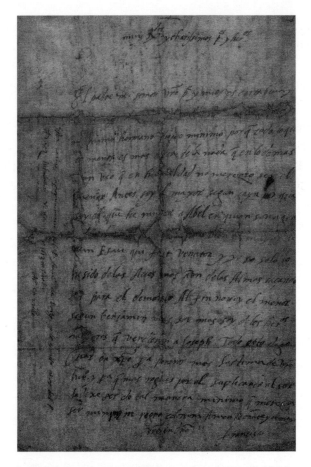

St Francis Borgia, autograph letter, signed, Oñate, 19 May [1551]. Talbot Collection, Georgetown University Library, Special Collections Division, Washington, DC.

In a passionate declaration of his sinfulness and humility, Francis addresses a group of Jesuits in Portugal: 'I have been like Esau, a mighty hunter, and chased not only birds, but souls, acting as beater for the Devil'. In 1565 he became Father General of the Order. He died in 1572, was beatified in 1624 and canonized in 1670.

son of Ercole and Renée, Alfonso II, whose three marriages – to Lucrezia de' Medici, Barbara of Austria and Margherita Gonzaga – illustrate both the interrelationship among Italian aristocratic families and the interest shown in Italian states by neighbouring powers. None of the marriages produced an heir. Among Alfonso's siblings, Anna was the wife of François de Lorraine, duke of Guise and leader of the Catholic side in the French Wars of Religion, while Lucrezia became duchess of Urbino through her marriage to Francesco Maria della Rovere. Their brother Liugi became archbishop of Ferrara and a cardinal. By means of the descendants of Lucrezia Borgia alone, therefore, the blood of Pope Alexander continued to course through the veins of the ruling elite of Italy, France and the Church.

Chapter 1. POPE PIUS III
(22 September–18 October 1503)
'I have been deceived'

'I had foreseen my father's death and made every preparation for it. But I had not anticipated that I should be, at that moment, wrestling with death myself.'[1] Thus spoke Cesare Borgia to Machiavelli. Alexander's death had deprived him of his greatest ally and protector. It also created a power vacuum in the Vatican where, upstairs, Cesare lay helpless, his face horribly violet, his skin peeling. Meanwhile Italy was in disarray. Gianpaolo Baglione and the Vitellis had taken up arms in Umbria. Camerino, Piombino and Urbino were in open revolt. Government of the Romagnol cities was on the verge of breaking down. Joyous at Alexander's death, both the Orsini and Colonna were riding hard for Rome, the centre of power, to win back all that had been 'theirs'. Francesco Gonzaga and the advancing French army were encamped at Viterbo, barely 40 miles north of Rome. The Spanish army, under the fearsomely competent Gonsalvo de Córdoba, was racing northwards from Naples. Cesare and his scattered forces were like a nut in a nutcracker. The previous week of terrible illness had prevented him from gathering his troops together, bringing them into Rome, smashing the remains of the Orsini and Colonna and gaining control of the city. Truly a week can be a long time in politics!

At least Cesare well knew the value of ready cash in a crisis. On Alexander's death, his henchman Michele Corella was dispatched to browbeat the papal treasurer and lay his hands on any available monies. Burchard records that some 100,000 ducats were seized, largely from Alexander's private treasure. But an attempt to take control of Castel S. Angelo and intimidate the cardinals was less successful. Roccamura, the castellan, refused to take sides in the power struggle. He confirmed this intention by closing the gates to everybody, remaining stubbornly indifferent to both bribes and threats.

Alexander had ruefully mused of Cesare, for whom triumph had come so spectacularly and so easily, 'I do not know if he will be able to keep what he has acquired'. For Cesare's survival, it was essential to secure the election of a pope favourable to him. Without papal support, he would be reduced to a common adventurer – and one with far too many powerful enemies to have any realistic hope of survival. So Cesare fought to influence the conclave. An attempt was made to stop Giuliano della Rovere reaching Rome. An alliance was forged with the Colonna, promising full restitution of their possessions and powers, in exchange for their support. In truth, this was merely a feint to disguise Cesare's real intention, which was to revive his relationship with the French. But the anti-Borgia backswell in the country gave the Italian cardinals confidence. Conversely, the Spanish cardinals lost confidence in their ability to secure another Spanish election.

Cesare had begun by trying force. When this failed, typically he made a volte-face, swearing loyalty to the electoral college and being confirmed as captain general. But it wasn't enough. Cardinal Carafa and his colleagues insisted that, as on previous occasions, a conclave would only take place when every army had removed itself to a safe distance from Rome. The Spanish and French ambassadors, desperate to sideline Cesare, quickly ensured that their armies complied with this stipulation. On 1 September, Cesare was forced to agree to withdraw his troops also. The following day they began to move out. Cesare left, the very same day, carried on a stretcher covered with crimson velvet. It was an ominous withdrawal for the tyrant who, in the previous few years, had turned Rome into a city of fear.

With Cesare and his entourage were his mother Vanozza and brother Jofré. All retired to the long-term Borgia stronghold of Nepi, from where Cesare forged an agreement with Louis XII. In exchange for personal and Romagnol protection, Cesare would support a French papal candidate. Meanwhile, the younger members of the family were taken to safety in the kingdom of Naples. Jofré's Neapolitan wife, Sancia, was the only Borgia left in Rome. Sancia and Jofré had never been compatible, and she had been effectively imprisoned in Castel S. Angelo towards the end of Alexander's pontificate. Before long she had become the mistress of Prospero Colonna, one of the Colonna who had been excommunicated by Alexander in 1501.

Although Cesare remained captain general of the Church and duke of the Romagna, the Romagnol vicars were busy attempting to reclaim their former lordships. Guidobaldo da Montefeltro in Urbino, Gianpaolo Baglione in Perugia, Giovanni Sforza in Pesaro and Pandolfo Malatesta in Rimini succeeded. Loyalty was at a premium in the Romagna – but to whom? Cesare's garrisons stubbornly held on to Cesena, Imola, Forlì and Faenza.

The conclave did not begin until 16 September. A most interesting cast of cardinals arrived from France. Georges d'Amboise and the triumphantly returning exile, Giuliano della Rovere, were about equally matched in terms of ambition for the papal tiara. Ascanio Sforza was released from prison in order to cast his vote for Cardinal Amboise, only to find the Roman crowds chanting his name instead! In the circumstances, neither a French nor a second successive Spanish pope was a sensible option (no matter how hard Georges d'Amboise lobbied on his own behalf or Cesare sought to revive the Franco-papal alliance by seeking the election of anyone who was not della Rovere). The Spanish cardinals grouped around Giovanni Vera, Cesare's former tutor, but were at a loss as to how to vote once Cesare declared himself an ally of France. In spite of being the 'French' candidate in 1493, della Rovere was no French stooge in 1503 and made his pitch as an Italian, not least because the election of an Italian pope was considered most likely.

For five days, della Rovere and Sforza fought each other for the papacy. But neither was strong enough. The compromise candidate, proposed by Amboise and accepted by the Spanish party, was Francesco Todeschini-Piccolomini, long-serving bishop of Siena. An experienced diplomat and protector of English and German interests at the Curia, with no strong French or Spanish connections, he was a wise choice. His election as Pius III on 22 September excited no fervent emotion, except relief after the frantic military activity of Alexander's pntificate. Pius was old and racked by gout. Soon he would surely die. And then the struggle for power would begin once more…

The first problem for the new pope was the legacy of the previous one. 'I wish no harm to the duke [Cesare] but I foresee that he will come to a bad end by the judgement of God.'[2] Pius, a well-meaning and decent man, was confronted by Cesare, the demonic prince, in crisis. The French army had gone to Naples, leaving the Borgia stronghold of Nepi unprotected. The Savelli and Orsini were preparing to attack. The feared *condottiere*, Bartolomeo d'Alviano, was advancing from Venice.

Cesare begged Pius to allow him to return to Rome; the Spanish cardinals pressed his case. Believing that Cesare was still badly ill, the kindly Pius took pity on him and relented. Still in command of the papal army, Cesare came back to Rome on 2 October. Pius quickly realized his mistake. Ruefully he admitted, 'I have been deceived. I am only a man and liable to err'.[3]

But Cesare was playing a dangerous game. Advancing his fortunes in Rome meant putting his head into the lion's den. His 'army' comprised a mere 1,000 men in the city, though more waited at Orvieto under Michelotto's command. Della Rovere threatened to arm his followers if Cesare did not remove his troops. The Orsini and Colonna, mutual antipathy momentarily cast aside, were united in their hatred for Cesare. Gianpaolo Baglione and Bartolomeo d'Alviano were now in Rome, ready to pounce. The entire city was turning against Cesare. The Orsini foiled an escape attempt at Orvieto. Alviano posted guards at every gate out of Rome. On 15 October, the Orsini stormed Cesare's palace in the Borgo. By secret passage, he fled with the two infant Borgia dukes and took refuge in Castel S. Angelo. On the day of Pius III's coronation, Cesare's gamble had appeared to pay off when Pius once more confirmed him as captain general and duke of the Romagna.

Yet no-one who saw Pius at the coronation on 8 October could have entertained any doubt of his physical frailty. Several ceremonies had to be omitted due to his ill-health. He survived for little over a week, dying in the early hours of 18 October. It was one of the shortest papacies on record – a mere 26 days. The nephew of Pius II, he had served the Church long and well. In 1464, Pius II had left him in charge of Rome and the papal states, when the former had gone to Ancona to lead the ill-fated crusade. For many years, he had been greatly esteemed by both England and Germany. He had consistently refused to be compromised by the Borgia. In the conclave of 1492, he had stubbornly retained his independence. Alexander had entrusted him with the delicate mission to Charles VIII, in 1494. Alone in the Sacred College, he had protested in 1497 against the transfer of papal realms to Alexander's son, Juan (Gandia). In short, he was a man of decency, culture and – not least – great integrity. Had he survived as pope, even for a few years, he might have called a General Council for desperately needed reform. But his papacy finished before it ever really began.

His death was a severe loss to the Church. And Cesare, for whom popes were merely protectors, was once more plunged into mortal danger.

Chapter 2. POPE JULIUS II (1503–13)
'Il terribile'

Through fear of assassination by Borgia supporters, Cardinal Giuliano della Rovere had spent an entire decade as an exile in France. During that decade, Italians came to perceive their society as passing through a period of profound crisis. The peninsular states, it was sensed, had been invaded and violated by foreign powers. Italy was becoming an economic backwater, at the expense of the recently unified Atlantic states. There was nothing particularly alarming about the fact that the Venetian Giovanni Caboto (anglicized as John Cabot) could sail from Bristol to Newfoundland in 1497, nor even that in 1500 the Portuguese Pedro Álavares Cabral could land on the coast of what was to become Brazil. But what sent a shiver down Venetian spines in particular was the news that another Portuguese, Vasco da Gama, had visited a sequence of east African ports, landed at Calicut in India in May 1498, and returned to Lisbon with valuable cargoes of spices. Venice may have been spared French or Spanish invasion, but she was not spared a sense of crisis.

Commentators grew nostalgic for the 'old days' before the French invasion, and thus evolved the myth of *quattrocento* Italy as a haven of peace and cultural prosperity, somehow presided over by Lorenzo de' Medici. Fifteenth-century political reality was sacrificed for superficially enticing images. Unfortunately for the Borgias, the subsequent perceived disasters occurred during the pontificate of that rare phenomenon, a non-Italian pope. When della Rovere returned to Rome for the first conclave of 1503, he represented a return to normality. When Pius III expired so quickly, it seemed to be a sign that della Rovere was meant to be the saviour of Italy.

The conclave following the death of Pius was very different from the one following the death of Alexander. The departure of the French army meant that there was no strong French candidate. At the previous conclave, della Rovere had distanced himself from the French faction and reinvented himself as an Italian candidate. Thus he was now able to secure the support of the other Italian cardinals. The Spanish cardinals, well aware of the hopelessness of a Spanish candidate, were reassured by della Rovere. The previous month, he had been the most powerful candidate. Now there was no creditable opposition. Della Rovere, who had coveted the papacy for so many years, was now poised to realize his life's ambition.

To seal the support of the Spanish cardinals, della Rovere made a deal to protect Cesare, still ensconced in Castel S. Angelo. Machiavelli, who had returned to Rome as a Florentine observer, stated at the time and later in *Il principe* that Cesare was a fool to trust della Rovere. But Cesare had little choice. There was no serious French contender. In truth, as the previous conclave had shown, Cesare had questionable power over the Spanish cardinals. Certainly he had no power to direct them to a creditable rival to della Rovere. Cesare did what pragmatists have always done in history – back the winning side. With his authority in tatters and his power waning by the hour, he was fighting for his very survival.

Della Rovere had beautifully laid the groundwork. The result was a forgone conclusion. He was elected unanimously in the shortest conclave on record – a single day, 1 November 1503. In contrast to the fragile Pope Pius, and although then aged 60, Julius II with his tall, athletic frame and thick beard had a commanding physical presence. Even more striking was the violence of his temper. The Venetian envoy noted:

> No one has any influence over him and he consults few or none. It
> is almost impossible to describe how strong and violent and difficult
> he is to manage. In body and soul, he has the nature of a giant.
> Everything about him is on a magnified scale, both his undertakings
> and his passions. He inspires fear rather than hatred, for there is
> nothing in him that is small or meanly selfish.[1]

On the same day as the election of Julius, Cesare surrendered Castel S. Angelo and moved back to the Vatican. Superficially, it seemed that his star was rising once again. But the reality was very different. Cesare had played his strongest card – his supposed control over the Spanish cardinals. With the election of Julius that card was severely devalued. On 5 November, Machiavelli met with Cesare. It was a revelation. The clear thinking, resolute and decisive prince was no more. In the telling words of another observer, 'he [Cesare] has lost his head and does not know himself what he wants to do'.[2] He was fretful and irresolute.

The supposed *rapprochement* between Cesare and Julius was yet another marriage of convenience in a seemingly endless Renaissance 'wilderness of mirrors'. The reality was that Cesare and the former della Rovere were deadly enemies, with a very short-term need of each other. Each was temporarily almost powerless – Cesare through the loss of Alexander and French influence, Julius because the papacy was near penniless, lacked any significant army and was confronted by enemies on all sides. The sternest enemy was Venice, already busy seizing territory in the Romagna. Despatching the helpless Cesare would leave a power vacuum in the Romagna and play straight into the Venetians' hands. So, for the time being, Pope Julius tolerated Cesare. Of Julius, whom he rated highly as an astute political operator, Machiavelli reported:

> He does not love il Valentino [Cesare], but nonetheless he strings him along for two reasons: one to keep his word, of which men hold him most observant, and for the obligations he has towards him, being recognizant to him for the good part of the papacy; the other, since it also seems to him that His holiness being without forces, the Duke is better placed to resist the Venetians.[3]

Julius issued the following blunt warning: 'I have always been a friend of Venice but, if the Venetians persist in robbing the Church of her property, I shall use the strongest measures and call all Christendom to help me'. For the irascible, outspoken Julius, diplomacy was most definitely war by other means. A stunned Venetian envoy reported to his political masters: 'Words fail me to describe with what resolution he [Julius] spoke, and not once, but again and again'.

For Julius, bluntness was no mere negotiating ploy; rather it was part of his character. He had no love for subtlety. Alexander, a shrewd judge of men, had commented that 'della Rovere has all the vices except duplicity'. Thus, by degrees, Cesare realized that Julius wanted direct papal control in the Romagna. Venice was to be squeezed out. And Borgia influence was also to be squeezed out. Cesare continued to play his cards skilfully – but they were increasingly weak. He had the goodwill of the Spanish cardinals but not, perhaps, control over them. Following Alexander's example, he tried to arrange marriages of alliance between Luisa, his daughter, and Francesco Maria della Rovere and between Giovanni Borgia and a niece of Venanzio Varano. His strongest card was the trio of Romagnol castles – Forlì, Cesena and Bertinoro – still under his control.

By mid-November, Cesare was offering his services to Florence as a *condottiere* against their enemy, Venice. However, Machiavelli had reported to his masters in Florence that Cesare was unlikely to enjoy any long-term support from Julius; consequently, his request was refused. Disappointed but undaunted, Cesare left Rome on 18 November. His plan was to sail with his troops from Ostia to Leghorn and march to the Romagna.

But Cesare's plan was overtaken by events. The Venetians were pressing ever harder in the Romagna, under a cynical flag of convenience that their sole aim was the removal of Borgia influence. When Julius learned that Faenza had surrendered to the Venetians, his fury knew no bounds. He sent a terse message to Cesare, ordering a handover of Forlì, Cesena and Bertinoro, lest they also surrender to the Venetians. Cesare refused, and was promptly arrested. A rumour soon circulated in Rome that he had been murdered and his body thrown in the Tiber; this was scotched when he was brought back to Rome. Fearing an ignominious death, he wept. Initially, however, Julius treated him kindly, hoping to gain more by being reasonable. Cesare agreed a handover of the castles, his strongest bargaining counters. He gave the necessary passwords. But when the governor of Cesena still refused to hand over the castle, the passwords were deemed suspect. An exasperated Julius threatened Cesare with imprisonment in Castel S. Angelo and relented only slightly by confining him in Torre Borgia in the Vatican, in the very room where the duke of Bisceglie had been strangled just over three years earlier. By December, only four months after Alexander's death, Borgia supporters were fleeing Rome. Machiavelli felt that Cesare's life would be forfeit once the castles were handed over. 'It seems to me that this duke of ours, little by little, is slipping down to his grave.'[4]

The case against the Borgia in general, and Cesare in particular, was made by initiating the blackening of the Borgia name, thus willingly sacrificing accuracy for the sake of gory fiction. The Venetian cardinal, Giovanni Michiel, had lived quietly in Rome throughout Alexander's pontificate and died on 10 April 1503. In December 1503, while Cesare was confined in the Vatican, one of Michiel's servants was arrested on suspicion of poisoning him, on Cesare's order. The timing of this revelation could hardly have been more significant. It is in episodes such as this that the myth of the Borgia, including their supposed penchant for poison, began to take root – just as the English myth of Richard III as an all-purpose villain dates back to the years immediately after his death, when Henry Tudor needed to justify his own usurpation of the throne. Sudden deaths of prominent men were routinely attributed to poison, but any attempt to accuse the Borgia of poisoning cardinals such as Michiel inevitably fails through lack of evidence. Cesare was undoubtedly a man of violence and ruthlessness – but he was almost certainly not a poisoner.

Amazingly, the good luck that had always favoured Cesare seemed to come his way again. On 28 December the Spanish general, Gonsalvo de Córdoba, won an overwhelming victory against the French at Garigliano. By the beginning of 1504, the French had lost Naples. These French reverses signalled a corresponding surge of Spanish influence. The large number of Spanish cardinals assumed greater power. Julius had to go back to Cesare with renewed vigour for a 'freedom for castles' deal. An agreement was hammered out that the three castles must be handed over within 40 days. Cesare would be put under the custody of the Castilian cardinal, Bernardin Lopez de Carvajal, the long-serving Roman agent of Ferdinand and Isabella. He would be held in Ostia and freed only when the castles were transferred. In April, Cesena and Bertinoro surrendered and the commander of Forlì had seemingly agreed to surrender. Feeling that Cesare had kept his side of the bargain, Carvajal allowed him to leave by galley for Naples. Here he was reunited with his brother Jofré and the Borgia cardinals. To Cesare, Gonsalvo de Córdoba gave respect but – significantly – little warmth.

With Cesare's new-found freedom, all his old confidence returned. Forlì had still not surrendered. If he could but reach the Romagna and use Forlì as a base, surely he would recover the territory lost to him? Disregarding the fact that he was already a throwback to a previous pontificate, and that Ferdinand needed to cultivate Pope Julius in order to secure investiture with the kingdom of Naples, Cesare assumed that Gonsalvo de Córdoba would offer him support for a military campaign to secure his Romagnol duchy. On the very eve of his planned departure from Naples, the great captain called his bluff and had him arrested and imprisoned in Castel Nuovo. It was a smoothly executed operation, which succeeded in raising King Ferdinand in the pope's sights. When a man of lesser loyalty might have taken the opportunity to stab his master in the back, Cesare's henchman, the dreaded Michelotto, resolutely defended him, even under torture, asserting that the duke of Bisceglie had been murdered on the order of the conveniently deceased Alexander.

For three months, the castellan at Forlì resisted surrender in the hope that the castle might still be of value to his master. But hope died. In early August, a secret message seems to have reached him that Cesare genuinely wished surrender. On 10 August the castellan of Forlì marched out with 200 archers and the Borgia standard fluttering defiantly. It was the end of the Borgia kingdom in the Romagna. Cesare's last bargaining chip had gone.

While his sister Lucrezia emerged as a popular duchess of Ferrara, the imprisoned Cesare dreamed of returning to the Italian stage that he had once commanded through fear and cunning – but he only succeeded in becoming something of a footnote in the history of Spain, where he was sent from Naples. Appropriately enough, his first place of Iberian incarceration was near Valencia, in the region from which the Borja had originally emerged.

As the kings of Aragon and France had reached a truce and divided the kingdom of Naples between them, Cesare could not revert to the ploy of playing one off against the other. To compound his humiliation, Louis stripped him of his French titles, including the dukedom of Valentinois. His only influential supporters were his sister, Lucrezia, in Ferrara and his brother-in-law, Jean d'Albret, king of Navarre, encouraged by stories that Cesare had made daring attempts to escape once more.

In Cesare's favour was the great political uncertainty that the Spanish kingdoms were experiencing. Isabella of Castile died at Medina del Campo on 26 November 1504, leaving the widowed Ferdinand bereft of power in her realms, where the new 'Queen proprietress' was their daughter, Juana, wife of Emperor Maximilian's son, Philip 'the Fair' (Felipe I of Castile). Castile became a Habsburg possession, in spite of Ferdinand's diplomatic initiatives to the contrary. All this demonstrated the limited degree of unity between the crowns of Castile and Aragon, but left Ferdinand free to take more direct involvement in the government of Naples.

But before heading across the sea to Naples, the wily monarch had one more card to play in the hope of outwitting the Habsburgs. In March 1506 he married Germaine de Foix, the 18-year-old niece of King Louis and potentially the bearer of a son who could, by some legal loophole or other, inherit the kingdom of Castile. Besides which, Ferdinand wanted to reincorporate the mountainous kingdom of Navarre into that of Aragon, as it had been in the days of his father. When Ferdinand succeeded Joan II in 1479, Navarre passed to his elder half-sister, Leonor, heir to her late mother. Leonor had married into one of the dominant families on the French side of the Pyrenees and was duly succeeded by her young grandson, François-Phébus de Foix, as king of Navarre. He, in turn, was succeeded by his sister Cathérine, wife of Jean d'Albret and consequently sister-in-law to Cesare's wife, Charlotte d'Albret. Germaine de Foix was a cousin of François-Phébus and Cathérine.

Jean d'Albret championed the cause of Navarrese independence from Aragon and consequently looked to the Habsburgs for support. Therein Cesare spied his opportunity. His transfer to a fortress close to Medina del Campo facilitated his plans, for it lay much closer to Navarre. Philip the Fair's death in September 1506 left the mentally unstable Juana unfit to rule alone, though she remained queen in name. Castile was ruled by a regency government until her eldest son, Charles (Carlos I) came of age. Charles himself remained resident in the Low Countries throughout this period, being groomed to succeed his paternal grandfather, the emperor.

Within weeks of Philip the Fair's death, Cesare lived up to his reputation as a daring adventurer by escaping from the castle of La Mota. The rope down which he made his descent was cut above him, so that he fell to the ground and was carried away unconscious by his servants. After escapades more suited to a fictional *picaro* than to a nobleman, let alone a former prince of the Church, he reached Pamplona, capital of Navarre, in early December. He had briefly been its bishop some 15 years earlier.

His last period of freedom was even shorter. By February he was in command of a small Navarrese army, fighting for Jean d'Albret. During the night of 11 March 1507, Cesare was caught in an ambush near Viana and stabbed to death by attackers. Ironically, they were ignorant of his identity. He was just 31 years of age. He was buried in the church of Sta Maria in

Viana. The Holy See inherited his possessions and thus, as Machiavelli caustically remarks, Cesare had indirectly worked to the aggrandizement of the Church.

For the seven remaining years of her life, Charlotte d'Albret mourned the husband she had hardly known. In 1517, her daughter Luisa married the distinguished military commander, Louis de la Trémoïlle, whose biography reads like a summary of the Italian Wars; but her six children were all by her second husband, Philippe de Bourbon. Thus could a significant number of the French aristocracy claim Borgia antecedents, alongside Luisa's grandson, César.

Cesare Borgia is one of the great 'might have beens' of history. He flitted across the world stage from the murder of his brother in 1497 to his own untimely end in 1507. At first, it seemed that he could do little wrong. After the death of Alexander, it seemed that he could do little right. Alexander the consummate strategist and Cesare the fearless man of action made one of the strongest teams in history. But Cesare's Achilles' heel was always his dependence upon a pope who would not live for very long. The huge success of the early part of his career had given him no 'wilderness years', no deep experience of failure and recovery from failure. The death of Alexander and the unrelenting enmity of Julius gave him too much failure, all at once. Despite his struggles, he never recovered from it.

Of father and son, Alexander is by far a more attractive personality than the proud and violent Cesare. But Machiavelli's verdict on Alexander had been scathing: 'The soul of the glorious Alexander was now borne among the choir of the blessed. Dancing attendance were his three devoted handmaidens: Cruelty, Simony and Lechery'. From their very first meeting, Machiavelli had been in awe of Cesare. Magnanimously, he decreed, 'When all of the actions of the duke [Cesare] are recalled, I know not how to blame him…' Countless widows and orphans in Italy, grieving the loss of husbands' and fathers' lives squandered to Cesare's futile ambitions, might have disagreed. They had severe cause to blame him. Cesare, an Icarus of history, wrote his story in blood. Had Alexander dreamed of the carnage that his son would cause, he would surely have questioned the worth of a Borgia dynasty. And, as Alexander's body went to dust, so did the Borgia dynasty follow it.

Sancia, arguably the most colourful of the Borgia women, died in 1506, leaving Jofré free to marry a woman more to his taste than the fiery princess. This was Maria de Mila, who was doubtless a cousin of some sort. Their four children – one son and three daughters – were fully integrated into the Neapolitan nobility. The fourth Borgia prince of Squillace had two daughters, the elder of whom married Francisco de Borja (count of Mayalde and viceroy of Peru), thereby uniting the Spanish and Italian branches of the dynasty.

Indeed, it is the Spanish branch that provides us with the thread running through the remainder of this chapter. The brief career in Spain of Alexander's son Juan Borgia, second duke of Gandia, was long enough to father two children by his wife, María Enríquez. Both María (who severed all contact with her husband's family in Rome) and her daughter Isabel duly joined the Poor Clares at Gandia, a house much favoured by the Borja dukes of Gandia over many generations. The other child was Joan, third duke of Gandia from infancy. This duke was twice married. His first wife was a granddaughter of King Ferdinand, through the king's illegitimate son, the archbishop of Zaragoza. Besides Francisco, the fourth duke of Gandia (general of the Jesuits, better known as St Francis), her children numbered a duchess, a viceroy of Catalonia, a cardinal (Enrique de Borja) and three nuns. Francisco and his siblings therefore had the distinction of being great-grandchildren of Pope Alexander and of King Ferdinand, 'the Catholic'. Among the 10 children of the third duke's second marriage, there was another cardinal (Rodrigo de Borja), a viceroy of Naples, an archbishop of Zaragoza and two more nuns.

Understandably, the beginning of Julius' pontificate is overshadowed by the increasingly desperate struggles of Cesare and the enforced demise of Borgia political influence by the new pope. Julius had always loathed the Borgias. Unsurprisingly, the first few years of his reign were devoted to their ruin. It was Julius who set in motion the Borgia myth, using calumny as a weapon to discredit Alexander. When Italy's leading historian Guicciardini, a faithful papal servant, accepted and continued the myth, it grew and grew as new stories began to be added to it. Stories qualified by *'on dit'* gradually became accepted statements of fact. (Was Guicciardini, however, a good judge? His persuading of Clement VI to back the king of France against the emperor – thus precipitating the sack of Rome – makes one wonder.)

In an age and place where duplicity and deception were the order of the day, Julius stood out like a virgin in a brothel. In speech, he was utterly direct; and, if he gave his word, he kept it. He was an outspoken, forceful character, feared and unloved. The 'awe' which he inspired in others was very real. He was known as *'il terribile'*, an Italian phrase with, in this context, no exact English equivalent except, perhaps, 'the awe-inspiring one'. As we have seen, he had spent most of the pontificate of his great rival, Alexander VI, in France, fearing assassination. He did his best to turn Charles VIII of France against Alexander. He also tried to organize a Council to depose Alexander. Ironically, considering the charges of simony against Alexander (in the course of a fairly prolonged and, initially, strongly contested conclave), Julius captured the papacy by straight bribery in a contest that ended almost as soon as it had begun. Once he had achieved the papacy, Julius calmly decreed that anyone who bribed the conclave should be deposed. There was no-one courageous enough to point out that this implied his own deposition.

Had it not been for the Borgia myth (successfully launched by himself to poison the memory of Alexander) Julius might qualify as a candidate for one of the least admirable popes. Paradoxically, however, he is far from short of champions, and many look back with awe and admiration at his masterful and grandiose vision for a magnificent Christian basilica and his limitless martial aspirations.

It must be remembered that Julius had to take vigorous – sometimes military – action because papal authority collapsed so rapidly in the papal states after the death of Alexander VI. His forcefulness was allied to a range of skills duly deployed in the revival of the temporal position of the papacy. Alexander had depleted the papal treasury in the course of his wars. Julius restored its fortunes through impressive fiscal competence. He also overhauled the administration of the papal states, and initiated agricultural improvements. Such achievements were impressive in themselves, but it should be remembered that the papacy now operated on more of a European and less of an exclusively Italian power political stage and was dwarfed by the might of France or Spain and even by the unwieldy bulk of the Empire. Thus, Julius' record would have been Herculean for a fifteenth-century pontiff, but was exceptionally brave and ambitious under sixteenth-century constraints. However grave his faults, Julius did not lack courage.

The most pressing concern at the beginning of Julius II's pontificate was to expel the Venetians from the Romagna, including Rimini and Faenza. To that end, he entered into an alliance with Maximilian and Louis XII, signed at Blois in September 1504. This was the first treaty of Blois; the second followed in 1513. Maximilian was slow to ratify the treaty and, even once he had done so, he showed no sign of joining the French for an attack on Venice. The republic was nevertheless cowed into negotiating with Julius, and sought the appointment of papal vicars in Rimini and Faenza. This optimistic offer was rebuffed. A firmer hand was evidently needed throughout the papal states, where inadequate papal government allowed the Baglione family to dominate Perugia and, most blatantly, the Bentivoglio to act as princes in Bologna.

Mindful of the feuds that could well break out in Rome in his absence, Julius made dynastic alliances with both the Orsini and the Colonna. His illegitimate daughter Felice was married to Giangiordano Orsini of Bracciano and a niece was found for Marcantonio Colonna. With this precaution taken, Julius led the entire Curia on an arduous expedition to Perugia and Bologna to oust the leading families. Perugia's strategic Umbrian location made it essential to the smooth operation of papal government in the region. The Baglione were not *signori* or papal vicars, but they were the most powerful faction and had a history of violence. In 1506, they surrendered to Julius without a fight.

The Bentivoglio operated in a different league, behaving like princes at home and abroad, and forging marriage alliances with princely families such as the Visconti, Sforza and Gonzaga. By 1506, they had been the dominant presence in Bologna for over a century, longer than living memory. Although they represented a direct threat to papal government, previous popes had lacked the military muscle to oppose them. Giovanni II Bentivoglio had ruled Bologna since 1463, making him one of the stable features of north Italian inter-state relations, but he fled to Louis XII in 1506 (though not before appealing for a General Council of the Church). Julius' triumphal entry into Bologna was arguably the symbolic climax of his pontificate, perhaps marred only by the news of Cesare's escape from La Mota and arrival in Navarre. The overwhelming success of this campaign gave Julius additional weight on the international stage.

Back in Rome the most conspicuous reminder of Spanish power was Bramante's tempietto, located by the side of the church of S. Pietro in Montorio on the supposed site of St Peter's martyrdom – half-way between St Peter's and S. Paolo Fuori le Mura (St Paul's Outside the Walls). The circular tempietto was constructed throughout the first decade of the sixteenth century, under the patronage of the Spanish monarchs. From the beginning of Julius II's pontificate, Bramante was also committed to a much more extensive project, for Julius wanted to extend the Vatican Palace on a scale unimagined by previous pontiffs and unequalled in execution since the time of ancient imperial Rome. In 1503 work began on the vast Cortile del Belvedere, created through linking the palace proper with Innocent VIII's villa on the summit of Monte S. Egidio by means of two long, thin buildings. To negotiate the rising ground, these two long arms stood three storeys high at the palace end, reducing to two storeys at an intermediate level and, finally, a single storey where they adjoined the villa – all of which could be appreciated as tamed Nature by the pope viewing the scene from his palace.

The cortile was not completed until 1563, but the long vista was soon disrupted by the building of Sixtus V's library. Bramante's energy was directed towards an even more conspicuous project, nothing less than entirely replacing the Constantinian basilica dedicated to the prince of the apostles. St Peter's was inevitably even more decayed than when Nicholas had addressed himself to the problems it posed. On 18 April 1506 Julius laid the foundation stone of the new St Peter's, which remained a building site throughout the sixteenth century and was not completed until 1614. Bramante's vision was of a centralized Greek cross plan, with four equal arms and a dome (inspired by that of the Pantheon in central Rome) over the crossing. The architect died the year after his patron and was duly succeeded by Raphael (originally from Urbino), Baldassare Peruzzi (Sienese) and Antonio da Sangallo the younger (Florentine), all of whom made their own adaptations to Bramante's basic idea.

With command over the papal states secured, Julius set about creating a capital city fit for a victorious ruler, principally through the creation of the via Giulia (begun 1507–08), parallel with the Tiber and connecting with his uncle Sictus IV's Ponte Sisto. Not only did this street stand in marked contrast to the dense urban warren within the Tiber bend, the likely scene of many a nefarious activity, but it was also the longest straight street to be created since antiquity. In 1507 Julius made known his desire to move out of the Appartamento Borgia. Alexander's portrait and the Borgia bull made distasteful companions, while the creations of Pinturicchio and his followers provided a standard which Raphael could be encouraged to surpass.

The first of the Raphael *stanze* (rooms) on the third floor of the Vatican Palace was therefore decorated between 1508 and 1511. This was the Stanza della Segnatura, designed to serve as the pope's private library. As in the Appartamento Borgia, Christian and pagan images were created in harmony with one another. On one wall is the *Disputa*, on the nature of the Eucharist, while on another *Parnassus* is shown as the home of Apollo and the nine Muses. A third wall carries the room's most famous image, the *School of Athens* (plate 5) in which Plato and Aristotle take centre stage, surrounded by a host of ancient sages who are thought to have been modelled on Raphael's artist contemporaries. Julius himself appears as Pope Gregory IX on the fourth wall, handing the *Decretals* of canon law to a jurist. The future popes, Giovanni de' Medici and Alessandro Farnese, can also be seen here.

At the risk of presenting it as something of an understatement, the years in which Raphael was at work in the Stanza della Segnatura were also those during which Michelangelo frescoed the Sistine Chapel ceiling with biblical and pagan prophetic figures, thereby providing the clearest element of continuity between the building projects of Sixtus IV and those of his nephew.

On 10 December 1508, a league was signed at Cambrai between Louis XII, Maximilian, Ferdinand of Aragon, the papacy and a number of smaller states. It was supposedly designed to unite them for a crusade against the Ottomans. In reality, the crusade was directed against Venice, one of the few Christian powers that had a recent history of fighting the Turks. Disregarding Venetian losses in the eastern Mediterranean, Venice's neighbours were united in resentment at the republic's acquisition of a land empire in Italy in the course of the fifteenth century, and were genuinely fearful of further Venetian expansion.

The republic's military strength was consistently overestimated but, in

1508, there was a conviction that only such a formidable coalition could defeat her. The proposed division of spoils was as follows: Louis was to receive Cremona, Crema, Brescia and Bergamo. Maximilian, piqued by the ease with which Venice had repulsed an imperial invasion of her territory earlier in the year, was to get Verona, Vicenza, Padua, Treviso and Friuli. Ferdinand, as king of Naples, was promised Venetian-held ports located down Italy's Adriatic coast. Julius claimed Faenza, Rimini and Ravenna. Mantua wanted territory lost in 1441. Ferrara was to be assured of Rovigo and Polesine, lost to Venice by the peace of Bagnolo in 1484. For good measure, Julius excommunicated the republic, which naturally responded with an appeal for a General Council.

The forces of the league, most of them French, met those of Venice at Agndello, near Crema, on 14 May 1509. The encounter is also known as the battle of Ghiaradadda. The Venetians were still commanded by the Orsini *condottieri*, the count of Pitigliano and Bartolomeo d'Alviano. Thus far in the Italian Wars, Venice had not shared the sense of crisis that haunted the other Italian states. The defeat at Agndello changed all that. Venice lost its *terraferma* possessions except Treviso. Like the Florentines of the 1490s, the Venetians experienced a bout of self-doubt and self-loathing. Military defeat was somehow attributed to luxurious living, and one response was to reinforce official condemnation of sodomy.

The Florentine government was among those who rejoiced at Venice's misfortune, though the lack of a shared border meant that there was no territorial reward to be reaped. Most immediately, it meant that Venice ceased to support the Pisan rebels, handing an easy victory to the Florentine militia. Since Piero Soderini's appointment as *gonfaloniere* (one of the nine citizens who formed the Florentine government) in 1502, the Florentine republic had been enjoying a period of peace and prosperity, facilitated by the death of Alexander and the fall of Cesare Borgia in 1503. The defeat of the Pisan rebels was the icing on the cake, not least for Niccolò Machiavelli, the most vocal advocate of a native Florentine militia whose loyalty and commitment was bound to be greater than that of hired mercenaries.

Although Julius achieved his objective, in that Venice surrendered the Romagna, he had not anticipated the sheer scale of the Venetian collapse and consequent extent of French power throughout northern Italy. It took Venice until 1517 to claw back its land empire, which thereafter remained intact until the Napoleonic invasion. One reason the republic's mainland fortunes revived so rapidly was that France had become too powerful in the region. The interdict against Venice was lifted in 1510. Julius' anti-French strategy meshed diplomatic initiatives with military action. Attempts were made to persuade the English government to break off negotiations with Louis and to dissuade Maximilian from a further French alliance. More successful was the offer of formal investiture with the kingdom of Naples, made to Ferdinand of Aragon. This put Spanish troops at the pope's disposal. Venice, meanwhile, had more cause than most to resist the French advance so, just months after Agndello, forces were sent to support the papal cause.

Throughout the summer and autumn of 1510, Julius plotted with Genoese exiles to foment uprisings against French power in Genoa. There was even a brief naval engagement in July, between a papal–Venetian fleet and a Franco–Genoese one, but each attempt ended in failure. The land war between France and the papacy was centred around Bologna and Ferrara. Alfonso d'Este of Ferrara was not merely a French ally; he was also an over mighty papal subject who had given shelter to the exiled Bentivoglio. Given the age-old tensions in that region, it was not difficult to persuade Venice to participate in a campaign against Ferrara. Julius' resolve to oust the French from Italy was such that he headed north to supervise the military campaign in person. However, a tertian fever kept him well behind the lines until January 1511, when he joined the fray at Mirandola. As Julius found repeatedly, the papal commanders were effectively useless. He much preferred dealing with those of Venice.

After the fall of Mirandola, Julius went first to Bologna, where Scottish and imperial envoys urged him to make peace, but met with no success. In May 1511 he left Bologna for Ravenna. After his departure, Giovanni Bentivoglio's son, Annibale, returned to Bologna, which revolted against papal rule. On 16 May Louis XII, in Milan, went further than many other secular princes had done when at odds with Renaissance popes. They had merely called for the summoning of a General Council of the Church – with the backing of a number of French and Francophile cardinals,

Louis actually summoned one. Technically, only a pope could do so. This latest council was to meet at Pisa. Louis was its only significant backer, for Ferdinand opposed the project, along with his son-in-law, Henry VIII of England. The excommunicated schismatic cardinals did not begin to arrive in Pisa until late October. By that time, Julius had trumped them by calling a technically valid General Council of his own (the Bull was dated 18 July). He had also negotiated a Holy League with Ferdinand and Venice for the recovery of Bologna and other lands of the Church occupied by the pope's enemies. The latter was signed on 4 October, and England ratified it the following month. By that stage, Louis, the 'Most Christian King', was beginning to feel squeamish about fighting against the Church. The Fifth Lateran Council duly opened on 3 May 1512.

The call for meaningful ecclesiastical reform was heard throughout the fifteenth and early sixteenth centuries and came, on this occasion, from two Venetian patricians – Paolo Giustiniani and Pietro Querini – who became Camaldolese hermits in 1511. Together with their friend and fellow patrician, Gasparo Contarini (who also experienced a spiritual crisis in 1511), they represent the fruit of the fifteenth-century Venetian monastic and spiritual tradition. The calling of the Fifth Lateran Council prompted Giustiniani and Querini to present their *Libellus a Leonem X*, urging thoroughgoing Church reform. Their call was not heeded, because there was insufficient pressure for change. Just five years later, that pressure began to be applied by the German Augustinian, Martin Luther.

In military and diplomatic terms, 1512 was a particularly dramatic year. The early months saw a sequence of military victories in northern Italy for the young French commander, Gaston de Foix, brother of Queen Germaine. These culminated in the battle of Ravenna, on Easter Sunday (11 April), but the spirit of the French forces was broken by news of the death of their commander. Julius was encouraged by assurances from Ferdinand and Henry that they were keen to continue fighting the French, but was even more encouraged by the arrival in the war zone of 18,000 troops from the Swiss Confederation. This last development caused the French armies to turn tail and leave Italy altogether.

The feared Swiss infantry, carrying pikes of up to three metres in length, had been much in demand as mercenaries since their defeat of Charles the

Bold at Nancy, in 1477. Their sheer numbers and the discipline of their pike squares provide us with a vital element in the move towards mass of troops on the battlefield and the defeat of armoured cavalry by infantry battalions.

Without French support, the Bolognese revolt collapsed. Milan was evacuated by the end of June, opening the way for Massimiliano Sforza, son of Ludovico il Moro, to be installed as duke. Parma, Piacenza and Reggio became incorporated into the papal states. The French retreat from Genoa gave Julius the keenest pleasure of all. Even Alfonso d'Este went to Rome to be reconciled with the pope.

Before the year was out, Italy witnessed one more revolution. Piero Soderini had led the Florentine government since 1502, long enough for many to resent his policies and choice of close associates. Typical of the disaffected was the patrician Francesco Guicciardini (whose father Piero had been a member of Lorenzo de' Medici's regime). He was concerned that the natural leadership skills of the patriciate were being ignored by Soderini. Guicciardini was atypical, in being steeped in Florentine history; his *Storie fiorentine (History of Florence)* was written in 1508–09. As Savonarola had done, Guicciardini favoured a mixed constitution with monarchical, aristocratic and democratic elements, albeit weighted towards the aristocratic. In his eyes, the Great Council was too popular, Soderini too autocratic. Thus evolved a body of pro-Medicean feeling in Florence, utilized in 1512 by Julius when he sent a Spanish army to induce Soderini's government to conform to his anti-French strategies. Soderini resisted. The Spanish troops sacked nearby Prato in August as a sign of what they could do to Florence itself. His enemies within and without the walls, Soderini elected to go into exile. The last decade of his life was spent in Dalmatia.

Within days the Medici, now headed by Cardinal Giovanni, were permitted to return to Florence. The constitution was again reformed; in addition to other changes, the *gonfaloniere di giustizia* would be appointed for a year at a time.

Some vicar of Bray types remained in continuous employment, but Niccolò Machiavelli was too closely associated with Soderini to hope for that. From time to time he endeavoured to ingratiate himself with the Medici, claiming that they were all ardent Florentine patriots together, but suspicion of collusion in an anti-Medicean plot in 1513 spoiled his chances.

Out of office, Machiavelli lived on a farm to the south of Florence, but returned to the city to mix with scholarly friends in an informal academy, and poured his enthusiasm for history and politics into his writings. First came *Il principe (The Prince)*, dedicated to Lorenzo de' Medici, duke of Urbino, but not published until 1532. Then followed *Discourses on the first decade of Livy, The art of war* and *The history of Florence*, interspersed by the stage plays for which he was best known among his contemporaries.

A final word about Julius' contribution to the architecture and beauty of Rome relates to Bramante's tempietto, as mentioned on page 229. From 1511 Raphael decorated a second *stanza*, for which Julius chose subjects to reflect the greatest triumphs of his pontificate. This is the Stanza d'Eliodoro. (The room takes its name from the apocryphal story of the expulsion of Heliodorus from the Temple in Jerusalem, which was selected by Julius as an allusion to his own expulsion of the foreign powers from the papal states). The pope himself appears as a witness to the eucharistic miracle which took place at Bolsena in 1263, when a consecrated host bled in the hands of a priest who had previously been unconvinced about transubstantiation. In reality, Julius prayed before this host on his way to Bologna in 1506, at Orvieto where it had been preserved. A wall is devoted to the repulse of Attila from Rome in 452, which Julius could easily have intended as an allusion to the repulse of the French at Ravenna, but which became more obviously so after Leo X's election, for the pope depicted in this scene is Pope (St) Leo I (reigned 440–61). As Cardinal Giovanni de' Medici, Leo X was present at the battle of Ravenna. In fact, he was captured after it, accounting for the image on another wall of the Stanza d'Eliodoro, that of the *Liberation of St Peter* (for whom read Leo X) from prison.

A long-time sufferer of gout and syphilis, Julius finally succumbed to fever on 21 February 1513. Towards the end of this life, this former exile – who had lived for almost a decade in France – became obsessed by hatred of France and the French 'barbarians' with their constant threat to Italy. On his deathbed, he repeatedly called out in his delirium, 'Out with the French! Out with the French!' A rough but not unkind ruler, he was mourned in Rome as a pope who compared favourably with his predecessors. The inevitable coming of another conclave reminded Romans of that which, through lavish bribery, had elected Julius. The two popes who bring to an end what may be called the Borgia Age proper were Julius II and his successor Leo X, whose combined pontificates lasted from 1503–21.

What are we to make of Julius II, the former Cardinal Giuliano della Rovere? Like all the great political popes, Julius realized that reform of the Church and the peace of Christian peoples would be possible only when the temporal power of the Holy See was firmly re-established. At the death of Alexander, the political status of the papacy had hardly ever been higher; conversely the status of the pope as a spiritual leader had rarely been lower. Julius carried on the work of making the papacy and its territories the primary power in Italy. To this end, he broke the Borgia dynastic ambitions. During the nine years of his pontificate, he gave unremitting attention to the financial reorganization of his state, practising strict economy and refraining from indulging in nepotism in connection with appointments to public offices. He warred or negotiated unceasingly with the factions in Rome and in the provinces, with the object of either suppressing or disarming them, and thus succeeded in re-establishing papal sovereignty. Machiavelli put it well when he wrote, 'There was a time when the least of the barons thought himself entitled to despise the Pope's power, but now that power is perforce respected by the King of France himself'. It was Julius who gave Henry VIII the dispensation that allowed him to marry his brother Arthur's widow, Catherine of Aragon. Alexander and Julius, such different entities, were united in moving the papacy to the centre of the world stage.

The image that Julius presented to the world differs considerably from what he was actually like as a person. Apart from the lies that he set in motion about Alexander, the irascible Julius would probably be easily remembered as the most unattractive figure of the Renaissance period. He was the bisexual father of a family, and a hard-drinking, hard-swearing, swashbuckling pederast. He loved his food – even during Lent he would eat the best caviar, tunny, prawns and lampreys from Flanders. The Emperor Maximilian did not mince his words, noting with disgust: 'Julius is a drunken and wicked Pope'. (Whatever else he was, Alexander was not a glutton or a drunkard; neither was he foul-mouthed, nor a sodomite. And, most tellingly, never would he have practised calumny against anyone in the way that Julius practised it against him.)

Julius has rightly gained fame as the patron of Michelangelo; but hereby hangs a tale. He persuaded the young sculptor to abandon his stonemason's craft and mercilessly goaded him into painting the ceiling of the Sistine Chapel. Julius had a keen appreciation of artistic greatness – or, as he put it, 'the humours of such men of genius'. This did not prevent him from working Michelangelo like a dog, and starving him of funds. When Michelangelo quit Rome in a rage, swearing that he would leave his work uncompleted, a horrified Florentine official admonished him: 'You have behaved towards the Pope in a way that the King of France himself would not have ventured upon. There must be an end of this. We are not going to be dragged into a war and risk the whole state for you. Go back to Rome!'

When a surly Michelangelo finally reappeared in Rome, a prelate tried to save him from the pope's wrath by pleading, 'Your Holiness should not be so hard on this fault of Michelangelo; he is a man who has never been taught good manners, these artists do not know how to behave, they understand nothing but their art'. Julius rounded on the prelate in fury, declaring that it was he who had no manners. From then on the arguments between Julius and Michelangelo were no less vehement, yet characterized by mutual respect. Julius would abandon all papal dignity to clamber up dusty ladders and crawl over grimy scaffolding so that he could confer with Michelangelo at the 'coal face'. The pair of them would stand together for hours, critically inspecting the frescoes that his 'man of genius' was creating. Five hundred years later, we owe a huge debt to both of them.

Were Julius and Michelangelo lovers? The question must be asked. Certainly both men were what we would now call gay. Julius, whatever might have been his relationship with Michelangelo, wore himself out in two hectic years 'among prostitutes and boys'. The master of ceremonies at the papal court had to prevent distinguished visitors from kissing the papal foot as it was so riddled with syphilis.

Contemporaries recognized Pope Julius to be a 'great sodomite'. According to a seventeenth-century tract, 'this man abused two young gentlemen, besides many others'. These particular young men were, it appears, two noble youths 'whom Anne, Queen of France, sent to Robert, Cardinal of Nantz, to be instructed'. Their instruction was taken over by the pope himself, who included 'that act' in their curriculum. He was liberal, moreover, when it came to other people's pleasures. He issued a papal Bull on 2 July 1510 establishing a brothel where young women could ply their trade. Leo X and Clement VII also condoned this establishment, on the condition that a quarter of the goods and chattels of the courtesans who worked there should belong, after their deaths, to the nuns of Ste-Marie-Madeleine.

Julius' main interest, however, was not religion, art or sex. It was war. Moreover, it was war for the intrinsic joy of conquest, not the resulting personal gain that the Borgia had pursued. He provided for his family; but he did not seek to advance them. The Holy See was the prime beneficiary of his military successes – although he viewed the interests of the Holy See as identical with those of Italian patriotism. Julius, the warrior pope, acted from conviction, not opportunism. In *Praise of Folly* (1509), Erasmus caricatured his military ardour. Guicciardini noted that, apart from his papal dress and title, there was nothing of the churchman about him. When Michelangelo suggested putting a book in the left hand of the pope's statue, his subject bluntly replied, 'Nay, give me a sword, for I am no scholar!' In blatant defiance of canon law, Julius donned armour and rode a charger into battle at the head of the papal army. When they took Mirandola from the French, he clambered over frozen ditches and through a breach in the wall, in full armour. Claiming the town for Christ, he yelled, 'Let's see who has the bigger balls, the King of France or the Pope!' The Italian made it quite clear that he was not talking about cannonballs.

Julius II's great ambition was to give the Church a new and mightier St Peter's basilica, for which purposes he turned the Church into a supermarket of indulgences, complete with vigorous promotions and special offers. He thus brought the Reformation an ominous step closer. His work in this regard was completed by his inglorious successor, Pope Leo X, who managed to do immense and permanent harm to the Church.

One final note about Julius II is that he enjoyed the services at his court of a brilliant theologian and preacher called Giles of Viterbo. The eminent Jesuit historian, John O'Malley, says of Giles that in contrasting – but, at the same time, comparing – Rome and the Vatican with Jerusalem and

Sion, he effectively enthroned Rome as the 'transcendent fulfilment of all that was imperfect and incomplete in the Synagogue'. This was an echo of the age-old Catholic theme that the Roman Church is the 'New Israel', the old Israel (i.e. in practice, the Jewish nation) having ceased to exist. It was believed that it had forfeited any right to exist by its mortal sin of murdering God; it could never again enjoy any right to recognition or to be an acceptable part of human history until it repented of this sin and recognized that it had been replaced by a greater body – the supreme and all-powerful Roman Church.

Chapter 3. POPE LEO X (1513–21)

'God has given us the papacy. Let us enjoy it!'

To his demoralized cardinals, the death of Julius came as a profound relief. They were weary of the rigours of continual war, and fed up with being hectored, bullied and browbeaten. In modern parlance, they yearned for a 'regime change'. They were virtually unanimous as to what kind of pope they wanted – the exact opposite of Julius. In short, they yearned for an easy life. They looked forward to a pope who would lift financial restrictions and rule in a civilized manner. Furthermore they expected their new pope to be considerate enough to die before too long, so that some of them could also enjoy bouts at the papacy.

On his deathbed, Julius had issued a Bull – with appropriate penalties – making simoniacal elections invalid. But his cardinals had paid dearly for their cardinals' hats; they wanted a payback. In a fit of inspiration they dusted down another Bull, whereby Paul II had allowed 200 ducats per month to all cardinals whose incomes fell below 4,000 ducats. As Julius had conspicuously failed to follow this injunction, they decided to help themselves to the arrears. Julius had left magnificent jewels, together with a large amount of money. He had deposited these in the Castel S. Angelo and instructed the commander to hand it over to nobody but his successor.

It says much for the force of Julius' personality that his instructions were followed to the letter, even after his death. The resolute commander of Castel S. Angelo stuck firmly to his brief. So the stymied cardinals had no option but to elect a pope who could be guaranteed to compensate them and usher in a prompt return to a life of ease, wealth and learning. These, not religion, were the true ideals of Renaissance Italy. Savonarola's attack upon this worship of sensuality had cost him his life. Nobody, in Italy at least, was bold enough to follow his example.

But the long arm of Julius once more reached out from the grave. He had debarred the nine Francophile cardinals who had attended the Council of Pisa from the conclave following his death. The remaining 25 cardinals entered the conclave on 4 March 1513. The absence of the French coterie left only two contending parties – the young and the old. The younger cardinals wanted Giovanni de' Medici; the older ones, including England's Cardinal Wolsey, backed by Henry VIII, supported one Cardinal S. Giorgio. Had it not been for his youth, Giovanni de' Medici would probably have been unanimously elected, but many of the older cardinals took umbrage at being ruled by a comparative stripling of 37. And, of course, it was highly likely that they would be signing away forever their own hopes of the papal crown. For many, this was far too bitter a pill to swallow.

The papal odds were posted at the Banchi as if for a race-meeting – Giovanni de' Medici with a staggering 25 to his opponent's 15. Many cardinals began by voting for the rankest outsider, in order to conceal their true intentions. An unintended farce ensued, when 13 of them chose the worthless Cardinal Arborense who consequently nearly became pope. This gave everybody such a shock that henceforth they opted for a straight Medici/Giorgio contest.

With Julius' stern injunctions about simony doubtless still ringing in their ears, the custodians of the conclave exercised unusual vigilance, almost amounting to sharp practice. Without warning, they cut the bell-rope communicating with the lower floor of the palace. This interrupted the passing of notes along a cord between the inmates and the outside world. Competition nevertheless remained intense. A silver dish belonging to the English Cardinal Bainbridge was smuggled into the conclave with the words 'S. Giorgio or Medici' scratched on it with a knife. After that, only earthenware vessels were allowed. As the days passed, the young party particularly grew impatient with their confinement, their boring vegetable diet and the lack of opportunities for personal cleanliness.

As a papal candidate, Giovanni de' Medici suffered from a grave handicap – poor health. Typically, some of his supporters managed to spin this into an advantage when it came to winning over votes from the older cardinals. Although he was young, if he was not expected to live for very long, then why not elect him? His weak constitution would guarantee a short pontificate... The older cardinals nibbled tentatively at the bait of ill-health.

His ill-health was certainly bad enough for him to be permitted to bring his medical attendants into the conclave with him. He was suffering from a painful complaint, which the commentator Varillas says was, 'in a part of the person that decency forbids one to mention'.[1] Among the many scurrilous stories that abound from this period (especially about Alexander VI) few, if any, can be safely accepted at face value. One story, often repeated, was that Giovanni de' Medici's anal complaint was brought about by his excessive sodomy. This is untrue. The complaint was a fistula, in association with piles. What is true, however, is that the condition was made worse by vigorous homosexual activity.

The unfortunate Medici had been carried into the conclave on a litter, lying on his side to alleviate the extreme discomfort of his chronic ulcers. As the days dragged by, the pain showed no sign of abating. When his attendants reported that the scars would not heal and might, at any moment, become gangrenous, the older cardinals, opposing Medici, finally took heart. They might well have won the day had it not been for the sudden volte-face on the part of one of their number – Cardinal Soderini (who, it was rumoured, had been interrupted in an amorous intrigue by the call of the conclave).

Soderini paid a discreet visit to Giovanni de' Medici's cell. Soderini was also Florentine, but had been exiled along with his family. Now he sided with Medici, on the promise of reinstatement. Soderini's action was pivotal; Giovanni de' Medici was elected Pope Leo X on the very next day. The result of the papal election was announced dramatically by Cardinal Farnese ('the petticoat cardinal') rushing out of the conclave into St Peter's Square, shouting, 'Balls! Balls!!!' Those present knew exactly whom he meant. The *palle* (balls) featured prominently on the Medici coat of arms.

Giovanni de' Medici belonged to one of the greatest families of medieval Italy. Originally bankers and merchants, the Medici had long been princes in all but name, with Florence as the centre of their power. The greatest of them was Lorenzo the Magnificent, Giovanni's father. The Medici were civilized, cultivated arts lovers; but when their political or financial interests were threatened, they quickly reverted to amoral ruthlessness.

'I have three sons', Lorenzo de' Medici had famously observed, 'One is good, one is shrewd and one is a fool'. Piero, the elder, was the fool; by capitulating to Charles VIII during the first French invasion, he had managed to get the Medici expelled. Giuliano, the good, remained forever in his brother's shadow. Giovanni, the shrewd, had been destined for the Church from childhood. He was made an abbot at the age of 7, took over the famous abbey at Monte Cassino at 11, and became a cardinal at 13. (He was the youngest cardinal ever, although Benedict IX had become pope by the age of 12.) Despite having been suspected by Alexander VI and cordially disliked by Julius II, his star had risen in the Sacred College. At the time of his election, he was also effectively ruler of Florence. Now he was ordained a priest on 15 March, consecrated as bishop of Rome on 17 March and crowned as pope on 19 March.

Leo's physical attributes and character traits present something of a parallel to the paradox of his pontificate. He was singularly unprepossessing in appearance, his head being huge, almost deformed, in size. His body was so massive that, when seated, he looked like a very large man. When standing, however, it could be seen that his legs were ludicrously short and spindly. His protuberant eyes, set in a fat, red face, were painfully shortsighted.

By contrast, however, his personality was extremely attractive. He was genuinely interested in people, regardless of their social standing. He spoke softly and clearly, in a gentle voice, often laughing spontaneously. All in all, he presented a striking contrast to the loud-mouthed and hard-swearing Julius II. But this amiable and smiling prince was, first and foremost a Medici and a Florentine. As a Medici, he had one overriding aim – the elevation of his family. As the ruler of Florence, he aimed to make as many states of Italy as possible subservient to it. Beneath his gentle manner and winning smile, lurked a truly Machiavellian duplicity. While Alexander had justly remarked, 'della Rovere has all the vices except duplicity', with Leo X, duplicity was making a comeback at the Vatican.

At the time, however, it merely seemed that normality was making a comeback, normality being a return to the Renaissance life of leisure and learning, as opposed to the constant warfare of the Julius regime. The change was symbolized by Leo, as with Julius, in spurning conventional pontifical robes. With Leo, however, the martial accoutrement of his predecessor was replaced with rich silks and velvets, ablaze with jewels and delicately perfumed. Leo's biographer, the Latinist and historian Paolo Giovio, described his reign as the 'Golden Age' of Italian culture. This perception has remained. Certainly men of genius flocked to Rome in an astonishing concentration of talent. But sumptuous outward appearances provided a frighteningly thin veneer of civilization, covering and disguising the corrupt behaviour of hedonists and gluttons. The unattractive private life of the pope remained largely hidden, just as it was not generally observed that the Church, during this pontificate, took a calamitous lurch towards being decimated by the forces of the Reformation.

When elected, Leo is said to have confided to his brother Giuliano, 'God has given us the papacy. Let us enjoy it!' This he most certainly did. Even the *Catholic Encyclopaedia* comments that Leo X 'looked upon the papal court as a centre of amusement'. To all intents and purposes an atheist, Leo remarked to Cardinal Bembo how lucky, through the ages, had been 'the fable' of Christ in that it had 'profited us and our associates'.

Leo's coronation took place in mean circumstances. A tent was erected in front of the dilapidated façade of the 1,000 year-old St Peter's. However, the coronation procession itself was more like that of an emperor than a pope. It was a fitting beginning for a man who intended to enjoy his time on the papal throne. Cardinal Farnese placed the papal tiara on Leo's head. Then, dressed in cloth woven with gold and covered with jewels, he rode on a white Turkish horse at the head of 2,500 troops and 4,000 prelates and nobles (including princes and kings), along a route sumptuously decorated with banners, bunting and statues of the saints interspersed with Roman gods. Past the Forum they all went, past the Colosseum, and so onwards to the Lateran palace. The wealthy banker, Agostino Chigi, had built a magnificent arch supported by eight columns and inscribed in gold: 'The time of Venus had passed: Gone, too, is Mars. Now is the rule of Minerva'.

Leo rode well, despite what must have been excruciating pain in his posterior. Behind him followed two chamberlains, with heavy bags of gold and silver coins that they threw to the crowd. Thus Leo's reign began with a shower of gold coins – the Golden Age had literally, as well as metaphorically, arrived. The entire ceremony cost 100,000 ducats, from the 700,000 ducat reserve which the thrifty Julius had amassed. Thus, one seventh of the financial reserves of the Vatican were dissipated in a single day! The evening was given over to feasting and fireworks. That night Leo privately celebrated his coronation in the Castel S. Angelo with his lover, Alfonso Petrucci, whom he had made cardinal of Siena.

Guicciardini reported that the new pope was excessively devoted to the flesh, 'especially those pleasures which cannot, with delicacy, be mentioned'. Leo X was much given to idleness, pleasure and carnal delights, whereby he had many bastard sons, all of whom he promoted to be dukes and great lords, and married them off well. Contemporary accounts claim that 'he was a lover of boys' and that he loved his liquor.

He seems to have been discreet at first about his sexual proclivities, only (as we would now say) 'coming out' when he was pope. Soon his interests were well known. His friend and biographer, Bishop Giovio, said openly: 'Nor was he free from the infamy, in that he seemed to have an improper love of some of his chamberlains, who were members of the noblest families of Italy, and to speak tenderly to them and make broad jokes'. He had plainly been a practising sodomite for years.

As a cultured Florentine and the favoured son of Lorenzo the Magnificent, Leo fully intended to teach Romans the meaning of splendour. To the thousands of weary pilgrims, Rome appeared a shabby, inhospitable place. But public squalor would prove no deterrent to private luxury. From the onset, Leo needed money, if only to hold his own in the orgy of conspicuous consumption which quickly engulfed Rome. The biggest spenders were the Florentine bankers, whose business skill primed the pump of commerce. Banquets thrown by the likes of Lorenzo Strozzi and Agostino Chigi would have financed a small state for a year.

Leo loved giving masked balls for his cardinals and their ladies, and he held huge banquets where naked boys would appear from puddings. One meal, reported the Venetian ambassador, consisted of 60 first courses. 'Scarcely had we finished one delicacy then a fresh plate was set before us.' He continues:

> Everything was served on the finest silver, of which his Eminence has an abundant supply. At the end of the meal, we rose from the table, gorged with rich food and deafened by the continual concert, carried on both inside and outside the hall and proceeding from every instrument that Rome could produce – fifes, harpsichords and four-stringed lutes, as well as the voices of the choir.

The dishes included monkeys' brains, parrot tongues, exotic fish from Constantinople, ape-meat, quails and venison, all prepared in exquisite sauces and served with aromatic wines and fruit from three continents. Leo tried to save on the washing up by having the silver dishes thrown into the Tiber after each course was finished. Count Chigi, however, the arranger of his dinner, instructed the servants to fix nets under the windows to catch the falling plates. Unsurprisingly Leo acquired a reputation for being wildly extravagant. When he played cards with his cardinals, he allowed the public to sit in as spectators and tossed huge handfuls of gold coins to the crowd whenever he won a hand.

Leo made no pretence of piety or reverence, and publicly embraced Aretino and Ariosto, the most licentious poets Italy had ever known. He was utterly disarmed by a timely jest, and would forgive almost any crime redeemed by a witty sally. 'It is difficult to judge whether the merits of the learned or the tricks of fools afford most delight to His Holiness', dryly noted Aretino. A Renaissance prince who loved books, music, art and the theatre, Leo restored Rome as cultural centre of the western world. Pietro Bembo, the Venetian scholar, was made a secretary of state. Although Machiavelli's comedies were popular, to his great chagrin his political philosophy was ignored. Not everyone was sufficiently politically well-connected to be successful – Erasmus of Rotterdam, *doyen* of the Renaissance, angled unsuccessfully for a position in Rome.

From Julius, Leo had inherited both Michelangelo and Raphael. Michelangelo was too intractable to make an amenable court painter but Raphael quickly slipped into the role, becoming a sort of propagandist for the Medici. Raphael's first commission was to immortalize the actions of Leo's great namesakes in history: Leo I who had halted Attila, Leo III who had crowned Charlemagne, Leo IV who had built the Leonine City – each was given the features of Leo X.

Among Leo's other passions were hunting and shooting. He had lavish and prolonged house parties at his sporting estate outside Rome, which excited the curiosity of the locals who inconveniently trespassed upon his property. They were promptly arrested and had their hands and feet cut off, which acted as an effective deterrent. In addition to his role as arts patron and *bon viveur*, Leo was also a practical joker. He could afford to be – as pope, he was, of course, immune from retaliation. He once had a carrion covered in a strong sauce; pretending it was a papal delicacy, he served it to the poor. He had an old priest called Baraballo, who was proud of his terrible verse, made poet laureate. After Baraballo was crowned, he was paraded around the capital on a white elephant, donated to the pope by the king of Portugal. In 1516, Aretino wrote a mock will for Hanno, Leo X's pet elephant, which left the animal's substantial genitals to one of the pope's more ludicrous cardinals.

Leo's antics, however, cost money. In time, personal extravagance and patronage of the arts forced him to pawn his palace furniture and gold plates. The papal finances were more dissipated by Leo's lavishness than the wars of Julius. The Holy See lived from hand to mouth off credit from Roman and Florentine bankers, such as Chigi, paying staggering interest rates of up to 40 per cent.

Leo lifted simony to a new height to raise the funds for his greatest of all projects. Against all advice he decided to pull down Constantine's basilica, which had been standing for over 1,000 years, to construct a new one. He began his fund-raising at prosaic levels. Even though there were 7,000 registered prostitutes in Rome for a population of less than 50,000, he discovered that the papal brothels were not bringing in enough cash. Leo was also happy to sell cardinals' hats to atheists, if need be, as long as they could come up with the right price. The going rate varied from 24,000 to 70,000 ducats, according to how much Leo felt he could fleece the aspirants.

Leo's lover, Alfonso Petrucci, did not, of course, have to pay for his hat but, once he was a cardinal, he realized that he was then just one small step from the papacy itself. In the summer of 1517 he bribed a Florentine doctor, Battista de Vercelli, to poison Leo by sticking venom up his back passage while operating on his sodomy-induced piles. Petrucci planned to replace Leo with Cardinal Raffaele Sansoni-Riario. Unfortunately for the conspirators, the papal secret police intercepted a note outlining the plan. Under torture, de Vercelli confessed and was hanged, drawn and quartered.

Realizing that the game was up, Petrucci fled. Leo sent the Spanish ambassador to him with a guarantee of safe conduct, provided he returned to Rome. Petrucci incautiously agreed. As soon as he arrived in Rome, Leo had him thrown in the infamous Sammarocco dungeon beneath the Castel S. Angelo. There he was tortured daily on the rack. When the Spanish ambassador complained that his word of honour, guaranteeing Petrucci's safe conduct, had been besmirched, Leo brusquely retorted 'No faith need be kept with a poisoner!'

In his confession, extracted under torture, Petrucci admitted, 'Eight times I, Cardinal Petrucci, went to a consistory with a stiletto beneath my robes, waiting for the opportune moment to kill Medici'. But it appeared that Petrucci was not the only conspirator. Under torture, he implicated more and more of his fellow cardinals. The accused were not peripheral figures; instead, they comprised some of the most senior and respected Churchmen of the age. Cardinal Riario, who had been a member of the Sacred College for more than 40 years, was seemingly implicated, as was Leo's fellow citizen, Cardinal Soderini, and his favourite, Cardinal Adrian of Corneto, together with Cardinal de Saulis.

At first, Leo had intended a dramatic exposure of Petrucci's guilt to his fellow cardinals, in consistory. However, he quickly became terrified at the breadth of the plot against him. His first step was the elimination of the ringleader, Cardinal Riario, whose arrest caused widespread shock. In the words of the commentator, Paris de Grassis:

> We could scarcely believe that Cardinal Riario, whose prudence and abilities were so well known, could have engaged in such a plot – or, if he had been guilty, that he would not have made his escape. We were therefore inclined to suppose that this accusation was made by the Pope as a pretext to revenge himself for former injuries.

The 'former injuries' referred to Riario's involvement in a plot against Leo's father – before Leo had even been born. Could any man, even a Medici, nourish revenge for an entire lifetime?

Leo's torturers continued their grisly work. His spies followed the web of involvement. Papal troops mustered at prominent street corners in Rome, ready to crush any rebellion. The pope shut himself up in Castel S. Angelo and asked himself the agonizing question, 'Why? Why had his most trusted colleagues plotted in secret against him?'

At a full consistory on 8 June, Leo asked this question: what had he possibly done to warrant such perfidy? The cardinals were sullen, frightened, resigned. One by one, each of them was called upon to affirm on oath whether he was guilty or not. Cardinal Soderini denied his guilt. Leo furiously challenged him, with a torrent of invective. Soderini threw himself to the floor and shamelessly begged for mercy. In the shocked silence, Leo declared that there was yet another conspirator. Under pressure from his colleagues, Adrian of Corneto admitted that he too had taken part in the treasonable discussions. In a rambling speech, Leo affirmed that, although the guilty parties deserved execution, he would nevertheless show mercy by fining them and pardoning them. His incredulous cardinals applauded the pope's unexpected generosity.

Soderini and Corneto, sensibly assessing Medici clemency for what little it was worth in practice, promptly fled Rome for self-exile, in Naples and Venice respectively. A few days later, Cardinals Petrucci, Riario and de Saulis were stripped of their dignities and handed over to the secular authorities for bloody punishment. Influential friends of Riario and de Saulis persuaded Leo to stand by his promise of mercy. But the unfortunate Petrucci, a convenient scapegoat, was sentenced to death. As the pope could not allow a Christian to lay a finger on a prince of the Church, he had his former lover strangled by a Moor. With due respect to Petrucci's station in life, a silk cord in cardinal's crimson was used to choke the life from him.

In truth, the Petrucci conspiracy had been a most curious affair. Each of the accused had nurtured a grievance against the pope. Cardinal Soderini's brother had been driven out of Florence by the Medici. Cardinal Riario had lost the papal election to Leo. Cardinals Adrian and de Saulis were related to the despoiled duke of Urbino. Yet probably most cardinals could have produced some grievance or other against their pope. The conspirators' motives were amazingly weak, in relation to the huge risk they took. Their assassination attempt had been feeble. There appeared to have been no credible backup for a second or third assassination attempt when the first one failed. The guilty parties remained in Rome as their guilt was uncovered. And abjectly, they confessed to their crimes. Their ineptitude seemed boundless.

Unsurprisingly, popular rumour ascribed the Petrucci conspiracy to a typically Medicean subterfuge, by which rivals could be promptly eliminated and desperately needed monies would be quickly gathered in. Confirmation for this view appeared when, less than a month later, Leo created 31 cardinals. This motley crew included three professional financiers. Ironically, the authority of individual cardinals was diminished by their sheer numbers; these newcomers were paying more money for less power. Each new appointment paid dearly; Leo's coffers swelled by an estimated 500,000 ducats. Even more important than the money was the fact that these new appointments owed everything to the Medici. Thus, in the Sacred College, Medicean enemies were greatly outnumbered by Medicean supporters. For the remainder of his pontificate, Leo would have no more trouble from his politically castrated College of Cardinals.

In addition to the estimated 500,000 ducats from the new appointments, Leo collected fines ranging from 5,000 to 50,000 ducats apiece from the guilty parties. Thus, he made even treachery pay – and pay well. It was sourly joked that he found ways of making money that even the Borgias had not explored. Ultimately, however, the joke would be on the Church. One of Leo's little schemes was to farm out indulgences, which were openly wagered in gambling halls across Europe. This was especially big business in Germany – with disastrous consequences, personified by a formerly obscure academic named Martin Luther.

Not that Leo was thinking of such things. After the excitement of the Petrucci plot, he comforted himself with the boy singer, Solimando, the grandson of Sultan Mehmet, the Turk who took Constantinople in 1453. (Solimando's father was Sultan Jem, whose untimely death, as we have seen, was maliciously and wrongly ascribed to Alexander VI.)

Playing on his family name, Leo had originally announced that, as pope, he would be a doctor ('*medicus*') healing the wounds of the Church and of Christendom. A factor in his elevation to the papacy was his independence from both the French and Spanish crowns, an independence he endeavoured to maintain throughout his pontificate, sometimes by means of extremely tortuous diplomacy. Rhetoric aside, Leo's primary political aim was much baser, amounting to little more than the elevation of his family. He wanted to set his brother on the throne of Naples (held by Spain) and his nephew in the duchy of Milan (constantly threatened by the French). Naturally this meant becoming involved in the power struggle then going on between the French and Spanish royal families for the leadership of Europe.

In the early years, he undoubtedly benefited from Louis XII, Ferdinand and Maximilian being past their military prime. However, all that changed when Louis was succeeded by Francis I in 1515, Ferdinand by his grandson,

Charles (already Carlos I in Castile) in 1516, and Maximilian by the same Charles, also his grandson, in 1519. Ironically, this made Leo something of an elder statesman, though he was only 37 at the time of his election in 1513. Another constant was Leo's preoccupation with the fate of Florence, synonymous, of course, with his family's fortunes. His first representatives there were his brother, Giuliano, duke of Nemours and his nephew, Lorenzo de' Medici, duke of Urbino, followed by Cardinal Giulio de' Medici (later Pope Clement VII), the illegitimate son of the Giuliano de' Medici who was murdered by the Pazzi conspirators in 1478. Between 1513 and 1517 the organs of Medicean government were restored, while the family themselves enjoyed greater power than they had done prior to 1494. Francesco Guicciardini was among the Florentines who enjoyed easy access to papal appointments, serving as Leo's governor of Modena (1516), Reggio (1517) and Parma (1519).

Leo may have resolved to restore Italy to health, but the extra-Italian powers had by no means finished treating the peninsular states as a battlefield on which to play out their various rivalries and ambitions. The anti-imperial second treaty of Blois was signed between France and Venice in May 1513, a prelude to Louis XII's last invasion of Milan. Venice was determined to recover Verona and Vicenza, still held by Maximilian as his reward after Agndello. The French were turned back by Massimiliano Sforza's Swiss protectors at Novara, west of Milan, on 6 June. This signalled the end of the French king's Pisan schism. French delegates were sent to the ongoing Lateran Council (1512–17) instead. By way of a balance, in 1514 Leo feared that Spain was becoming too powerful a force in Italy and cultivated France as the most obvious counterweight.

Eager for military glory at the start of his reign, Francis I renewed his predecessor's alliance with Venice and sent his troops back into the traditional French hunting ground of Milan. This time, Massimiliano's Swiss infantry were broken at Marignano, near Milan, on 13–14 September 1515. The duchy reverted to French control, as did Genoa later in the year. Francis entered Milan on 11 October and thereupon sought to press home his advantage by proposing a meeting at Bologna with Leo, who had been allied with the defeated Massimiliano. Leo arrived at the rendezvous on 7 December, Francis following four days later. Their meeting lasted until 15

December and witnessed the compilation of the Concordat of Bologna to define the relationship between France and the papacy and thereby replace the Pragmatic Sanction of Bourges (1438). Francis obtained powers over the nomination to major benefices, together with the right to levy taxes on the French clergy. While he was in the area, the king also persuaded Maximilian to withdraw his imperial garrisons from the Veneto, thereby aiding Venetian recovery of their *terraferma* state.

Leo suffered a reverse closer to home when Francesco della Rovere, duke of Urbino since 1508, conspired with France and rebelled against his papal overlord. Wanting to maintain good relations with Rome, Francis I abandoned the rebel, who was formally deposed on 14 March 1516. Urbino was given instead to the pope's nephew, Lorenzo, as previously mentioned. But Urbino rose against the Medici the following year, Francesco reoccupying it in Lorenzo's absence. Leo suspected France or Venice of having a hand in this reversal. War over Urbino continued throughout the year, until Francis ceased to lend secret support to Francesco, who was finally obliged to give up his quest and retire to Mantua.

Histories of Renaissance Italy and Reformation Germany are rarely to be found within the same covers. That 1517 is generally taken to be the start of the Lutheran Reformation is of little consequence as far as Italianists are concerned, for it was certainly of little consequence in Italy at the time. Whereas Leo saw the Petrucci conspiracy as a threat to his papacy, he failed to realize that the Protestant Reformation would prove a much greater challenge to the Church as a whole.

For many years, there had been a glaring rift between spirituality and secularism, with Leo being a prime example of the latter. There had also been deep rifts between morality, immorality and amorality. Again Leo was a prime example of the latter. It is also notable that whereas the High Renaissance (thanks to Michelangelo, Leonardo and Raphael) completed, in Italy, the refinement of all that had gone earlier in the Renaissance, the situation was different in northern Europe. Late Gothic art continued, mostly in Germany, completely untouched by Renaissance innovations. There had also been a cultural rift between Italy and Germany, exacerbated by the centralization and Italianization of the papal administration. With hindsight, some kind of serious rebellion was long overdue. All it needed was a catalyst.

Martin Luther's hostility to many aspects of the institutional Church was of much more recent standing. He had visited Rome as a humble pilgrim in 1511 and later castigated himself bitterly for his naïveté. 'I dashed like a madman between one church and another, believing all their filthy nonsense...If there is a hell, then Rome is built upon it.' Lurid tales of 12 naked girls serving the papal court titillated Luther and his fellow Germans. Luther became professor of biblical studies at the new university of Wittenberg, a post he retained for the rest of his life thanks to the continual protection of the elector of Saxony. From 1512 he developed the central tenet of his theology, that of justification by faith alone *(per solam fidem)*. This refers to the means by which the sinful human soul is sanctified by God's grace.

What tipped Luther over the edge was the indulgence initiated by Leo, in 1516, to finance the rebuilding of St Peter's. The archbishop of Mainz charged the Dominican, Johann Tetzel, with preaching in favour of indulgences. Luther travelled from Saxony to hear the preacher assure his audience that a cash payment would guarantee the donor deliverance from purgatory, where the faithful expected their souls to be purged, prior to entering heaven. Tetzel had reduced complex theology on indulgences to a simple formula, neatly summed up by a contemporary satirical couplet:

As soon as the coin in the coffer rings,
the soul from out the fire springs.

Tetzel was what we would now describe as a marketing man of the highest order. The state of the art invention of the printing press was used to churn out indulgence slips. It was no longer necessary for seekers after salvation to make long and tiring journeys to Rome, as had the naïve Luther only a few years previously. Now, courtesy of Tetzel, indulgences were brought to your very door. The Tetzel roadshow went from town to town, as would the fabled snake-oil salesmen of nineteenth-century America. Indulgences were big business. But, of the hundreds and thousands of little indulgence slips, some were discreetly passed to the 34-year-old doctor of theology at Wittenberg university. Would Dr Martin Luther care to comment upon the validity of this most curious means of salvation?

It was against this non-scriptural belief, and other Catholic doctrines, that Luther compiled his famous 95 theses and nailed them to the door of the Schlosskirche at Wittenberg on 31 October 1517. The thud of Luther's hammer on the oak door has taken on vast dramatic import, a Hollywood image of a decent man defying a sinister, corrupt and all-powerful organization. As so often happens in history, the truth is much more prosaic. The church door was regularly used for the display of public notices. All that Luther intended – and all that he was understood to intend – was an offer to defend, in debate, 95 points which purported to establish the illegitimacy of the current use of indulgences.

It must be admitted, though, that some of Luther's points were hard for the pope to swallow, particularly his swipe at the Medici wealth. Yet, when Leo heard of the 'monkish squabble', as he called it, he was unperturbed. Luther was doubtless yet another in a seemingly endless array of misanthropes over the centuries, all busily protesting about this or that aspect of the Church. Some had been kicked upstairs and canonized; others, such as Savonarola, burned. Although these surly opposition figures came and went, the Church continued regardless. Doubtless Luther was yet another; a tiresome pest perhaps but, to a worldly pope, the sort of problem that went with the territory.

With hindsight, we can marvel at Leo's consummate misreading of the situation. True, a host of fiery friars and surly monks had come and gone. But one thing was certain – if the Church resolutely refused to clean out its own stables then, sooner or later, an aspirant reformer would resonate enough with the public to do real damage. Indeed Savonarola had nearly achieved this, particularly in Leo's very own Florence. Savonarola's supporters had been drawn from the most volatile members of a volatile race. Conversely, Luther's supporters were serious, earnest Germans, far less prepared to drop the cudgels once they were taken up. And the German ruling class had a vested interest in making capital out of any situation that would increase their hegemony in European politics. They were as prepared to use Luther as their tool as their successors in the 1930s were to use Adolf Hitler.

When Leo belatedly realized that Luther was a problem that was simply not going to go away, he amended the Church's position. Yes, the doctrine of indulgences had been grossly oversimplified – an edict was issued, condemning its abuse. The nuncio, Karl von Miltitz, savagely castigated poor Tetzel for his marketing zeal, which had raised so much cash for the Church. For a while, it seemed as though differences might be smoothed over; Leo would safely rid himself of a troublesome monk and business could carry on as normal.

'I do not know how it has happened, but it is certain that those who first opposed Luther were also the enemies of learning, and therefore the friends of scholarship were less averse to him, lest by assisting his enemies, they should injure their own cause'. No less a personage than Erasmus of Rotterdam made this candid admission. There was no shortage of intellectual muscle to crush Luther, or a dozen Luthers, and tie them up in ontological puzzles for evermore. Was not Leo the benefactor of one of the most glittering arrays of scholarly talent ever assembled? And yet these men of supposed genius all stood silent.

Guicciardini spoke with a candour equal to that of Erasmus:

> No man is more disgusted than I am with the ambition, the avarice and the profligacy of the priests...Nevertheless, my position at the court of several Popes forced me to desire their greatness for the sake of my own interest. But, had it not been for this, I should have loved Martin Luther as myself – not in order to free myself from the laws which Christianity lays upon us but in order to see this swarm of scoundrels put back into their proper place, so that they may be forced to live without vices or without power.[2]

Leo's array of intellectuals suffered from self-interest, consequent 'bad faith' (in the existential sense), consequent mixed motives and consequent moral cowardice. They idly stood by and did nothing. Erasmus idly stood by and did nothing. They were no less deserving of the scorn that Erasmus received, in the stinging insult: 'He [Erasmus] laid the egg which Luther hatched'.

It is intriguing to wonder with what finesse Alexander VI would have managed Luther. But events were allowed to follow their weary course. In April 1518, Luther was called to defend his position at the Heidelberg Disputation, an act that merely succeeded in attracting others, most notably the Dominican, Martin Bucer, to his cause. The Dominicans had long provided the Church's principal theologians, and it was a notable commentator on Aquinas who was sent on a legatine mission from Rome to interview Luther later in 1518. This was Cardinal Tommaso de Vio (known as Cajetan), one of the host of new cardinals created at the height of the Petrucci conspiracy. Protected by Elector Friedrich, Luther refused to recant. In July 1518, Luther was summoned to appear in Rome; again he refused.

In Leo's eyes, the most pressing German matter was still not Luther; it was the imperial election following the death of Maximilian on 12 January 1519. His successor, as previously mentioned, was his grandson, Charles – head of the house of Habsburg who had been king of Castile since 1506 and of Aragon since 1516. He had not been formally invested with the kingdom of Naples, though he was its *de facto* ruler. Leo was acutely aware of the dangers of the emperor doubling up as king of Naples, and tried to persuade the electors to choose one of their own number instead. However Charles was elected unanimously on 28 June 1519. In September of that year, Leo entered into a secret treaty with Francis. Meanwhile Luther was called to dispute at Leipzig with the German theologian, Johann Eck. If the authorities hoped to halt the spread of Lutheranism by breaking Luther, they miscalculated. In 1519 Ulrich Zwingli began preaching on the New Testament in Zurich, thereby starting the Reformation in the Swiss Confederation.

On 12 June 1520, Rome threatened Luther with excommunication in the Bull, *Exsurge Domine*. His teachings on indulgences, purgatory, papal authority and related matters were denounced, and his writings ordered to be burned. But in Wittenberg, on 10 December, the papal Bull was burned instead. Luther's excommunication followed swiftly, on 3 January 1521, by means of the Bull *Decet Romanum pontificem*. In consequence, he was summoned to appear before the imperial Diet meeting at Worms. It is uncertain whether he actually uttered the statement, 'Here I stand. I cannot do otherwise. God help me. Amen', but it is certain that he still refused to recant and was formally condemned by the Diet on 26 May. Again the elector of Saxony gave him protection, and the comfort in which to live quietly while translating the New Testament into German.

Lutheranism became a political force during the Peasants' Revolt of 1524–25, which spread throughout much of central and southern Germany. The peasants had a range of grievances against their lords, but also attacked monasteries and claimed to be espousing the teachings of Luther, who had abandoned his Augustinian habit in 1523. In reality, Luther supported the princes of the Swabian League who defeated the peasants in battle. While Lutheranism was beginning to convulse Germany and, with each passing year, was taken more seriously in Rome, one region where it had made no impact by 1520 was Iberia, where the young Francisco de Borja, duke of Gandia, was being educated in ignorance of the challenge it posed.

Francisco de Borja is better known as Francis Borgia, great-grandson of Pope Alexander VI – and later general of the Jesuits. Hereafter, we will refer to him by his more popular name.

Reform of the Spanish Church had been a priority of Cardinal Francisco Jiménez de Cisneros, the austere Franciscan archbishop of Toledo, confessor to Queen Isabel and staunch advocate of mass baptism for the Moorish population of Granada. Consequently, there was a conviction in high places that no reform movement was required, least of all one originating outside the peninsula. The aged Cisneros also served as regent in the Spanish kingdoms, prior to the arrival of King Carlos (Charles of Ghent) in September 1517. Ferdinand's anti-Habsburg designs had failed spectacularly when Germaine de Foix only gave birth to one stillborn son. Castilians had resented rule by Ferdinand and his Aragonese officials, but now saw themselves destined for perhaps greater ignominy – domination by Charles' Flemish advisers. A group of nobles attempted to proclaim Charles' younger brother as king, for he had been brought up in Spain. However, Cisneros foiled their scheme. Castilian fears were borne out when men like Guillaume de Croy and Jean le Sauvage were given priority at the new king's court.

The prospect that Charles should succeed Maximilian on the imperial throne sparked further anxiety in Spain, for it could easily mean rule by a permanently absentee monarch. The contrast with the days of Ferdinand and Isabella, when two monarchs were constantly travelling around their domains, could scarcely have been more marked. In 1520 a new session of the *cortes* of Castile was convened to vote Charles money to finance his forthcoming voyage to Germany to claim his imperial inheritance. The *cortes* effectively consisted of representatives of the kingdom's major cities. Protests were made; nevertheless Charles sailed from La Coruña, leaving the regent, his former tutor Adriaan Florenszoon Dedal (Adrian Florent, the future Pope Hadrian VI) to deal with the widespread uprising known as the revolt of the *comuneros* (citizens who organize an armed uprising).

Towns and cities banded together to defend the *bien comun* (common good) against high taxation, royal absenteeism and the king's foreign advisers. Thus was the nationalism that had been so consciously cultivated by Ferdinand and Isabella turned against their own grandson. Valencia experienced a simultaneous uprising, the Germanía, during which the duke of Gandia's palace was sacked and young Francisco was sent to the household of his uncle, the archbishop of Zaragoza. Like others of his social background, the duke fought for the king's cause against the rebels. In Castile, the *comunero* army went down to a massive defeat in battle at Villalar, near Valladolid, on 23 April 1521, after which its leaders were executed. Both in Castile and Valencia, the revolts concluded with the crown and the aristocracy ranged against the civic authorities. Indeed the duke of Gandia was created one of the 20 grandees of Spain, the highest ranking aristocrats who boasted the privileges of being addressed as 'brother' by the king and allowed to wear their hats in his presence.

Within a few weeks of the battle of Villalar, there occurred another martial episode that had profound consequences for Francis Borgia. In May, Ignacio de Loyola (Ignatius Loyola), a Basque nobleman, was wounded during the defence of Pamplona from an invading French army. As is fondly related by historians of the Society of Jesus, Ignatius read many devotional works during his long convalescence. There followed his pilgrimage to the great Catalan shrine at Montserrat and his stay at Manresa, where he complied the *Exercitia spiritualia* (*Spiritual Exercises*), the very heart of Ignatian piety. The chapter containing Ignatius's ghoulishly vivid description of the eternal torments of hell supplied spiritual medicine that proved appropriate for the period.

Thus was sown arguably the most fruitful of the seeds of the Counter – or Catholic – Reformation. Indeed, now that the confessional mists have largely cleared, it is possible to appreciate the Protestant and Catholic Reformations as twin manifestations of spiritual and ecclesiastical renewal. This renewal can be traced in Rome at precisely the same time as it can in Wittenberg, for it was also in 1517 that a number of leading Curial figures founded the Oratory of Divine Love. They included Gian Pietro Carafa, who became Pope Paul IV, and the Ferrarese humanist, Jacopo Sadoleto, who acted as secretary to the Medici popes (Leo X and Clement VII).

Leo X died of malaria on 1 December 1521. He showed no inclination whatsoever to receive the sacraments on his deathbed. His death caused widespread ruin in Rome. He left an empty papal treasury and debts of 800,000 ducats. His sister promptly fled with whatever jewels she could lay her hands on. The Holy See was confronted with stark bankruptcy.

253

Leo had viewed his role in terms of secular splendour and the furtherance of humanist culture. He had demonstrated little flair for politics. His wavering and incessant double-dealing had won him scant respect. Even the Italian rulers who had befriended the Medici in times of need were tricked and despoiled by him. Certainly Henry VIII of England, Francis I of France, and the Emperor Charles V all knew him for what he was. (Perhaps this partially explains why Charles treated Luther so leniently.) Domestically, Leo had earned the hatred and contempt of his fellow Romans. During his pontificate, his cardinals must often have thought with regret of the gruff, bellicose Julius II. Leo's Golden Age was merely a veneer of civilization, concealing immense cruelties and depravities.

Even more insensitive in religious than political matters, Leo had failed to take heed of the warning signs that the spiritual authority of the Church was in mortal danger. His insouciance and failure to grasp reality left Italy in political turmoil and northern Europe poised to erupt into religious conflict. Fittingly, yet ironically, Leo was buried first in St Peter's. It had been a significant source of his debts and the inspiration of nefarious money-making schemes, plunging the Church into disrepute and hastening the Reformation. In 1536, his remains were transferred to the basilica of Sta Maria sopra Minerva, where a monument was erected. Truly, the reign of Minerva had come...and gone.

Chapter 4. POPE HADRIAN VI (1522–23)
'We will see'

The death of Leo X, after a lifetime of riotous spending, had left the papacy penniless. In desperation Vatican furniture was pawned. A miserable few thousand ducats were borrowed from the banker Chigi to pay for a bodyguard, 500 strong, to guard the dazed and bewildered cardinals. At Leo's funeral, the candles were the remains of the ones used at the funeral of Cardinal S. Giorgio the day before. Had the wealthy, powerful and well-connected S. Giorgio only lived a few weeks longer, he would undoubtedly have won the papal tiara that Leo had cunningly wrested from him. Such are the whims of history.

Cardinals who were abroad hastened to Rome. Thus the conclave began a few days late, on 28 December 1521. When it did, the mood was savage. 'There cannot be so much hatred and so many devils in hell as among these cardinals', the imperial envoy reported. Although the Holy See was effectively bankrupt, there was no shortage of aspirants for the papacy. Thirty-nine cardinals entered the conclave. Of these, 15 were Medici supporters, favouring Cardinal Giulio de' Medici. Of the remaining 24 cardinals, 18 wanted the crown for themselves. With 19 active contenders – almost 50 per cent of the conclave – the scene was set for a notable power struggle.

The band of 19 aspirants certainly contained interesting characters. Cardinal Farnese (dubbed 'the petticoat cardinal') owed his red hat to the intercession of his sister, Giulia Farnese, with her lover, Alexander VI. A convicted forger, he had swapped prison for the Sacred College. He might well have been able to offer technical advice to his opponent, Cardinal Flisco, whose supreme ambition was to see his own papal image on coins. Cardinal Colonna had two contrasting passions – war, and the pleasures of the boudoir. A poor loser, as it turned out, he would later win the papal crown. The fearsomely obese Cardinal Mantova lived for food in general and oysters in particular. Cardinal Egidio, a martinet, was obsessed by a crusade against the Turks. Cardinal Grimani – that *rara avis* for the time, a principled man – was, unfortunately, far too principled to make much headway in this nest of unprincipled knaves. Cardinal Wolsey, egged on by his supposed supporter, Cardinal Campeggio, had yet to learn that an overbearing Englishman had no chance of becoming pope in Rome.

Cardinal Soderini, who had decided the result of the last conclave, was back in Rome after his exile following the Petrucci conspiracy. Driven by hatred and revenge, he rallied the opposition and put paid to Giulio, the Medici candidate. The latter, acknowledging the hopelessness of his position, declared himself a supporter of Farnese. Cardinal Grimani's request to leave the conclave on the supposed grounds of ill-health was granted. It was widely viewed as a silent protest against the infamous Farnese becoming pope.

Day after day passed in weary deadlock. In the depths of winter, the Vatican was freezing. The frosted window panes were almost all boarded up; very little light penetrated the gloomy interiors. These men of immense power, who had lived such lives of indulgence under Leo, were reduced to living like animals. They could not wash properly. They could not eat properly. They lived in a seemingly perpetual half-night, dreaming of a warmth that was denied them, locked in a fierce battle of wills. Outside, at the Banchi stockmarket, Cardinal Farnese remained favourite. Inside the conclave, he remained in deadlock, too strong to beat but not quite strong enough to win. All it needed, at any time, was a tactical advance and the erstwhile forger would have scooped the biggest prize in Rome. When word leaked that Cardinal Cesarini had sneaked a message out of the conclave to the Banchi, to put another 1,000 ducats on Farnese, the waverers started coming over to the 'petticoat cardinal'. He was close, so very close...

At this, the doughty Cardinal Edigio forgot about the Turks for long enough to consider the perilous state of Christendom. He came forward and verbally flayed his fellow cardinals. Farnese was little more than a career criminal. Edigio listed the crimes which the assembly knew about; and then he listed still more crimes that the assembly had not known about. Edigio had formerly been Farnese's confessor. As such, his revelations were instantly accepted. Was he breaking the sanctity of confession? Certainly it would appear so. The essence of Edigio's arguments boiled down to this: How could the papacy possibly be granted to a convicted forger? What confidence could anyone have in such a person? By the time Edigio had finished his character assassination, Farnese's hopes of the papacy had collapsed. For the exhausted and bewildered cardinals, there was no other recourse but to return to the seemingly interminable deadlock.

Now was the ripe psychological moment for Cardinal S. Sisto to come forward with a letter from the Emperor Charles, stating his wishes for his former tutor, Adrian Florent, to be elected pope. To state that Florent was a dark horse in the conclave, or even a rank outsider, would be to overstate his position. Of all the names that had been read out as a papal candidate in the conclave, his had never been heard. Indeed he was not even present at the conclave. Apart from S. Sisto, nobody in Rome seemed to know him. The best that could be said of him was that, as a near-unknown, he had no enemies!

S. Sisto was evidently a salesman of some distinction, for he talked up the supposed virtues of the absent, unknown Florent. Voting for Florent meant voting oneself into the emperor's good graces – a sound argument for many of the elderly cardinals, eagerly seeking a benefactor to see them through their days. Knowing that the choice would enrage many of their younger, ambitious colleagues gave a delectable sense of *schadenfreude*. If both Charles and S. Sisto vouched for the unknown Florent, they might finally escape, with advantage, from this dark, freezing, filthy Vatican.

Thus were the votes of the elderly contingent assured. Certainly the Medici faction was a tougher nut to crack but, nevertheless, the redoubtable S. Sisto cracked it. At 62, Florent was 'the right age'. Nevertheless the old health card was skilfully deployed; Florent's reign, S. Sisto broadly hinted, was unlikely to last very long. (In this, as it happens, he was entirely correct.) The young contenders would not be signing away their own hopes but merely earning a breathing space. It was obvious that Giulio de' Medici couldn't win, this time around. But maybe next time? In other words, Florent was that old staple of the papacy – a compromise candidate.

S. Sisto sealed the deal by informing Giulio de' Medici that the emperor had given him authority to award him a pension of 10,000 ducats per year and his support in the next conclave. A surly Medici accepted. Consequently, Adrian Florent, the darkest of dark horses, a cardinal who was neither in the conclave nor even in the country, was elected pope.

If Florent's election had come unexpectedly to the conclave, it came even more unexpectedly to the citizens of Rome, many of whom had lost good money betting on the failed 'petticoat cardinal' Farnese. The announcement of the new pope was greeted with catcalls, howls and snarls of derision. How dare the greatest city in the world be insulted by the papal election of some nobody from afar? The stunned cardinals seemed to be suffering from 'buyer's remorse' – S. Sisto's smooth arguments waned in the light of day. Cursed by the Roman mob, the cardinals slunk away from the Vatican, which was promptly festooned with placards offering 'Palace to let!'

When Adrian Florent learned of his elevation to the papacy, he sent letters from Spain informing the Sacred College that, as pope, he chose to retain his name. This was a blatant breach of papal etiquette. Thus, Hadrian VI started as he continued – on the wrong foot. When he wrote earnestly asking if somewhere could be found for him to live in Rome, his request was greeted with dismay, then derision. Surely this was taking unworldliness a little far! As it happened, his pontificate lasted a mere 20 months – and 7 of these elapsed before he managed to set foot in Italy, never mind Rome. The plague which was then raging provided a good excuse for dispensing with the cost of the normal celebrations (which the papacy could still ill afford). Thus the unobtrusive Hadrian entered the Vatican with as little fuss as he might have wished. Curiously however, he allowed the cardinals to kiss his feet three times, rather than offering his hand and cheek after the first kiss. Again this was a viewed as a breach of papal etiquette. Whatever other qualities he might possess, Hadrian most definitely lacked charm.

The shocked cardinals quickly realized that following a libertine (Alexander), a war-monger (Julius) and a spendthrift (Leo), they now had someone far worse in the Vatican – a monk! The lowly born Hadrian had raised himself in the Church by the simple virtues of hard work and blameless living; both qualities were, of course, utter anathema to those who had paid dearly for their red hat passports to a life of splendour and ease. For many years, Hadrian had lived a Spartan, monkish existence. As pope, he saw no reason to change his ways. After only a few hours rest, he rose each dawn to say Mass. Every day, he carefully took a single crown from his purse and gave it to his disgusted major-domo for the following day's catering. (Under no circumstances was this budget to overrun.) His cooking, cleaning and washing were all done by one person – his old Flemish housekeeper.

Hadrian liked silence. He liked solitude. And he liked contemplation. He was slow to move and slower to speak, in a barbarously pronounced Latin, well nigh unintelligible to Italians. His inner circle was Flemish. Neither he nor they had any understanding of the secular world. None of them had any appreciation of Rome. And all of them were hopelessly out of their depth when it came to managing world affairs. Of the cardinalate, only Giulio de' Medici, the vice-chancellor (and future Pope Clement VII), seemed to have Hadrian's ear. It was Medici who tactically suggested Hadrian for pope, certain that he would be rejected and hoping, himself, to gain thereby.

In short, no less suitable an occupant of the papacy could possibly have been envisaged. The stiff, taciturn Hadrian was useless when it came to winning the hearts of men. His simple life earned derision. Shocked by the permissiveness of Renaissance art, he threatened to have the Sistine Chapel whitewashed and the *Laocoon* thrown in the Tiber. Swingeing staff cutbacks at the Vatican left him with an army of embittered critics. Unfortunately his headcount reductions were indiscriminate. Having dispensed with the services of crucial administrators, he was starved of expertise when it came to making vital decisions. All this made him seem gauche and ridiculous.

Ironically, when it came to rooting out systematic corruption at the Sacred College, Hadrian scarcely knew where to begin. Moreover, if he stopped the cardinals from milking the system, they would demand refunds of the cost of their red hats. Refunds were impossible, as Leo had squandered the money. The sale of indulgences, which had resulted in the Lutheran Reformation, continued unabated, for the Holy See had desperate need of money.

Reform of the Sacred College would have required a strong, worldly but incorruptible leader. Certainly Hadrian was incorruptible; but he lacked the other requisite qualities. Surrounded by difficulties with which he could not get to grips, he did what all weak rulers have done throughout history. He immersed himself in irrelevant detail, in his case ordering the young cardinals to shave their Julian beards and lead better lives. He steadfastly refused to make decisions, endlessly prevaricating with a supposedly lofty 'We will see…', which fooled nobody.

Incompetent in domestic affairs, he proved an innocent in international ones. Like his predecessor Leo, he utterly failed to grasp the gravity of Luther's German rebellion. At the Diet of Nuremberg in December 1522, he authorized the admission that the Curia was primarily at fault; this admission has become regarded as the first step towards the Counter-Reformation. Yet he persisted in attempts to stamp out doctrinal change, insisting that Luther, whose opinions he condemned *in absentia* as Inquisitor in Spain, be punished for heresy. Clearly, Hadrian was not the man to offer an olive branch.

His attempts for a European coalition against the Turks were likewise stymied by diplomatic gaucherie. He managed to alienate his former pupil and the man who had gained him his papacy, the Emperor Charles V. When the Turks captured Rhodes, he tried to impose a three-year truce upon the Christian states. Alas, he lacked the authority to do so. Arresting Cardinal Soderini, who was plotting with Francis I of France, was not, in retrospect, the cleverest of moves. It succeeded not only in alienating Francis but turning him into an active aggressor. Francis made ready to invade Lombardy and, in August 1523, a startled Hadrian was pushed into a defensive alliance with anybody he could lay his hands upon – Milan, Austria, even England.

The next month, exhausted by his ineffectual efforts, Hadrian, like many a pope before him, fell foul of summer heat and fever. His cardinals rushed to his deathbed – not for his last blessing, but to discover the whereabouts of his vast treasure. For them, avarice could be the only conceivable reason for his austere lifestyle. The dying Hadrian vainly assured them that his entire worth consisted of no more than 1,000 ducats. Enraged, they refused to believe him; their interrogation grew ever more forceful. Eventually the duke of Sessa had to terminate an ugly scene. The discomfited cardinals withdrew and the pathetic Hadrian died.

Hadrian would have made an admirable monk; but his papacy was a damp squib. No pope had held greater ideals, yet probably none had achieved less. Lonely and isolated, he had not made a single friend in Rome. The Roman mob exulted in the poor man's death, joking that a statue should be erected to his doctor. The inscription on his tomb was one of the late pope's wry quotes, 'How much depends on the times in which even the best of men are cast'. With a Medici enjoying good odds in the next conclave, Romans excitedly looked forward to a return of the good times. Certainly the cardinals were weary of foreign popes – it was to be 450 years before they elected another. The unhappy Hadrian went in the earth and was promptly forgotten. He was a good man, in the wrong place, at the wrong time.

Chapter 5. POPE CLEMENT VII (1523–34)
'He listens to everyone and then does just as he pleases'

A furious Roman mob jostled the fearful cardinals entering the conclave following Hadrian's death. Another foreign pope? 'No!!!' And, if the holy cardinals could not make up their minds, the mob would batter down the doors of the Vatican and make up their minds for them. On 1 October 1523, 34 cardinals scuttled into the relative safety of the conclave. Two days later, they learned that the duke of Ferrara had taken the papal town of Reggio and was getting ready to occupy Modena. A plea went out for bankers. Terms were agreed through the wicket gates; money was sent to defend Reggio.

On 6 October, three French cardinals arrived to attend the conclave, which had, of course, deliberately started without them. Booted, spurred and filthy from travelling, they rode straight to the Vatican, demanding to be admitted. The disapproving custodians had no option; consequently the French faction increased to 22 out of the 37 cardinals. However, the French suffered from the grievous fault of being divided. Some Italian members were there merely out of hatred for the Medici. Cardinal Colonna led this contingent, ably supported by Cardinal Soderini. Hadrian had imprisoned Soderini, following his exposure in a plot to hand over Naples to the French. He had left a stern injunction that Soderini was not to have a vote at this conclave. Whereas the dictates of Julius had been followed after his death, nobody took any notice of Hadrian's wishes. Soderini was promptly released from prison and allowed to vote. Thus, in death, did the cardinals continue to show Hadrian the contempt that they had given him in life.

Colonna's followers met in his cell and bound themselves with a solemn oath not to elect the Medicean candidate under any circumstances whatsoever. Heedless of the wishes of the Roman mob and ignorant of their influence, England was pushing hard for Cardinal Wolsey; money was changing hands at a brisk pace. France had two candidates, Monti and Farnese, and seemed to think that one or the other would be a foregone conclusion. (Alas, they had much to learn.) Charles V, the emperor and king of Spain, had agreed, two years previously, to support Giulio de' Medici – and he kept his word to the letter. Giulio de' Medici had been a keen supporter of Spain throughout both previous papacies. The Spanish faction, although numerically smaller at only 17 votes, had a massive advantage over the French one. It was united and could be relied upon to stay united in the cause of the emperor's candidate. Thus the conclave, like Europe, was divided between the emperor and the king of France, with England as the rank outsider.

Giulio de' Medici's stall was, either by accident or design, situated beneath Perugino's portrait of St Peter receiving the keys. The then Cardinal della Rovere had launched his successful bid for the Vatican while occupying the same cell. Whether an omen or not, by the end of the first week of the conclave, serious voting had not even begun.

The Roman mob viciously denounced the dilatory cardinals and demanded strict adherence to the regulations for meals, thus hoping to hit the cardinals where it could would hurt most – in their stomachs. Another two weeks passed. To the joy of the French contingent, Monti amassed 19 votes. But Giulio de' Medici stated firmly that he and his 17 supporters would die in the Vatican rather than give up the struggle. Without their support, there could be no pope. When this titbit of gossip was sneaked out of the supposedly hermetically sealed conclave, voting at the Banchi shifted away from who would become pope to how long the conclave might endure.

Hoping to speed things up, the city magistrates informed the custodians that ever more rigorous measures would be needed. Conversely, almost four weeks into the conclave, the four principal French cardinals staged a protest against the draconian nature of the conclave. They appealed for two hours' exercise, morning and afternoon. The conclave was officially suspended for 24 hours, while an inspection was made of the filthy interior. At the end of this suspension, the four hours' exercise was curtly refused and conditions were deliberately worsened. Food was restricted to a single dish for midday and evening, then further reduced to bread, wine and water. After a month without fresh air or natural light, the cardinals, many of them old men, now had malnutrition to contend with. A fine incentive for considered decision-making…

However, the suspension had allowed news of the greatest import to penetrate the conclave. In northern Italy, where the forces of Francis I were locked in conflict with those of the Emperor Charles V, the French were retreating from Monza. This was enough for some of Monti's irresolute 'French' supporters to switch sides abruptly. The leaders of the French contingent proposed Farnese but, by the middle of November, a breakthrough still had not been made. The disgusted Roman mob had grown still more irate. Hostile demonstrations had been made in front of the Vatican; the Medici faction had needed to use their influence in Rome to stop rioting.

Pompeo Colonna, leader of the Italian cardinals, attempted to break the deadlock by bringing forward Cardinal Jacobacci as a compromise candidate. The French faction pretended to accept his proposal. Now he needed Medici support. His argument was blunt. One way or another, a pope must be elected. If neither faction would give way, an outsider was the only solution. Giulio de' Medici considered his opponent's argument, and agreed to it. But he made one stipulation. He would transfer his faction's votes to Jacobacci – but Colonna must agree that, if Jacobacci still failed, his faction would support Medici. For Colonna this stipulation was an irrelevance; he knew he had the French votes for Jacobacci. So he willingly gave Medici a written promise to agree with his condition. Thus was a binding deal struck between mortal enemies.

Unbeknown to Colonna, Medici knew from a spy in the French faction that Cardinal de Lorraine, while pretending to accept Jacobacci as pope elect, had ordered his subordinate cardinals to vote against him. Thus, with typically Medicean cunning, the wily Colonna was trapped.

At the next scrutiny, Jacobacci duly failed to achieve the required majority. Colonna, realizing he had been duped, flew into a rage and had to be prevented from making a physical attack on the faithless French contingent. Medici observed the debacle and calmly told Colonna that he expected their written agreement to be honoured. Colonna was now in an untenable position. Early on in the conclave he had pushed his followers into binding themselves together with a solemn oath not to elect Medici under any circumstances whatsoever; conversely, he had signed an undertaking to support Medici now that Jacobacci had fallen by the wayside.

For three days Colonna agonized over which covenant to break. Finally, on 18 November, word reached the conclave that the French had been badly defeated by the emperor's army. The Empire was the winning side to choose. Colonna and his faction went to the chapel and mutually absolved themselves from their formerly binding vows. The following day, after a seven week conclave, Giulio de' Medici was elected Pope Clement VII. In an attempt at conciliation, Colonna was made vice-chancellor and given the Riario palace. Soderini, the plotter, saw his possessions restored. And each of the cardinals received 1,000 ducats to compensate them for the prolonged rigours of the conclave. The Spanish ambassador wrote to Emperor Charles V: 'This Pope is entirely your majesty's creature – so great is your majesty's power that even stones become obedient children'. In this judgement, however, the ambassador was greatly mistaken. The consequences of his mistake would be catastrophic for Rome.

Giulio de' Medici had always been lucky. Luck had taken him from a Florentine slum to the Medici palace and thus to the Vatican. He was born of a dalliance between an unknown Florentine girl and the young, handsome and popular Giuliano de' Medici, brother of Lorenzo. According to the mores of the time, illegitimacy was not a social stigma. Young noblemen married well for political and commercial advantage. Before then, they sowed their wild oats. Typically, illegitimate children were brought up in the father's household, denied familial power, but well provided for. Young Giulio was probably destined to be brought up in Giuliano's household, before becoming a well connected, minor Florentine official. Fate intervened. In April 1478, Giuliano was stabbed to death at the cathedral of Florence, in the Pazzi conspiracy. Riven by grief, Lorenzo learned that his dead brother had left a son by an unknown girl. In a city of only 100,000 people, Lorenzo found her. She was persuaded to let her son be brought up by the ruler of Florence.

Lorenzo kept his side of the bargain, treating Giulio almost as his own. When Lorenzo died, Giulio was 14. In many families, the demise of a patron would have meant relegation to the sidelines of power. But Medici loyalty was strong. Lorenzo's second son, Giovanni, only three years older than Giulio, became his guardian. The two boys shared a close bond of friendship. The withdrawn, shy Giulio hero-worshipped his confident and articulate cousin, Giovanni. When the latter became Leo X, he legitimized Giulio's illegitimacy in the eyes of the Vatican (for there was a ban on illegitimate cardinals, let alone popes). Documents were produced which somehow satisfied the supposed rigour of the Sacred College. Leo evidently considered that half a Medici was worth as much as any other man. He made his protégé cardinal, vice-chancellor and lord of Florence. Leo made policy; Giulio administered it. In time, due to his administrative talents, Giulio succeeded in winning respect, if not affection. Although owing his elevation to nepotism, he refrained from practising it. When he commissioned Machiavelli to write a history of Florence, he stipulated that the Medici should be subject to critical scrutiny, not the normal hagiography.

Ironically, Leo, the legitimate Medici, had physically in no way resembled the exemplar of a Renaissance prince; Clement VII, the illegitimate Medici, much more closely looked the part. He was tall, handsome and slender. But, whereas Leo's personality had been charm personified, Clement had an air of sour suspicion about him. Guicciardini, who nevertheless liked him, wrote that: 'He was rather morose and disagreeable, reputed to be avaricious, by no means trustworthy and naturally disinclined to do a kindness'.

But if Clement was merely acceptable to the Vatican, he was a hero to the Roman mob. Aghast at the demise of Leo's 'Golden Age' and the wretchedly parsimonious Hadrian, they confidently expected a return to the good times. They were to be disappointed. Clement was a hard-working, efficient administrator. No sexual scandal was attached to his name. He was pious. He was universally respected. And, as vice-chancellor to the two previous popes, he had been an excellent second-in-command. But, as chief executive of the Vatican, he was disastrous.

It was soon apparent that, while he could execute policy competently, he could not initiate it. Nearly all his life he had been able to look up to his cousin and benefactor. Even with the over-promoted Hadrian, there was still somebody above him. But now he was seemingly paralysed by the responsibility of overall authority; hopelessly indecisive when it came to making vital decisions. And, like Leo, he was apparently unable to grasp that the papacy's power was fast eroding. Worse, it was in mortal danger from the challenge of Luther. As the great European nations increasingly bypassed the Vatican, its state rooms were decorated with Raphael's frescoes of the *Donation of Constantine* and the supposed omnipotence of Rome. In the *Baptism of Constantine*, Clement appeared as St Sylvester, the legendary inheritor of Constantine's Empire of the West. Given what was to come, no greater irony could possibly have been devised.

During Hadrian's abysmal papacy, the writers and artists whom he had made redundant at the Vatican had flocked to the Medici palace as to a shrine of culture. Now, with Clement's pontificate, like the Roman mob they anticipated another Golden Age. Culture was back in vogue in Rome. Clement struck up a friendship with that dark genius, Benvenuto Cellini, perhaps the greatest silversmith in history. Cellini, ever quick to tarnish reputations, is virtually the only contemporary to praise Clement. In Cellini's company, lost in the intricacies of design, Clement seemed to find his true *métier*. But, whereas Julius could lose himself with Michelangelo in the intricacies of the Sistine Chapel and still discharge his papal duties, the unfortunate Clement could not. Marco Foscari, the Venetian ambassador, closely observed Clement for four years. His judgement is damning:

> The Pope is 48 years old and is a sensible man but slow in decision, which explains his irresolution in action. He talks well, he sees everything, but is very timid. He suffers no control in state affairs – he listens to everyone and then does just as he pleases. He is just and God-fearing. If he signs a petition, he never revokes it – as did Pope Leo, who signed so many. He withdraws no benefices and does not give them in simony. He gives away nothing, nor does he bestow the property of others. But he is considered avaricious. Pope Leo, however, was very liberal – he presented and gave away a great deal but this Pope is the opposite and therefore people grumble in Rome. He gives largely in alms, but is nevertheless not liked. He is very abstemious and is a stranger to all luxury…Since he has been Pope, he has only twice left Rome…His entire pleasure consists in talking to engineers about waterworks.[1]

Lacking charm, Clement's virtues were stigmatized (as had been Hadrian's). If he was frugal, then certainly frugality was fitting; the Vatican was bankrupt. Leo would have used charm to borrow more money – and he would have spent it. But, when Clement ran a papacy that lived within its means, the Roman mob merely felt cheated out of the renewal of a Golden Age to which they believed they had a divine right. They did not attack Clement; instead, they spurned him.

CHAPTER 5. Pope Clement VII (1523–34)

Unpopular in Rome, Clement failed to attract respect elsewhere. The Venetians derisively referred to him as, 'I will and I won't', in response to his vacillations, which were little better than poor Hadrian's 'We will see'. Guicciardini, who had respected him as a cardinal, ended up despising him as pope. He gave Clement salutary advice: 'It is bad to make a bad decision – but worse to make none at all'. By trying to please everybody, he would succeed in pleasing nobody.

In Europe, there were two predominant rulers, both of whom Clement vainly attempted to please. In 1523, the year of Clement's election to the papacy, King Francis I of France was 29 years of age, while the Emperor Charles was a mere 23. In character, they had nothing in common. As to their shared youth, Charles already possessed a maturity that Francis would never achieve.

Francis, like so many other French monarchs, was an exponent of the divine right of kings. It was an attitude that would one day lead to the guillotine and the French republic. Blinded by this attitude, his intelligence, sensitivity and scholarship were all rendered futile. The king considered himself above mere human laws. Whether right or wrong by lesser standards, as a monarch, he was always right in the greater scheme of things. His normally astute mother, Louise of Savoy, had a mother's blind spot where Francis was concerned; she indulged him. The Emperor Charles V was a very different man. By birth he could not have been more favoured, for he was born at the intersection of the greatest bloodlines in Europe. In 1506, at six, he inherited the Netherlands from his father. At 16, he inherited Spain and Naples from his mother. At 19, on the death of his grandfather, Maximilian, he became archduke of Austria and emperor. Francis received the great gift of France; Charles received even more.

Unlike Francis, Charles was a man whose character was as rare as the singular gifts he possessed. As the servant of God, to whom he prayed every day of his life, power was, above all else, duty. For Francis war was a chance to win honour, whereas for Charles it was merely another means to an end. With great moral and physical courage, Charles could trace the most complex and hazardous policies through to fruition. Conversely, if need be, he could stake his crown – and his life – on a single combat. Unlike Francis, he had no intrinsic need to be a ruler. In the autumn of his life, he would voluntarily abdicate, deliberately shunning the splendours of his reign to become a private citizen.

From the moment of his election, Clement was caught between the rivalries of these two very different men. While each of them was too strong to be attacked on their home ground, each laid claim to Milan. If pretext were needed, this left both of them with Italy as a battleground. Clement may have appeared the creature of Charles; certainly Charles' support had been instrumental in securing him the papacy. And Leo, in his pontificate, had supported the Spanish effort to drive the French from Italy. But whereas Charles, as king of Spain, was a useful papal ally, Charles as emperor was simply too powerful. He had legal claims on both Milan and Naples. If he secured both the north and south of Italy, Rome would be caught in a pincer movement. To avoid this contingency, Clement adopted Leo's divide and rule policy of threatening Charles with Francis and Francis with Charles. With Leo, this policy had worked; with Clement, it led to disaster.

At the onset of his papacy, Clement professed neutrality. But while he was negotiating with Charles, he made an alliance with Francis. In this, he was only following typical Medicean – and Italian – policy of making simultaneous alliances with sworn enemies. But when Charles learned of Clement's duplicity, he took a very different view. He did something almost unprecedented for him – he lost his temper. 'I shall go into Italy and revenge myself on those who have injured me, particularly on that fool of a Pope! Martin Luther, perhaps, was not so far wrong.' Clement had chosen the wrong man with whom to break faith. His punishment would be savage – and it would be twofold. The Lutheran fire would become a blaze, which would engulf virtually all of northern Europe. And the emperor's forces would invade Italy with macabre consequences, which have resonated throughout history.

In the autumn of 1524, two armies were converging upon Milan. Emulating Hannibal, Francis had crossed the Alps, dragging cumbersome artillery with him in a grandiose gesture. The enemy army came from the southwest, led by the renegade Constable of Bourbon. The French made the first sally by quickly capturing Milan, from which the imperial garrison fled. Francis promised Clement that he would not encroach upon the papal states; furthermore, he would protect Medici rule in Florence.

Conversely Clement would recognize Francis as duke of Milan and the French army would receive safe passage through the papal states to attack the Spanish in Naples.

The imperial army had come to Italy demoralized from losing a battle near Marseilles. Now they saw their enemies snatch victory once more. Their advance stopped. By February, however, it began again. This time, the French were pushed on the defensive at Pavia. The French generals urged their king to retreat to Milan. Why risk battle when hunger would destroy their poorly provisioned enemy? Clement urged the same wise policy. But as we have seen, for Francis war was a chance to win honour, whereas for Charles it was merely an expedient. The stakes were horribly high. An encounter at Pavia would be no isolated skirmish; instead, it would be a battle to the death between France and Spain. Whoever lost the battle would also lose the war. If Francis lost, Clement had no desire to be taken down with him. In Rome, the papal nuncio to Francis was implored to use every scrap of influence to prevent his master from engaging in battle. And there was a veiled threat: 'As no sailor ever risks the storm of the open sea with one anchor only, so the Pope, confident though he is in the strength of King Francis, will not stake all on the single throw of a battle before Pavia'.

The battle took place on 25 February 1525. For France, Pavia was a calamity comparable to Agincourt. The French army was destroyed. Francis was captured. When news of the disaster was brought to Clement the following evening, he was dazed with horror. He had backed the loser. If the imperial army came south, Rome was at their mercy. In jubilant anticipation, in Rome the imperialist Colonna savaged their age-old enemies, the Orsini, who had backed the French. Inevitably Clement was blamed for choosing the wrong side. Cardinal Farnese succinctly noted, 'This willing and not willing has brought the inevitable result. All Rome is dismayed and dreads the ruin that may easily follow'.

By now Charles had recovered from his rage at Clement's duplicity; he gave the pope a second chance. There was good reason behind his policy; better to have the papacy as an ally than crush it altogether. On 1 April 1525, three months after signing a treaty with Francis, Clement signed a counter-treaty with Charles, recognizing him as lord of Milan with the right to bestow it upon whomsoever he chose. Charles promised protection to the papal states and to Medici rule in Florence, for which pleasure the Florentines would pay 100,000 florins.

Throughout the summer of 1525, the imperial power of Charles was much in evidence. Clement was at his wits' end trying to devise a means by which he might recover autonomy. Machiavelli neatly summed up the impasse in which Clement found himself: 'The Church, being possessed of a temporal sovereignty in Italy, was not sufficiently powerful to unite the rest of Italy under her sceptre – yet feared to forfeit that temporal dominion by invoking a potentate who would defend her against the mighty ones of the land'.

Charles had reinstated the Sforza in Milan. Francesco Sforza, the duke of Milan, held his position only through Charles' protection. He had a secretary, one Girolamo Morone, possessed of great political expertise and few scruples. Morone devised an ingenious scheme. The commander-in-chief of the imperial forces in Italy was the marquis of Pescara. Pescara was Italian by birth, though he now served Charles. But if Pescara could be offered a big enough bribe – the crown of Naples – and he accepted it, then at one fell swoop Charles would have lost military control of Italy.

Morone needed a backer; he went to Clement. Clement not only endorsed the scheme, he promoted it. Truly this was a plot of Medicean cunning. Pescara heard the proposals, considered them and agreed in principle. Understandably, he asked for more details. While these were being furnished, he kept Charles minutely informed of the plot. Charles was a shrewd judge and leader of men. Another monarch might have taken fright or, more likely, usurped Pescara and taken personal control of the situation. Charles did neither. He delegated full operational control to the loyal Pescara. No wonder his men held him in such high regard.

Pescara invited Morone to meet him, and arrested him. Sforza had to flee Milan, which was promptly reoccupied by the Spanish. With a fine disregard for loyalty, Clement cursed Pescara as a 'double traitor'. Once more, he waited for retribution from Charles. None came. Charles had Italy under control and would attend to it in due course, when he had settled affairs elsewhere. Clement, taking the lack of retribution as a good sign, foolishly entered a third, final and fatal deception.

After Pavia, Francis had been reduced from king to captive. 'All is lost save honour', he plaintively wrote to his mother. But Francis had an elastic sense of honour; for him, possessed of the divine right of kings, it meant doing as he pleased. After a year of captivity, Charles offered him freedom, though stern conditions were attached. By law of conquest, Charles pointed out, he could make a claim to France; however, he would reclaim only those territories he considered his own. Burgundy was to be given back to the Empire and French claims to any part of Italy were to be renounced. Generations of French blood had been shed pursuing royal claims to Milan, Genoa, Naples and Asti. Heedless of their sacrifice, Francis gave his word. As he crossed the border into France, he cried triumphantly, 'Once again I am King!' He left two sons behind as hostages to an oath which he had not the slightest intention of keeping.

Clement sent a papal nuncio to intercept Francis. Would the young king be prepared to perjure himself? Or perhaps perjury was too strong a term? After all, had not the oath been made under duress? If he would break this oath and once again take up arms against Charles, then Francis would be assured of papal absolution. In truth, Francis needed no papal absolution to break his oath. He was king, he could do as he liked – although Clement's offer to release him from a charge of perjury was convenient and welcome.

At Cognac, on 22 May 1526, a holy alliance was agreed between the papacy, Venice, Milan and France against Emperor Charles V. Clement had committed the Vatican to a war of which even the bellicose Julius might have thought better: 'This war is not for a point of honour or for a vendetta, or for the occupation of a city: this war concerns the well-being or the servitude of all Italy'. Thus spoke one commentator. Machiavelli was equally forthright, imploring Guicciardini to use his influence with Clement to the maximum, 'For the love of God, do not allow this chance to slip by!' And Guicciardini, in turn, urged Clement to throw off the yoke of the Empire and hurl the foreign troops out of Italy.

Guicciardini's place in history is that of a man who always aimed at scrupulous objectivity and was generally of sound judgement. But urging Clement to fight Charles showed abysmal judgment (of which Guicciardini later bitterly repented). Similarly we have seen chinks in Guicciardini's objectivity, with his seductively idyllic portrait of 1490s Italy, his anti-Borgia bias and his candid admission of his own compromises. Undoubtedly Guicciardini was an impressive man – but, like all men, he was fallible.

Nowhere was his fallibility more evident than in his unquestioning acceptance of the slurs so craftily laid by Pope Julius II to launch the great Borgia myth. Or perhaps one should say that so successful was Julius' deceptive technique that even Guicciardini was taken in.

Clement, however, was busy turning fallibility into an art form. Severely miscast in the role of patriotic leader of Italy, throwing off the yoke of the hated Spanish invaders, his eternal vacillation drove others to fury. For years Machiavelli had nourished the dream of a loyal, nationally motivated militia and an end to dependence on self-serving mercenaries. When he took the scheme to Clement, the pope first embraced it, than dallied. After all, war had not yet been declared, diplomatic solutions were still possible, it might be better not to antagonize Charles. Machiavelli well knew that Charles had been antagonized enough already. Wearily, he went back to increase the fortifications of Florence, of which Clement seemed to care more than he did for Rome or Italy. Machiavelli implored Guicciardini to tell the pope, 'he does not know what he is talking about', at least when it came to civic defences.

In truth, Charles did make diplomatic overtures to Clement but they were rejected. Italy had suffered invasion after invasion since 1494. The bitterness of the vanquished, the occupied and the repressed had swelled into nationalistic fervour. Inevitably this would have happened sooner or later. The tragedy for Italy was that it happened at the time of Clement, the wrong leader, and Charles, the wrong enemy.

On 20 June 1526, after yet another diplomatic *contretemps*, the Spanish ambassador quit the Vatican in a rage. As he rode off, his court fool mocked the entourage. Three days later, filled with patriotic fervour, Clement wrote a vituperative letter to Charles denouncing the emperor's actions and justifying his own. The letter was duly passed to Charles in Spain. Characteristically, Clement changed his mind. Two days after sending the first letter, he sent another, much more moderate. But, by then, the damage had been done.

With the onset of war, Clement's first mistake was to select the duke of Urbino as commander-in-chief of the papal armies. The dukes of Urbino had bad memories of the Medici. This duke of Urbino soon displayed his own agenda by withholding his army from engagement while a rebellion in Milan was being savagely repressed.

Meanwhile, on 20 September, Cardinal Colonna, whom Clement had so nimbly outwitted in the conclave, rode into Rome with a posse of raiders. He intended to stage a coup, overthrow Clement and seize the papacy for himself. Foolishly, the Romans greeted the incursion as entertainment. A mob of 5,000 gathered outside the Colonna palace, baying for Clement's blood. He appealed to the populace to defend him; with contempt, they ignored him. With a flicker of courage, he stated that he would meet his enemies as Boniface had met the Colonna at Anagni – throned, robed and crowned. Then he changed his mind and sought refuge in Castel S. Angelo, while the mob plundered and despoiled various churches in Rome, including St Peter's. Nor were the Roman citizens exempted from the fury and lasciviousness of the invading mob. They realized, too late, they would have done far better to defend themselves.

The next day, Clement hastily signed a treaty of convenience with the same Spanish ambassador who had quit the Vatican not three months previously. Clement would break faith once more by withdrawing from his anti-imperial alliance for four months. The Colonna would, incredibly, be pardoned for despoiling Rome. Laden with plunder, they reluctantly retreated. Clement had paid a high price for their withdrawal. Little did he imagine that this invasion of Rome was merely a prelude of much worse to come.

> 'We are on the brink of ruin. Fate has let loose upon us every kind of evil, so that it is impossible to add to our misery. It seems to me that sentence of death has been passed upon us and that we are only waiting its execution which cannot be long delayed.'

Thus did the papal nuncio in England learn of the situation in Rome, in December, only three months after the raiders had departed. Typically Clement had once more broken his word, by rejoining the very allies he had betrayed; and, as before, their faith was scarcely better than his. Francis talked a good fight and the duke of Urbino continued to advance his own agenda of self-interest. The duke of Ferrara grew weary of Clement's duplicity and defected to the immeasurably more steadfast Charles. Setback followed setback. The Milanese wrote dourly of Clement, 'He looks to me like a sick man whom the doctors have given up'.

Finally Charles replied to Clement's letter in like vein. Clement was charged with causing a needless war in Italy. He was threatened with a General Council. Clement knew full well that Cardinal Colonna was waiting like a buzzard for the papal crown that he regarded as his by right. He knew that, if he tried to flee Rome, Colonna would seize him – with disastrous consequences.

Clement was in a political trap, and he was also in a military one. An imperial fleet of hated Spaniards was approaching Italy and, in Germany, bands of mercenaries (known as *landsknechts*) were preparing for invasion. These *landsknechts* were Lutheran but they were loyal to Catholic Charles, at least in the matter of dealing with duplicitous Italians and a corrupt, faithless pope. General Frundsberg, the victor of Pavia, crossed the Alps in winter with 12,000 *landsknechts*. Exhausted from their struggle, weak with hunger, on the plains of Lombardy they were confronted by a deadly enemy – the feared Black Bands mercenaries, commanded by the *condottiere*, Giovanni de' Medici. A junior member of the great family, he had been ignored by Clement, who felt threatened by him. But Machiavelli, ever a patriot, had begged Clement to put the defence of Lombardy in this man's competent hands.

In one of those accidents of history, a stray imperial bullet killed Giovanni de' Medici and the Black Bands' defence crumbled. Frundsberg urgently requested funds from Bourbon in Milan. Bourbon raised them by the simple expedient of threatening the Milanese with the very terror he had curtailed. Thus funded, the German and Spanish armies united on 7 February 1527 with an army of 25,000 men advancing on Rome from the north. By now, the Spanish fleet had landed half-way between Rome and Naples. Swollen by Italian enemies of Clement, it was advancing from the south. Trapped in the middle, Clement received imperial and French envoys on the same day. The imperial envoy, with the bargaining power of two converging armies, threatened. The French envoy carried yet more empty promises – and no funds – from Francis. Strapped for cash in such a crisis, Clement considered selling some cardinals' hats. As ever, he vacillated, then he sanctimoniously but unconvincingly decided that he could not possibly compromise his principles. For this, he won the savage contempt of Guicciardini. Bourbon, in Naples, had given a harsh lesson in how funds could be quickly raised.

Clement made yet another blunder. Having broken his former treaty with the Spanish ambassador, he made a new one – abandoning his allies once more and agreeing to an eight-month armistice. He would withdraw his army from Naples, he would pardon the Colonna (yet again!) and, crucially, he would pay 60,000 ducats to the by now penniless and starving *landsknechts,* on one condition – that they withdrew from Italy immediately.

Clement's proposed ransom was akin to putting a fire out with petrol. All the way across the Alps in winter and through a blood-soaked country filled with hate, the *landsknechts* had chased a *conquistador* dream of avarice – a great ransom from Rome, or the plunder of Florence. Now their treasure was to be a mere two ducats apiece. Furiously, they mutinied. Frundsberg appealed to their loyalty but, of course, as mercenaries their only loyalty was to themselves. Frundsberg, who had loved them, was shouted down, even threatened. He collapsed and died, it was said, of a broken heart. Bourbon was now in command. If the *landsknechts* had broken loyalty to their Germanic tribal chieftain, Frundsberg, then what chance had a French renegade of controlling them? The Spanish viceroy came to the camp to try to keep Clement's treaty intact. Bourbon flatly stated that he needed at least 250,000 ducats to buy off the *landsknechts.* Clement, all too hastily, vetoed this and the combined army advanced. Their original plan had been to attack Florence, but after decades of warfare (and Machiavelli's strengthening) the fortifications were forbidding. Rome was far less well prepared, for who would possibly dare to attack it? Somehow ignoring the recent Colonna raid, Clement, unaccountably optimistic, decided to save money. He disbanded his troops – and the last great line of defence was removed from Rome as a gold-fevered, hate-filled army of 25,000 descended upon it.

The attack came on 6 May 1527, at 6am. It was a cold morning; a thick mist disguised the enemy approach. Benvenuto Cellini, the legendary silversmith and friend of Clement, was also a master gunner. He was with a party of defenders on the walls. Hampered by the fog, they could see little. He was just about to leave when, through the tendrils of mist, he caught a glimpse of an enemy cohort trying to raise scaling ladders against the wall. He alerted his companions:

> and then, directing my arquebus where I saw the thickest mass of men, I aimed exactly at one who seemed to be higher than the rest – the fog prevented me from seeing whether he was on horseback or on foot...When we had fired two rounds apiece, I crept cautiously up to the rampart and, observing an extraordinary confusion among

> the enemy, I discovered afterwards that one of our shots had killed
> the Constable of Bourbon.[2]

If Cellini's account is to be believed, he (or his companions) had killed the leader of the imperial army and the only person who might have been able to restrain the carnage that followed.

Within a few hours, the city had fallen. But Clement was still living in a fantasy world. Cellini reports that Clement 'had refused to leave the Palace of St Peter earlier, being unable to believe that his enemies would effect their entrance into Rome'. Clement, as ever, was doing the wrong thing at the wrong time – praying in his chapel when he should have been in command of the defences, such as they were. Surprised at prayer by the invaders, he dashed out of the Vatican Palace. Giovio, the historian, threw his violet cape over Clement's papal vestments to give him some disguise from enemy snipers as they ran for the safety of Castel S. Angelo. His Swiss Guard fought and died to the last man to buy the pope time. His cardinals raced after him, struggling desperately to get through the gates to safety. With Clement inside, the order was given to drop the portcullis against the enemy throng. Many of the cardinals were still on the wrong side of the portcullis. A battered Cardinal Pucci was desperately shoved in through a window by his faithful servants. Cardinal Armellino was dragged up in a basket. The other poor souls, so close to refuge, found themselves victims in a world of unimaginable horror.

On 10 May, only a few days into the enemy occupation, a Venetian wrote: 'Hell has nothing to compare with the present state of Rome'. The German army was running amok, robbing, stabbing, raping, burning. They stabled their horses in St Peter's and the Sistine Chapel. They scribbled Luther's name over Raphael's painting in the Vatican *stanze*. They dressed in the robes of cardinals and popes and obscenely denounced these sacred offices. Cardinal del Monte, who would become Pope Julius III, was hung up by his hair. Anybody who looked as if they could be ransomed was ransomed. When the ransom was paid, often they would be captured again and ransomed again, over and over. On 12 May, another Venetian piteously appealed to his brother for money:

> For God's sake, do not abandon me. I am a prisoner of the Spaniards
> who have fixed my ransom at 1,000 ducats. They have already

tortured me twice and finished by lighting a fire under the soles of my feet. Dear brother, do not let me perish thus miserably. If I do not pay the ransom in 26 days, they will hack me to pieces. For the love of God and the blessed Virgin, help me. All the Romans are prisoners, and if a man does not pay his ransom, he is killed. Help me, dear Antonio, help me for God's sake.[3]

The Germans behaved brutishly but, not knowing the value of their prisoners, they could often be fobbed off with puny ransoms. Not so the cruel Italians and Spaniards, who could assess wealth and importance to the last ducat. The Lutheran Germans took particular pleasure in desecrating the sacred churches of Rome. The popes' tombs were defiled. Unable to get their hands on Clement, the barbarians took their revenge upon his defenceless priests and nuns. An ass was dressed as a bishop and a priest was urged to offer it the Host. He swallowed the Host himself and paid for his courage with death by horrible, lingering torture. Nuns were repeatedly raped, then killed. In a mock ceremony, Luther was declared pope. A horde assembled beneath Clement's window at Castel S. Angelo, jeering that they would eat him.

When Cardinal Colonna entered Rome, even he was horrified. Shocked at the despoliation of his native city, he offered to rid it of the invaders and restore it to papal control. But Clement refused. The condition was, of course, that he would be in Colonna's power. And this he could never envisage. He valued his position as pope more than the welfare of his fellow Romans. Meanwhile in Florence, the Medici had been overthrown and a republic proclaimed. Elected as perpetual sovereign of the city was none other than Jesus Christ. Clement seemed more disturbed by this bizarre and unexpected reverse than by the sack of Rome. His priorities were, as ever, possession of the papacy and advancement of the Medici, with Florence as their vehicle.

Back in Rome, the soldiers became ever richer with plunder. Over greasy rags, they pulled exquisite robes. They stuffed their hats with gold coins. Filthy sacks clanked with precious *objets d'art* from Roman palaces. Rome had not been looted for 400 years. It was a treasure store beyond compare. Ironically, a fraction of what was plundered would have provided adequate defence. Within a month, thousands of Romans had been wantonly butchered. Corpses were lying in the streets and floating in the Tiber. Rome was a charnel house. In the words of one horrified observer: 'No bells ring, no churches are open, no masses are said. The stench of dead bodies is terrible – men and beasts have a common grave and, in the churches, I have seen corpses that dogs have gnawed'.

With the summer heat, the foul corpses brought plague to the survivors. And now there was another enemy – famine. With commercial life brutally halted, there were no food supplies. The plunderers reaped a bitter reward for their murders as, increasingly, their own lives became forfeit. Thus do charnel houses consume their creators.

On 5 June Clement signed his last treaty – one of unconditional surrender to Charles. On 8 June a Spanish envoy blithely discussed the future of the papacy with a pope who now lacked any credibility whatsoever. Clement spent that terrible summer effectively a prisoner in Castel S. Angelo, while his future was debated elsewhere. Destruction of the papacy, while it must have seemed tempting indeed to the emperor, would nevertheless create a power vacuum; and Charles was too wise a man to want the risky uncertainty of power vacuums. As emperor, he was horrified by what his army had done in his name. And, however much Clement had been despised, much of Europe was mortified by the sack of Rome. Corrupt and rotten it may have been, but no civilized person could ever condone what had happened. Erasmus, who had been scathing about papal sins of the flesh, led a chorus of critics deploring the killing and destruction.

By the end of October, after almost six months of hell in Rome, Charles decided its ultimate fate. He would withdraw his troops from the city and from all papal territories. In return, Clement would remain politically neutral. He would give hostages. And he would agree to a Council for reform of the Church.

Cellini, who had shared Clement's refuge of Castel S. Angelo, used his silversmith's skills to melt gold and remove precious jewels from their settings. All the surviving papal tiaras, save that of Julius II, went into the melting pot. They were needed for the fine of 400,000 ducats Clement had to pay to regain his freedom. (The original 250,000 ducats to buy off the *landsknechts* must, in retrospect, have seemed a bargain.) Now the papal treasury was empty; nor had Clement any troops. His former Italian allies were like rats turning on each other, fighting for his territories. The citizens of his native Florence had revolted and exiled the two young Medici bastards whom he had installed as proxies. Clement's follies had been great; but his punishment was worse.

On 8 December Pope Clement, disguised as a merchant, was taken from Rome to Orvieto, 80 miles north. Almost his first visitors were envoys of Henry VIII of England, soliciting his help in releasing their king from his Spanish marriage to Catherine of Aragon. Clement was as indecisive as ever; but now, the envoys reported, his situation was truly pitiful:

> The Pope lieth in an old palace of the bishops of the city, ruinous and decayed, as we came to his privy chamber we pass three chambers, all naked and unhanged, the roofs fallen down, and, as one can guess, 30 persons – riffraff and others – standing in the chambers for a garnishment. And as for the Pope's bedchamber, all the apparel in it was not worth 20 nobles…it were better to be in captivity in Rome than here at liberty.[4]

Seven months later, through starvation, Clement and what remained of his entourage had to leave Orvieto for Viterbo, where he would live for another two years. They went through a land of death, where predators preyed and they themselves became prey. The only civilizing force in Italy was that of Charles. Clement crowned Charles as emperor in Bologna, in December 1529. He would be the last pope to crown an emperor. With the assistance of imperial troops, the newly created republic of Florence was attacked. For almost a year, it held out. But, without allies, its fall was merely a matter of time. Finally starvation and sickness decided the issue. Clement promised amnesty and the city surrendered. Like the great rulers of Europe, the survivors of Florence learned how valueless was Clement's word. His vengeance was merciless. All possible opposition was crushed and the throne given to Alessandro de' Medici, Clement's 'nephew' whom he undoubtedly loved and who was thought by many to be his son. Italy might have been destroyed. The papacy might have been extinguished. But at least the Medici fortunes were restored.

Clement still faced the ordeal of a possible Church Council. Again he returned to Bologna, a foul journey in the bitter depths of winter. He was accompanied by an English envoy, for the vexing problem of Henry's marriage would not go away. Henry's marriage was the very last problem that Clement needed. If he had not been Charles' creature at the beginning of his pontificate, he most certainly was now. Granting a dissolution to the marriage of Catherine, the emperor's aunt, was for Clement a sheer political impossibility. Characteristically, he prevaricated and wriggled. But, on the matter of a General Council, Clement would do more than wriggle; he would do anything to stop it. The Venetian ambassador at Bologna read the pope well when he stated bluntly to his political masters:

> As far as the Council is concerned, Your Serenity can be assured that Clement will avoid it by any means. Indeed, the fear of it, more than any other thing, vexes the soul of His Holiness – so much so that he is prepared to forfeit the friendship of the Emperor and the others, and even his own life.

Clement had won his papacy through political finesse in the conclave. Thereafter, he had shown himself to be a man of straw. Now he showed the paradoxical obstinacy that weak men sometimes display when their closest interests are threatened. His closest interests were his personal occupancy of the papacy and the advancement of the Medici, not the fate of the papacy itself or even that of Italy. Now, bizarrely, this obstinacy served him well. He wriggled out of a General Council. Charles, with all his resolution, could not stop him, for he realized that Clement would cling to the papal tiara at any cost – *any* cost – even if it meant that Rome was obliterated. Charles, a rational and wise man, could not risk Clement's madness in this respect.

Clement succeeded in clinging to the papacy – but at the price of religious division across Europe. Certainly a General Council was fraught with danger; but, without a General Council, the politicization of religion became an uncontrollable fire. Religious civil war erupted in Germany and Switzerland. Protestantism spread to the Netherlands, to Scandinavia, to France, even to Spain and to Italy. The advance of Catholicism in Central and South America was a consolation of sorts.

With supreme irony, Clement lost the very country that was once a bastion of Catholic orthodoxy. When the challenge of Lutheranism had grown significant, Henry VIII of England used intellectual heavyweights to tie Luther and his supporters up in theological knots. For his personal attack upon Luther, Leo X had given him the title, *'Fidei Defensor'* (Defender of the Faith), which would remain upon British coinage for nearly 500 years. But Henry's marriage to Catherine of Aragon had produced no issue. Understandably, he wanted a son and heir to continue the Tudor bloodline. Catherine had been the widow of Henry's older brother, Arthur, and under canon law, marriage to a dead brother's wife was forbidden. However, Julius II had given Henry a dispensation. Henry now rationalized his position by believing that, from God's law, written in scripture, there could be no dispensation, even by a pope. (Catherine's inability to produce an heir was evidence of God's disapproval.) Thus, his marriage was illicit and he should be released from it – to remarry and, hopefully, produce a male heir.

Henry's theological rationalization took no account whatsoever of a niggling political obstacle. Catherine of Aragon had a favourite nephew – the emperor Charles. And, once the pope had become *in truth* the creature of the emperor, Henry's wishes would never be carried out. Clement delayed and delayed. Finally, he made the only politically possible decision for him – he refused Henry release from his unwonted marriage. Henry promptly renounced the power of Rome and appointed himself head of the Church in England. The erstwhile Defender of the Faith prepared the way for England to become a Protestant country. As in Europe, religion would become markedly politicized – with a legacy of hatred and violence, which has continued for five centuries to our very own day.

Clement, who would not fight like a man for the Holy See or for Italy, had fought like a madman for his occupation of the papal throne. To add to his twisted triumph, he now added a *coup* for his other great love – the advancement of the Medici. With Charles' permission, he secured an arranged marriage between Catherine de' Medici, the great-granddaughter of Lorenzo, and Henry of Orléans, the son of Francis I of France. And he secured another arranged marriage, between Alessandro de' Medici and Charles' daughter. This double marriage alliance with the two, mortally opposed, greatest forces in Europe was an amazing feat, showing that Clement still possessed world-class political finesse, when it suited him. Alas for the papacy, it only suited him when his closest interests were involved. Even so, these diplomatic successes late in his reign, after such a calamitous litany of failure, are quite remarkable.

In 1533 Clement went to Marseilles and personally celebrated the first dynastic marriage between Catherine and Henry. Worn out by his exertions, he returned to Rome in December and soon fell ill, remaining so through most of 1534. As his vitality ebbed from him, his final thoughts were, typically, unconcerned with the future of the papacy but only with that of Medici advancement. Towards the end, he wrote a begging letter to Charles, commending Alessandro to his protection, 'since I fear that the position which your magnanimity has bestowed on him may be destroyed by those enemies who are encouraged by the fact that his marriage to your daughter has not yet taken place'.

Towards the very end, Clement's old friend Cellini came to see him. They had always had a shared love of great workmanship and now Cellini brought some medals for Clement's inspection. Cellini's description evokes the pathetic nature of their meeting:

> He ordered his spectacles and a candle to be brought in, but nevertheless he could discern nothing of my workmanship. So he set to examine the medals by the touch of his fingers, but, after feeling thus for some length of time, he fetched a deep sigh, and told one of the courtiers he was sorry for me, but, if it pleased God to restore his health, he would make me a satisfactory payment. Three days later he died and I had only my labour for my pains.[5]

So Clement had the last laugh, where another of his great interests were concerned. He died on 25 September 1534, aged a mere 56. Only half of his dynastic coup remained in place. Catherine de' Medici did indeed become queen of France. But, of his two nephews, one poisoned the other and was murdered in turn, so the second dynastic marriage came to nothing.

It has been said that Clement was a victim in a Greek tragedy. The sins of so many preceding popes abruptly resurfaced and had to be paid for during his pontificate. As with Hadrian, he was in the wrong place, at the wrong time. But, again like Hadrian, indecision was his fatal weakness. If we compare his record with the political brinksmanship displayed by Alexander VI when the French invaded Rome, the crucial difference between the two becomes quite clear. Both men were world-class statesmen. But Alexander, crucially, had an inner strength, a moral courage, which gave him the ability to back his actions to the hilt, to play for keeps, with every fibre of his being. Clement had no such resolution. Ironically the greatest exemplar from whom he might have learned was the emperor Charles, the very man whom he constantly turned into his greatest enemy. Clement was forever the stage-struck 'younger brother' to Pope Leo, Giovanni de' Medici. He was always the Medici man, who must advance his family above all else. Under more favourable circumstances, he might have been a competent pope. As it was, his papal incompetence was breathtaking.

Leo had failed to recognize the danger of Luther. The pathetic Hadrian had failed to get to grips with it. Clement inherited an inevitable consequence of Lutheranism – the use of religious difference for political gain. Forever caught between the two deadly Catholic opponents, Charles and Francis, Clement failed to deal with Lutheranism as a political entity. He also failed to deal with it as an imperative for reform.

After the sack of Rome, the Venetian ambassador had tried to put some spirit into the demoralized Clement. His words were as compassionate as they were wise:

> Your Holiness must not imagine that the welfare of the Church of Christ rests in this little State of the Church: on the contrary, the Church existed before she possessed the State, and was the better for it. The Church is the community of all Christians; the temporal State is like any other province in Italy and therefore Your Holiness must seek all to promote the welfare of the True Church which consists in the peace of Christendom.[6]

Pathetically, Clement agreed with every word of this sage advice: 'As a conscientious man, I know that I ought to act as you tell me'. But he simply could not. For him, the temporal State came first and the welfare of the True Church came nowhere. How ironic therefore that, having neglected the welfare of the Church, he should now also lose so much of the value of the temporal State. Even after the sack of Rome, he still had not learned his lesson, and he continued to refuse to learn it. His defence to the Venetian ambassador was a pathetic mixture of self-interest and denial. Clement considered that, if he had attended to the welfare of the Church first:

> I would have been plundered to the last farthing, unable to recover anything of my own. I repeat – I see clearly that the way you point out is the right way, but in this world the ideal does not correspond to reality, and he who acts from amiable motives is nothing but a fool.[7]

If there is a lesson we can learn from the tragedy of Clement, it is surely this – if, in life, one deviates from the right way, one is a far greater fool. Clement's loyalty to the Medici overwhelmed his loyalty to the papacy. His love of the temporal overwhelmed his duty to the spiritual. His great political finesse was directed to his own ends, not those of the Church.

Guicciardini, his former ally, left a damning judgement on Clement: 'He died, loathed by the Curia, distrusted by monarchs, leaving behind him a hated and oppressive memory'. Each night his tomb was despoiled; each morning it had to be cleaned again. Likewise, the inscription was nightly defaced and a painter was kept permanently occupied rewriting it. Had it not been for the ominous presence in Rome of Clement's nephew, Cardinal de Medici, it is probable that his tomb would have been ripped open and his body ravaged. As the pope responsible for the sack of Rome, Clement evoked an enduring memory of hate.

Guicciardini's judgement is correct – as far as it goes. But his judgement ignores the tragedy of Clement. As vice-chancellor, putting policy into practice, he had been excellent and, in this role, he would very probably have continued to do an excellent job. He was a superb second-in-command who flunked the challenge of the top job. In another era, his endless vacillation might have got him by, but not in this one. Unluckily for Clement in his pontificate, at least three great themes of previous papacies finally burst forth together. Religious division became political, the papacy was crushed in the nutcracker of opposing European superpowers and the price of family loyalty finally became exorbitant. One wonders what manner of pope might have overcome these challenges; certainly he would have had to be immensely more decisive and he would have had to act with the full courage of his convictions. Clement's greatest weaknesses were self-doubt and indecision. Those weaknesses brought ruin to the papacy, the Church and to Rome. Pope Clement VII will be remembered eternally – for all the wrong reasons.

Chapter 6. POPE PAUL III (1534–49)
'This is not a pope, but a papacy in abeyance!'

Back in the conclave of 1522 Cardinal Farnese came within a whisker of winning the papacy, but by the time Cardinal Edigio had finished his character assassination, Farnese's chances of the papacy were finished. The disastrous pontificates of Hadrian and Clement had followed. Now 12 years had passed, and much had changed. At 67, Farnese was the oldest cardinal. Loyal service to the Church had mitigated the former notoriety to which Edigio had alluded. As dean of the Sacred College, Farnese was now a highly respected figure. After years of waiting, he felt that his chance had finally come. He had been involved in the five previous papal elections. He knew how things worked. This time, he meant to make no mistake.

Tactically, Farnese needed the support of Cardinal Giovanni de' Medici, who held the votes of Clement's former cronies. Medici was scheming for the overthrow of his cousin Alessandro, who ruled Florence. Farnese offered him a deal – in exchange for his support, when elected he would cede to him Ancona, with the legation of the Marches. He would also use all the papal forces and influence at his command to help Medici gain Florence. Furthermore, should the cardinal choose to leave the Church, Farnese would grant him the necessary dispensations and give him the hand of his daughter, Victoria, with a regal dowry.

Farnese had done his homework well. He had thought through Medici's situation and come up with viable solutions. Nor were these solutions empty promises. Farnese had drawn up a deed, signed and sealed, to stand by all that he promised. Hundreds of years later, Sam Goldwyn would wryly remark, 'Verbal contracts are worth the paper they're not written on'. Farnese spared Medici any such embarrassment.

With Medici and his creatures' votes spoken for, the papacy seemed assured but was not certain. Farnese, however, was thorough, very thorough indeed. He sent a solemn assurance to Charles V that, upon his election, his first priority would be to convene a General Council, of the type that Clement had so strenuously resisted. This would surely be a strong incentive for the emperor to lend his support. Strangely enough, Charles declared himself disinterested in this particular papal election. His previous two candidates had won, yet turned out to be hopeless. When it came to selecting military men, Charles seemed to possess acute judgement; but when it came to selecting popes, his judgement had been disastrous. Also, by this time Charles had assumed a quasi-spiritual authority himself. Certainly, after the faithless Clement, he viewed the role of Vicar of Christ with a jaundiced eye. The emperor was content merely to wish that the Sacred College would elect a good man. He would not stand in Farnese's way, but he would not actively support either him or any other candidate.

With the emperor neutral, Farnese now looked to the French contingent. Here, he was in favour. Cardinal Trivulzi, the leader of the French-supporting Italian cardinals, was particularly well disposed to him – not from any laudable aims, but from pure self-interest. Trivulzi wanted that staple of the papacy – a pope who would not last long. Afterwards, he wanted the papacy for himself. Farnese duly promised to pave the way for Trivulzi as his successor. Against this general background, the immediate circumstances in which Farnese was elected are almost comical.

Farnese appeared like a pope who, if elected, would not last long. Bent almost double, he walked with extreme difficulty. His breathing was little more than a gasp. His face was that of a man at death's door. When the cardinals had gathered together in the chapel after the conclave had opened, and the cardinal-dean was making obeisance before the altar, the silence was breached by the rhythmic tap, tap, tapping of a stick on marble flag stones. The pitiful figure of the white-bearded Cardinal Farnese hobbled into view. At the entrance he faltered helplessly, as though about to collapse. It was a deeply moving sight. The nearest cardinals quickly clutched the ancient prelate to stop him falling and help him into his stall. Trivulzi triumphantly whispered to the surrounding cardinals, 'This is not a Pope but the papacy in abeyance!' Farnese's entrance proved a compelling argument, which won over the last few waverers. After a conclave of only two days, Cardinal Farnese was unanimously elected. He took the name of Paul III.

As it turned out the papacy agreed admirably with Paul, for he lived for another 15 years. Great was the chagrin of Trivulzi and his ilk. Nor were these years a 'papacy in abeyance' – far from it. Paul's pontificate corresponded to a time of much needed renewal in the Church. After Hadrian and Clement, in particular, there was a return to something of the vigour of Alexander and Julius. Whereas Alexander and Julius had put their energies into much needed strengthening of the Church as a temporal institution, Clement had shown how calamitous this approach could be when mismanaged. Paul's energies were, perhaps more wisely, employed in addressing the spiritual concerns of the Church. This is the primary theme of his pontificate. The new religious congregations described in the last chapter were clear manifestations of the reforming element that existed within the Church in Italy. In 1534, that party gained a pope highly sympathetic to their cause.

On the face if it, Paul was an unlikely reformer. As we have already seen, he was not only a long-term Curial insider, but was popularly thought to have been created a cardinal in 1493 simply because of his sister's liaison with Alexander VI. (Paul never forgot Alexander; to the end of his life, he had Masses said for Alexander's soul.) Paul may have deserved the soubriquet of 'the petticoat cardinal', but his pontificate shows quite clearly that he was no petticoat pope. He displayed steely strength and determination at a time when the Church had grave need of these qualities.

The Farnese were a well-known *condittiere* family, with estates situated near Viterbo and Lake Bolsena. Although powerful, they were overshadowed by their Orsini neighbours. The then cardinal's early career was that of an ecclesiastical prince, whose only experience of trade was that in benefices. Sixteen bishoprics had him as their non-resident pastor at one time or another. He had no particular vocation, entering the Church to please his mother; he thereupon underlined his unsuitability by fathering at least four illegitimate children. Clerics such as the young Alessandro Farnese remained in the higher echelons of the Church throughout the sixteenth century, as can be seen through the continued practice of uncles resigning bishoprics to their nephews in order to keep the revenue in the family.[1]

Even before his papal election, he proved to be a Janus figure – looking back, on the one hand, to the archetypal characteristics of the Renaissance papacy and, on the other, forward to those of the Catholic Reformation. In a manner somewhat reminiscent of Pius II, his way of life changed quite dramatically in what would now be regarded as middle age. In 1513, he broke off relations with his mistress and began to put his private life in order. In 1519, he was ordained a priest, although this was not essential for cardinals at that time. Their chief functions were not the cure of souls but the election and advice of popes. From then onwards, he associated himself with the reform party in the Curia. But as we have seen, he had not distanced himself enough from his former life to attain the papacy in 1552.

Paul had been reared in the court of Lorenzo the Magnificent. A true Renaissance pope, he was well-educated, clever and cultured. Affable and charming, his worldliness lent him an enviable maturity. The papacy would once more resonate with the culture of some of the greatest artists the world has ever seen. Carnivals, banquets and masked balls signalled a much-needed return to social and business confidence in the capital. But unlike predecessors such as Leo, Paul would never allow frivolity, or even culture, to dominate. Always there was an inner steel. In some ways, he is reminiscent of Alexander, an Alexander who succeeded in renouncing the pleasures of the flesh. Sadly, his family would also ultimately lead him to grief.

Paul's appearance is well known to us through Titian's unfinished portrait of the pontiff with two of his *nipoti*.[2] There had been no papal sons since those of Alexander VI. The new pope combined thoroughgoing reform of the Church with the unreserved nepotism of old. An early sign of this was the appointment of his son, Pierluigi Farnese as captain general of the Church. When Paul created Pierluigi duke of Parma and Piacenza in 1545, he founded a dynasty that ruled until 1731. This was a considerable achievement, in comparison with the short-lived states of Girolamo Riario and Cesare Borgia in the Romagna. (Of the other papal families, that of the della Rovere survived as dukes of Urbino only until 1631.) As with Riario and Borgia though, Pierluigi also met a violent end.

Paul III's greatest dynastic coup was the marriage of Pierluigi's son Ottavio Farnese, duke of Camerino, to Charles V's illegitimate daughter, Margaret, in 1539 – though the mismatch between the bride and groom was obvious to all concerned. Their son was Alessandro Farnese, duke of Parma, who was Philip II's commander in the Low Countries in the 1580s. Pierluigi's third son, Orazio, was made duke of Castro and married an illegitimate daughter of Henri II of France.

Pierluigi's three sons were all well provided for by their grandfather, who created the eldest, Alessandro, a cardinal at the age of 14. This Alessandro inherited his namesake's ambitious Roman building project, the Palazzo Farnese, which took so long to complete that its successive architects were Antonio da Sangallo the younger, Michelangelo, Giacomo della Vignola and Giacomo della Porta. Cardinal Alessandro complemented it by commissioning from Vignola a rural counterpart, the palatial Villa Farnese at Caprarola, north of Rome, dating from 1556.

The Palazzo Farnese, together with the rearrangement of neighbouring streets to create a vista to and from the palace, was not Paul III's only contribution to the physical development of Rome. Michelangelo was commissioned to renovate the Campidoglio, the seat of the city's civic government, to which the impressive equestrian statue of Marcus Aurelius was moved to provide a centrepiece. As with the Palazzo Farnese, Michelangelo succeeded da Sangallo as architect of St Peter's basilica. He made more drastic changes than had his predecessors, but nevertheless retained the Greek cross plan, and contributed the distinctive hemispherical dome. His *Last Judgement* on the altar wall of the Sistine Chapel (plate 10) had been commissioned by Clement. It was executed for Paul between 1536 and 1541. In common with the chapel ceiling, it conveys what might be called – quite literally – muscular Christianity.

Michelangelo returned to Rome in 1534, and his faith became his principal source of inspiration during the last two decades of his long life. In the late 1530s he developed a mutually creative friendship with the noblewoman Vittoria Colonna, who assuaged her grief after the death in 1525 of her husband, Ferdinando Francesco d'Avalos, marquis of Pescara, by writing sonnets. Some of her later works were dedicated to the artist, as was one of his Crucifixion drawings to her. It is through her, therefore, that we enter the world of the *spirituali*, the Italian religious reformers with whom Juan de Valdés sought sanctuary from his Spanish persecutors.

As the term '*Evangelisme*' is used to refer to the thought and priorities of the circle of Marguerite d'Angoulême in France, so '*Evangelismo*' refers to the same phenomenon in Italy. The individuals concerned can be placed on the confessional cusp between Catholicism and Protestantism; some actually became Protestants, but others did not. An Italo-French connection existed in the person of Renée de France, duchess of Ferrara, who antagonized her husband by providing shelter for her fellow Protestants.

Many of the adherents of Italian Evangelism (which must not be confused with Evangelicalism) gravitated towards Naples. It was there that Valdés settled after a short period in Rome. One of his contacts was Giulia Gonzaga, a noble widow who abandoned her estates in 1533 and retired to a convent near Naples. Another was the Florentine Pietro Carnesecchi, who served Clement VII as papal secretary but followed Valdés to Naples in 1536. Bernardino Ochino, general of the Franciscan Order, was yet another contact of Valdés. Ochino was an Observant Franciscan, but yearned for greater strictness than even that branch of the Order provided. In 1534 he joined the recently founded Capuchin friars. Like others of the Valdés circle, he sympathized with Luther on the key issue of justification by faith alone.

From the Augustinian tradition came another Florentine, Pietro Martire Vermigli, whose father had been a follower of Savonarola. In 1533 he became prior of an Augustinian house in Naples, where he read works by Bucer and Zwingli. As a student at Padua, Vermigli had struck up a friendship with one of the university's more notable members. This was the English king's 'cousin', Reginald Pole,[3] son of Margaret, countess of Salisbury, and consequently great-nephew of Edward IV and Richard III. Henry VIII paid for Pole's Paduan studies in the 1520s, and subsequently sought a return on his investment by seeking his support for the royal divorce. The archbishopric of York was offered as an additional inducement. Pole finally put his learning into his *Pro ecclesiasticae unitatis defensione (In Defence of Church Unity)* of 1536, a work highly critical of Henry's break with Rome. Pole completes our circle of *spirituali* because he acted as spiritual adviser to Vittoria Colonna.[4]

The last years of Clement VII's pontificate and the first years of Paul III's coincided with the onset of ecclesiastical revolution in Pole's homeland. Cardinal Wolsey had conspicuously failed to get the royal marriage annulled, so was ousted from power and died shortly afterwards. In 1532 Thomas Cromwell emerged as Henry VIII's chief adviser, and was responsible for the legislation that cut England's financial and legal ties to Rome. From 1536 Cromwell oversaw the first phase of the dissolution of the monasteries and the royal acquisition of monastic wealth, which was subsequently alienated to ambitious laymen. When the northern counties rose in revolt against the dissolution, Paul III hoped that Reginald Pole would be able to spearhead the reclamation of England from Rome, but his legation was a complete failure in that respect.

Of more direct and immediate relevance for Anglo-papal relations was the 1534 Act of Supremacy and accompanying oath – which the chancellor, Thomas More, and John Fisher, bishop of Rochester, refused to take on the grounds that it was a direct threat to papal supremacy. By denying the king's title and authority over the Church in England, as approved by Parliament, More and Fisher found themselves condemned as traitors. Paul made an 11th hour attempt to help Fisher by promoting him to the cardinalate, but it did not save him. Both men were executed in the summer of 1535.

Contemporaneously, the debate about religion also reached a crisis in France, where a spate of anti-Catholic broadsides appeared in Paris and other cities during the night of 18 October 1534. This was the *Affaire des Placades*, which finally forced Francis off the confessional fence. From then onwards, the authorities came down heavily on the Protestant minority and a number of Huguenots were burned for their beliefs. Positions hardened on both sides, and the *evangelisme* of the associates of Marguerite d'Angoulême was forced into becoming a decision between Protestant or Catholic. The middle way was no longer a viable option.

From 1536 the embattled Huguenots were fortified by the first edition of Calvin's *Institutio religionis christianae* (*Institutes of Christian Religion*), the core text of non-Lutheran reformed theology. Also in 1536, Luther drew up the Schmalkaldic Articles, designed to supplement the Augsburg Confession as a statement of reformed belief and to be presented to the pope. In matters of religion, the German-speaking lands were considerably more divided than France, where Catholicism was coming to mean loyalty to the Crown and Protestantism disloyalty. In the patchwork of states that made up the Holy Roman Empire, these things were determined by the choice of individual princes. Beyond Germany, Lutheranism soon held sway throughout Scandinavia. The Catholic episcopate was abolished in Denmark in 1537.

As he strove vainly to impose the imperial will throughout the Empire, Charles V was forced to withdraw his support for anti-clerical Erasmians and reach an accommodation with the papacy. With Paul observing from a distance, Charles led military campaigns in Germany against the Lutheran princes. This gave the ecclesiastical and secular heads of Christendom a unity of purpose and reason enough for rather more personal encounters than their predecessors had enjoyed. As emperor, Charles also had a holy mission to defend Christendom against the external enemies of the faith. This meshed neatly with his Spanish responsibilities and inheritance, part and parcel of which was the crusading tradition.

The Ottoman Turks were allied to the Barbary corsairs of the North African coast; they were a constant danger to Spanish maritime interests in the western Mediterranean. It is important to remember that the Mediterranean was more of an Islamic than a Christian lake in the sixteenth century, and that a greater proportion of the coastline was in Islamic hands. As king of Spain, Charles ruled a large, discontented Morisco population that had not been fully assimilated into Christian culture. Spanish Christians were genuinely fearful that the Moriscos would mount an insurrection with the support of international Islam. It was a fear that was not quelled until the final expulsion of the Moriscos from Spain in 1609–14. Thus it was that Charles came to conduct sporadic naval campaigns, beginning with the recovery of Tunis from Khair-ed-Din 'Barbarossa' in 1535, and to meet Paul when he made his victor's entrance into Rome the following year.

Although the papacy had great need of Charles as a champion of Christianity against the infidel, and of Catholicism against German Protestantism, nothing could really allay Pope Paul III's fears about the sheer extent of Spanish/imperial power in Italy, nor had Francis I quite finished attacking his old adversary on the peninsula-wide battlefield. At the death of Francesco II Sforza in 1535, Charles granted the Milanese duchy to his son, Philip. Francis responded by occupying the neighbouring duchy of Savoy-Piedmont the following year. In 1538 hostilities between the two powers were halted by means of the truce of Nice, brokered by Paul in the hope that they would unite in the name of a crusade. When Perugia revolted against papal rule in 1540, over the price of salt, the rebels sought support from both France and Germany but were forced to surrender to a papal army.

One pressing issue on which it proved difficult to reconcile the competing interests of the secular powers was Paul's proposal for a General Council to determine the means by which thoroughgoing reform of the Church might be effected. It is ironic that secular princes had spent generations threatening to call Councils and institute reformation by force but, when the pope took the initiative, Charles presented a series of obstacles. Paul addressed the subject of a Council in the very first consistory of his pontificate and went on to raise reform-minded clerics such as Pole and Sadoleto to the Sacred College in 1536. He appointed a commission of cardinals and prelates to address the question of non-Protestant reform, and they presented their *Consilium de emendenda ecclesia (Advice on Church Reform)* in 1537. From January 1538 nine cardinals made preparations for the General Council, which finally opened in the north Italian city of Trent in 1545.

A description of the opening of this historic Church Council makes curious reading to modern eyes. It affords a vivid picture of prevailing Renaissance behaviour, whether ecclesiastical or ordinary. Archbishop Mandruzz of Trent gave a sumptuous banquet to welcome 'his' guests to Trent. Ladies were invited and the archbishop himself, in gorgeous robes, led the dancing that followed the dinner. Early (and infrequent) sessions of the Council attracted only a handful of delegates and proceedings only really got going properly after much delay.

While this process was in train, that most distinctive of Counter-Reformation organizations, the Society of Jesus, was coming into being. In 1537, the same seven men who had vowed themselves to poverty in Paris in 1534 had met again in Venice, from where they hoped to make a pilgrimage to the Holy Land. Their plan was frustrated, but it was at this point that they were ordained. In 1538 Ignatius and his small band of colleagues met Pope Paul at Frascati, outside Rome, and placed themselves 'unreservedly at the disposal of the Pope'. Herein lay the origins of the Jesuits' fourth vow, that of loyalty to the pope. The Society's constitutions were submitted for examination by the Roman authorities and duly confirmed by Paul, in the Bull *Regimini militantis ecclesiae (Norms for the Church Militant)*, dated 27 September 1540. Ignatius was elected as the first general of the Order.

As we have seen, the Society was not founded as an anti-Protestant initiative and much of its earliest missionary work was in Asia and Brazil. However, the Dutch-born Jesuit, Petrus Canisius, was soon at work in Austria, Bavaria and Bohemia, converting Protestants and reinforcing the faith of Catholics. Canisius was a patristic scholar[5] who held a series of academic posts, one of which was in the first Jesuit school, founded at

Messina in 1548. Jesuit schools and colleges proliferated by the end of the century, contributing to the size of the Society itself, which boasted more than 8,500 members throughout the world by 1600. As the Order of which he was to be the third general came into being, Francis Borgia was still a layman and, from 1539, Charles V's viceroy in Catalonia.

The last serious attempt to reconcile the doctrinal differences between Rome and the German Lutherans occurred in 1541, at the Diet of Regensburg (known to the English as Ratisbon). The key figure here was Gasparo Contarini, who had already served on the preparatory committee for the General Council. As an habitué of *spirituali* circles, Contarini was well placed to bring about reconciliation, providing sufficient common ground could be found. Taking his cue from the German Catholic theologian Johann Gropper, Contarini advocated the concept of double justice *(duplex iustitia)*, which was not too far from Luther's insistence on justification by faith alone. Had this position been advanced 20 years earlier, Luther argued, it might have provided a viable compromise, but it had come too late. It was too late for Bernardino Ochino and Pietro Martire Vermigli, who 'came out' as Lutherans in 1541. It was too late, in another sense, for Margaret, countess of Salisbury, who was executed on 27 May of that year for her loyalty to Rome.

1541 saw the completion, but not publication, of two immensely influential works by Spanish authors. The first of these was the *Spiritual Exercises* of Ignatius (already mentioned), a work with which Francis Borgia was to become intimately associated; and the second was the *Brevísima relación de la destrución de las Indias* (*Short Treatise on the Destruction of the Indies*) of Bartolomé de Las Casas. The latter was designed to persuade Prince Philip, who was effectively ruling Spain in his father's absence, to stop the abominable practices of the Spanish New World settlers, who were allegedly responsible for the deaths of millions of the indigenous population. The settlers resorted to immense cruelty in their quest for gold and silver, some of which went to their own enrichment, while some effectively paid for Charles V's wars. The *Brevísima relación* partly inspired the New Laws of 1542, by which the Spanish government endeavoured to improve conditions for the native population, and was duly published in 1552. Las Casas, a Dominican, presented perfectly conventional arguments that all men were made in the image of God, but found himself under concerted attack from those whose interests he threatened. Francis Borgia, meanwhile, had thrown in his lot with the other principal Order of friars by becoming a Franciscan tertiary – that is, as close as he could come to joining the Order while remaining a layman.[6]

Back in the heart of Europe, Protestant anti-Catholicism and Catholic anti-Protestantism were becoming institutionalized and codified, confirming a mutual reluctance to compromise. In 1541 Calvin was invited to settle in Geneva, where he presided over a theocratic government for the remaining 23 years of his life. Church attendance was compulsory and a lifestyle was enforced that could come to be regarded in a British context as 'puritanical'. Dancing and gambling were among the forbidden activities.

On the Roman side, 1542 saw the foundation of the Holy Office of the Inquisition, the specifically *Roman* Inquisition, as distinct from the Spanish or Portuguese Inquisitions that were essentially branches of secular government. As with their medieval precedent, which was created to root out Catharism, all these bodies were designed to detect and eliminate heresy of one sort or another. The Roman Inquisition was intended to have jurisdiction in France and the German-speaking lands, but could not operate there in any meaningful sense. What it could and did achieve was the swift elimination of Protestantism in Italy.

Juan de Valdés died in Naples in 1541. His followers rapidly dispersed; Ochino and Vermigli fled to Switzerland. Ochino went first to Geneva, before travelling widely throughout northern Europe and dying among the Moravian Anabaptists. The persecution they faced in Italy was personified in Gian Pietro Carafa (later Pope Paul IV), the leading light behind the Roman Inquisition and, ironically, every bit as austere and rigorous as the most thorough of Genevan Calvinists. Paul III not only continued to hope that a middle way might be found through the General Council at Trent, but also continued to avoid puritanical extremes by hosting lavish entertainments in the Vatican and reviving the Roman carnival.

During the winter of 1542–3, bishops began to trickle into Trent, located in the border lands where Italian and Germans speakers met. The imperial chancellor, Granvelle, arrived in January 1543, though it was still possible that negotiations between Paul and Charles would break down and the Council would be suspended even before it had undertaken any real business. It was December 1545 before the first session of the Council actually opened at Trent. When it did so, the Fathers had to decide whether to deal first with dogma, the teaching of the Church, or with reform of its structures and practices. The pope wanted them to give primacy to dogmatic issues, regarding these as more fundamental, but the imperialists took the opposite approach, preferring to address the external expressions of Christianity. A compromise was reached whereby both issues were dealt with simultaneously, while matters of faith were said to be at the forefront of the debate.

Beginning with the canon of Scripture, the Council of Trent went on to be extremely thorough in its examination of the Church and its teaching. By January 1546 the Fathers had got as far as laying down rules on the depiction of Christian subjects in the visual arts, which caused parts of Michelangelo's *Last Judgement* in the Sistine Chapel to be reworked, just five years or so after its completion. Trent was the Church's response to the gauntlet thrown down by Luther, but the Protestant representatives withdrew from Trent within weeks of Luther's death, early in 1546. The Society of Jesus, on the other hand, retained a significant presence and the Council provided a timely medium through which bishops learned of its work and invited Jesuits to operate in their dioceses.

By 1543 Francis Borgia had corresponded with Ignatius for some time. He had also studied the *Spiritual Exercises* and given hospitality to Jesuits in Barcelona, where he resided in his capacity as viceroy of Catalonia. When in that year his father died and he inherited the dukedom of Gandia, he resigned the viceroyalty, retired to his estates and devoted himself all the more assiduously to asceticism and the spiritual journey. The next stage on that journey was made possible by the death of his wife, Leonor, on 27 March 1546. He forthwith resolved to join the Society of Jesus, of which he was already a significant patron. At Gandia he founded a Jesuit college, the better to confirm the converted Moors of the region in their new religion. Until this point Jesuit education was provided only for members of the Order; Gandia represented a broadening of their mission. In 1547 Paul III raised the new foundation to university status.

The duke's desire had been to join the Society immediately, but it was agreed that he should begin with withdrawing from public life, settling his worldly affairs and waiting until his eldest son was old enough to assume the burden of the ducal estates. At the same time, Ignatius could not conceal his delight at this prestigious acquisition and the Jesuits in Spain were said to treat the duke 'like a trophy'.[7] He made his solemn procession at Gandia on 1 February 1547, but his status was kept secret for a while longer. In the same year, he paid for the Roman publication of the *Spiritual Exercises*.

Outside Spain and Italy, in the later 1540s the religious affairs of Europe were in a state of flux. In England, Henry VIII died on 28 January 1547, but Pope Paul's hopes that a line could then be drawn under its religious rebellion were dashed with the accession of Edward VI and government by a hard-core of convinced Protestants. Within weeks, in France Henry's old rival, Francis, was also dead. Henry II succeeded his father on 31 March.

In Germany, Charles V was preoccupied by war with the Protestant princes of the Schmalkaldic League. In the summer of 1546 the League was advancing sufficiently to fuel fears that Trent might be attacked by Protestant troops. As events transpired, it was an outbreak of epidemic that actually forced the Fathers to flee from Trent to Bologna, in March 1547. Charles was displeased by this move into the papal states, but was soon cheered by a notable victory, for the battle of Mühlberg (24 April 1547) was sufficiently decisive to bring an end to the Schmalkaldic War. On that occasion, Charles was allied with one branch of the divided house of Wettin against the other, as his army and that of Moritz, duke of Saxony, defeated that of Johann Freidrich I, elector of the same. By way of celebration the emperor summoned Titian to paint him at Augsburg, where the Diet was in session, the result being the equestrian portrait now in the Prado, *Charles V at the battle of Mühlberg*. Gratifying though the victory was, Charles recognized that bringing the Protestant states back within the Catholic fold was beyond his capabilities and that toleration of Protestantism was a more viable course. This was a further cause of tension between pope and emperor. The Diet of Augsburg drew up an 'Interim' declaration that satisfied neither the Catholic nor Protestant members, and underlined the difficulties in finding common ground.

As we have seen, in 1545 Paul III made his son Pierluigi duke of Parma and Piacenza. Pierluigi was to Paul as Cesare Borgia was to Alexander – a man of wild and violent character. Pierluigi may have lacked Cesare's overarching ambition, but he more than made up for it by his cruelty. Parma and Piacenza were papal, not personal, possessions; granting them to a family member was, therefore, inappropriate. But nepotism had always been Paul's Achille's heel. Charles V remonstrated with him. When such remonstration proved futile a coup was plotted, allegedly by *agents provocateurs* of the imperial governor of Milan. In September 1547 the inhabitants of Piacenza overthrew Pierluigi and assassinated him. Paul, as with Alexander and his murdered son Gandia, was riven by grief. To escape Paul's retribution, Pierluigi's murderers placed themselves under the protection of the emperor. As a loving father first and pope second, it was impossible for Paul to forgive Charles for what he saw as complicity in his son's death.

Paul's enmity with Charles changed papal policy in favour of France. Charles acidly remarked that, 'most men take the French disease in their youth but the Pope caught it in his old age'. But by now Paul was in no mood for witty quips. There is a tale that he tried to send Charles a mechanical box which fired bullets upon being opened. Allegedly, Cosimo de' Medici learned of the murder attempt and foiled it. No friend of the Medici at heart, it seems that Paul subsequently also regarded Cosimo with enmity and hatred.

Although Piacenza was under the emperor's protection, the Farnese still occupied Parma, upon which Charles was casting covetous eyes. Paul decided to return it to the Holy See, thus depriving Charles of a pretext for seizing it. However Ottavio, his grandson, flatly disobeyed him by refusing to pass it over. Incredibly, Ottavio was found to be entering into an alliance with Charles and Pierluigi's murderers. The worst blow of all came when Paul discovered that his favourite grandson, Cardinal Farnese whom he had trusted implicitly, was also involved. He sent for Farnese, snatched the biretta from his hands, ripped it into pieces and flung them to the ground. Raving and cursing the traitor, Paul utterly drained himself of emotional and physical energy. A few hours later, the poor man died. His love for his family had literally destroyed him.

The manner of Paul's demise was a particularly sad ending for a pope who had done much to restore confidence in the Church. Summoning the Council of Trent and authorizing the Society of Jesus were milestones of the greatest importance. Farnese may indeed have come to the cardinalate through the petticoats of his sister, Giulia the Beautiful. But Paul III, repenting of the sins of his youth, was a more worthy pope than three out of four of his predecessors. Flaws he possessed, but his virtues were far greater.

Chapter 7. POPE JULIUS III (1550–55)

'And what could you see in me to make me Pope?'

By the time Paul III died on 10 November 1549, the Council by which he had set such great store had held eight sessions and defined Catholic teaching on a wide range of subjects, including justification and the sacraments. However, the confessional positions were much more entrenched than they had been at the time of his election. As the ensuing conclave amply demonstrated, the antagonism of the French and imperialists was hardly less pronounced than in the latter stages of the Italian Wars.

Early modern conclaves grew increasingly protracted as a reflection of the sheer numbers of cardinals involved. The astonishingly complicated and drawn out conclave of 1549–50 provided a portent of things to come. Each scrutiny saw the advancing of a different candidate, his chances being pitted against those of his fellows. Scores of scrutinies came and went without any results being achieved. A fifteenth-century conclave would have produced a result in good time for the new pontiff to inaugurate the Jubilee year, but the Christmas season passed with the electors in deadlock. A fifteenth-century conclave would also have taken place without the participation of non-Curial cardinals. From the sixteenth century onwards, the practice evolved of waiting for such voters to arrive from a distance, the intervening time being spent in lobbying and politicking, in effect, 'laying the groundwork'.

If the imperialists' will had prevailed, the conclave that followed Paul III's death would not have contributed to this trend; their plan was to force a result before the arrival of a party of French cardinals. Conversely, the French ambassador played for time. Reginald Pole, the quasi-royal English cardinal, emerged from the first scrutiny with 25 out of the 28 votes needed to win, from the 45 cardinals at the conclave. He was championed by the imperialists, though undertook no lobbying on his own behalf. When the arrival of the French cardinals seemed imminent, his supporters prepared to elect him by acclamation and his victory seemed so certain that papal vestments were prepared for him. Yet many of the Italians were unenthusiastic about the prospect of a 'foreign' pope, and their xenophobia blocked Pole from being elected. Once the French cardinals arrived, the prospects of victory for Pole receded.

It was a tragedy that Pole was not elected pope. He combined many of the qualities that were desperately needed by the Church of his time. He was both Catholic and catholic. He was pious, yet tolerant. He had great integrity but was not at all bigoted. He was absolutely the right man for the job. Sadly, his promotion in the conclave became part of the powerplay between the scheming Cardinal Farnese and the French. Cardinal Chieti, Italian but in the French camp, was used as the mouthpiece for a virulent attack upon Pole, charging him with heresy. At the gravity of the charges, he lost seven supporters. Cardinals Farnese and Trento, his 'backers', then made him an offer. They would push through his election in the middle of the night, when their fellow cardinals were too befuddled to have a keen grasp on what was happening. This was classic 'conclave diplomacy', i.e. Machiavellian duplicity. As a man of honour, Pole would not agree. He replied that he would not enter the Vatican like a burglar, but properly by the open door – or not at all. Quietly, yet firmly, he withdrew himself as a candidate.

The Florentine envoy was delighted yet incredulous at the self-elimination of a feared rival. The dignity of Pole's behaviour elicited the contemptuous remark, 'What can be done to help a man who will not help himself?' Charles V, who had rediscovered an interest in conclaves, was severely unimpressed by the politicking. He made his wishes quite clear: 'Pole or Burgos'. However, Pole was out of the running and Burgos was a political impossibility – he was a Spaniard, whose brother-in-law was ruler of Naples. The Sacred College had bad memories of Spaniards and rulers of Naples.

Some of the antics in the conclave were burlesque, verging upon farce. Cardinal d'Este, renowned for his stupidity, fancied himself as the next pope. He was in league with his brother, Ruggiero, the duke of Ferrara's agent in Rome. As ever, the conclave was supposed to be hermetically sealed from the outside world; in practice, it leaked like a sieve. But poor Ruggiero took all at face value. Hoping to outwit the custodians (whom everybody else simply bypassed or ignored), he resorted to James Bond tactics. His reports to his master reveal the dangers of 'climbing by a small ladder on to the roof of the Vatican and slipping about among the tiles, perilous expeditions from which he returned more dead than alive'. Naturally the conclave was well aware of Ruggiero's 'secret' escapades, which quickly became the subject of general hilarity.

D'Este himself provided more amusement for the assembled cardinals. As his hair and beard were dropping out in clumps, his colleagues summoned him to a meeting where, with mock solemnity, he was interrogated as to the possibly sexual nature of his disease. D'Este, furiously trying to protect his supposed election chances, swore that he had been chaste for more than a year and it was the great heat of the previous summer that was causing his hair to fall out. Once again, the mood of the conclave was leavened by hilarity. No more was heard of d'Este as a papal contender. Ruggiero wrote, with resignation, to the duke of Ferrara: 'This little indisposition has come at an awkward moment for his most reverend Highness, as the cardinals say that it is impossible to elect a Pope attacked with the ringworm'. The 'little indisposition' meant that Ruggiero could stop slithering across Vatican roofs in the middle of the night.

Hilarious or not, the conclave dragged on, laden with plots and intrigues for over two months. As ever, the Roman mob was disgusted by the cardinals' lack of progress. A bread and water regime to speed up decision-making was somehow transmuted to a one-course meal – the one course, however, allowing any number of dishes. Finally, a deal was struck between Cardinal Farnese for the Italian faction and Cardinal de Guise for the French one. Ottavio Farnese would get Parma and Piacenza, courtesy of the French. And the French would get a lazy and indulgent pope, from whom they would have nothing politically to fear. A suitable candidate existed in the obscure and undistinguished Cardinal Giovanni Maria Ciocchi del Monte. On the next day, 8 February, he was elected as Julius III, in honour of Julius II. With a new pope, the Jubilee of 1550 was finally inaugurated on 24 February.

One virtue may safely be ascribed to Julius III – what you saw was what you got. When the former Cardinal del Monte had been legate at Parma, he had kept a large monkey as a pet. One day, the monkey grabbed a young boy in the street and set about him as though trying to kill him. The boy struggled free and, not being content with this, attacked the monkey in turn. The cardinal saw the whole episode. He was so delighted with the boy's spirited performance that he instantly adopted him. The youth was given the monkey as a playfellow. Later on, he became a constant companion to the cardinal. Del Monte had once joked to some of his fellow cardinals, 'If you make me Pope, I warn you that the very next day I give you the *Prevostino* for brother member'. This was Julius' nickname for the boy (literally, '*prevostino*' was the diminutive of the Italian word for provost!). At 17 the former child of the streets became the new Cardinal del Monte. Charles V was not the only one to be appalled by Julius, his *Prevostino* and his monkey.

The new pope had studied law at Perugia and Siena. He had been chamberlain to Julius II, and had become archbishop of Siponto in 1511 and bishop of Pavia in 1520. Twice, under Clement VII, he had been governor of Rome. (As mentioned earlier, during the sack of Rome he had been hung up by his hair.) He had been one of the three legates to the Council of Trent in 1545 and had been instrumental in moving it to Bologna in 1547 – thereby earning Charles V's severe disapproval.

Julius, like many another Renaissance pope, was a complex Janus-faced character. One aspect of him was the familiar pleasure-loving pope, devoted to his family's advancement, spending his time hunting, going to the theatre and organizing sumptuous banquets. But he was also keenly aware of the need for Church reform. In this, he represented a continuation of Paul III's priorities. Before the conclave he had been one of a group of 14 cardinals who swore an oath to resume the suspended Council of Trent. In this, he was successful. After delicate negotiations and the eventual support of Charles, he called on the Council to reassemble on 1 May 1551. Although several sessions were held, some with German Protestants present, Henry II vetoed French participation.

Sadly the Council became a victim of national politics. As we have seen, Pope Paul III was bitterly betrayed by his grandchildren. On his deathbed he had expressed a desire for the faithless Ottavio Farnese to be reinstated in Parma. However, Charles claimed Parma for the Empire; conversely the French backed Ottavio's claim. Combined papal and imperial armies failed to defeat the French. Meanwhile Charles faced a revolt in Germany in 1552. A beleaguered Julius had to sue for peace with France. Parma was given back to Ottavio. In an atmosphere of such heightened political tension, Julius had little option but to suspend the Council indefinitely. Although he tried to be an honest broker between Charles and Henry, he merely succeeded in being mistrusted by both of them. Discouraged by political impasse, he contented himself with more domestic reforms, such as reorganization of the Curia and the restoration of monastic discipline. The latter was ironic for a pontiff who practised severe indiscipline in his private life.

Certainly Julius' hedonism found favour with the citizens of Rome. In the promotion of his family, he was as assiduous as the most nepotistic of his papal predecessors, while his lavish spending suggested a return to the building projects of the last Pope Julius. Whereas Julius II had built to the greater glory of the papal monarchy, Julius III built for sheer pleasure. His Villa Giulia stands outside Rome's Porta del Popolo and belongs to the same category of pleasure palace as the Palazzo del Té at Mantua or the Villa Farnese at Caprarola.

The inspiration for villas and villa life came from descriptions of antique villas, found especially in the younger Pliny. The villa life was urbane, combining the luxury of the city with the health and beauty of the countryside, but without the stench and toil of agriculture. Villas proliferated within easy travelling distances of all the principal Italian cities, perhaps most conspicuously in the Veneto. Here, Andrea Palladio created rural temples for the Venetian patriciate, who took to living like princes, turning their backs on the lifestyle of their merchant ancestors. Villas were therefore a means by which the elite could distinguish themselves from the rest of society.

Villa life certainly agreed with Julius. With the Council of Trent in abeyance, with France and the Empire locked in permanent conflict and with the government of the Church in the hands of capable administrators, the pope could devote himself to a life of pleasure. Even this was Janus-faced. On the one hand, we have the arts patron liaising with Michelangelo as chief architect of St Peter's and the bibliophile Marcello Cervini (later, Pope Marcellus II), librarian at the Vatican. On the other, we have an uncouth sodomite obsessed with the worthless and criminal *Prevostino*. The antics of the latter were so dreadful that the cardinals were moved to remonstrate with their pope, who promptly flew into a rage. When asked what he saw in the boy, Julius gave a caustic and cynical riposte: 'And what could you see in me to make me Pope? Fortune favours whom he pleases and this boy perhaps might have as much merit as I'. It would appear that Julius, unlike the idiotic Cardinal d'Este, entertained few illusions as to why he was capable of attaining the papacy.

The Roman mob began to refer to Julius as Jupiter and his boy as Ganymede, the mythical king of Troy who was taken by the gods for his beauty and used as a catamite. The famous poem *In Praise of Sodomy*, by Cardinal della Casa, is dedicated to Julius. A proposal to make Aretino the pornographer a cardinal moved the Emperor Charles to astounded hilarity. Julius contented himself with publicly kissing Aretino on the lips.

Julius has been described as hedonistic, yet frugal, reclusive, yet a lover of banquets. Seemingly endlessly Janus-faced, the key perhaps is his determined pursuit of a life of pleasure. With his villa, his boys and the pleasures of Rome at his whim, he had little need of anything else. A long-term sufferer of gout, as his pontificate progressed he became increasingly unable to digest the culinary delicacies in which he had previously delighted. A life of pleasure requires a body capable of absorbing it.

Francis Borgia, duke of Gandia, arrived in Rome on 23 October 1550 and stayed with his Jesuit confrères. This excited no exceptional interest, as it was generally thought that he was in Rome merely for the Jubilee. With the reconstruction of St Peter's continuing apace and many tombs being lost in the process, the duke expressed a desire to rebury his kinsmen, Calixtus and Alexander. The mortal remains of Calixtus III and Alexander VI were eventually given a home in Rome's Catalan church, Sta Maria di Monserrato, but not until the nineteenth century when the Borgia myth was at last beginning to crumble. A Roman monument made possible by Borgia munificence was the Jesuits' Collegio Romano, 'an educational establishment which soon overshadowed the University of Rome, in the wealth of its teaching power and the excellence of its curriculum'.[1] It is now the celebrated Gregorian University.

The duke of Gandia travelled to Rome in August 1550 after passing the examination for his doctorate in theology. This was also the month in which his eldest son, Carlos, reached maturity. Carlos was married to Magdalena de Centelles and their eldest son, the sixth duke, was born in 1551. With the dynasty's future secure, the emperor gave permission for his 'brother' to relinquish his worldly status. Pope Julius was as excited by the opportunities presented by so illustrious a 'catch' as were Ignatius and the Jesuits, to whom the pope was well disposed. Julius sought to make him a cardinal, the greatest gift at his disposal. Francis Borgia opposed this, even to the extent of fleeing to a small Basque town to escape contact with the outside world. It was there, on 11 May 1551, that he renounced all his titles and estates, donned a simple habit and began to beg for alms.

For a grandee of Spain to become an ordinary priest upset the natural order of things, in a century that saw a distinctive narrowing of the socio-political elite and its increasing economic and cultural separation from mainstream society. Whatever his personal impulses, Borgia was not allowed to become anonymous. His first public Mass, celebrated in the open air, took place six months later on 15 November and attracted 1,200 people. In the course of his short pontificate, Julius made repeated attempts to bestow the red hat on Borgia and was repeatedly frustrated by the ex-duke's opposition and the persuasive arguments of Ignatius about not putting any unnecessary obstacle between the new Jesuit and his service of God.

By 1551 the Jesuits were serving God in China, where St Francis Xavier had wished to go on to from Japan. In India, meanwhile, they compiled the first grammar of the Tamil language, which was published in 1554. Back in Europe, it was also in 1554 that the Carmelite mystic Teresa of Ávila first came into contact with the Society of Jesus. This was the year before she started to experience the visions that prompted her to lead the reform of her Order in Spain. One country in which the Jesuits conspicuously did not operate, at that time, was the England of Mary I (who succeeded her half-brother, Edward VI, in July 1553).

Edward's government had ordered the removal of all visible signs of Catholic worship, which was duly restored at the accession of the Catholic queen. Mary's piecemeal attempts to restore the old order included the reopening of a few monastic houses and the restoration to their dioceses of deposed bishops, such as Stephen Gardiner of Winchester. But they did not include the introduction of any alien movements or organizations that had come into being since the onset of the Reformation and had no place in English history. This precluded the Society of Jesus, which nevertheless offered its services to Reginald Pole in his capacity as Julius III's legate to England and Mary's archbishop of Canterbury. The Jesuits were to be crucially concerned, as we shall see, in the succeeding reign of Queen Elizabeth I.

Whether or not the English experience can properly be termed a 'Counter-Reformation' – and there has been a division of scholarly opinion on this – the essential characteristics of that phenomenon proceeded apace in Italy. Julius III's desire to reconvene the Council of Trent duly bore fruit in 1551–52 (sessions 9 to 14), though he had to negotiate a diplomatic minefield to persuade the major powers to co-operate. Relations between Paris and Rome were particularly strained during this period, as was underlined during the War of Parma (1551–52), when the Farnese rulers of that state allied with France against the papacy and the emperor. Another of the new religious congregations had its origins in this pontificate, when the Florentine Philip Neri moved to the Roman hospital of S. Girolamo della Carità, where the community of priests evolved into the Congregation of the Oratory (known as the Oratorians, and quite distinct from the Oratory of Divine Love).[2] Neri had long been resident in Rome, but was a key figure in the Florentine community there, and never forgot his education in the Dominican house of S. Marco, Florence, where the influence of Savonarola survived.

As we have seen, Julius was a long-term sufferer of gout. Increasingly unable to digest his favourite foods, he gradually became enfeebled and emaciated. This lover of food and much else died, largely through starvation, on 23 March 1555. Shortly before, at the request of Charles V, he had sent Cardinal Morone to the Diet of Augsburg in an attempt to bring Germany, like England, back into the papal fold. Sadly, it was not to be. Julius died as he lived, leaving behind him yet another impasse in the turbulent mixture of religion and politics.

Chapter 8. POPE MARCELLUS II
(9 April–1 May 1555)
'The first true reform pope'

The new conclave assembled on 5 April 1555. Julius III's supporters were leaderless. Cardinal del Monte had been an embarrassment. Most cardinals were sickened by the behaviour of their late pope, and were resorting to one of the staples of the papacy – a new pope as unlike his predecessor as possible.

Cardinal d'Este again fancied his chances; in truth, they were non-existent. The unfortunate man simply lacked the intelligence to realize this. Quite apart from his stupidity, his noble birth was enough to preclude him. The powerful French contingent wanted a grateful recipient of their support, not a lordly prince. And they wanted a pope who would conduct himself with decorum.

As before, conflict in the conclave mirrored that in the outside world, with the opposing French and imperialist factions being fairly equally balanced. This balance meant that the reform party was successful with its candidate – a man of spotless reputation and resolute character, acceptable to all. On 9 April, after a mere four-day conclave, Cardinal Marcello Cervini was unanimously elected as Pope Marcellus II. He kept his baptismal name, but this does not seem to have caused offence as it had done in the case of poor Hadrian VI.

Marcello Cervini was born in 1501 into a relatively humble but respectable family. A scholar and bibliophile, he had revised a calendar for Pope Clement VII. Pope Paul III made him tutor to his favoured nephew, Cardinal Alessandro. He was a key participant in diplomatic missions to the French and imperial courts. Although often absent from his sees, he was conscientious, both in his duty of care and in promoting reform. Under Paul, he had been one of the three co-presidents of the Council of Trent, where his staunch support of the papacy won him the disapproval of Charles V. Subsequently he was given the more enjoyable task of reorganizing the Vatican Library, but he was also made a member of Paul's reform commission. Under Pope Julius III, he became president of this commission. As a man of integrity, this brought him into conflict with Pope Paul's shameless hedonism and nepotism. Politically it became necessary for him to retreat to his diocese of Gubbio.

Pope Marcellus was a tall, lean man with a bald head. Aged only 54, his frail aspect made him seem much older. His character was quiet, yet determined. He was a listener first, a talker second. Scholarly, learned and well informed, he was not shy of practical matters. At once, he drastically decreased the costs of his coronation and reduced the size of the Curia. He put a moratorium on petitions for favours and made it be known that, henceforth, justice would be impartially carried out. To prevent nepotism, he banned his numerous relatives from coming near Rome. He initiated a collection of all reform documents from the previous pontificate to assemble a comprehensive reform Bull. And all of this happened within some three weeks of his election.

But then he died of a stroke. The rigours of Holy Week, with its long, exhausting ceremonies, took their toll on the delicate health of a man facing huge responsibilities and a massive work load. As a desperate measure he was wrapped in the still steaming skins of sheep, which had been flayed alive. Evidently, neither this nor any other palliative could save him. His reign was a paltry 22 days. Already he had shown not only the promise of an election candidate but the mettle of the first true reform pope. All the signs were that he would have continued the reforming work of his patrons, Paul III and Julius III, albeit with greater personal austerity than they had exhibited. He might have accomplished marvels – how unfortunate was the Church, first to lose Cardinal Pole as pope, then Marcellus.

Ironically, yet perhaps fittingly, Pope Marcellus is now better known than most sixteenth-century pontiffs, however long they lived, thanks entirely to the *Missa Papal Marcelli* by that prolific setter of the Mass, Giovanni Pierluigi da Palestrina. The great composer, then a singer in the Sistine choir, had written the Mass in response to a complaint by Marcellus about the quality of Good Friday liturgical chants.

Chapter 9. POPE PAUL IV (1555–59)
'His arm is dyed in blood to the elbow'

Gian Pietro Carafa, who wore the triple tiara as Pope Paul IV, has the unique distinction in papal history of placing on the *Index of Forbidden Books* a composition of which he himself was the author. The circumstances in which this happened were somewhat bizarre, and related to the pontificate of Paul III. Paul had appointed Carafa to lead a team of nine cardinals to engage in a rigorous investigation of heterodoxy in matters of faith and morals. It was a key part of the Farnese pope's general programme of reform. The report so commissioned was to be as wide-ranging and candid as possible, being a confidential document for the pope's eyes only. Unfortunately for the Holy See this document was leaked to the world at large, and fallen upon with glee by Protestant activists for reform.

The document was entitled *Consilium* (*Advice*), consisting of counsel proffered to the Holy Father on areas most urgently in need of reform. There were many. Included were excessive papal absolutism, simony, abuses in the bestowal of bishoprics on unworthy candidates and much else besides. The pope himself thus became, in theory, a prime candidate for investigation. In practice, his mistress, his illegitimate children, his gifts of red hats to his grandson and two nephews – the latter aged 14 and 16 – were, by tacit agreement, kept apart from the general condemnation. It was, nevertheless, an explosive piece of writing, especially as, since 1450, books had been pouring off the newly invented printing presses with increasing prolificness.

The damning indictment of the state of the Roman Church contained in *Consilium* could not, having been leaked, be kept secret from Protestants. The only recourse was to ensure that Catholics should, if possible, be prevented from reading it. Paul IV thus realized that he had no option but to place on the *Index* the composition of which he had been the principal author. The final irony was that it was he himself who created the *Index* as a powerful instrument in the hands of the Congregation of the Inquisition.

Gian Pietro Carafa was born near Benevento on 28 June 1476, the scion of a Neapolitan baronial family. Being committed to the concept of 'reform', as then understood, he combined strict personal asceticism with humanist interests and corresponded with Erasmus; as a Neapolitan, he nourished an aversion to Spain and Spanish ascendancy. Returning to Rome, he joined the Oratory of Divine Love and worked to amend abuses in his dioceses. Chosen by Hadrian VI to collaborate with his projected reform programme, he renounced his bishoprics in 1524 and with Gaetano da Thiene (also known as Cajetan) founded the Theatines. They were dedicated to strict poverty, to restoring the apostolic way of life and to reforming abuses in the Church. He became their first superior.

His election was hailed by partisans of genuine reform, but their hopes were not fulfilled. Autocratic and passionate, inspired by a medieval conception of papal supremacy, he relinquished his predecessors' neutrality and – in his revulsion to Spanish rule in Italy – was led by his nephew, Carlo Carafa, to ally himself with France and make war on Spain. The papal forces were defeated by Fernando Álvarez de Toledo (duke of Alba, viceroy of Naples), and the papal state was overrun. Paul was forced to accept the, fortunately generous, treaty of Cave on 12 September 1557. That Rome was spared the horror of another sacking was in no way to the pope's credit. He was very lucky that the hatred that he had attracted toward the Holy See was only narrowly overcome by the pious respect of the duke of Alba toward the centre of the Church.

In spite of his advanced age – 79 at the time of his election and the oldest pope of the sixteenth century – Paul was a man of quick temper and violent language. He was also acutely conscious of the papal dignity, *vis à vis* the secular princes, and thought of himself as being in the tradition of Innocent III (reigned 1198–1216), under whom papal power reached its medieval apogee. As something of a matter of course, considerable power was put in the hands of the Carafa *nipoti*, particularly the ambitious Carlo Carafa, who tended to operate his own foreign policies independent of, and without the knowledge of, the pope. The various *nipoti* gained notorious reputations in Rome, but it was only in the dying days of his pontificate that Paul's eyes were opened to their crimes. In conformity with the rigour he practised and demanded from prelates and Curialists, he stripped his three nephews of their offices and banished them from Rome.

Unlike his three immediate predecessors, Paul had no particular desire to reconvene the Council of Trent. His reluctance was partly attributable to his distrust of the newly founded Society of Jesus. This antagonism toward the Jesuits was not merely that of 'healthy' rivalry between congregations or jealousy of the Society's phenomenal achievements over a brief span of time, but lay in the fact that they were still essentially a Spanish organization. The Carafa pope was motivated, above all else, by hostility towards Spain, the power that had occupied his native Naples for over half a century. His advanced age put him in the rare position of being able to remember things as they were before the Spanish occupation.

Reform, he thought, could be instituted through other means, and a large reform congregation was created in 1556. In reality, it operated like a Council in miniature, but did so under the eagle eye of the pope himself, not from distant Trent. His age may well have made him a pope in a hurry, who could not wait for the long deliberations of the Council. Cardinals were urged to reside in Rome and bishops to have no other benefices. A second means at Paul's disposal was the Roman Inquisition. Even as pope he continued to attend its weekly tribunals. Genuine Protestants were in short supply in mid-sixteenth-century Italy, but those who could be found were dealt with severely, as was anyone suspected of heresy. As in the time of the Cathars, the inquisitors were Dominicans. This brings us back to the *Index*.

There was a strong Dominican presence among the theologians who were charged with drawing up the *Index* of prohibited books, which Paul IV promulgated in 1559. It took its cue from a similar *Index* published in Venice ten years earlier. There was no doubt among the theologians that all the works of Luther and other Protestant writers should be condemned. The entire output of Erasmus also appeared on the Roman *Index*, since Erasmian humanism was generally thought to have emboldened Luther and opened the way to the German Reformation. Greater doubt and greater debate surrounded the published works of that thorn in the flesh of the second Borgia pope, Girolamo Savonarola. The Fifth Lateran Council of 1512–17 might have condemned him as a heretic and a schismatic, but actually failed to do so. Consequently, his writings were quite freely printed for some decades. Some of his sermons appeared in the Venetian *Index* and reappeared in the Roman version. While Luther and Erasmus had no-one to plead their causes in Rome, Savonarola had his confrères in the Dominican Order who defended his orthodoxy. Chief among his defenders was Cardinal Michele Ghislieri, the future Pius V.

Towards the beginning of Paul IV's relatively brief pontificate, the cause of Church reform was, to a great extent, sacrificed to the pope's determination to rid Italy of Spanish occupation and Spanish/imperial domination. In his imperial capacity, Charles V continued to be more realistic about the need to reach an accommodation with the Lutheran princes. In 1555, the Peace of Augsburg recognized that the Empire contained both Catholic and Lutheran elements and advocated a *modus vivendi*, whereby citizens followed the confessional choice of their princes. This was a notable Protestant triumph, but it also reflected the increasingly Protestant character of the German-speaking regions. Paul was livid.

As we have seen, he waged war with the Spanish occupying forces. He did so in alliance with the France of Henry II (this was the very last phase of the Italian Wars which dated back to the French invasion of Naples in 1494). When the French and imperialists signed an armistice in 1556, Paul's schemes appeared to be thwarted, and Rome found itself poorly defended against the army of the duke of Alba, which crossed the border between Naples and the papal states in September. Alba was a veteran of the Spanish victories at Pavia (1525) and Tunis (1535), but was then Charles' commander-in-chief in Italy. With such a record, perhaps it was little wonder that the Romans feared another sack of their city and prepared for a siege. Ostia fell, but Rome survived.

From about 1540, Italy had ceased to feature heavily in Charles' sights. By the 1550s, bowed down by the unparalleled burdens of his personal 'empire', he was prematurely aged and determined to relinquish control of his various domains. The example of his 'brother', the fourth duke of Gandia, may well have inspired him in this respect. Naturally enough, Charles wanted his only son (Philip) to succeed him in the Empire, the imperial title ranking higher than that of king of Spain. His brother Ferdinand had gained vast experience as the emperor's lieutenant in Germany, and he realized that the essentially Spanish Philip would not be welcome there. Thus it was that Charles relinquished the Netherlands, Castile, Aragon and Sicily to Philip, but the Empire to Ferdinand, in 1555–56. Ferdinand reigned as emperor until 1564, Philip as King Philip II until 1598. In 1556, Charles sailed from the Netherlands to Spain and his retirement in the Jeronimite monastery at Yuste, where he died on 21 September 1558. It was the ex-duke of Gandia who preached at the ex-emperor's funeral in Valladolid, some months later.

In 1557 there was an overlap between Pope Paul IV's war against Spain and his personal crusade against heresy. Cardinal Giovanni Morone had been legate to the Diet, which agreed the Peace of Augsburg two months previously. This brought him into contact with Lutherans, and the accusations subsequently made against him suggested that he harboured Protestant sympathies on justification by faith and other contentious matters. Morone was arrested and imprisoned in Castel S. Angelo, where he remained until Paul's death. The accusations were without foundation and the next pontiff, Pius IV, absolved Morone from all guilt and employed him on further missions to the Empire. Giovanni Morone and Reginald Pole had both been created cardinals by Paul III in 1536, as part of that pope's reforming initiatives. They moved in the same sort of circles as the then Cardinal Carafa. In 1557, Paul recalled to Rome all papal representatives in Spanish-held dominions. This included England, because Philip of Spain was married to England's Queen Mary Tudor. It was a recall of ambassadors in time of war, but also a means of bringing Pole, the legate to England, under closer papal scrutiny.

Paul felt convinced that Pole was of a similar stamp to Morone, mixing rather too freely with heretics in England, as he had mixed with *spirituali* of dubious orthodoxy during his long years in Italy. Feeling betrayed by his old friend, Pole resigned the legation and Mary ensured his protection in England. It was a stand-off that lasted until the queen and the archbishop died on the same day, 17 November 1558.

Paul IV made a last desperate stand for Italian independence from Spanish rule, but it ended in failure. The treaty of Cateau-Cambrésis (2–3 April 1559) brought a formal conclusion to the Italian Wars and confirmed Spanish Habsburg hegemony in the peninsula. On 10 July Henry II died (as a result of receiving a wound to the head when tilting). This left France with a minority government, as Henry's son, Francis II, was only 14 at the time of his accession. Philip II was the undisputed master of western Europe. His hopes frustrated, Pope Paul expired on 18 August 1559. The Roman mob celebrated the event by attacking the headquarters of the hated Inquisition and by destroying the pope's statue on the Campidoglio.

As with the other popes of this period, there is a division between general political events and those trends and developments that particularly illustrate the character and outlook of the pope himself. It was in his attitude toward Jews that Paul IV was to be seen at his most repressive and repulsive. His solemn declaration *Cum nimis absurdum* (17 July 1555) is an interesting example of a Bull which never appears in pious anthologies of papal documents. It was nevertheless a landmark in the history of anti-Semitism. It earned him the description he himself had invented concerning his nephew, Carlo Carafa: 'His arm is dyed in blood to the elbow'. During his pontificate, the Jewish population of Rome was halved.

Paul IV had expert knowledge of the history of the Jews, as affected by Catholic policy. Their welfare and status in Roman times had been transformed after the coming of Christianity. By the Roman Imperial Edict of Caracalla in AD 212, Jews in the Empire had been awarded full Roman citizenship. A century later, when Constantine became a Christian, Jewish persecution began. This became steadily worse in every succeeding century. It was given a tremendous boost by the deliberation of the Fourth Council of the Lateran, as influenced by the 'great medieval pope' Innocent III. But it is probably true that the biggest momentum to Christian anti-Semitism was that which was given by Paul IV, who stressed that Jews, as Christ-killers, were by nature slaves and should be treated as such.

For the first time in the papal states, Jews were to be confined to a particular area called, after the Venetian Foundry, a 'ghetto'. Each ghetto was to have but one entrance. Jews were obliged to sell all their property to Christians at knockdown prices. Forbidden to engage in commercial activity or deal in corn, they could otherwise sell food and secondhand clothes (*strazzaria*); thus was their status reduced to that of rag-pickers. They were allowed one synagogue in each city; 7 out of the 8 in Rome were destroyed and, in the Campagna, 18 out of 19. They were obliged to wear, as a distinguishing mark, a yellow hat in public. They were to use only Italian and Latin in speech, in their calendars and accounts. They were not to give medical treatment to Christians, nor receive from them so much as the services of a wet-nurse. They were not to be called *signor* (sir), even by beggars.

Since Roman times, Jews had tended to live in the same districts. There they could build their ritual slaughterhouse and baths, their synagogues, their study-places, their courts, their own burial-grounds. Now they were forced to live in one place like cattle; to have to return by nightfall; to own neither the land nor their homes. Roman Jews suffered especially, in that their ghetto was a stretch along the right bank of the Tiber, malarial and frequently as waterlogged as Venice. Paul died in 1559, but his Bull had set a pattern that was to last for three centuries. In 1581 Gregory XIII concluded that the guilt of Jews in rejecting and crucifying Christ 'only grows deeper with successive generations, entailing perpetual slavery'.

In the Romagna two priests, ex-Jews, were delegated to force their way into synagogues on the Sabbath. In an act of desecration they placed a crucifix in front of the Ark and preached Jesus as God and Messiah. Any excuse was good enough for sending the head of a Jewish family to the 'House of Catechumens' for brainwashing. A Jew who approached the building without permission – such as a rabbi seeking to dissuade his fellows from converting – was savagely beaten.

In 1639, a certain Jew in Rome was chatting amicably with a Dominican priest when, as a joke, he offered to have his child baptized, provided the pope acted as godfather. His flippancy cost him both his boys, one still in the cradle. This insult to their race caused a riot in the ghetto, which was ruthlessly repressed. Between 1634 and 1790, 2,030 Jews in Rome 'converted'. Benedict XIII baptized 26 as a sign of his favour. Conversions were attended by fireworks displays and processions in the neighbourhood of ghettos where Jews, mostly reduced to silence, were insulted and humiliated.

Paul IV justified, in real life, the forbidding image he radiates in a bust where he broods, vulture-like over his victims. It may be said that he could not help himself, since every kind of 'heresy', as he saw it, blinded him to all facts and consequences. Heresy was a plague; it had to be burnt out and exterminated. No human considerations of any kind could stand in the way. Though Paul IV was absent from many functions, he never missed, every Thursday, the meetings of the Holy Office, the Inquisition. Set up originally to deal with heretics, the inquisitors now began sentencing to death fornicators, sodomites, actors, buffoons, lay folk who failed to maintain the Lenten fast and even, in one case, a sculptor who had carved a crucifix judged to be unworthy of Christ.

One reason for this sudden proceeding by the Inquisition against sexual offenders was the revolution, at this time, in Vatican thinking. Paul repented from his promiscuous early life to become a sexual prude of the most extreme, even perverted, kind. He particularly turned his attention to irregularities of a sexual nature occurring, or alleged to have occurred, in the course of the administration of the sacrament of penance. Priests thus came to be increasingly accused of 'soliciting' in confession. But the inquisitors had to define what exactly was meant by soliciting. Was it touching hands or playing footsie? Passing love letters or making lewd suggestions? Or did the priest have to fondle the penitent's breasts or grope her? For example, when a woman fainted during confession and the priest seized the opportunity to rape her, the Inquisition found that this, technically, was not a case of soliciting.

There were numerous instances of the priest, acting as *flagellant*, ordering a penitent to take off her clothes so that he could whip her. Sometimes the confessor decided that he was a sinner too. Both of them took off their clothes and whipped each other. Yet very few of the clerical offenders were punished. The inquisitors reckoned that, for men who had been deprived of sex since they joined a seminary in their early teens, sitting in the dark listening to some attractive young lady confess the details of her sexual misdemeanours was more than flesh and blood could stand.

This unattractive phenomenon can be more readily understood by reference to the manner in which the sacrament of penance was administered before the Council of Trent. The priest, as a general rule, would sit in some secluded and darkened part of the church, with the penitent kneeling in front of him. What the late medieval priest wore underneath his cassock is a question in line with that facetiously asked in the matter of a Scotsman's kilt. The opportunities for irregularities are only too embarrassingly obvious. The only real canonical strictness applied to such misbehaviour at this time was that a priest adjudged to be guilty could not absolve his 'accomplice', but had to send her to another confessor. The big change (at least in this particular regard) made by the Council of Trent was the introduction of the 'confessional box'. This curious type of church furnishing ensured that penitents should be separated from the priest by a partition containing a grille.

As to Pope Paul IV's personal life, we owe much to the description given by the historian Navigero:

> His temperament is dry and bilious. He has incredible gravity and grandeur in his demeanour. He seems born to command. He is very healthy and robust, being all sinews and no flesh. His expression and all his movements have the litheness of youth. Although 79 years old, he seems to skim along the ground sooner than to walk. He has two bodily ailments, the flux and the rheum; but the first dispenses him from taking medicine and the second he overcomes by eating Parmesan cheese. He is very scholarly; speaks excellent Latin, Greek and Spanish, besides expressing himself in the purest and choicest Italian. His memory is prodigious, and he is an authority on the scriptures, etc. His eloquence is remarkable and his private life blameless. He admits of no contradiction; for not only does he consider that, as Pontiff, his word must be law, even to Kings and Emperors, but he is acutely conscious of his superior learning, his exalted birth and the rectitude of his conduct. He consults no one, treating the cardinals as dust beneath his feet. He is keen in all his pursuits, but in none as much as in the Inquisition. He has no fixed time for meals. He dines whenever he chooses, often in the middle of the night, and expects to be served, with the greatest luxury and punctilio, a number of courses never inferior to 25. He drinks freely and always a coarse Neapolitan wine, as thick as broth. At dessert, he washes out his mouth with Malmsey. He frequently sits for three hours at his meals, discoursing incessantly. He retires to bed when he is sleepy and remains there till he wakes. No one would be bold enough, under any circumstances, to enter his room before he had rung, whatever the time of day. He never admits anyone into his presence until he is fully dressed, which is a lengthy business, as he is most meticulous and washes his beard with the greatest care. He spends hours at his devotions and in sleep; and when, at last, he gives an audience, he talks so persistently that his visitor, not daring to interrupt him, rarely gets an opportunity of explaining his business. He keeps ambassadors waiting for hours and they rarely manage to see him more than once a year. He is dilatory in all affairs but in those of the Inquisition. Nothing is ever allowed to interfere with the weekly conference he holds on the Thursday with the Inquisitors and which seems to be the greatest interest in his life.

Despite such achievements during his pontificate, as described by the more tolerant of chroniclers, the unseemly popular reactions following the death of Pope Paul IV are not difficult to account for. He died on 18 August 1559. The populace, who had raised a statue to him in his lifetime, gave themselves up to a 12-day orgy of rioting, smashing the statue and sacking the Palace of the Inquisition. A party of Jews placed a yellow hat on the severed head of his fallen statue. Urchins spat on it and used it as a football, before it was dragged through the streets and thrown in the Tiber. In view of the ugly public mood, the authorities hurriedly buried his body in the dead of night and mounted a guard.

Chapter 10. POPE PIUS IV (1559–65)
'Nothing can be allowed to interfere with God's justice'

Before his unlamented death, Pope Paul IV appointed the menacingly austere Dominican, Michele Ghislieri, to be in charge of his favourite administrative department of the Holy See – the Holy Office of the Inquisition. This guaranteed a continuation of the reign of terror that the Carafa pope had put in place. It not only continued but intensified, as we shall see, in the next reign but one. The intervening pontiff was elected in 1559, after four months of troubled deliberation by a divided and, in some ways, extraordinary conclave.

The conclavists were united only in one particular, namely their resolve to elect someone as different as possible from the universally detested Paul IV. There was no obvious favourite among the 51 cardinals who assembled on 5 September of that year. At least 20 of them secretly hoped to be elected. All of them had to reckon with the overriding influence of Cosimo de' Medici, the duke of Florence. With the astute help of a sort of 'professional' conclavist named Lottino, and by patience, discretion and the gradual elimination of other candidates, the duke's protégé was eventually selected. But it turned out to be a long and exhausting process. The conclave, moreover, was filled with events and characteristics that may be numbered as among the most unorthodox and extraordinary of the period.

To begin with, the concave witnessed a struggle between d'Este, backed by the French party, and Carpi, supported by the Spaniards. The prestigious Farnese, because of his animosity toward the Ferrarese, had transferred his support to the Spanish faction. He even resorted to one of his surprise nocturnal stunts in favour of Carpi. His agent, however, was surprised to find that some of the more vigilant cardinals had sent out their own scouts with lanterns to see what was being attempted. Not surprisingly, the ploy came to nothing.

319

Proceedings, at this early stage, were interrupted by an incident descending almost into farce. Apart from the claustrophobia, stench and discomfort, one of the disagreeable features the inmates had to suffer was boredom. The scrutinies began to mount up (two every day) without any clear result, and the conclavists were pleased to be supplied by a sort of 'court jester' to the conclave – the Spanish Cardinal La Queva, with his various distractions. He was full of fun and games, and the younger cardinals especially were always flocking to his cell. Lightweight though he was in political and ecclesiastical terms, La Queva thought he might as well turn his popularity to his own advantage. Like every other cardinal, he retained his own private 'conclavist' or agent, who duly did the rounds among the other cardinals to elicit support for his principal. Token support was all that was being sought; a mere *voto di onore* to acknowledge the harmless popularity of this particular cardinal. It would give great personal satisfaction to the genial La Queva.

But the conclavist's mission was so successfully carried out that this wholly unsuitable cardinal might easily have been elected, had it not come, by chance, to the ears of one of the more elderly cardinals. The plot, if this is what it can be called, collapsed.

So the conclave dragged on. There were many cases of illness. Two cardinals died and another left the conclave in a serious condition. Some possibly decisive action was occasioned by the late arrival of Cardinal de Guise. He decided that Carafa, nephew of the previous pope, might hold the key to the impasse. He duly offered him the not inconsiderable sum of 30,000 ducats if he would throw his support behind the French party. A further offer of the marquisate of Salerna and confirmation of all his Italian possessions was added to the bribe, but Carafa wanted more. The initiative failed only when the de Guise faction got fed up with Carafa's excessive demands.

Various irregularities now began further to complicate the unruly scene. Discipline was more lax than at any previous conclave. Several boards were taken down from the windows and the cardinals could be clearly seen from the outside, 'gesticulating like puppets'. Desiring even closer concourse with the outside world, they even knocked a hole in the masonry to facilitate communication. On the Rialto, Rome's medieval Wall Street, the scene was considerably less lively. The Banchi (Stock Exchange) had to put up its shutters for lack of business. The usual 'book' on who might be elected pope was abandoned – or rather, never really got started – for want of viable competitors. Most of the voting papers in the twice-daily scrutinies continued to be marked *nemini* (no-one).

Autumn gave way to winter and the conclavists began to think that Christmas would come and go without one of their number being elected. Then, suddenly, came unexpected movement. A letter arrived from King Philip II of Spain, directed to Cardinal Colonna. The imperial fief of Palliano was to be restored to the Colonna family. This represented a dramatic reversal of policy, inasmuch as Paul IV had brutally despoiled the Colonna of their castles to give them to his nephews. This had a sort of domino effect among the cardinals, reactivating their various conflicting ambitions and objectives. Carafa now regretted his former snubbing of de Guise and agreed to support the French faction. He managed to rally Farnese to their cause. The latter's consequent enthusiasm even resulted in a disagreement on the subject with some of the other cardinals, which led to fisticuffs in the chapel. Vargas, the Spanish envoy, was continually appearing at the breach in the conclave wall, if only to urge the cardinals on to greater activity. The lethargy of the preceding weeks was thus replaced by a state of frenzied activity. The de Guise faction, however, was too proud and independent to enter into the fray, and thus the chances of the cardinal of Rheims sank without trace.

In desperation, the electors now turned to a possible Spanish compromise candidate, in the person of Cardinal Pacheco. The only effect of this, however, was to galvanize the Italian and French cardinals into vocal opposition. The former protested vehemently that they would not accept a 'foreign' pope; the latter leapt on to their stalls to try and revive Gallic aspirations. No further scrutinies could take place until the pandemonium had been quelled. A further delay thus set in and, suddenly as it seemed, it was Christmas Eve.

Lottino had been keeping his master, Cosimo de' Medici, fully acquainted with events. The latter now decided to make a direct intervention to try and break the deadlock. He wrote, both to de Guise and Carafa, recommending his namesake (though no relation) – Angelo de' Medici. Simultaneously

Catherine de' Medici, France's queen, sent new instructions to de Guise that he should abandon d'Este and support Medici. She also sent a large consignment of gold, which proved extremely useful for buying up a few stray votes. And so it was that, on Christmas Day, a new pope was duly elected as Pius IV.

As mentioned above, Angelo de' Medici was no blood relation of the powerful Florentine family. He may have had some link, by way of adoption by an obscure member of the family, but this is doubtful, in view of his palpably mean extraction. This he overcame by his resourcefulness and nimble brain. His brother had been a stable hand in the service of the Morone, but he was an unscrupulous ruffian who murdered one of the Visconti, against whom his employers had a grudge. This brother then disappeared, at least temporarily, with the considerable sums he had received from the Morone. The latter then tried to exact vengeance by luring Medici into a trap. He was meant to meet a grim fate in a stronghold, from which, however, he escaped.

Angelo de' Medici emerged from all this cloak and dagger activity with enhanced prestige, thanks to his quick wits. He was granted the fortress and marquisate of Marignano by the duke of Milan and, having successfully taken to the study of law, managed, by his scholarly attainments, to mix advantageously with clerics and men of learning. He became secretary to Farnese (the future Paul III), then his intimate companion, and thus eventually became a cardinal.

In looking for the exact opposite of Paul IV, the conclavists of 1559 had succeeded. The new Pope Pius IV displayed none of the arrogance and haughtiness of his predecessor, and his disposition was outwardly easy-going and affable. But this seemingly easy-going disposition disguised some distinctly meretricious and less attractive traits in his character, as will be seen below.

The absolution of Cardinal Morone was one example among many reversals of Paul IV's policies. Pius was more of a statesman than a theologian, and was considerably more diplomatic than his immediate predecessor. That Paul had resisted calls for the Council of Trent to be reconvened was reason enough for Pius to express enthusiasm for it and ensure that its work continued. Paul's *Index* of prohibited books was too rigorous to be workable, so the Council was duly entrusted with creating a new version, the effect of which was to free some authors from censure. The revival of the Roman carnival reflects something of the contrast between the popes in their domestic policies. The clearest line to be drawn under the previous regime was the execution of Carlo Carafa and some of his associates but this, as we shall see later, can also be understood as a reflection of the darker side of Pius' nature.

In the tradition of the genuine Medici and other popes of the Renaissance period, Pius swiftly summoned numerous relatives to Rome, among them a young nephew who was made cardinal, archbishop of Milan and secretary of state at the age of just 22. In this case, accusations of nepotism have been mitigated by the fact that the *nipote* in question was the exceptionally gifted and later canonized Carlo Borromeo. However it was not, as has often been asserted, Borromeo whose influence ensured the reconvening of the Council of Trent. This was done on Pius' own initiative. When Francis Borgia was summoned to Rome in 1561 to assist Laínez, the Jesuit general, he found a good friend in the young but earnest Borromeo. While Laínez attended the Council at Trent, Borgia was the Society's vicar general in Rome.

Following his brief visit to Rome in 1550, Francis Borgia had spent the 1550s in Iberia, preaching, lecturing at Valladolid and strengthening the organization of the Society of Jesus throughout Spain. Late in the decade, he had been forced to flee to Portugal when his enemies denounced him to the Inquisition on the grounds that he was too lenient towards the relatively small number of Lutherans who emerged at Valladolid at that time. Ignatius had died on 31 July 1556 and Laínez was elected as the second general of the Order at a general congregation held in Spain, almost two years later. On balance, Borgia was better placed in Spain than in Rome, with Pope Paul IV having been so highly suspicious of the Society.

The Council reopened on 18 January 1562 and 11 sessions were held. Decrees were duly published on many aspects of the Church and the Christian life, including the hierarchy, Holy Orders and the education and training of priests. The Council of Trent achieved much, defined much and provided unprecedented unity for those parts of Christendom that remained loyal to Rome. The other parts of Christendom, including Geneva (where

Calvin died on 27 May 1564), were further away from Roman authority and practice than they had ever been. If Trent was intended to spur reunification, it failed.

As the Council drew to its close, Borromeo chose to abandon the pomp and ceremony that went with his office as the pope's right-hand man. He received Holy Orders, adopted an altogether stricter mode of life and expressed a desire to reside in his archdiocese as a thoroughly Tridentine pastoral bishop. This was more in the style of Paul IV than Pius IV, who was not impressed. Borromeo finally left Rome for Milan in 1565, but hurried back when he heard of the pope's fatal illness. Could Pius simply not manage without him?

While individual bishops were keen to reside in their sees and found diocesan seminaries along the lines prescribed by Trent, the secular princes tended to be less enthusiastic about the implementation of its decrees in their realms. If the Church reasserted itself, it could only be at the expense of the temporal powers. None could match Philip II's global power, which continued to expand. The Philippines were added to his Empire in 1564. He deferred to no-one and was more inclined to rule the Church – in Spain, if not in Rome – than to protect it. From 1564 the Austrian Habsburgs were headed by Emperor Maximilian II, whose religious views can best be understood as post-Erasmus Erasmianism. So keen was he to seek reconciliation between Catholics and Protestants, that he advocated marriage for the Catholic clergy. He refused to license publication of the Tridentine decrees in the Habsburg lands.

In France, the regent and queen dowager, Catherine de' Medici, was equally resolute in her opposition to the decrees as she had been to the reconvening of the Council in the first place. Catherine was the consort during the reigns of her young sons. Francis II died on 5 December 1560 and his teenage wife, Mary Stuart,[1] returned home to the Scotland of John Knox. Pope Pius sent her the golden rose, in recognition of the challenges she faced as Catholic queen of a Calvinist kingdom, but could offer no more practical support.

Francis' brother was aged 10 when he became King Charles IX (reigned 1560–74) and it was during his reign that there occurred the first of the civil conflicts known as the Wars of Religion (1562–98). Like her imperial counterparts, Catherine recognized the desirability of an accommodation between Catholics and Protestants, to which end she convened the Colloquy of Poissy in 1561. The Catholic disputants on that occasion included the Jesuit general Laínez, while the Protestants were led by Théodore de Bèze and Pietro Martire Vermigli. The debate stalled, but Catherine nevertheless made significant concessions to the Huguenots. The Catholic 2nd duke of Guise opposed any toleration of Protestants, massacred one of their congregations and sought to impose his will on the king and queen. Thus did the wars begin.

Other leaders of the Catholic party were the duke's brother, Cardinal Charles de Guise, so prominent at the conclave which elected Medici, and the 3rd duke. The Huguenot response was led by first cousins of the de Guises, Louis de Bourbon, prince of Condé, and his brother Antoine de Bourbon, king of Navarre by virtue of his marriage to Jeanne d'Albret, the Huguenot daughter of Marguerite d'Angoulême.

Antoine was an early casualty in the conflict, and was succeeded as champion of the Protestant cause by his son, the future Henry IV of France. External support came from Elizabeth I of England, who had already indicated her attitude towards Rome by refusing to admit a papal nuncio into her kingdom. The first war was concluded by the treaty of Amboise (19 March 1563), but seven others ensued.

Four years after the Colloquy of Poissy, Laínez died and was succeeded by his second-in-command, Francis Borgia. He was to be general of the Society of Jesus until his own death in 1572. Ideally Borgia wished to finish his life not as an administrator in Rome but as a missionary in India, but the fact was that he had the necessary skills to continue strengthening the Society and preparing it for future missions.

Carlo Borromeo came closer to realizing his ambitions. The next pope (Pius V) granted Borromeo's request that he might reside in Milan. The city had not had a resident archbishop for eight decades. There Borromeo put the Tridentine decrees into operation, reordering his cathedral, establishing a seminary and entrusting educational endeavours to the Jesuits and Barnabites. He also founded his own order of oblates.

The most lastingly important event of Pius IV's pontificate was the reconvening of the Council of Trent which, with all its limitations, ended of medieval ecclesiastical thinking. As a spearhead of the Counter-Reformation, its essential weakness is encapsulated in the latter description. The prefix 'Counter' implies the negative and adversarial character of the whole movement: a *counter-attack* in fact, against Protestantism.

The Church, tragically, had to wait four more centuries before it embarked, at the Second Vatican Council, on a programme of thorough internal renovation.

Pius IV was 62 at the time of his election. Of medium height, build and colouring, he had a pleasant, sympathetic countenance, bright eyes and a sprightly manner. He was possessed of extraordinary physical energy. He was always up and active. He enjoyed strong wine and coarse food and plenty of both; he is reported to have drunk as much as 12 pitchers of wine at a single meal and to have indulged in other exhausting dissipations. But he was obsessively secretive about his private life and kept his three illegitimate children strictly in the background. The great amount of exercise he took kept him lean. He was a great walker and went for long rambles, morning and evening.

It was in his treatment of the Carafa that the less admirable side of his nature was revealed. They were certainly guilty of serious crimes and spoliations and, of course, as creatures of the hated Paul IV they continued to be held in opprobrium during the reign of his successor. Moreover, King Philip of Spain was bent on revenge against the Carafa for their uncle's enmity toward him and his country.

Philip thus requested – virtually ordered – the pope to bring the Carafa to book. Had Pius been, deep down, as easy-going as he seemed on the surface, he might have jibbed at or even refused Philip's wish. He had, after all, given the Carafa a solemn promise of immunity at the conclave in return for their support. When Pius agreed to Philip's subsequent request to move against the Carafa, Cosimo de' Medici was incensed at so flagrant a breach of faith. He remonstrated with the pope and reminded him that, without Carafa's help, he would not have been elected.

Cosimo also expostulated with King Philip. He appealed to him, as a fellow sovereign, not to commit this grave breach of faith and thus bring dishonour on his word. For the king, in the early days of the troubled and drawn-out conclave, had also promised Carafa immunity from retribution. Philip, however, was not the sort of man to be impressed by Medici's scruples. On top of all this, Pius wrote that nothing could be allowed to interfere with God's justice. At the very least, this statement can only be looked on as one of extreme unction.

The Carafa were accordingly committed for trial and treated with the utmost severity. The duke of Polliano and two of his brothers were condemned to decapitation, and Cardinal Carafa to strangulation. (He was not even judged worthy of being strangled with a crimson cord, as had the attempted murderer of Leo X, Alfonso Petrucci, back in 1517.) All the Carafa's possessions were naturally confiscated, and the executions took place on the spot.

Despite his differences from the Carafa pope, Pius left most of his ecclesiastical apparatus in place. The work of the Inquisition went on, but without the active participation of the Holy Father. The latter's chief preoccupation was building, which swallowed up enormous sums. Though Pius is remembered for the reconvening of Trent, he left the Fathers mostly to their own devices, harbouring for himself no pretensions toward theological expertise. The work of doctrinal definition, for which the Jesuits at Trent were chiefly responsible, slammed the door shut against the Protestants and gave the Catholics on the inside a new sense of 'patriotism' and militancy. Here, ominously, lay the seeds of the Wars of Religion, which were to darken future years.

After the Council, even the old pope relaxed his good intentions; he became more fond of his dinner and more prone to make bad jokes. A conspiracy against his life, led by the fanatic Benedetto Accolti, failed when it came to the point because the conspirators were over-awed by the outward majesty of the papacy.

Carlo Borromeo carried on the work of government faithfully as before and with undistinguished discretion. When his uncle died, in 1565, Carlo managed to secure the election of one for whom he had a greater respect and who was already well known in Rome for his 'piety and aestheticism'. Such alleged virtues, however, as practised by this next pope – Pius V – took on a curious and sinister character.

This pontificate, in circumstances invariably misunderstood, proved to be a disaster for the Church, with tragic repercussions, especially in England, even up to modern times. He was none other than the 'menacingly austere' Michele Ghislieri, mentioned at the very beginning of this chapter.

Chapter 11. POPE PIUS V (1566–72)
'He who reigns in heaven'

Coming to the end of this survey of papal reigns, full of paradoxes, it may be said that the pontificate of Pius V appears as the most paradoxical of all. For this reason, it presents something of a problem for the historian in producing an equitable overall picture.

To tackle this problem, the first step is to present as objective as possible a summary of the pope's background, character and achievements. The second step is to subject this record to something of an analysis in depth. Thus revealed is a substantial further dimension, many of whose features and implications have, in the past, been considered infrequently and often with faulty conclusions by commentators.

A balanced assessment of this dimension, however, supplies a vital key to the official mind of the Church as the Renaissance in Rome was drawing to an end. It also affords a valuable key to many issues that are still very much alive – and hotly debated – in the Church of today. The Council of Trent was, in fact, a torrential watershed in Catholic history. It threw up an array of issues, not all of which have been finally settled, even to this day. What, for example, in real terms is truly 'old' and what is demonstrably 'new' in Catholic history and thought? What is genuinely 'traditional', as opposed to being only seemingly so? In putting into operation the decrees of Trent – and then bequeathing us the 'Tridentine' Church – Pope Pius V provided many answers. These 'answers', however, contained tantalizing time bombs and implied further questions, which are still being vehemently debated. In certain important respects, the pontificate of Pius V is more relevant to the modern Church than that of almost any other pope.

Antonio Ghislieri was born of poor parents on 17 January 1504, at Bosco near Alessandria. He was a shepherd until he became a Dominican at 14, taking the name Michele. After studying at Bologna, being ordained (1528) and lecturing for 16 years at Pavia, he was made inquisitor for Como and Bergamo. His zeal brought him to the notice of Cardinal Gian Pietro Carafa, on whose recommendation Julius III appointed him commissary general of the Roman Inquisition in 1551. When Carafa became Pope Paul IV, he named Ghislieri bishop of Nepi and Salvi (1556), cardinal (1557) and finally inquisitor general. He was less in favour with Pius IV because of his intimacy with the Carafa family, but his earnestness, asceticism and evangelical poverty suggested, even to the Spanish ambassador to the Holy See, that he would one day be the pope called for by the times. Nevertheless, his actual election was by no means a foregone conclusion.

The only man of outstanding personality and influence at the conclave, which convened in the middle of December 1565, was Carlo Borromeo, the late pope's nephew. He was an honest, virtuous, narrow-minded man of unmistakable sincerity, who made it clear that he did not desire the papacy for himself. However, it soon became obvious that no serious opposition would be offered to any candidate he selected.

His first nomination was Morone. This caused some surprise, since Morone, though a learned cleric of excellent character, had incurred disfavour with the Inquisition because of wrongful accusations against him, along with England's Cardinal Pole, of being friendly with heretics. Morone, however, was opposed by the erstwhile foes, Farnese and Ferrara. It is interesting, even amusing in its own way, to look at the reasons for the opposition to Morone on the part of these two powerful cardinals, as it exemplifies the comparatively trifling circumstances that can sometimes influence important events. Morone had once been the successful rival in a love affair conducted by Carpi,[1] Farnese's most intimate friend. In the case of Ferrara (who, some years earlier, had been legate at Bologna), Morone had sided with the city against Ferrara in some trivial dispute concerning a water conduit.

Farnese and Ferrara therefore buried the hatchet in their own private feud and, on grounds of conscience (entirely feigned), pointed out to Borromeo that Morone was suspected of liberal tendencies. Borromeo's response, not in the least expected or desired as a result of the Farnese-Ferrara initiative, was to switch his support to the cardinal-archbishop of Alexandria, the forbidding Ghislieri. Farnese and Ferrara were aghast at the suggestion but realized grimly that, once having appealed to Borromeo, they would find it difficult to change his mind. Their desperate appeal to Borromeo to accept the nomination himself having failed, the name of Ghislieri became known to the other conclavists, among whom there now spread a cloud of horror and apprehension.

Ferrara and Farnese were hoisted by their own petard. Such was the awe in which Borromeo was held, there was now no going back. The cardinals, moreover, did not want to appear lukewarm toward Borromeo's robust ideas of reform. Their sudden conversion to such ideas was little less than volcanic and there was a positive rush toward Ghislieri's cubicle. Panic was drowned with an exaggerated show of mock enthusiasm, in remarkably short order.

Ghislieri's election as Pope Pius V (on 7 January 1556) had an extremely unsettling effect on the papal states. There were few subjects who did not have cause to fear this pope, a man of so forbidding a reputation. Among those most reduced to fear were the mendicant friars who infested Rome and the provinces. They knew that they would immediately be ordered to return to their monasteries and conform to the ascetic rules of their Orders, instead of staying on in lodgings in Rome and elsewhere. Here they had done no 'work' except to say Mass daily, in return for the stipends they begged from pious believers desiring Masses to be said for the departed souls of their relations. The rest of their time was spent in taverns or brothels.

As for the clergy higher up, they too could expect an abrupt change in their lifestyle. They did not, in the event, convert to a more virtuous routine but only to a semblance thereof. This, human nature being what it is, often proved more difficult and more irksome. Nor could they, as had been done in the case of Hadrian VI, treat the new pope's wishes with ridicule and contempt. Ultimately, Ghislieri was 'one of them' as well as, into the bargain, being a reformer of unbreakable will and stubbornness. He was personally devoid of any of those weaknesses of the flesh that might have provided a point of contact with his fellow creatures. It was true that, in earlier days, he had fathered at least three illegitimate offspring. But his conversion had sent him to the other extreme and he was now inaccessible to compassion of any kind. In appearance, Pius V was a bundle of yellow skin and shaking bones, bald, with a big white beard and great beak of a nose.

The reign of terror presided over by his predecessor but one now returned with a vengeance. It is surprising that Ghislieri did not take the papal name of Paul, instead of that of the more easy-going Pius. He ostentatiously reversed the efforts of the latter; moreover, he illogically rehabilitated members of the disgraced Carafa family. This brought him political unpopularity, as did his uncompromising stand against any form of state control over the Church. His exalted claims for overriding papal power were inconvenient for the secular rulers, whose support he needed. Nothing, however, was allowed to divert him from his pitiless crusade against heresy.

His immediate subjects, in and around Rome, suffered in a number of small but significant ways. Doctors were forbidden to attend patients who had not confessed within three days. Blasphemy was punished with heavy fines for the rich and flogging for the poor. He sent his spies and informers into every corner. No one was safe. Even the mentally deficient were subjected to examinations on their orthodoxy and condemned to the rack for their drivellings. Pontifical procedures were devoid of any vestige of Christian love or compassion. The commander of the small force which Pius sent to assist the French Catholics was instructed to take no Huguenot prisoners but, instead, to slaughter them all on the spot.

This pope's natural ally was his fellow fanatic, King Philip II of Spain, especially in their mutual hatred of England. This was to have important and lastingly evil consequences, as we shall soon see. For the time being, however, the Spanish king was preoccupied with unrest in various parts of his far-flung dominions. In one example of this, we are faced with the spectacle of his cruelty being so excessive as to attract a rebuke from the normally ruthless Supreme Pontiff.

The Spanish government used the Inquisition as a political as well as a religious weapon. Calvinism had made some headway in the northern part of the Spanish Netherlands and Pius at first encouraged the Spanish to crush the dissenters. This, however, was carried out with such excessive cruelty that even the pope was moved to protest at the excessiveness of their 'zeal'.

Pius devoted his time to pontifical matters out of necessity. But his true heart was in the rooting out of all weakness and evil, as he saw it, in every corner of the Church. Minute regulations were issued as to every branch of the behaviour of the clergy, who could no longer attend theatres or frequent taverns. All bishops had to reside within their sees or risk severe punishment. The pope carefully scrutinized episcopal elections and prevented several scandalous ones. He, for instance, prevented the canons of Halberstadt in northern Germany from electing a six-year-old relative of the duke of Brunswick as their bishop.

As a Dominican, he shared his Order's devotion to St Thomas Aquinas and declared him a Doctor of the Church in 1567. His preoccupation with this, however, was disciplinary rather than scholarly. The new presentation of that medieval theologian's works, in 17 volumes, was badly edited and severely defective. This even had repercussions, as we shall see, in the pope's later liturgical initiatives. His version of Aquinas' works had to be revised in the time of Leo XIII and again, more recently.

Even his attitude toward art was influenced more by austerity than any form of pleasurable attraction. He recoiled from all appearances of taking any aesthetic, let alone sensual, satisfaction from his contemplation of art. It was an appropriate coincidence, in fact, that his pontificate came almost exactly half-way through that period of art (roughly from 1530 to 1590) referred to as Mannerism.

This latter phase represented not so much a reaction against Renaissance art, at its most spectacular, as a transitional stage between this and the eighteenth century, associated with the ornate but voluptuous and naturalistic styles of Baroque and Rococo. There was something of a shifting of the traditional art form favoured by and appropriate to the Italian genius – painting and sculpture – toward music and literature. The former trend is reflected in Pius V's most notable contribution to the arts – his patronage of the musical genius, Palestrina. He made him master of the papal chapel and gave him every encouragement. Thus the mighty composer's work played a key part in the presentation of western liturgy, as definitively 'reformed' by Pius V, for the next four centuries.

After putting away the short-lived sexual laxity of his earlier years, Pius devoted every fibre of his being to the cause of 'reform' as he saw it. Reform of the Church was a counterpart, in his scheme of things, to reform of the person, starting with himself. Under his papal robes the pope continued to wear not only his rough Dominican habit but also a hair-shirt. He looked upon suffering and physical pain as a normal and necessary means of salvation. Just as he welcomed this for himself, he regarded it with complete indifference and lack of all compassion in others. The sight of the most terrible tortures, the cries of agonized humanity, left him unmoved. He led the life of an anchorite, incorruptible and unmovable. He has been accused of taking a sadistic delight in inflicting and witnessing the excruciating torments practised on his hapless victims, but it is far more likely that they produced no reaction whatever on his petrified feelings. He was, one might say, a monomaniac of forcible salvation.

Although Pius V did not distinguish himself as a patron of the arts (apart from his encouragement for Palestrina), he was a supporter of scholarly writers – invariably those still employing Latin, thus reflecting the drift in cultural taste toward the cerebral away from the visual. As to those writers who followed the fashion originally set by Dante and wrote in Italian, Pius was chronically on the look out for compositions excessively humanist in the secular sense, as well as for the slightest whiff of heterodoxy or irreverence. His punishment for blasphemers was that their tongues should be pierced with a red-hot poker. He personally revised and extended the *Index of Forbidden Books* and elevated its status by creating the Congregation of the Index with seven cardinals to vet every new piece of literature that appeared. He tried to destroy all the ancient monuments around Rome, on the grounds that they were the work of heathens.

His 'reforms' penetrated into every corner of people's most private lives. Bachelors were forbidden female servants and nuns were not allowed to keep male dogs. Sexual misconduct of any kind was punished with the utmost ferocity, and sodomites were burned. He was only dissuaded, at the last minute, from making adultery a capital offence. He was shocked by the amount of brothels in Rome, and set in motion a relentless pursuit of prostitutes, especially those catering to prelates. His first plan was that all prostitutes in Rome should be expelled; but this was resisted by the Senate. It was argued that there was always licentiousness where there was celibacy and that, if the prostitutes were banished, no respectable woman would be safe from the attentions of the clergy. Instead, the pope ordered that all prostitutes in the city must be either married or flogged. Those who died under the lash were to be buried in a dungheap without, of course, the benefit of any spiritual ministrator. The survivors were confined to special areas, where they would be seen by as few people as possible. Clerical incontinence was heavily cracked down on by the pope; however, this resulted in a disastrous increase in sodomy among the clergy and he eventually abandoned this particular campaign.

CHAPTER 11. Pope Pius V (1566–72)

With a Dominican in charge of the Vatican, it was natural that the religious Orders should now experience an intensive bout of reform. Branches of certain Orders, some of which had split in the preceding century, were combined, with conventional houses placed under the direction of observants. Teresa of Ávila and her Discalced Carmelites[2] fitted squarely within this context, but just as Teresa and her younger colleague, John of the Cross, encountered trenchant opposition to reform from within their own Order in Spain, so did Pius and Borromeo in their imposition of reform on the religious Orders in Italy. The Humiliati were a small Order based in northern Italy, with a history of splintering into yet smaller parts: precisely the sort of organization that the pope and the cardinal were keen to reform. It was these endeavours that led to the assassination attempt on Borromeo by members of the Order in 1569. He was shot at in his chapel, but escaped. Indeed, his survival was considered to be miraculous and this claim led first to his cult and then to his canonization. The Humiliati were duly suppressed completely, in 1571. By way of contrast, it may be noted that Pius praised the work of the Jesuits and was a personal friend of Borgia (St Francis), which made for smooth relations between the Jesuits and the Holy See during the generalate of one and the pontificate of the other. In 1568 the Society acquired the site in central Rome on which the church of the Gesù was built by Vignola and della Porta.

One of the guiding principles of Pius V's pontificate – as it had been for Charles V and so many other leaders – was peace among Christians and war against the Turk. However, the death of Sultan Süleyman 'the Magnificent' in 1566 brought a lull in the sporadic naval war in the Mediterranean, while peace among Christians was as elusive as ever. Indeed, the shedding of Christian blood on account of confessional differences plumbed new depths of barbarity during Pius' time. The scene of the greatest slaughter was the Low Countries. Philip II left the Netherlands in 1559 and never returned. There was rising tension, on the one hand between the Spanish governors and the native nobility and, on the other, between the Catholic rulers and Calvinist subjects. Native nobles, such as William of Orange, and religious dissenters came increasingly to make common cause against the Spanish. In 1566 Calvinists in the Spanish Netherlands systematically attacked Catholic churches, especially in the more southerly provinces. These were the Iconoclastic Riots, the opening salvos in the Revolt of the Netherlands

(1567–1609). They were followed by bloody reprisals exacted by the duke of Alba. Those opposition leaders who did not go into exile were executed. As already noted, even the pope protested at the severity of Spanish methods.

Although, militarily speaking, Alba's campaigns achieved many of the government's aims, the human cost was immense, as entire communities were slaughtered or fled. As in France, Elizabeth of England provided support for the Protestant rebels. Her opposition towards the papacy had been confirmed in 1561 when she refused to admit a papal nuncio into her realm. Pius IV was minded to excommunicate her on that occasion, but Philip dissuaded him, partly because England could be of use against France and partly because the king thought there was still a chance that Elizabeth might declare for Rome after all. Pius V was not so cautious and issued his Bull of excommunication in 1570. The tragic and long-lasting consequences of this fateful document are considered in more detail below.

With all that has been said about Pius V – mostly unfavourable – how is it that he has been accorded so honoured a place in papal history by most writers? The short answer to this is that he was officially a saint, the only pope to be canonized between Celestine V (1294–96) and Pius X (1903–14). (Benedict XI looked to be in the running for the honour but only made it as far as beatification, by Pope Clement XII, in 1776.)

Pius V, it is true, personified to perfection the criteria for sainthood as then conceived by the Church. In an age of licentiousness, his sexual behaviour was exemplary, to the point of excess. His devotions were lengthy and his mortifications rigid. And he conformed totally to the required characteristics of an ideal reformer. His efforts against not only individual heretics but also heretical countries were hailed as heroic.

What then of that hidden 'dimension', of which we have spoken, to the conventional record of his pontificate? The fact that his achievements were considered to be heroic and saintly tells us much about the official mind of the Church when reviewing an aberrant period in its history. The methods, however, whereby he accumulated glory for the Church were, in some cases, little short of barbaric. Herein lies the ultimate paradox of this particular papal reign.

Reference in detail to one particular achievement on the part of Pius V has been deferred until now because of its tremendous importance in Christian history. Successive popes in the fifteenth and sixteenth centuries were urged to be vigorous and unflinching in their prosecution of the great crusade against the infidel. History had been changed for ever, in 1453, by the fall of Constantinople to the Ottoman Turks. Christian Europe had never been the same since this fateful date. The haemorrhage of Greek scholarship from the Orthodox East is seen by many writers as the real inspiration for the Renaissance in the West. It had ever been the ambition, since 1453, to recapture Constantinople for Christianity, and otherwise to push back the growing advance of the Turks. The latter, by the mid-sixteenth century, had become virtual masters of the sea.

The 1571 battle of Lepanto was an illustrious victory, attracting the admiring attention of many writers, including Miguel Cervantes who was actually present. Years later, it produced a rousing lyric poem from G.K. Chesterton who wrote:

> The Pope has cast his arms abroad for agony and loss
> And called the Kings of Christendom for swords about the cross...

The Turks had attacked Cyprus and looked like making the Mediterranean their private lake. The pope's pleas fell on deaf ears as far as France and Germany were concerned, but were enthusiastically received in Spain and Venice. On 7 October the Turkish fleet was engaged at Lepanto by a combined Christian fleet, commanded by Philip II's natural brother, Don John of Austria and Marcantonio Colonna. The magnificent victory was not without onerous loss. The pope personally sent several caravels to join the Spanish and Venetian fleet, which amounted to 250 vessels, without counting the convoys. The victory cost the lives of 25,000 to 30,000 men, with 80 galleys sunk and 117 captured. The Turks, however, lost their command of the sea.

Though the Turks had a superior number of galleys, their weapons consisted mostly of bows and arrows, inefficient against armour. The fact that, even so, they proved difficult to defeat is a witness to the ferocity of the hand-to-hand fighting. The galley slaves on the Spanish and Venetian vessels begged for their liberty to join the fray and fought like demons. They liberated their Christian fellow-sufferers in the Turkish vessels, who turned on their captors and hastened the victory. The sea, says one chronicler, was dyed with blood for leagues around.

The victory of the Cross over the Crescent was a notable turning point. Don John of Austria became the most popular hero of Christendom. For Pius V, it was a matter of consummate satisfaction and he bathed in the reflected glory. All the bells in Rome peeled in jubilation and commands were issued for public rejoicings. It was the most important single event in allowing Pius V's pontificate to be remembered with apparent glory.

It is sad to have to recall, however, that despite the rejoicings over Lepanto nothing could dispel the gloom brooding over the papal states at this time. Every man, woman and child lived in constant fear. The horror of the Inquisition, ever present on the doorstep, made the Turkish menace seem very remote to the average citizen of Rome. Severe as were the sufferings of this pope's Christian subjects, those of his Jewish ones were even worse, as the humiliations heaped on them by Paul IV were continued and, in some cases, intensified.

The two aspects of Pope Pius V's pontificate which had the most significant long-term results are, ironically, those which have been the least written about. One was the effect of his policy, as part of his fanatical campaign against heresy, as regards England. The other was his work in the theological-liturgical life of the Church. They are not treated here with the extensiveness which they intrinsically deserve, because a detailed exposition might prove tedious to those not particularly interested in matters of largely internal Roman Catholic concern. Any description of Pius V's pontificate, however, that did not take some account of them would be seriously incomplete. Furthermore, both matters have, for various reasons, been distinctly underrated as to their effect on Catholic history, particularly by Roman Catholics themselves. One of the matters in question particularly concerned England.

Pius V was a convinced misogynist, but he reserved a special hatred for Queen Elizabeth I of England. In his eyes, she was not only a heretic but also a sinner. She was, moreover, he claimed, illegitimate and not the rightful monarch of England. This distinction belonged rather to the Catholic Mary Stuart, daughter of King James VI of Scotland, later James I of England. It was for this reason that Pius embarked on a policy that was, in every way, disastrous and, for English Catholics, needlessly tragic.

The pope's mistaken policy was partly based on the fact that he was woefully ill-advised on the actual situation of Roman Catholics in England. It is true that the ascendancy of Protestantism in England had been firmly established soon after Elizabeth had come to the throne (in 1558). The Act of Supremacy was passed, confirming the official position of the Church of England, of which the queen was declared supreme governor. Non-adherence to the Anglican Church, however, was not subject to sanctions more onerous than fairly nominal fines. For the first 12 years of Elizabeth's reign, Protestants and Catholics lived side by side in undisturbed amity. None was molested for his attendance at church, even Catholic, provided it was done discreetly. All was changed as of 1570, when the pope issued a pronouncement whose evil consequences for England lasted for over two centuries and still have reverberations today. For it was in this year that the pope solemnly excommunicated the English queen and purported to depose her. One particular passage of his corresponding Bull, *Regnans in excelsis (Reigning in Heaven)* is worth quoting as it starkly affirms the exorbitant nature of papal claims at this time.

Pius V solemnly proclaimed that:

> He who reigns in heaven, to whom is given all power in heaven and on earth, the one Holy, Catholic and Apostolic church, outside of which there is no salvation, is to be governed in the fullness of authority to one man only, that is to say to Peter, the Prince of the Apostles and to his successor, the Roman Pontiff. This one ruler He established as prince over all nations and kingdoms, to root up, destroy, dissipate, scatter, plant and build, so that the Holy Spirit might bind together a faithful people, united in the bond of mutual charity, and present it safe and sound to the Saviour.

The pope not only presumed to 'dethrone' the English queen but – and herein lay the most devastating and tragic part of his declaration – he solemnly absolved all her Catholic 'subjects' of any legitimate allegiance to her. Worse still, he went further and burdened them in conscience with the obligation, binding under danger of grave sin, to rebel against her and do all in their power to ensure her removal. 'Removal' did not mean merely deposition but, if necessary, elimination by murder. The Catholics of England, from that moment onwards, were handed a 'licence to kill' that was to prove immensely dangerous, ultimately to themselves. Indeed, it was more than just a licence; it was a duty. And, as such, it caused endless hardship, bloodshed, hatred and misery.

English Catholics, despite themselves, were turned overnight into traitors if they remained loyal to their country. It is herein that the situation emerged which has since been so often underestimated and misunderstood, particularly by Catholics. Those members of the 'ancient faith' who, mostly under Queen Elizabeth I, suffered a horrible death, have long been honoured by their co-religionists for their bravery in dying for the faith. The supreme irony, however, is that it was not for their *faith* as such that they died. They were executed as traitors. And it is in this respect that lies the vital difference between the fate suffered by these Catholics and by those Protestants burned at the stake by Elizabeth's predecessor, Mary Tudor. For the victims of 'Bloody Mary' were executed as heretics. This was a capital offence in the eyes of the regrettably fanatical Catholic queen. The resultant severity with which she dealt with so large a number of 'heretics' in her realm (including the archbishop of Canterbury, Thomas Cranmer) has never been forgotten.

Queen Elizabeth's victims, on the other hand, were hanged (rather than burned, as was Mary's preferred method) as traitors – which, thanks to the action of the pope, they were. The courageous but foolhardy men, and some women, who suffered under Elizabeth I have been remembered with glory in English Catholic folklore as the English Martyrs, and have been duly canonized. Owing, however, to the pope's active encouragement that they should rebel against their crown and government, there were several serious traitorous conspiracies during this reign, such as the Ridolfi plot, the Casket plot and the Babington conspiracy. The most elaborate conspiracy of all, coming in the following reign, became one of the most famous of its kind in all history, namely the Gunpowder plot. The hardship and misery, along with the several hundred unnecessary and fruitless deaths, brought upon England by Pope Pius V, is truly heart-breaking.

The pope compounded his guilt in this regard by attempting, with the help of King Philip of Spain, to mount an invasion of England. Philip was too preoccupied elsewhere to co-operate actively at this time in any such enterprise. The ill-fated (from the Spanish point of view) Armada did not sail until 1588. The pope contented himself, meanwhile, by sending his 'spies' to England to carry on the work of subverting the government. Sturdy, punitive legislation against them was, not unnaturally, provoked. The victims, many of them Jesuits such as the celebrated Edmund Campion, suffered death not, as many Catholics hold, for the 'crime' of celebrating Mass but for that of plotting against the throne.

The other important matter with which Pius V was concerned was the implementation of the decrees of the Council of Trent. One of his principal actions in this regard was to authorize the official form of the 'Tridentine Mass' (sometimes, though misleadingly, referred to as the 'Latin Mass'). Primarily as a rejection of various new Protestant ideas as to how the central Christian act of worship should be observed, the Council decreed that the form of the Eucharist, as it had developed in medieval times, should henceforth be normative. Thus enshrined for 400 years was a form of the Catholic Eucharist, or Mass as it had come to be called, which many modern 'traditionalist' Catholics consider to be a time-honoured and venerable expression of Catholic antiquity and even apostolic integrity. By a similar token, they consider the Mass that replaced the Tridentine version, by order of Pope Paul VI in 1969, to have been something entirely new and in conflict with traditional Catholic theology and liturgy.

Nothing could be further from the truth. The so-called 'new' Mass is in fact based, in modern form, on the Eucharist as celebrated by the Christians of the earliest centuries. Called 'The Breaking of Bread' or 'Lord's Supper', it began to disappear in the early Middle Ages. The Mass became more and more the preserve of the clergy, to serve the principles of priesthood (or 'priestcraft' as the enemies of such a form of religion call it). The people became increasingly separated from the action of the Mass, as reflected in the architecture of medieval churches. The doctrine of transubstantiation brought an appearance of magic to the manner in which the real presence of the Lord took place upon the altar.

No magic, of course, was actually involved, but its very semblance was enough to symbolize the great gap that opened up between Catholics and Protestants over how their central act of worship should be conducted. Eventually a pope (Leo XIII, at the end of the nineteenth century) declared Anglicans incapable of conducting a 'valid' eucharistic service. In declaring Anglican Orders 'null and void', he thus preserved and indefinitely extended the Catholic-Anglican rift.

All of this, indirectly, can be traced to the work of Pius V. Modern 'traditionalists' – at least those of the more extreme kind – eschew many of the recent liturgical reforms. They tend, for example, to sit staring po-facedly ahead of them when the congregation is exhorted to exchange a sign of peace. Little do they realize that there is no older practice in the whole of Christian history. The first Christians, being pacifists, greeted each other with this sign on meeting and at the beginning of every eucharistic service. They were forced to abandon their pacifist ideals when Christianity became, in the fourth century, the official religion of the Roman Empire. Soon afterwards, St Augustine of Hippo developed the theory of the 'just war', responsible, as it has been through history, for so many millions of deaths.

One last point on this general theme is that Latin is still the official language of the Church though, in practice, its liturgy is now ordinarily performed in the local language – the vernacular. This is to conform, as desired by Pope Paul VI, with the very ancient principle that the worship of the Church should be carried out in language that the ordinary Christians could understand. The very first such language was Aramaic, then Greek and finally Latin – as this was, for the next 1,000 years, the language of the man in the street in what we now call western Europe, i.e. the territory equating roughly to the Roman Empire, before the transfer of Rome as a capital to Constantinople.

While the principle of using the vernacular language is thus very ancient, the use of Latin was not meant to be normative or perpetual and would have been abandoned had it not been for the espousal of the vernacular by Protestantism. Any concession to the latter, real or imagined, was and is still strongly resented by triumphalist and hard-core traditionalists. They have never entirely relinquished their literal adherence to the (long since heavily qualified) proposition that the Church of Rome is the one true Church, outside which there can be no salvation.

It is hoped that these points have not been commented upon in too much detail, directly relevant as they are, now more than ever, to the pontificate of Pius V, effectively the last of the Renaissance popes. Three weeks after he died, on 1 May 1572, there occurred the death of a genuine saint. He was a man whose outlook and career ushered in a new and more salubrious period of Catholic history. He was none other than the great-grandson of Alexander VI, St Francis Borgia.

APPENDIX I: HENRY CHARLES LEA

The author Henry Charles Lea deserves a short section to himself. He was a distinguished Episcopalian scholar from Philadelphia, whose works today are comparatively unknown to Catholic readers. Theirs is the loss. According to W.E.H Lecky (author of *History of European Morals*, Watts, London, 1869; LECKY 1869), Lea's history of celibacy was the most important work of its kind to come out of the New World. The Anglican bishop Mandell Crichton (see CREIGHTON 1897) said of Lea, 'If you don't know Lea's books, read them, for no one knows more about the institutions of the medieval Church'. Historian Lord Acton (1834–1902), notoriously backward in commending the works of others, wrote: 'Lea has made the most important contribution of the new world to the religious history of the old... Nothing in European literature can compare with this, the centre and substratum of Mr Lea's great history'.

Henry Charles Lea's works include:

The Eve of the Reformation, Cambridge Modern History, Cambridge, 1902 (LEA 1902).

A History of Auricular Confession and Indulgences in the Latin Church, 2 vols, Lea Brothers, Philadelphia, 1896; reprinted Greenwood Press, New York, 1968 (LEA 1896a).

A History of the Inquisition in Spain, 4 vols, Macmillan, New York and London, 1906–07 (LEA 1906–07).

A History of the Inquisition of the Middle Ages, 3 vols, Harper Brothers, New York, 1887; reprinted Russell & Russell, New York, 1958 (LEA 1887).

Materials Toward a History of Witchcraft, 3 vols, University of Pennsylvania Press, Philadelphia, 1939; reprinted T. Yoseloff, New York, 1957 (LEA 1896b).

Studies in Church History, H.C. Lea, Philadelphia, 1883 (LEA 1883).

APPENDIX II: TIMELINE

1434	Cosimo de' Medici returns from exile to Florence
1447	Election of Nicholas V
	Visconti line in Milan dies out
1448	Concordat of Vienna
1449	Felix V (anti-pope) abdicates in Avignon
1450	Nicholas V declares a Jubilee Year
1452	Friedrich III crowned Emperor of the Holy Roman Empire
1453	Stefano Porcari plot to set fire to the Vatican and end papal rule
	Turks take Constantinople
1455	Nicholas V grants exclusive rights to explore the African coast to the Portuguese
	Election of Calixtus III
1458	Election of Pope Pius II
1459	Serbia and the Morea (Peloponnese) fall to the Ottomans
1460	Congress at Mantua
1461	Coronation of Louis XI of France
1463	Bosnia falls to the Ottomans
1464	Election of Paul II
1470	Coronation of Charles VIII of France
1471	Election of Sixtus IV
1478	Pazzi conspiracy
	Sixtus issues Bull sanctioning new inquisition in Castile (becomes the Spanish Inquisition)
1484	Election of Innocent VIII
	Innocent issues Bull ordering inquisition in Germany to deal severely with witches
1492	Fall of Granada to the Spanish
	Election of Alexander VI
	Cibo castles affair
	Decoration of the Appartamento Borgia begins

1493	Marriage of Lucrezia Borgia (Alexander's daughter) and Giovanni Sforza, Lord of Pesaro
	Alexander issues Bull to determine division between Portugal and Spain of new land discoveries
	Maximilian I becomes Emperor of the Holy Roman Empire
1494	Coronation of Alfonso II, King of Naples
	French army invades Italy
	Medici family exiled from Florence
	Savonarola preaches a series of powerful sermons on the reform of the Florentine constitution
	French army marches into Rome on 31 December
1495	Alexander regains control of Rome through peaceful negotiation (January)
	French army marches to Naples
	Alfonso II abdicates in favour of his son, Fernando II (Ferrantino); both flee to Sicily
	Charles VIII of France crowns himself King of Naples
	Formation of the Holy League (Milan, Venice, Spain, the papacy and Emperor Maximilian), ostensibly to fight the Turks but in reality to defend Italy, the papacy and the Holy Roman Empire
	French driven out of Naples; King Ferrantino restored to the throne
1497	Lucrezia Borgia and Giovanni Sforza divorce
	Juan Borgia, duke of Gandia and favourite son of Alexander, is murdered in Rome
1498	Trial and execution of Savonarola
	Death of Charles VIII of France; coronation of Louis XII
	Marriage of Lucrezia Borgia and Don Alfonso of Bisceglie
	Cesare Borgia renounces the priesthood and becomes Duke of Valentinois ('il Valentino')
1499	Marriage of Cesare Borgia and Charlotte d'Albret
	French army takes Milan, with Cesare Borgia at French king's side. Borgias see this as an opportunity to bring recalcitrant papal states to heel.
1500	Jubilee Year in Rome
	Treaty of Granada divides kingdom of Naples between France and Spain
	Don Alfonso is attacked, and later dies
	Cesare Borgia takes cities of Pesaro, Rimini and Faenza
1501	Naples surrenders to Cesare and the French army; in accordance with Treaty of Granada, Louis XII of France becomes King of Naples
1502	Marriage of Lucrezia Borgia and Alfonso d'Este

1503	Death of Alexander VI; Cesare seriously ill Election of Pius III Election of Julius II
1504	1st Treaty of Blois – alliance between Julius II, Maximilian and Louis XII to expel the Venetians from the Romagna
1506	Julius II ousts the ruling Baglioni family from Perugia and the Bentivoglio from Bologna Julius lays the foundation stone of the new St Peter's
1507	Cesare Borgia murdered, near Viana
1508	League signed between Louis XII, Maximilian, Ferdinand of Aragon, the papacy and a number of smaller states – supposedly to unite against the Ottomans, but in reality directed against Venice
1509	Battle of Ghiaradadda
1512	The Medici return to Florence Start of the Lateran Council (continues until 1517)
1513	Election of Leo X 2nd Treaty of Blois – alliance between France and Venice
1515	Francis I is crowned King of France Concordat of Bologna
1517	Alfonso Petrucci conspiracy to poison Leo X Martin Luther nails his 95 theses to the door of the Schlosskirche at Wittenberg
1519	Charles (King of Castile since 1506 and of Aragon since 1516) becomes Holy Roman Emperor on death of Maximilian I
1521	Luther excommunicated
1522	Election of Hadrian VI Diet of Nuremberg
1523	Election of Clement VII
1524	Peasants' Revolt, Germany French army captures Milan
1525	French army defeated at Pavia Emperor Charles V reinstates Sforza in Milan
1526	Holy alliance agreed between the papacy, Venice, Milan and France against Emperor Charles V Attempted coup by Cardinal Colonna to overthrow the papacy

1527	German and Spanish armies unite and march on Rome
	6 May: Sack of Rome
	5 June: Clement VII surrenders to Charles V
1533	Clement refuses to allow dissolution of Henry VIII's marriage to Catherine of Aragon
1534	Election of Paul III
	Act of Supremacy in England – Thomas More and John Fisher executed for refusing to take accompanying oath
1536	Thomas Cromwell oversees first phase of the dissolution of the monasteries
	John Calvin publishes Institutio religionis christianae (Institutes of Christian Religion)
	Luther draws up the Schmalkaldic Articles
1537	Catholic episcopate abolished in Denmark
1540	Constitutions of Society of Jesus (Jesuits) submitted for examination; confirmed by Paul III. Ignatius Ioyola elected as the first General of the Order
1541	Diet of Regensburg
	Ignatius Ioyola completes Spiritual Exercises
1542	Bartolomé de Las Casas publishes Brevísima relación de la destrución de las Indias (Short Treatise on the Destruction of the Indies)
	Foundation of the Holy Office of the Inquisition
1545	Council of Trent opens
1546	Francis Borgia founds a Jesuit college at Gandia
1547	Coronation of Edward VI of England
	Coronation of Henry II of France
	Assassination of Paul III's son, Pierluigi
	Council of Trent moved to Bologna due to epidemic
1550	Election of Julius III
1551	Council of Trent reassembled
1552	Council of Trent suspended
1555	Election of Marcellus II
	Election of Paul IV
1559	Treaty of Cateau-Cambrésis concluded to the 'Italian Wars', begun in 1494
	Election of Pius IV
1562	Re-opening of the Council of Trent
	Start of the Wars of Religion (ran until 1598)

1566	Election of Pius V
	Death of Sultan Süleyman 'the Magnificent'
1567	Pius V declares St Thomas Aquinas a Doctor of the Church
1570	Pius V excommunicates Elizabeth I, turning English Catholics into traitors if they remained loyal to their country
1571	Battle of Lepanto

APPENDIX III: THE ROAD TO THE PONTIFICATE

Nicholas V (1447–55)	Formerly Cardinal Tommaso Parentucelli, having been papal legate at the Diet of Frankfurt
Calixtus III (1455–58)	Formerly Cardinal Alfonso Borja; uncle of Alexander VI
Pius II (1458–64)	Formerly Cardinal Aeneus Silvius Piccolomini; uncle of Pius III
Paul II (1464–71)	Formerly Cardinal Pietro Barbo; nephew of Eugenius IV
Sixtus IV (1471–84)	Formerly Cardinal Francesco della Rovere; uncle of Julius II
Innocent VIII (1484–92)	Formerly Cardinal Giovanni Battista Cibo
Alexander VI (1492–1503)	Formerly Cardinal Rodrigo Borgia; vice-chancellor to five popes; nephew of Calixtus III
Pius III (22 September – 18 October 1503)	Formerly Cardinal Francesco Todeschini-Piccolomini; nephew of Pius II
Julius II (1503–13)	Formerly Cardinal Giuliano della Rovere; nephew of Sixtus IV
Leo X (1513–21)	Formerly Cardinal Giovanni de' Medici (son of Lorenzo the Magnificent)
Hadrian VI (1522–23)	Formerly Adriaan Florenszoon Dedal, tutor to Emperor Charles
Clement VII (1523–34)	Formerly Cardinal Giulio de' Medici (nephew of Lorenzo the Magnificent)
Paul III (1534–49)	Formerly Cardinal Alessandro Farnese, due to intercession of his sister, Giulia Farnese (lover of Alexander VI)
Julius III (1550–55)	Formerly Cardinal Giovanni Maria Ciocchi del Monti
Marcellus II (9 April – 1 May 1555)	Formerly Cardinal Marcello Cervini
Paul IV (1555–59)	Formerly Cardinal Gian Pietro Carafa

Pius IV (1559–65)	Formerly Cardinal Angelo de' Medici, having been secretary to Paul III
Pius V (1566–72)	Formerly Cardinal Antonio Ghislieri, inquisitor general under Julius III

NOTES

PART I: POPES OF THE EARLY RENAISSANCE

Chapter One

1.   PASTOR 1901–53, vol. 2 (1952), p. 166.
2.   *Collectionis Bullarum Brevium aliorumque Diplomatum sacrosanctae Basilicae Vaticannae.* Vol II (Rome, 1760), pp 123–24. Quoted in WESTFALL 1974, p. 19.
3.   DUFFY 1998, p. 137.
4.   PASTOR 1901–53, vol. 2 (1952), p. 166.
5.   Treaties made between the papacy and a secular power are known as *concordats*, a well-known one being that between Pope Pius XI and Germany, on 20 July 1933.

Chapter Two

1.   Rome, Archv Cent. Stato, cited in Jane Turner (ed.), *The Dictionary of Art* (Grove, New York, 1996), vol. 26, p. 267.
2.   JOHNSON 1981, p. 43.
3.   FUSERO 1972, p. 85.

Chapter Three

1.   MITCHELL 1962, p. 46.
2.   PICCOLOMINI/GABEL & GRAGG 1988.
3.   Pius' only major Roman building project, the Benediction loggia at St Peter's, dates from the same middle years of the pontificate. Inspired in design by the Colosseum, the loggia was probably intended to extend right across the façade of the basilica, but only a portion of it was completed prior to the demolition of old St Peter's.
4.   PICCOLOMINI/GABEL & GRAGG 1988.
5.   PICCOLOMINI/GABEL & GRAGG 1988.
6.   PICCOLOMINI/GABEL & GRAGG 1988.
7.   PICCOLOMINI/GABEL & GRAGG 1988.
8.   PICCOLOMINI/GABEL & GRAGG 1988.
9.   PICCOLOMINI/GABEL & GRAGG 1988.

Chapter Five

1.   HOWE 1978, p. 64.
2.   GRAFTON 1993, p. xiii.

Chapter Six

1.   CREIGHTON 1897, vol. IV, p. 148.

2. COFFIN 1977, p. 95.

3. The Villa Belvedere was connected to the Vatican Palace, in the sixteenth century, by Bramante's Cortile del Belvedere. Its interiors were substantially altered in the eighteenth century by Pius VI. The one open-air vaulted loggia now forms the Galleria delle Statue of the Vatican Museums.

4. INFESSURA/TOMMASINI 1890, p. 279.

5. COFFIN 1977.

6. J. Schulz, 'Pinturicchio and the Revival of Antiquity', *Journal of the Warburg and Courtauld Institutes*, vol. XXV (1962), p. 40.

7. VASARI/BONDELLA 1998, p. 253.

8. Agostino Taja, *Descrizione del Palazzo Apostolico Vaticano* (Rome, 1750): G.B. Chattard, *Nuova Descrizione del Vaticano* (Rome, 1767).

9. VASARI/BONDELLA 1998, p. 247

10. COFFIN 1977.

PART II: POPE ALEXANDER VI (1492–1503)

Chapter One

1. GUICCIARDINI/ALEXANDER 1972, p. 1490.

2. GUICCIARDINI/ALEXANDER 1972, p. xviii. Italics added.

3. Stefano Infessura, *Diarium Romanae Urbis* (Rome, 1494).

4. FERRARA 1942, p. 108.

5. FERRARA 1942.

6. FERRARA 1942, p. 109.

7. JOHNSON 1981, p. 88.

8. Jacopo Nardi, *Istorie Florentine*, Book I (Florence, 1838–41), p. 9.

9. FERRARA 1942, pp 113–14.

10. A. Leonetti, *Papa Alessandro VI*, vol. 1 (Bologna, 1880), p. 106.

11. *Secret Archives of the Vatican: Innocentius VIII*, register 682, folio 251, quoted in FERRARA 1942. Italics added.

12. Benedetto Croce, *La Spagna nella vita Italiana*, quoted in FERRARA 1942, p. 9. Italics added.

13. In Spain, Jews who had converted to Christianity were popularly known as Marranos. This was not a term of respect for those who had made morally courageous decisions. Rather, it was a term of racist abuse.

14. JOHNSON 1981, p. 64.

15. JOHNSON 1981.

16. Gaspare da Verona, *Le vite di Paolo II*, quoted in MALLETT 1969, p. 81.

17. William Shakespeare, *The Tragedy of Julius Caesar*, edited by Horwood Furness Junion

(The New Variorum Shakespeare, Philadelphia, 1913).

18. Pope Alexander VI, *Statua et novae reformationes Urbis Romae* (Book IV, folio 1).

Chapter Two

1. Peter De Roo, as example – see ALFANO 2002 for reference.
2. JOHNSON 1981, p. 94.
3. FERRARA 1942, p. 123.
4. JOHNSON 1981, p. 96.
5. It may be recalled that Alexander lifted the censures against Pico, the arch-syncretist of the later fifteenth century.
6. Some enthusiasts have tried to identify Pinturicchio's exceptionally beautiful Virgin Mary as 'la bella Giulia' Farnese, Alexander's mistress at the time the room was decorated, or even with Vanozza Catanei.
7. Two paintings by Bartolomeo Veneto have been supposed to be portraits of Lucrezia: *Flora* (Frankfurt, Stadelsches Kunstinstitut) and *Portrait of a Woman* (London, National Gallery).
8. Biblioteca Apostolica Vaticana, Borg. Lat. 425.
9. Madrid, Museo Nacional del Prado.
10. Prague, Narodni Galerie v Praze.
11. Antwerp, Koninklijk Museum voor Schone Kunsten
12. Quoted in CECCHI 1982, p. 9.

Chapter Three

1. Discussed by N. Rubinstein, 'Savonarola on the Government of Florence', in FLETCHER & SHAW 2000**,** pp 42–54.
2. L. Alberi, *Relazioni Venete*, series I, vol. 4 (Venice, 1840), pp 15 and 16.
3. FERRARA 1942, pp 193–94.
4. JOHNSON 1981, p. 108.
5. JOHNSON 1981, p. 113.

Chapter Four

1. JOHNSON 1981, p. 115.
2. VILLARI 1888.
3. VILLARI 1888, p. 384.
4. FERRARA 1942, pp 235–36.
5. FERRARA 1942, p. 236.
6. JOHNSON 1981, p. 126.
7. FERRARA 1942, p. 248.
8. FERRARA 1942, p. 250.
9. JOHNSON 1981, p. 128.

10. CELANI 1906 (under the date of 14 February 1498.)
11. FERRARA 1942, p. 254.

Chapter Five

1. Quoted in BAUMGARTNER 1996, p. 51.
2. Quoted in GREGOROVIUS 1948, p. 106.
3. Quoted in GREGOROVIUS 1948, p. 111.
4. PARKER 1963, p. 194.

Chapter Six

1. GREGOROVIUS 1948, p. 159.
2. JOHNSON 1981, p. 167.
3. JOHNSON 1981, p. 169.
4. Dispatch of Giustinian of 7 August 1502.
5. BERTELLI 1964, pp 386–87.
6. BERTELLI 1964, p. 392.
7. GIUSTINIAN/VILLARI 1876, vol. 1, p. 298.
8. Bernardino Zambotti, *Giornale Ferrarese*, 6 January 1503.
9. FERRARA 1942, p. 395.
10. JOHNSON 1981, p. 175.

Chapter Seven

1. MALLETT 1969, p. 13.
2. PARKER 1963, pp 225–26.
3. ALFANO 2002.
4. Quoted in HILLGARTH 1996, p. 119.
5. Quoted in HILLGARTH 1996, p. 120.
6. ALFANO 2002.
7. GREGOROVIUS 1948, pp 187–88.
8. V. Nutton, 'The rise of Medical Humanism: Ferrars, 1464–1555', *Renaissance Studies* 11, 1 (1997).
9. GREGOROVIUS 1948, pp 187–88.
10. *Lord Beaconsfield's Letters*, 1830–52, ed. R. Disraeli (John Murray, London, 1887), p. 139.
11. ALFANO 2002.

Chapter Eight

1. FERRARA 1942, p. 27.
2. FERRARA 1942, p. 20.
3. FERRARA 1942, p. 32.

4. FERRARA 1942, p. 30.
5. FERRARA 1942, p. 35.
6. FERRARA 1942, p. 65.
7. FERRARA 1942, p. 66.
8. FERRARA 1942, p. 211.
9. FERRARA 1942, p. 248.
10. FERRARA 1942, p. 255.
11. FERRARA 1942, p. 259.
12. FERRARA 1942, p. 157.
13. FERRARA 1942, p. 105.
14. FERRARA 1942, p. 149.
15. FERRARA 1942, p. 409.
16. FERRARA 1942, p. 414.
17. JOHNSON 1981, p. 189.
18. MALLETT 1969

PART III: POPES OF THE HIGH RENAISSANCE AND COUNTER-REFORMATION

Chapter 1

1. JOHNSON 1981, p. 179.
2. JOHNSON 1981, p. 181.
3. JOHNSON 1981, p. 181.

Chapter 2

1. JOHNSON 1981, p. 182.
2. BERTELLI 1964, vol. II, pp 631–32.
3. Quoted in BRADFORD 1976, p. 252.
4. JOHNSON 1981, p. 183.

Chapter 3

1. PIRIE 1935.
2. For a full account of the Petrucci 'conspiracy', see LOWE 1993, pp 104–13.
3. GUICCIARDINI/ALEXANDER 1972, p. xviii. Italics added.

Chapter 5

1. CHAMBERLAIN 1970, p. 260.
2. CELLINI/BULL 1999.
3. CHAMBERLAIN 1970, p. 278.

4. CHAMBERLAIN 1970, p. 280.
5. CELLINI/BULL 1999.
6. CHAMBERLAIN 1970, p 285.
7. CHAMBERLAIN 1970, p. 285.

Chapter 6

1. See HALLMAN 1985 for this and other practices.
2. Museo Nazionale, Naples.
3. Pronounced 'Pool'. A bitter enemy of Pope Paul IV, Pole was nearly elected pope in 1549 and was the last (Roman) Catholic Archbishop of Canterbury.
4. Another name that could be added is that of the neo-Latin Marcantonio Flaminio (1498–1550), who was briefly Pole's secretary.
5. His chief field of study was the early 'Fathers' of the Church.
6. Religious Orders, such as the Franciscans and Carmelites, consisted of first Orders and second Orders respectively, made up of priests and nuns, and a third 'Order' of laymen, or 'tertiaries'. The Benedictine equivalents of tertiaries were called oblates.
7. O'MALLEY 1993b, p. 72.

Chapter 7

1. PASTOR 1901–53, vol. XIII, p. 178. The buildings date from 1585.
2. The Congregation of the Oratory was founded in 1564.

Chapter 10

1. Known to history as Mary, Queen of Scots.

Chapter 11

1. Girolamo da Carpi, Ferrarese painter (1501–66).
2. Discalced meant reformed (literally 'without socks', i.e. wearing sandals).

BIBLIOGRAPHIC HANDLIST

ABULAFIA 1995. David Abulafia (ed.), *The French Descent into Italy, 1494–95: Antecedents and Effects*, Ashgate Publishing, Aldershot, 1995.

ADY 1913. Cecilia M. Ady, *Pius II*, Methuen, London, 1913.

ALEXANDER 1969. Sydney Alexander: *The History of Italy*, Princeton University Press, Princeton, NJ, 1969.

ALFANO 2002. *I Borgia*, ed. Carla Alfano, Learco Andalò and Felipe V. Garín Llombart, exhibition catalogue, Electa, Milan, 2002.

ANGLO 1969. Sydney Anglo, *Machiavelli: A Dissection*, Paladin, London, 1969.

ANTONOVICS 1970. A.V. Antonovics, 'Counter-Reformation cardinals, 1534–1590', *European Studies Review* 2 (1970), pp 301–27.

ATWATER 1939. Donald Atwater, *A Dictionary of Popes*, London, 1939.

BAIGENT & LEIGH 1999. Michael Baigent and Richard Leigh, *The Inquisition*, Viking, London, 1999.

BAINTON 1950. Roland H. Bainton, *Here I Stand: A Life of Martin Luther*, Mentor, New York, 1950.

BATAILLON 1966. Marcel Bataillon, *Erasmo y Espag a: estudios sobre la historia espiritual del siglo xvi*, Mexico, 1966.

BAUMGARTNER 1996. Frederic J. Baumgartner, *Louis XII*, Macmillan, Basingstoke, 1996.

BELLONCI 1939. Maria Bellonci, *Lucrezia Borgia: sua vita e suoi tempi*, Milan, 1939.

BELLONCI/WALL 1953. Maria Bellonci, *The Life and Times of Lucrezia Borgia*, tr. Bernard and Barbara Wall, Phoenix Press, London, 1953.

BEAN ET AL 1964. J.M.W. Bean and others, *The Popes: A Concise Biographical History*, Burns & Oates, New York, 1964.

BENZI 1997. Fabio Benzi, *Palaces of Rome*, Thames & Hudson, London, 1997.

BERTELLI 1964. *Le legazioni e commissarie di Niccolo Machiavelli*, ed. Sergio Bertelli, Milan, 1964.

BOSSY 1985. John Bossy, *Christianity in the West, 1400–1700*, Oxford University Press, Oxford, 1985.

BRADFORD 1976. Sarah Bradford, *Cesare Borgia: His Life and Times*, Macmillan, London, 1976.

BRAUDEL 1976. Fernand Braudel, *The Mediterranean World in the Age of Philip II*, 2 vols, Collins, London, 1976.

BRECHT 1985–93. Martin Brecht, *Martin Luther*, 3 vols, English translation, Fortress, Minneapolis, 1985–93.

BREISACH 1967. Ernst Breisach, *Caterina Sforza, a Renaissance Virago*, University of Chicago Press, Chicago, 1967.

BURCHARD 1963. Johann Burchard, *At the Court of the Borgias*, Folio Society, London, 1963.

BURCHARD/PARKER 1963. Johann Burchard, *At the Court of the Borgia* (abridged), ed. and trans. Geoffrey Parker, Folio Society, London, 1963.

CAMERON 1991. Euan Cameron, *The European Reformation*, Oxford University Press, Oxford, 1991.

CAMPBELL 2003. Gordon Campbell, *The Oxford Dictionary of the Renaissance*, Oxford University Press, Oxford, 2003.

CARLI 1960. Enzo Carli, *Il Pinturicchio*, Electa, Milan, 1960.

CASTIGLIONE/BULL 2004. Baldassare Castiglione, *The Book of the Courtier (Il libro del cortegiano)*, ed and trans George Bull, Penguin, London, 2004.

CATHOLIC ENCYCLOPEDIA 1907. *The Catholic Encyclopedia*, Catholic Encyclopedia Press, New York, 1907.

CATHOLIC ENCYCLOPEDIA 1966. *The New Catholic Encyclopaedia*, McGraw-Hill, New York, 1966.

CECCHI 1982. Alessandro Cecchi, *The Piccolomini Library in the Cathedral of Siena*, Scala, Florence, 1982.

CELANI 1906. *Johannis Burckardi liber notarum*, ed. E. Celani, 2 vols, *RIS* 32, 1, 1–2, Città di Castello, 1906.

CELENZA 1999. Christopher S. Celenza, *Renaissance Humanism and the Papal Curia: Lapo da Castiglionchio the Younger's De Curiae commodis*, University of Michigan Press, Ann Arbor, 1999.

CELLINI/BULL 1999. Benevenuto Cellini, *Autobiography*, ed and trans George Bull, Penguin, London, 1999.

CHAMBERLAIN 1970. E.R. Chamberlain, *The Bad Popes*, Hamish Hamilton, London, 1970.

CHAMBERS 1997. D.S. Chambers, *Renaissance Cardinals and their Worldly Problems*, Ashgate Publishing, Aldershot, 1997.

CHASTEL 1983. André Chastel, *The Sack of Rome 1527*, Princeton University Press, Princeton, 1983.

CHEETHAM 1982. Sir Nicholas Cheetham, *A History of the Popes*, Dorset Press, New York, 1982.

CLOULAS 1990. Ivan Cloulas, *Jules II*, Fayard, Paris, 1990.

COBBAN 1975. A.B. Cobban, *Medieval Universities, their Development and Organisation,* Methuen and Co, London, 1975.

COCHRANE 1988. Eric Cochrane (ed. Julius Kirschner), *Italy 1530–1630,* Longman Press, London, 1988.

COCHRANE 1989. Eric Cochrane, *Early Modern Europe,* Chicago University Press, Chicago and London, 1989.

COCKE 1993. Richard Cocke, *From Magic to High Fashion: The Classical Tradition and the Renaissance of Roman Patronage, 1420–1600,* Mill Hill Publications, Norwich, 1993.

COFFIN 1977. David R. Coffin, *Pope Innocent VIII and the Villa Belvedere, Studies in Late Medieval and Renaissance Painting in Honor of Milliard Meiss,* New York University Press, New York, 1977.

COLUMBUS/COHEN 1992. Columbus, *The Four Voyages,* trans J. M. Cohen, Penguin, London, 1992.

CONTI 1883. Sigismondo de' Conti, *Le storie de' suoi tempi (1475–1510),* 2 vols, Rome, 1883.

CORTESI 1510. Paolo Cortesi, *De cardinalatu,* Castro Cortesio, 1510.

CREIGHTON 1897. Mandell Creighton, *A History of the Papacy from the Great Schism to the Sack of Rome,* London, 1897.

CRESTI 1963. Carlo Cresti, *Ville e Palazzi di Roma,* Magnus, Udine, 1998.

CROSS & LIVINGSTONE 1997. *The Oxford Dictionary of the Christian Church,* ed. F.L. Cross and E.A. Livingstone, 3rd edn, Oxford University Press, Oxford, 1997.

D'AMICO 1983. John D'Amico, *Renaissance Humanism in Papal Rome: Humanists and Churchmen on the Eve of the Reformation,* Johns Hopkins University Press, Baltimore and London, 1983.

DANDELET 2001. Thomas James Dandelet, *Spanish Rome 1500–1700,* Yale University Press, New Haven and London, 2001.

DE ROO 1924. Peter De Roo, *Material for a History of Pope Alexander VI: His Relatives and his Time,* Desclée de Brouwer & Company, Bruges, 1924.

DE ROOVER 1963. Raymond De Roover, *The Rise and Decline of the Medici Bank,* Harvard University Press, Cambridge, Mass., 1963.

DIAZ/COHEN 1969. Bernal Diaz, *The Conquest of New Spain,* trans J. M. Cohen, Penguin, London, 1969.

DICKENS 1974. A.G. Dickens, *The German Nation and Martin Luther,* Edward Arnold, London, 1974.

DICTIONNAIRE CANONIQUE 1903. *Dictionnaire du droit canonique,* Paris, 1903

DICTIONNAIRE D'HISTOIRE 1912. *Dictionnaire d'histoire et geographie ecclesiastique,* Paris, 1912.

DIZIONARIO BIOGRAFICO 1960. *Dizionario biografico degli italiani,* Rome, 1960.

DÖLLINGER 1869. J.H. Ignaz von Döllinger, *The Pope and the Council*, Rivingtons, London, 1869.

DUFFY 1998. Eamon Duffy, *Saints & Sinners: A History of the Popes*, Yale University Press, London and New Haven, 1998.

ELLIOTT 1963. J.H. Elliott, *Imperial Spain, 1469–1716*, Edward Arnold Publishers, London, 1963.

ERASMUS/PASCAL 1968. Desiderius Erasmus, *Julius exclusus*, trans. P. Pascal, Indiana University Press, Bloomington, 1968.

ETTLINGER 1965. Leopold David Ettlinger, *The Sistine Chapel Before Michelangelo: Religious Imagery and Papal Primacy*, Clarendon Press, Oxford, 1965.

EVENNETT 1968. H. Outram Evennett, *The Spirit of the Counter-Reformation*, Cambridge University Press, Cambridge, 1968.

FARROW 1950. John Farrow, *Pageant of the Popes*, Sheed & Ward, New York, 1950.

FENLON 1972. Dermot Fenlon, *Heresy and Obedience in Tridentine Italy*, Cambridge University Press, Cambridge, 1972.

FENLON 1989. Iain Fenlon (ed.), *Man and Music: The Renaissance*, Macmillan, London, 1989.

FERRARA 1942. Orestes Ferrara, *The Borgia Pope, Alexander The Sixth*, translated by F.J. Sheed, Sheed & Ward, London, 1942.

FIRPO 1991. Massimo Firpo, 'The Cardinal', in Eugenio Garin (ed.), *Renaissance Characters*, University of Chicago Press, Chicago and London, 1991, pp 46–97 (originally published as L'uomo del rinascimento, Bari, 1988).

FLETCHER & SHAW 2000. Stella Fletcher and Christine Shaw (eds), *The World of Savonarola: Italian Elites and Perceptions of Crisis*, Ashgate Publishing, Aldershot, 2000.

FUSERO 1972. Clemente Fusero, *The Borgias*, Pall Mall Press, London, 1972.

GAIDA 1913–15. *Liber de vita Christi ac omnium pontificium*, ed. G. Gaida, *RIS* 3, 1, Città di Castello, 1913–15.

GAIDA 1917–33. *Liber de vita Christi ac omnium pontificium*, ed. G. Gaida, *RIS* 3, 1, Bologna, 1917–33.

GENSINI 1994. S. Gensini (ed.), *Roma capitale (1447–1527)*, Pisa, 1994.

GILL 1959. Joseph Gill, *The Council of Florence*, Cambridge University Press, Cambridge, 1959.

GIUSTINIAN/VILLARI 1876. Antonio Giustinian, *Dispacci*, 3 vols, ed. Pasquale Villari, Florence, 1876.

GOFFEN 1986. R. Goffen, 'Article on Sixtus IV', *Renaissance Quarterly*, vol. xxxix, New York, 1986, pp 218–62.

GOLLIN 1971. James Gollin, *Worldly Goods: The Wealth and Power of the American Catholic Church, the Vatican, and the Men Who Control the Money*, Random House, New York, 1971.

GONTARD 1964. F. Gontard, *The Popes*, Barrie & Rockliff, London, 1964.

GRAFTON 1993. Anthony Grafton (ed.), *Rome Reborn: The Vatican Library and Renaissance Culture*, Yale University Press, New Haven & London, 1993.

GRAMICK 1990. *Homosexuality and the Priesthood*, ed. Jeannie Gramick, Crossroad, New York, 1990.

GREGOROVIUS 1874. Ferdinand Gregorovius, *Lucrezia Borgia*, Stuttgart, 1874.

GREGOROVIUS 1948. Ferdinand Gregorovius, *Lucrezia Borgia, A Chapter from the Morals of the Italian Renaissance*, London, 1948.

GREGOROVIUS/HAMILTON 1900–02. Ferdinand Gregorovius, *History of the City of Rome in the Middle Ages*, trans. from the 4th German ed. by A. Hamilton, London, 1900–02 (originally published as *Geschichte der Stadt Rom im Mittelalter*, Stuttgart, 1869–72).

GRENDLER 1989. Paul F. Grendler, *Schooling in Renaissance Italy: Literacy and Learning 1300–1600,* Johns Hopkins University Press, Baltimore and London, 1989.

GRIMAL 1997. Pierre Grimal, *Churches of Rome*, Tauris Parke, London, 1997.

GUICCIARDINI/ALEXANDER 1972. F. Guicciardini, *Storia d'Italia*, translated, edited and with notes and introduction by Sidney Alexander (Sheed & Ward, London, 1972).

GUIDONI AND PETRUCCI 1997. Enrico Guidoni and Giulia Petrucci, *Urbanistica per i giubilei: Roma, via Alessandrina: una strada 'tra due fondali' nell'Italia delle corti (1492–1499)*, Rome, 1997.

HALE 1961. John Hale, *Machiavelli and Renaissance Italy*, English Universities Press, London, 1961.

HALE 1993. John Hale, *The Civilization of Europe in the Renaissance*, Simon & Schuster, London, 1993.

HALLMAN 1985. Barbara McClung Hallman, *Italian Cardinals, Reform, and the Church as Property, 1492–1563*, University of California Press, Berkeley, Los Angeles and London, 1985.

HAY 1976. Denys Hay, 'The Renaissance Cardinals: Church, State, Culture', *Synthesis* 3, 1976, pp 35–46.

HAY 1977. Denys Hay, *The Church in Italy in the Fifteenth Century*, Cambridge University Press, Cambridge, 1977.

HAY 1989. Denys Hay, *Europe in the Fourteenth and Fifteenth Centuries*, 2nd edn, Longman, Harlow, 1989.

HAY & LAW 1989. Denys Hay and John Law, *Italy in the Age of the Renaissance, 1380–1530*, Longman, London, 1989.

HERSEY 1993. George L. Hersey, *High Renaissance Art in St Peter's and the Vatican: An Interpretative Guide*, University of Chicago Press, Chicago, 1993.

HILLGARTH 1978. J.N. Hillgarth, *The Spanish Kingdoms, 1250–1516*, vol. 2, Clarendon Press, Oxford, 1978.

HILLGARTH 1996. J.N. Hillgarth, 'The Image of Alexander VI and Cesare Borgia in the Sixteenth and Seventeenth centuries', *Journal of the Warburg and Courtauld Institutes* 59 (1996), pp 119–29.

HOGUE 1998. John Hogue, *The Last Pope*: *The Prophecies of St Malachy for the New Millennium*, Element, Shaftesbury, 1998.

HOLLINGSWORTH 1994. Mary Hollingsworth, *Patronage in Renaissance Italy: From 1400 to the early Sixteenth Century*, John Murray, London, 1994.

HOLLINGSWORTH 1996. Mary Hollingsworth, *Patronage in Sixteenth-Century Italy*, John Murray, London, 1996.

HOLMES 1969. George Holmes, *The Florentine Enlightenment 1400–50*, Oxford University Press, Oxford, 1969.

HOOK 1972. Judith Hook, *The Sack of Rome*, Macmillan, London, 1972.

HOOK 1979. Judith Hook, *Siena: A City and its History*, Hamish Hamilton, London, 1979.

HOOK 1984. Judith Hook, *Lorenzo de' Medici: An Historical Biography*, Hamish Hamilton, London, 1984.

HOUSLEY 1992. Norman Housley, *The Later Crusades*, Oxford University Press, Oxford, 1992.

HOWE 1978. Eunice D. Howe, *The Hospital of Santo Spirito and Pope Sixtus IV*, Garland Publishing, New York and London, 1978.

INFESSURA/TOMMASINI 1890. *Diario della città di Roma di Stefano Infessura Scribasenato*, ed. O. Tommasini, Rome, 1890.

JEDIN 1949–75. Hubert Jedin, *Geschichte des Konzils von Trent*, 4 vols, Herder, Freiberg, 1949–75.

JEDIN/GRAF 1957–61. Hubert Jedin, *A History of the Council of Trent*, trans. by Ernest Graf, Nelson, London, 1957–61.

JOHNSON 1981. Marion Johnson, *The Borgias*, Penguin Books, London, 1981.

KAMEN 1971. Henry Kamen, *The Iron Century: Social Change in Europe 1550–1660*, Weidenfeld & Nicholson, London, 1971.

KAMEN 1997a. Henry Kamen, *Philip of Spain*, Yale University Press, New Haven and London, 1997.

KAMEN 1997b. Henry Kamen, *The Spanish Inquisition: An Historical Revision*, Yale University Press, Newhaven and London, 1997.

KAMEN 2003. Henry Kamen, *Spain's Road to Empire: The Making of a World Power 1492–1763*, Allen Lane, London, 2003.

KELLY 1986. J.N.D. Kelly, *The Oxford Dictionary of the Popes*, Oxford University Press, Oxford, 1986.

KNECHT 1982. R.J. Knecht, *Francis I*, Cambridge University Press, Cambridge, 1982.

KNECHT 1996. R.J. Knecht, *The Rise and Fall of Renaissance France, 1483–1610*, Fontana Press, London, 1996.

KOENIGSBERGER 1968. H.G. Koenigsberger, George L. Mosse and G.Q. Bowler, *Europe in the Sixteenth Century*, Oxford University Press, London, 1968.

KRAUTHEIMER 1980. Richard Krautheimer, *Rome: Profile of a City, 312–1308*, Princeton University Press, Princeton, 1980.

KRAYE 1996. Jill Kraye (ed.), *The Cambridge Companion to Renaissance Humanism*, Cambridge University Press, Cambridge, 1996.

KRISTELLER 1956–93. Paul Oskar Kristeller, *Studies in Renaissance Thought and Letters*, 3 vols, Edizioni di Storia e Letteratura, Rome, 1956–93.

LA TORRE 1933. F. La Torre, *Del conclave di Alessandro VI, papa Borgia*, Florence, 1933.

LARNER 1965. John Larner, *The Lords of the Romagna*, Eyre & Spottiswoode, London, 1965.

LAS CASAS/GRIFFIN 2004. Bartolomé de Las Casas, *A Short Account of the Destruction of the Indies*, trans Nigel Griffin, Penguin, London, 2004.

LAVAGNINO 1920a. Emilio Lavagnino, *Santa Maria del Popolo*, Treves Dell' Anonima Libreria Italiana, Rome, c.1920.

LAVAGNINO 1920b. Emilio Lavagnino, *Santa Maria Maggiore*, Casa Editrice 'Roma', Rome, c.1920.

LEA 1883. Henry Charles Lea, *Studies in Church History*, Lea Brothers, Philadelphia, 1883.

LEA 1887. Henry Charles Lea, *A History of the Inquisition of the Middle Ages*, 3 vols, Harper Brothers, New York, 1887; reprinted Russell & Russell, New York, 1958.

LEA 1896a. Henry Charles Lea, *A History of Auricular Confession and Indulgences in the Latin Church*, 2 vols, Lea Brothers, Philadelphia, 1896; reprinted Greenwood Press, New York, 1968.

LEA 1896b. Henry Charles Lea, *Materials Toward a History of Witchcraft*, 3 vols, University of Pennsylvania Press, Philadelphia, 1939; reprinted T. Yoseloff, New York, 1957.

LEA 1906–07. Henry Charles Lea, *A History of the Inquisition in Spain*, 4 vols, Macmillan, New York and London, 1906–07.

LEA 1902. Henry Charles Lea, *The Eve of the Reformation*, Cambridge Modern History, Cambridge, 1902.

LECKY 1869. W.E.H Lecky, *History of European Morals*, Watts, London, 1869.

LEE 1978. Egmont Lee, *Sixtus IV and Men of Letters*, Edizioni di storia e letteratura, Rome, 1978.

LIBER/DAVIS 1992. *Liber Pontificalis*, trans. by Raymond Davis. Liverpool University Press, Liverpool, 1992.

LOVETT 1986. A.W. Lovett, *Early Habsburg Spain, 1517–1598*, Oxford University Press, Oxford, 1986.

LOWE 1993. K.J.P. Lowe, *Church and Politics in Renaissance Italy: The Life and Career of Cardinal Francesco Soderini, 1453–1524*, Cambridge University Press, Cambridge, 1993.

LUCIANI 1996. Roberto Luciani, *Santa Maria Maggiore e Roma,* Fratelli Palombi, Rome, 1996.

MACHIAVELLI/BULL 1961. Machiavelli, *Il principe (The Prince),* ed and trans George Bull, Penguin, Harmondsworth, 1961.

MACK 1987. Charles R. Mack, *Pienza: The Creation of a Renaissance City,* Cornell University Press, Ithaca, 1987.

MAGNUSON 1958. Torgil Magnuson, *Studies in Roman Quattrocento Architecture*, Almqvist & Wiksell, Stockholm, 1958.

MALLETT 1969. Michael Mallett, *The Borgias: The Rise and Fall of a Renaissance Dynasty*, Bodley Head, London, 1969.

MALLETT 1974. Michael Mallett, *Mercenaries and their Masters: Warfare in Renaissance Italy*, Bodley Head, London, 1974.

MALLETT 1981. Michael Mallett 'Diplomacy and War in Later Fifteenth-century Italy', *Proceedings of the British Academy*, 67, 1981, pp 267–88.

MANN 1925. Horace K. Mann, *The Lives of the Popes in the Early Middle Ages,* Kegan Paul & Co, London, 1925.

MARTINES 2003. Lauro Martines, *April Blood, Florence and the Plot Against the Medici*, Jonathan Cape Ltd, London, 2003.

MASI 1999. Stefano Masi, *Rome and the Vatican*, Bonechi, Florence, 1999.

MASSON 1965. Georgina Masson, *The Companion Guide to Rome*, Collins, London, 1965.

MATTINGLY 1962. Garrett Mattingly, *Renaissance Diplomacy*, Jonathan Cape, London, 1962.

MCGRATH 1987. Alister E. McGrath, *The Intellectual Origins of the European Reformation*, Blackwell Publishers, Oxford, 1987.

MCGRATH 1988. Alister E. McGrath, *Reformation Thought: An Introduction*, Blackwell Publishers, Oxford, 1988.

MCGRATH 1990. Alister E. McGrath, *A Life of John Calvin*, Blackwell Publishers, Oxford, 1990.

MCNAIR 1967. Philip McNair, *Peter Martyr in Italy: An Anatomy of an Apostasy*, Clarendon Press, Oxford, 1967.

LORENZO DE' MEDICI/FUBINI 1977–. *Lettere*, 9 vols, ed. Riccardo Fubini, Nicolai Rubinstein, Michael Mallett and Humfrey Butters, Istituto Nazionale di Studi sul Rinascimento in collaboration with I Tatti, the Renaissance Society of America, and the Warburg Institute, Florence.

MIGLIO ET AL 1986. M. Miglio, P. Niutta, D. Quaglioni, C. Ranieri (eds), *Un pontificato ed una città: Sisto IV (1471–1484)*, Littera antiqua 5, Vatican City, 1986

MITCHELL 1962. Rosamund Joscelyne Mitchell, *The Laurels and the Tiara: Pope Pius II 1458–1464*, Harvill Press, London; Doubleday, New York, 1962.

MULLETT 2000. Michael A. Mullett, *The Catholic Reformation*, Routledge, London, 2000.

MÜNTZ 1882. Eugène Müntz, *Les arts à la cour des Papes pendant le Xve et le XVIe siècles*, 3 vols, Paris, 1882.

NEWMAN 2000. Paul Newman, *A History of Terror*, Sutton Publishing, Thrupp, 2000.

O'MALLEY 1979. John W. O'Malley, *Praise and Blame in Renaissance Rome: Rhetoric, Doctrine and Reform in the Sacred Orators of the Papal Court, 1450–1521*, Duke University Press, Durham, NC, 1979.

O'MALLEY 1993a. John W. O'Malley, *Religious Culture in the Sixteenth Century: Preaching, Rhetoric, Spirituality and Reform*, Ashgate Publishing, Aldershot, 1993.

O'MALLEY 1993b. John W. O'Malley, *The First Jesuits,* Harvard University Press, Cambridge, Mass., and London, 1993.

OLIN 1969. J.C. Olin (ed.), *The Catholic Reformation: Savonarola to Ignatius Loyola: Reform in the Church, 1495–1540*, New York: Harper & Row, 1969.

PARTNER 1958. Peter Partner, *The Papal State under Martin V*, British School at Rome, London 1958.

PARTNER 1972. Peter Partner, *The Lands of St Peter*, University of California Press, Berkeley and London, 1972.

PARTNER 1976. Peter Partner, *Renaissance Rome, 1500–1559: A Portrait of a Society*, University of California Press, Berkeley, Los Angeles and London, 1976.

PARTNER 1980. Peter Partner, 'Papal financial policy in the Renaissance and Counter-Reformation', *Past and Present* 88, 1980, pp 17–62.

PARTNER 1990. Peter Partner, *The Pope's Men: The Papal Civil Service in the Renaissance*, Oxford University Press, Oxford, 1990.

PARTRIDGE 1996. Loren Partridge, *The Renaissance in Rome 1400–1600*, Weidenfield & Nicolson, London, 1996.

PARTRIDGE 2002. *A History of Orgies*, by Burgo Partridge. Prion Books, London, 2002.

PASCHINI 1940. Pio Paschini, *Roma nel Rinascimento*, Cappelli, Bologna, 1940.

PASCHINI 1948. *Il carteggio fra il card. Marco Barbo e Giovanni Lorenzi (1481–1490)*, ed. P. Paschini, Studi e testi 137, Vatican City, 1948.

PASTOR 1901–53. Ludwig von Pastor, *The History of the Popes from the Close of the Middle Ages*, 40 vols, London, 1901–53.

PELLEGRINI 2002. Marco Pellegrini, 'A Turning-point in the History of the Factional System in the Sacred College: The Power of Pope and Cardinals in the Age of Alexander VI', in Gianvittorio Signorotto and Maria Antonietta Visceglia (eds), *Court and Politics in Papal Rome 1492–1700*, Cambridge University Press, Cambridge, 2002, pp 8–30.

PHILLIPS 1977. Mark Phillips, *Francesco Guicciardini: The Historian's Craft*, Manchester University Press, Manchester, 1977.

PICCOLOMINI/CHERUBINI 1997. I. Ammannati Piccolomini, *Lettere (1444–1479)*, 3 vols, ed. P. Cherubini, Pubblicazioni degli Archivi di Stato, Fonti 25, Rome, 1997.

PICCOLOMINI/GABEL & GRAGG 1937–57. *Commentaries*, edited by Lorna C. Gabel and Florence A. Gragg, Smith College Studies in History, vols XXII, XXV, XXX, XXXV and XLIII, Northampton, Mass, 1937–57.

PICCOLOMINI/GABEL & GRAGG 1988. *Secret Memoirs of a Renaissance Pope. The Commentaries of Aeneas Sylvius Piccolomini, Pius II*, with introduction by Leona C. Gabel, translated by Florence A. Gragg, Folio Society, London, 1988.

PICOTTI 1928. G.B. Picotti, *La giovinezza di Leone X*, Milan, 1928.

PIETRANGELI 1993. Carlo Pietrangeli, *The Vatican Museums: Five Centuries of History*, Quasar Biblioteca Apostolica Vaticana, Rome, 1993.

PIETRANGELI ET AL 1986. C. Pietrangeli et al, *The Sistine Chapel: the Art, the History and the Restoration*, Harmony Books, New York, 1986.

PILLININI 1970. G. Pillinini, *Il sistema degli stati italiani, 1454–94*, Venice, 1970.

PIRIE 1935. Valerie Pirie, *The Triple Crown*, Sidgwick & Jackson, London, 1935.

PLATINA 1645. B. Platina, *The Lives of the Popes*, London, 1645.

POLIZZOTTO 1994. Lorenzo Polizzotto, *The Elect Nation: The Savonarolan Movement in Florence 1494–1545*, Oxford University Press, Oxford, 1994.

PONTANO/TONI 1907–08. Giovanni Pontano, *Il diario romano*, ed. D. Toni, *RIS* 3, 2, Città di Castello, 1907–8.

PONTIERI 1975-76. E. Pontieri (ed), *Storia di Napoli*, vols 2–3, Naples, 1975–76.

POTTER 1995. David Potter, *A History of France, 1460–1560: The Emergence of a Nation State*, Macmillan, Basingstoke, 1995.

PRODI 1987. Paolo Prodi, *The Papal Prince*, Cambridge University Press, Cambridge, 1987.

RABIL 1988. Albert Rabil (ed.), *Renaissance Humanism: Foundations, Forms and Legacy*, 3 vols, University of Pennsylvania Press, Philadelphia, 1988.

RAMSEY 1982. P.A. Ramsey (ed.), *Rome in the Renaissance: the City and the Myth*, Papers of the 13th Annual conference of the Center for Medieval and Early Renaissance Studies, Binghamton, NY, 1982.

RANKE 1840. Leopold von Ranke, *The Ecclesiastical and Political History of the Popes of Rome, during the Sixteenth and Seventeenth Centuries*, trans. by Sarah Austin. 3 vols, John Murray, London, 1840.

RANKE 1990. Cita Ranke, *Eunochs for the Kingdom of Heaven*. Heinemann, New York, 1990.

RICCI 1902. Corrado Ricci, *Pintoricchio*, Heinemann, London, 1902.

RIDOLFI 1959. Roberto Ridolfi, *The Life of Girolamo Savonarola*, Alfred A. Knopf, New York, 1959. RIDOLFI 1963. Roberto Ridolfi, *Life of Niccolò Machiavelli*, Routledge & Kegan Paul, London, 1963.

RIDOLFI 1967. Roberto Ridolfi, *Life of Francesco Guicciardini*, Routledge & Kegan Paul, London, 1967.

ROLFE 1901. F.W. Rolfe (Baron Corvo), *Chronicles of the House of Borgia*, Adam and Charles Black, London, 1901.

ROSA 1988. Peter de Rosa, *Vicars of Christ*, Bantam Press, London, 1988.

ROSCOE 1846. Thomas Roscoe, *The Life and Pontificate of Leo X*, Henry G. Bohn, London, 1846.

RUBENSTEIN 1997. Nicolai Rubinstein, *The Government of Florence under the Medici (1434–94)*, 2nd edn., Oxford University Press, Oxford, 1997.

RUTHVEN 1978. Malise Ruthven, *Torture: The Grand Conspiracy*, Weidenfeld & Nicolson, London, 1978.

RYDER 1976. Alan Ryder, *The Kingdom of Naples under Alfonso the Magnanimous: The Making of a Modern State*, Clarendon Press, Oxford, 1976.

SCHOECK 1990. Richard J. Schoeck, *Erasmus and Europe: The Making of a Humanist*, Edinburgh University Press, Edinburgh, 1990.

SERVADIO 2005. Gaia Servadio, *Renaissance Woman*, I.B. Tauris, London and New York, 2005.

SHANKLAND 1987. *The Prettiest Love Letters in the World: Letters between Lucrezia Borgia and Pietro Bembo*, trans. Hugh Shankland, Collins Harvill, London, 1987.

SHAW 1993. Christine Shaw, *Julius II: The Warrior Pope*, Blackwell, Oxford, 1993.

SIGNOROTTO AND VISCEGLIA 2002. Gianvittorio Signorotto and Maria Antonietta Visceglia (eds), *Court and Politics in Papal Rome 1492–1700*, Cambridge University Press, Cambridge, 2002.

SKINNER 1981. Quentin Skinner, *Machiavelli*, Oxford University Press, Oxford, 1981.

SKINNER 1988. Quentin Skinner et al, *The Cambridge History of Renaissance Philosophy*, Cambridge University Press, Cambridge, 1988.

STINGER 1985. Charles L. Stinger, *The Renaissance in Rome*, Indiana University Press, Bloomington, In, 1985

STRATHERN 2003. Michael Strathern, *The Medici, Godfathers of the Renaissance*, Jonathon Cape, London, 2003.

SYNAN 1965. Edward A. Synan, *The Popes and the Jews in the Middle Ages*, Macmillan, New York, 1965.

THOMSON 1980. John A.F. Thomson, *Popes and Princes, 1417–1517: Politics and Policy in the Late Medieval Church*, Allen & Unwin, London, 1980.

TRUE HISTORY 1679. H.M. and R.T. *A True History of the Lives of the Popes*, London, 1679.

VAILLANCOURT 1980. Jean-Guy Vaillancourt, *Papal Power*, University of California Press, Berkeley, 1980.

VALERA 1904. Cypriano de Valera, *Popery*, London, 1904.

VASARI/BONDELLA 1998. Georgio Vasari, *The Lives of the Artists*, trans Julia Conway Bondanella and Peter Bondanella, Oxford University Press, Oxford, 1998.

VERONA/ZIPPEL 1904. Gaspare da Verona, *Le vite di Paolo II*, ed. G. Zippel, *RIS* 16, 3, Città di Castello, 1904.

VILLARI 1878. Pasquale Villari, *Life and Times of Niccolò Machiavelli*, C. Kegan Paul & Co, London, 1878.

VILLARI 1888. Pasquale Villari, *Life and Times of Girolamo Savonarola*, London, 1888.

VOLTERRA/CARUSI 1904–06. Jacopo Gherardi da Volterra, *Il diario romano*, ed. E. Carusi, *RIS* 23, 3, Città di Castello, 1904–06.

WEIL-GARRIS 1980. Kathless Weil-Garris and John F. D'Amico, 'The Renaissance Cardinal's Ideal Palace: A Chapter from Cortesi's *De cardinalatu*', in Henry A. Millon (ed.), *Studies in Italian Art and Architecture, 15th through 18th centuries. Memoirs of the American Academy in Rome* 35 (1980), pp 45–123.

WEINSTEIN 1970. Donald Weinstein, *Savonarola and Florence: Prophecy and Patriotism in the Renaissance*, Princeton University Press, Princeton, NJ, 1970.

WEISS 1958. Roberto Weiss, *Un umanista veneziano: Papa Paolo II*, Istituto per la Collaborazione Culturale, Venice, 1958.

WELCH 1997. Evelyn Welch, *Art and Society in Italy 1350–1600*, Oxford University Press, Oxford, 1997.

WESTFALL 1974. Carroll William Westfall, *In this Most Perfect Paradise: Alberti, Nicholas V and the Invention of Conscious Urban Planning in Rome, 1447–55,* Pennsylvania State University Press, Pennsylvania, 1974.

WOODWARD 1913. W.H. Woodward, *Cesare Borgia,* London, 1913.

YEO 1936. M. Yeo, *The Greatest of the Borgias,* Bruce Publishing Co., New York, 1936.

GENERAL BIBLIOGRAPHY

The following list is deliberately extended so as to cover material for further reading, in view of the complexity and controversial nature of the subject matter.

The history of Europe in the fifteenth and sixteenth centuries is well served by reference works, aimed at a variety of audiences. The most recent and most comprehensive single-volume reference work is Gordon Campbell, *The Oxford Dictionary of the Renaissance*, Oxford University Press, Oxford, 2003 (CAMPBELL 2003), which contains thousands of biographies and short essays. For papal history, see J.N.D. Kelly, *The Oxford Dictionary of the Popes*, Oxford University Press, Oxford, 1986 (KELLY 1986). *The Oxford Dictionary of the Christian Church*, ed. F.L. Cross and E.A. Livingstone, 3rd edn, Oxford University Press, Oxford, 1997 (CROSS & LIVINGSTONE 1997) is an excellent point of departure for all ecclesiastical topics. More specialized information can be found in the *Dictionnaire d'histoire et geographie ecclesiastique* (DICTIONNAIRE D'HISTOIRE 1912), *Dictionnaire du droit canonique* (DICTIONNAIRE CANONIQUE 1903) and *Dizionario biografico degli italiani* (DIZIONARIO BIOGRAFICO 1960).

For a general history of Europe during the period of the Borgia ascendance, see Denys Hay, *Europe in the Fourteenth and Ffifteenth Centuries*, 2nd edn, Longman, Harlow, 1989 (HAY 1989). An appreciation of the cultural dimension of European experience throughout the late medieval and early modern period is provided by John Hale, *The Civilization of Europe in the Renaissance*, Simon & Schuster, London, 1993 (HALE 1993). In his *Christianity in the West, 1400–1700*, Oxford University Press, Oxford, 1985 (BOSSY 1985), John Bossy wields a similarly broad brush to equally impressive effect.

Another pan-European study, albeit with a tighter chronological focus, is John A.F. Thomson, *Popes and Princes, 1417–1517: Politics and Policy in the Late Medieval Church*, Allen & Unwin, London, 1980 (THOMSON 1980). This provides a useful survey of the governmental, administrative and financial structures of the western Church in the century prior to the Reformation. A further form of interaction between the Church and the secular powers is addressed by Norman Housley, *The Later Crusades*, Oxford University Press, Oxford, 1992 (HOUSLEY 1992) that contains accounts of the abortive crusading enterprises of the fifteenth century. For a survey of French history, see R.J. Knecht, *The Rise and Fall of Renaissance France, 1483–1610*, Fontana Press, London, 1996 (KNECHT 1996). David Potter, *A History of France, 1460–1560: The Emergence of a Nation State*, Macmillan, Basingstoke, 1995 (POTTER 1995) is particularly useful for the organs of government.

J.H. Elliott, *Imperial Spain, 1469–1716*, Edward Arnold Publishers, London, 1963 (ELLIOTT 1963) remains the standard point of departure for an examination of the land that gave birth to the Borgia. J.N. Hillgarth, *The Spanish Kingdoms, 1250–1516*, vol. 2, Clarendon Press, Oxford, 1978 (HILLGARTH 1978) contains more detailed coverage for the fifteenth century. For the princely states and republics which the Borgia family encountered on their move to Italy, see Denys Hay and John Law, *Italy in the Age of the Renaissance, 1380–1530*, Longman, London, 1989 (HAY & LAW 1989). Studies of individual Italian states in the fifteenth century are too numerous to be mentioned here, but mention ought to be made of Rome's nearest neighbours, Naples, Florence and Siena. On these, see Alan Ryder, *The Kingdom of Naples under Alfonso the Magnanimous: The Making of a Modern State*, Clarendon Press, Oxford, 1976 (RYDER 1976); E. Pontieri (ed), *Storia di Napoli*, vols 2–3, Naples, 1975–76 (PONTIERI 1975-76); Nicolai Rubinstein, *The Government of Florence under the Medici (1434–94)*, 2nd edn., Oxford University Press, Oxford, 1997 (RUBENSTEIN 1997); Judith Hook, *Lorenzo de' Medici: An Historical Biography*, Hamish Hamilton, London, 1984 (HOOK 1984); Judith Hook, *Siena: A City and its History*, Hamish Hamilton, London, 1979 (HOOK 1979).

Although the vicariates of the Romagna were within the papal states, the vicars themselves frequently took advantage of papal weaknesses and operated as independent princes. On this region, see John Larner, *The Lords of the Romagna*, Eyre & Spottiswoode, London, 1965 (LARNER 1965). Inter-state relations between the peace of Lodi and the French invasion are examined more closely by G. Pillinini, *Il sistema degli stati italiani, 1454–94*, Venice, 1970 (PILLININI 1970). Resident diplomats began to replace ad hoc embassies in the later fifteenth century, on which see Garrett Mattingly, *Renaissance Diplomacy*, Jonathan Cape, London, 1962 (MATTINGLY 1962), supplemented by Michael Mallett 'Diplomacy and War in Later Fifteenth-century Italy', *Proceedings of the British Academy*, 67, 1981, pp 267–88 (MALLETT 1981). As Mallett argues, diplomacy and warfare were two sides of the same coin. For the organization and practice of war, see Michael Mallett, *Mercenaries and their Masters: Warfare in Renaissance Italy*, Bodley Head, London, 1974 (MALLETT 1974).

Turning more specifically to the history of Rome and the papacy in the fifteenth century, the Vatican and other archives contain a wealth of primary source material, a portion of which has been edited and published. A number of chronicle sources dating from the latter years of the century, supplemented by copious notes, are available in the *Rerum Italicarum Scriptores* series (hereafter RIS): Gaspare da Verona, *Le vite di Paolo II*, ed. G. Zippel, *RIS* 16, 3, Città di Castello, 1904 (VERONA/ZIPPEL 1904); Jacopo Gherardi da Volterra, *Il diario romano*, ed. E. Carusi, *RIS* 23, 3, Città di Castello, 1904–6 (VOLTERRA/CARUSI 1904–6); *Johannis Burckardi liber notarum*, ed. E. Celani, 2 vols, *RIS* 32, 1, 1–2, Città di Castello, 1906 (CELANI 1906); Giovanni Pontano, *Il diario romano*, ed. D. Toni, *RIS* 3, 2, Città di Castello 1907–8 (PONTANO/TONI 1907–8). Between them, Gherardi and Burchard provide coverage of comings and goings at the papal court and information about who was present at liturgical celebrations in the papal chapel.

Not all Roman diarists and historians of their own times have received such thorough editorial treatment. They include Sigismondo de' Conti, *Le storie de' suoi tempi (1475–1510)*, 2 vols, Rome, 1883 (CONTI 1883) and the Colonna partisan, Stefano Infessura, in *Diario della città di Roma di Stefano Infessura Scribasenato*, ed. O. Tommasini, Rome, 1890 (INFESSURA/TOMMASINI 1890). Bartolomeo Sacchi, known as Il Plastina, was no more impartial in the latter sections of his *Liber de vita Christi ac omnium pontificium*, ed. G. Gaida, *RIS* 3,1, Città di Castello, 1913–15 (GAIDA 1890), and Bologna, 1917–33 (GAIDA 1917–33).

Equally unreliable, but equally readable, are the autobiographical *Commentaries* of Pius II. Unlike the other primary sources listed here, they are available in English translation, edited by Lorna C. Gabel and Florence A. Gragg, Smith College Studies in History, vols XXII, XXV, XXX, XXXV and XLIII, Northampton, Mass, 1937–57 (PICCOLOMINI/ GABEL & GRAGG 1937–57). More accessible is the abridged version published in one volume as *Secret Memoirs of a Renaissance Pope. The Commentaries of Aeneas Sylvius Piccolomini, Pius II*, with introduction by Leona C. Gabel, translated by Florence A. Gragg, Folio Society, London, 1988 (PICCOLOMINI/GABEL & GRAGG 1988). The correspondence of two later fifteenth-century cardinals, Jacopo Ammanati Piccolomini and Marco Barbo, provides fascinating insights into the minutiae of Curial life: I. Ammannati Piccolomini, *Lettere (1444–1479)*, 3 vols, ed. P. Cherubini, Pubblicazioni degli Archivi di Stato, Fonti 25, Rome, 1997 (PICCOLOMINI/CHERUBINI 1997); *Il carteggio fra il card. Marco Barbo e Giovanni Lorenzi (1481–1490)*, ed. P. Paschini, Studi e testi 137, Vatican City, 1948 (PASCHINI 1948). For interaction between the Italian states, both in peace and war, the letters of Lorenzo de' Medici are in the course of publication: *Lettere*, 9 vols, ed. Riccardo Fubini, Nicolai Rubinstein, Michael Mallett and Humfrey Butters, Istituto Nazionale di Studi sul Rinascimento in collaboration with I Tatti, the Renaissance Society of America, and the Warburg Institute, Florence, 1977 onwards (LORENZO DE' MEDICI/FUBINI 1977–).

The history of the papacy has inspired a number of multi-volume histories, of which that of Ludwig von Pastor, *The History of the Popes from the Close of the Middle Ages*, 40 vols, London, 1901–53 (PASTOR 1901-53) – originally published as *Geschichte der Päpste seit dem Ausgang des Mittelalters*, Freiberg, 1886 – remains the most authoritative, providing that allowance is made for the author's distinction between the 'good' Christian and 'bad' pagan Renaissance and similar labelling of the major players in papal history. Volumes 1–5 take the story through to 1492. An alternative perspective is provided by the Anglican bishop of London, Mandell Creighton, in his *A History of the Papacy from the Great Schism to the Sack of Rome*, London, 1897 (CREIGHTON 1897). A recent distillation of these and others works in a single-volume history of the papacy is Eamon Duffy's *Saints & Sinners: A History of the Popes*, Yale University Press, London and New Haven, 1998 (DUFFY 1998). The Borgia Age forms but a fraction of the highly readable saga related by Duffy.

For ecclesiastical organization throughout the Italian peninsula, see Denys Hay, *The Church in Italy in the Fifteenth Century*, Cambridge University Press, Cambridge, 1977 (HAY 1977). The return of the papacy to Rome in the early fifteenth century can be appreciated through Peter Partner, *The Papal State under Martin V*, British School at Rome, London 1958 (PARTNER 1958). In *The Lands of St Peter*, University of California Press, Berkeley and London, 1972 (PARTNER 1972), Partner examines the temporal power of the papacy in a wider chronological context. Also see Peter Partner, 'Papal financial policy in the Renaissance and Counter-Reformation', *Past and Present* 88, 1980 pp 17–62 (PARTNER 1980). From these studies, it was a natural development for Partner to analyse the careers of those clerics who administered the papal states, for many of whom the civil service was a route to episcopal promotion and even to a cardinal's red hat: Peter Partner, *The Pope's Men: The Papal Civil Service in the Renaissance*, Oxford University Press, Oxford, 1990 (PARTNER 1990). Much valuable information about the financial affairs of the papacy can be gleaned from Raymond De Roover, *The Rise and Decline of the Medici Bank*, Harvard University Press, Cambridge, Mass., 1963 (DE ROOVER 1963). For the full range of the pope's powers, temporal and otherwise, see Paolo Prodi, *The Papal Prince*, Cambridge University Press, Cambridge, 1987 (PRODI 1987). Individual fifteenth-century pontiffs have not been well served by biographers, an exception being Cecilia M. Ady, *Pius II*, Methuen, London, 1913 (ADY 1913). Joseph Gill, *The Council of Florence*, Cambridge University Press, Cambridge, 1959 (GILL 1959), covers the most crucial episodes of the pontificate of Eugenius IV. For a defence of Paul II against the attacks of Platina, see Roberto Weiss, *Un umanista veneziano: Papa Paolo II*, Istituto per la Collaborazione Culturale, Venice, 1958 (WEISS 1958).

For the Borgia family, including Pope Calixtus III and Cardinal Rodrigo Borgia, up to 1492, the best overall account in English remains Michael Mallett, *The Borgias: The Rise and Fall of a Renaissance Dynasty*, Bodley Head, London, 1969 (MALLETT 1969). In addition to being extremely accessible, it contains an annotated bibliography of works directly relating to the Borgia family. A further study of the family collectively is that of Clemente Fusero, *The Borgias*, Pall Mall Press, London, 1972 (FUSERO 1972), translated from the Italian original (*I Borgia*, Milan, 1966), but this does not add substantially to the Mallett volume. Although quite widely available, F.W. Rolfe (Baron Corvo), *Chronicles of the House of Borgia*, Adam and Charles Black, London, 1901 (ROLFE 1901) should perhaps be read as much for a study of Rolfe as for one of the Borgia, and not even attempted by readers uninitiated in the author's style.

The fruits of recent research can be found in Spanish and Italian publications produced to mark the 500th anniversaries of the election of Rodrigo Borgia to the papacy in 1492, the Jubilee of 1500 and the death of the second Borgia Pope in 1503. The most recent example of this is the exhibition catalogue, *I Borgia*, ed. Carla Alfano, Learco Andalò and Felipe V. Garín Llombart, Electa, Milan, 2002 (ALFANO 2002). In addition to the letters of Cardinals Barbo and Ammannati Piccolomini, various studies have shed light on the Sacred College, during the cardinalate of Rodrigo Borgia, not least those of D.S. Chambers, collected as *Renaissance Cardinals and their Worldly Problems*, Ashgate Publishing, Aldershot, 1997 (CHAMBERS 1997). Among the articles reprinted in that volume, 'The economic predicament of Renaissance cardinals' is of particular significance, and first appeared in *Studies in Medieval and Renaissance History* 3, 1966, pp 287–311. Other surveys of Borgia's red-hatted colleagues include: Denys Hay, 'The Renaissance Cardinals: Church, State, Culture', *Synthesis* 3, 1976, pp 35–46 (HAY 1976), and Massimo Firpo, 'The Cardinal', in Eugenio Garin (ed.), *Renaissance Characters*, University of Chicago Press, Chicago and London, 1991, pp 46–97 (FIRPO 1991; originally published as *L'uomo del rinascimento*, Bari, 1988).

The city of Rome, its architecture and social composition, has generated a considerably larger body of secondary literature than has the Sacred College of Cardinals. Among the more venerable studies, there remains Ferdinand Gregorovius, *History of the City of Rome in the Middle Ages*, trans. from the 4th German ed. by A. Hamilton, London, 1900–02 (GREGOROVIUS/HAMILTON 1900-2; originally published as *Geschichte der Stadt Rom im Mittelalter*, Stuttgart, 1869–72). Richard Krautheimer's interests predated the Borgia Age, but his *Rome: Profile of a City, 312–1308*, Princeton University Press, Princeton, 1980 (KRAUTHEIMER 1980) is, nevertheless, an indispensable guide to understanding its evolution in the Christian era.

Study of the visual arts in later fifteenth-century Rome requires a documentary base, and this has long been provided by the collection of documentary sources assembled in Eugène Müntz, *Les arts à la cour des Papes pendant le Xve et le XVIe siècles*, 3 vols, Paris, 1882 (MÜNTZ 1882). Three volumes of essays are worth highlighting for the wealth of research they contain about the pan-European melting pot that was Rome: P.A. Ramsey (ed.), *Rome in the Renaissance: the City and the Myth*, Papers of the 13th Annual conference of the Center for Medieval and Early Renaissance Studies, Binghamton, NY, 1982 (RAMSEY 1982): M. Miglio, P. Niutta, D. Quaglioni, C. Ranieri (eds), *Un pontificato ed una città: Sisto IV (1471–1484)*, Littera antiqua 5, Vatican City, 1986 (MIGLIO ET AL 1994); S. Gensini (ed.), *Roma capitale (1447–1527)*, Pisa, 1994 (GENSINI 1994). Useful accounts of the major architectural developments in the city are provided by Torgil Magnuson, *Studies in Roman Quattrocento Architecture*, Almqvist & Wiksell, Stockholm, 1958 (MAGNUSON 1958), and Loren Partridge, *The Renaissance in Rome 1400–1600*, Weidenfield & Nicolson, London, 1996 (PARTRIDGE 1996). More detailed coverage of architectural projects and urban development is provided by Carroll William Westfall, *In this Most Perfect Paradise: Alberti, Nicholas V and the Invention of Conscious Urban Planning in Rome, 1447–55*, Pennsylvania State University Press, Pennsylvania, 1974 (WESTFALL 1974).

At a certain level, the reputation of Pope Sixtus IV continues to rest on his patronage of architecture in Rome, on which see Eunice D. Howe, *The Hospital of Santo Spirito and Pope Sixtus IV*, Garland Publishing, New York and London, 1978 (HOWE 1978); Leopold David Ettlinger, *The Sistine Chapel before Michelangelo: Religious Imagery and Papal Primacy*, Clarendon Press, Oxford, 1965 (ETTLINGER 1965); C. Pietrangeli et al, *The Sistine Chapel: the Art, the History and the Restoration*, Harmony Books, New York, 1986 (PIETRANGELI ET AL 1986). Together with cultural patronage in Florence, Venice and the Italian courts, papal patronage of the arts is surveyed by Mary Hollingsworth, *Patronage in Renaissance Italy: From 1400 to the early Sixteenth Century*, John Murray, London, 1994 (HOLLINGSWORTH 1994). For general coverage on the visual arts in fifteenth-century Italy, see Evelyn Welch, *Art and Society in Italy 1350–1600*, Oxford University Press, Oxford, 1997 (WELCH 1997). Both Hollingsworth and Welch include thorough bibliographies.

Another aspect of Sixtus IV's pontificate has been featured in the volume now presented in accordance with the overall objective of telling a fully rounded story. For literary culture in fifteenth-century Rome, see Christopher S. Celenza, *Renaissance Humanism and the Papal*

Curia: Lapo da Castiglionchio the Younger's De Curiae commodis, University of Michigan Press, Ann Arbor, MI, 1999 (CELENZA 1999) and Egmont Lee, *Sixtus IV and Men of Letters*, Edizioni di storia e letteratura, Rome, 1978 (LEE 1978). In terms of the cultural life of Rome, the ever-flexible term 'Renaissance' has tended to be applied more frequently to the early *cinquecento* than to the *quattrocento*. Information on the earlier period may be gleaned from: John O'Malley, *Praise and Blame in Renaissance Rome: Rhetoric, Doctrine and Reform in the Sacred Orators of the Papal Court, 1450–1521*, Duke University Press, Durham, NC, 1979 (O'MALLEY 1979); Charles L. Stinger, *The Renaissance in Rome*, Indiana University Press, Bloomington, In, 1985 (STINGER 1985); Anthony Grafton (ed.), *Rome Reborn: The Vatican Library and Renaissance Culture*, Yale University Press, New Haven & London, 1993 (GRAFTON 1993). For the cultural impact of the curia in Florence during the pontificate of Eugenius IV, see George Holmes, *The Florentine Enlightenment 1400–50*, Oxford University Press, Oxford, 1969 (HOLMES 1969).

There is no shortage of guides to the wider world of Renaissance humanism, of which the following are good examples: Jill Kraye (ed.), *The Cambridge Companion to Renaissance Humanism*, Cambridge University Press, Cambridge, 1996 (KRAYE 1996); Quentin Skinner et al, *The Cambridge History of Renaissance Philosophy*, Cambridge University Press, Cambridge, 1988 (SKINNER 1988); Albert Rabil (ed.), *Renaissance Humanism: Foundations, Forms and Legacy*, 3 vols, University of Pennsylvania Press, Philadelphia, 1988 (RABIL 1988); Paul Oskar Kristeller, *Studies in Renaissance Thought and Letters*, 3 vols, Edizioni di Storia e Letteratura, Rome, 1956–93 (KRISTELLER 1956–93). For education, see: Paul F. Grendler, *Schooling in Renaissance Italy: Literacy and Learning 1300–1600*, Johns Hopkins University Press, Baltimore and London, 1989 (GRENDLER 1989); A.B. Cobban, *Medieval Universities, their Development and Organisation*, Methuen and Co, London, 1975 (COBBAN 1975). At the risk of presenting it as an appendage to the cultural life of the time, for a consideration of music in the Borgia Age see Iain Fenlon (ed.), *Man and Music: The Renaissance*, Macmillan, London, 1989 (FENLON 1989).

Alexander VI, his family and his pontificate

Of the primary sources listed above, the diary of Johannes Burchard, the papal master of ceremonies, is the most detailed for the period 1492 to 1503 (CELANI 1906). Quotations from Burchard, incorporated in the present work, have been taken from the heavily abridged English translation, *At the Court of the Borgia*, ed. and trans. Geoffrey Parker, Folio Society, London, 1963 (BURCHARD/PARKER 1963). Sigismondo de' Conti, *Le storie de' suoi tempi (1475–1510)*, 2 vols, Rome, 1883 (CONTI 1883) continues to provide an alternative contemporary perspective on the second Borgia pontificate.

Archival sources for the nine years of Alexander's pontificate are manifold, with published selections including the extensive collection assembled by Peter De Roo, *Material for a History of Pope Alexander VI: His Relatives and his Time*, Desclée de Brouwer & Company, Bruges, 1924 (DE ROO 1924) and Antonio Giustinian, *Dispacci*, 3 vols, ed. Pasquale Villari, Florence,

1876 (GIUSTINIAN/VILLARI 1876). Giustinian was Venetian ambassador to the Curia and Villari's edition covers the years 1502–3. Many of Niccolò Machiavelli's insights into the character and career of Cesare Borgia came from his dispatches as a diplomatic agent of the Florentine republic: *Le legazioni e commissarie di Niccolo Machiavelli*, ed. Sergio Bertelli, Milan, 1964 (BERTELLI 1964). More accessible is Machiavelli's *Il principe (The prince)*, available in various editions and translations, including that of George Bull, Harmondsworth, 1961 (MACHIAVELLI/BULL 1961). Francesco Guicciardini's *Storia d'Italia (1534)* has been edited and translated by Sydney Alexander: *The History of Italy*, Princeton University Press, Princeton, NJ, 1969 (ALEXANDER 1969). An English translation of immediate relevance to the life of Lucrezia Borgia is that of her correspondence with Pietro Bembo: *The Prettiest Love Letters in the World: Letters between Lucrezia Borgia and Pietro Bembo*, trans. Hugh Shankland, Collins Harvill, London, 1987 (SHANKLAND 1987).

Many of the secondary works already cited cover the pontificate of Alexander VI. The opening phases of the Italian Wars have inspired a sequence of quincentenary volumes, beginning with David Abulafia (ed.), *The French Descent into Italy, 1494–95: Antecedents and Effects*, Ashgate Publishing, Aldershot, 1995 (ABULAFIA 1995), and continuing with Stella Fletcher and Christine Shaw (eds), *The World of Savonarola: Italian Elites and Perceptions of Crisis*, Ashgate Publishing, Aldershot, 2000 (FLETCHER & SHAW 2000). The latter contains essays by leading scholars, including Lauro Martines, Alison Brown, Nicolai Rubinstein, Gigliola Fragnito, Michael Mallett, Loren Partridge and Iain Fenlon, on the political, social and cultural impact of war in Italy in the 1490s. There is every sign that the 500th anniversaries of phases of the conflict in the first half of the sixteenth century will be marked in similar scholarly fashion.

For a continuous narrative of interstate relations during Alexander's pontificate, a more recent version can be found in Frederic J. Baumgartner, *Louis XII*, Macmillian, Basingstoke, 1996 (BAUMGARTNER 1996). Among the Italian players, few have attracted greater biographical attention than Savonarola, the drama of whose life can be traced through successive nineteenth and twentieth-century studies: Pasquale Villari, *Life and Times of Girolamo Savonarola*, London, 1888 (VILLARI 1888); Roberto Ridolfi, *The Life of Girolamo Savonarola*, Alfred A. Knopf, New York, 1959 (RIDOLFI 1959); Donald Weinstein, *Savonarola and Florence: Prophecy and Patriotism in the Renaissance*, Princeton University Press, Princeton, NJ, 1970 (WEINSTEIN 1970). The friar's contribution to Florentine history did not end with his death, as Lorenzo Polizzotto has demonstrated in *The Elect Nation: The Savonarolan Movement in Florence 1494–1545*, Oxford University Press, Oxford, 1994 (POLIZZOTTO 1994). Roberto Ridolfi was also the biographer of the Florentine historian Guicciardini: *Life of Francesco Guicciardini*, Routledge & Kegan Paul, London, 1967 (RIDOLFI 1967). On Guicciardini also see Mark Phillips, *Francesco Guicciardini: The Historian's Craft*, Manchester University Press, Manchester, 1977 (PHILLIPS 1977).

Of the industry that is the study of Machiavelli's life and works, it is reasonable to skim the surface and mention some of the classic studies: Pasquale Villari, *Life and Times of Niccolò*

Machiavelli, C. Kegan Paul & Co, London, 1878 (VILLARI 1878); Roberto Ridolfi, *Life of Niccolò Machiavelli*, Routledge & K. Paul, London, 1963 (RIDOLFI 1963); J.R. Hale, *Machiavelli and Renaissance Italy*, English Universities Press, London, 1961 (HALE 1961); Sydney Anglo, *Machiavelli: A Dissection*, Paladin, London, 1969 (ANGLO 1969); Quentin Skinner, *Machiavelli*, Oxford University Press, Oxford, 1981 (SKINNER 1981). Among biographies of subjects whose paths crossed those of the Borgia, mention can also be made of Ernst Breisach, *Caterina Sforza, a Renaissance Virago*, University of Chicago Press, Chicago, 1967 (BREISACH 1967), and G.B. Picotti, *La giovinezza di Leone X*, Milan, 1928 (PICOTTI 1928).

As the present work illustrates, there have been scores of pseudo-biographical romances, more or less loosely based on the lives of Alexander VI, Cesare and *Lucrezia Borgia*. Serious Borgia scholarship can be said to begin with Ferdinand Gregorovius, Lucrezia Borgia, Stuttgart, 1874 (GREGOROVIUS 1874) which appeared in English translation as *Lucrezia Borgia, A Chapter from the Morals of the Italian Renaissance*, London, 1948 (GREGOROVIUS 1948). The other notable study of Lucrezia is that of Maria Bellonci, *Lucrezia Borgia: sua vita e suoi tempi*, Milan, 1939 (BELLONCI 1939), which first appeared in an abridged English version as *The Life and Times of Lucrezia Borgia*, tr. Bernard and Barbara Wall, Phoenix Press, London, 1953 (BELLONCI/WALL 1953).

The best English-language biography of Cesare remains W.H. Woodward, *Cesare Borgia*, London, 1913 (WOODWARD 1913), though that of Sarah Bradford, *Cesare Borgia: His Life and Times*, Macmillan, London, 1976 (BRADFORD 1976) is eminently readable. In spite of the detailed coverage of the years 1492 to 1503 provided by MALLETT 1969, the most obvious biographical lacuna concerns Alexander VI, whose pontificate deserves the most thorough archival treatment that contemporary scholarship can afford. As a full-scale biography in English translation, that of Orestes Ferrara, *The Borgia Pope, Alexander The Sixth*, translated by F.J. Sheed, Sheed & Ward, London, 1942 (FERRARA 1942), is particularly important for reasons stated elsewhere, despite minor inaccuracies. (See, in particular, Part II, chapter 8). The immediate 'afterlife' of Alexander and the most famous of his sons is charted with full bibliographical references by J.N. Hillgarth, 'The Image of Alexander VI and Cesare Borgia in the Sixteenth and Seventeenth centuries', *Journal of the Warburg and Courtauld Institutes* 59 (1996), pp 119–29 (HILLGARTH 1996).

For the nature and organs of papal government, which witnessed no substantial changes between 1492 and 1503, see above. Pastor's coverage and assessment of Alexander's pontificate appears in vols 5–6 of his *The History of the Popes* (PASTOR 1901-53), and includes some of the classic expressions of anti-Borgia propaganda. Important reappraisal of the conclave which elected Rodrigo Borgia to the papal throne came with the publication of the voting patterns in the first three scrutinies: F. La Torre, *Del conclave di Alessandro VI, papa Borgia*, Florence, 1933 (LA TORRE 1933). Picotti's detailed study of the life of the future Leo X has useful insights into the careers of the socio-political elite (PICOTTI 1928).

Three recent studies may also be cited to illustrate the role of cardinals during the Borgia pontificate: Barbara McClung Hallman, *Italian Cardinals, Reform, and the Church as*

Property, 1492–1563, University of California Press, Berkeley, Los Angeles and London, 1985 (HALLMAN 1985); K.J.P. Lowe, *Church and Politics in Renaissance Italy: The Life and Career of Cardinal Francesco Soderini, 1453–1524*, Cambridge University Press, Cambridge, 1993 (LOWE 1993); Marco Pellegrini, 'A Turning-point in the History of the Factional System in the Sacred College: The Power of Pope and Cardinals in the Age of Alexander VI', in Gianvittorio Signorotto and Maria Antonietta Visceglia (eds), *Court and Politics in Papal Rome 1492–1700*, Cambridge University Press, Cambridge, 2002, pp 8–30 (PELLEGRINI 2002).

For the visual arts in the Rome of Alexander VI, the more venerable work of Müntz and the more recent analysis of Partridge are still relevant. The 2002 *I Borgia* exhibition catalogue (ALFANO 2002) concentrates heavily on Borgia portraiture and material remains from Rome and the papal states during Alexander's pontificate. It also provides a reliable guide to recent scholarship in these fields. For Pinturicchio, see Enzo Carli, *Il Pinturicchio*, Electa, Milan, 1960 (CARLI 1960), and Alessandro Cecchi, *The Piccolomini Library in the Cathedral of Siena*, Scala, Florence, 1982 (CECCHI 1982). The most significant urban development of the period was that of the via Alessandrina, through the Borgo. A detailed study of the properties bordering that road and of those destroyed in the process has been undertaken by Enrico Guidoni and Giulia Petrucci, *Urbanistica per i giubilei: Roma, via Alessandrina: una strada 'tra due fondali' nell'Italia delle corti (1492–1499)*, Rome, 1997 (GUIDONI AND PETRUCCI 1997).

A more general picture of the city and its inhabitants is supplied by Peter Partner's *Renaissance Rome, 1500–1559: A Portrait of a Society*, University of California Press, Berkeley, Los Angeles and London, 1976 (PARTNER 1976). A similar survey, taking examples from both the fifteenth and sixteenth centuries, is Pio Paschini, *Roma nel Rinascimento*, Cappelli, Bologna, 1940 (PASCHINI 1940). For the literary and intellectual life of Rome between 1492 and 1503 GRAFTON 1993, O'MALLEY 1979 and STINGER 1985 remain useful, with the last boasting a particularly thorough bibliography. To these may be added John D'Amico, *Renaissance Humanism in Papal Rome: Humanists and Churchmen on the Eve of the Reformation*, Johns Hopkins University Press, Baltimore and London, 1983 (D'AMICO 1983).

From Renaissance to Catholic Reformation

A cornucopia of edited primary sources exist for Italian history and culture in the period from the pontificates of Pius III and Julius II through to that of Pius V. Among those readily available in English translation are: Baldassare Castiglione, *The Book of the Courtier (Il libro del cortegiano)*, ed and trans George Bull, Penguin, London, 2004 (CASTIGLIONE/BULL 2004), the classic guide to courtly accomplishments; and Benevenuto Cellini, *Autobiography*, ed and trans George Bull, Penguin, London, 1999 (CELLINI/BULL 1999) which contains a memorable account of the sack of Rome in 1527 and ample opportunity for scholars to tease fact from fiction. Less easily accessible is Paolo Cortesi, *De cardinalatu*, Castro Cortesio, 1510 (CORTESI 1510). Like Machiavelli's *Il principe*, this is an example of the 'mirrors for princes' genre, the princes in this case being cardinals. A portion of it has been translated and edited by Kathless Weil-Garris and John F. D'Amico, 'The Renaissance Cardinal's Ideal Palace: A Chapter from Cortesi's *De cardinalatu*', in Henry A. Millon (ed.), *Studies in Italian Art and Architecture, 15th through 18th centuries. Memoirs of the American Academy in Rome* 35 (1980), pp 45–123 (WEIL-GARRIS 1980).

Among the biting satires directed at the Church by the Dutch humanist, Desiderius Erasmus, none was more personal than that inspired by Pope Julius II: Desiderius Erasmus, *Julius exclusus*, trans. P. Pascal, Indiana University Press, Bloomington, 1968 (ERASMUS/ PASCAL 1968). Among the best known literary works produced in the Spain of St Francis Borgia were those relating to the exploration, conquest and exploitation of Castile's New World possessions: Columbus, *The Four Voyages*, trans J. M. Cohen, Penguin, London, 1992 (COLUMBUS/COHEN 1992); Bernal Diaz, *The Conquest of New Spain*, trans J. M. Cohen, Penguin, London, 1969 (DIAZ/COHEN 1969); Bartolomé de Las Casas, *A Short Account of the Destruction of the Indies*, trans Nigel Griffin, Penguin, London, 2004 (LAS CASAS/ GRIFFIN 2004).

While many of the works already cited bridge the fifteenth and sixteenth centuries, others focus on the later period. General histories of sixteenth-century Europe include: H.G. Koenigsberger, George L. Mosse and G.Q. Bowler, *Europe in the Sixteenth Century*, Oxford University Press, London, 1968 (KOENIGSBERGER 1968); Eric Cochrane, *Early Modern Europe*, Chicago University Press, Chicago and London, 1989 (COCHRANE 1989); Henry Kamen, *The Iron Century: Social Change in Europe 1550–1660*, Weidenfeld & Nicholson, London, 1971 (KAMEN 1971). A wealth of information is also to be found in Fernand Braudel, *The Mediterranean World in the Age of Philip II*, 2 vols, Collins, London, 1976 (BRAUDEL 1976). In addition to HAY & LAW 1989 for the early part of the century, see Eric Cochrane (ed. Julius Kirschner), *Italy 1530–1630*, Longman Press, London, 1988 (COCHRANE 1988) for an overview of the Italian states.

For Spain, ELLIOTT 1963 remains useful. See also: A.W. Lovett, *Early Habsburg Spain, 1517–1598*, Oxford University Press, Oxford, 1986 (LOVETT 1986); Henry Kamen, *Philip of Spain*, Yale University Press, New Haven and London, 1997 (KAMENa 1997); Henry Kamen, *Spain's Road to Empire: The Making of a World Power 1492–1763*, Allen Lane, London, 2003 (KAMEN 2003). In addition to BAUMGARTNER 1996 (on Louis XII) and the general histories of KNECHT 1996 and POTTER 1995, French foreign and domestic policies can also be appreciated by means of R.J. Knecht, *Francis I*, Cambridge University Press, Cambridge, 1982 (KNECHT 1982).

The religious turmoil of the sixteenth century has resulted in a wealth of local, regional and pan-European studies of the Reformation and Counter-Reformation or, as they are now sometimes known, the 'Reformations'. Euan Cameron, *The European Reformation*, Oxford University Press, Oxford, 1991 (CAMERON 1991), deals with these phenomena as a whole and provides recent bibliographical coverage. See also the works of Alister E. McGrath, especially *The Intellectual Origins of the European Reformation*, Blackwell Publishers,

Oxford, 1987 (MCGRATH 1987), and *Reformation Thought: An Introduction*, Blackwell Publishers, Oxford, 1988 (MCGRATH 1988). Biographical studies of Luther include: Martin Brecht, *Martin Luther*, 3 vols, English translation, Fortress, Minneapolis, 1985–93 (BRECHT 1985–93) and Roland H. Bainton, *Here I Stand: A life of Martin Luther*, Mentor, New York, 1950 (BAINTON 1950). For wider perspectives, see A.G. Dickens, *The German Nation and Martin Luther*, Edward Arnold, London, 1974 (DICKENS 1974). Biographies of Calvin include: Alister E. McGrath, *A Life of John Calvin*, Blackwell Publishers, Oxford, 1990 (MCGRATH 1990).

Turning to reform in a Catholic context, a useful survey is Michael A. Mullett, *The Catholic Reformation*, Routledge, London, 2000 (MULLETT 2000). See also J.C. Olin (ed.), *The Catholic Reformation: Savonarola to Ignatius Loyola: Reform in the Church, 1495–1540*, New York: Harper & Row, 1969 (OLIN 1969). At the heart of the Catholic Reformation was the Council of Trent, on which: Hubert Jedin, *Geschichte des Konzils von Trent*, 4 vols, Herder, Freiberg, 1949–75 (JEDIN 1949–75), the first two volumes of which have been translated as *A History of the Council of Trent*, trans. by Ernest Graf, Nelson, London, 1957–61 (JEDIN/GRAF 1957–61). See also H. Outram Evennett, *The Spirit of the Counter-Reformation*, Cambridge University Press, Cambridge, 1968 (EVENNETT 1968), and the collected essays of John W. O'Malley, *Religious Culture in the Sixteenth Century: Preaching, Rhetoric, Spirituality and Reform*, Ashgate Publishing, Aldershot, 1993 (O'MALLEY 1993).

Among regional studies, the religious history of Spain offers important works such as Marcel Bataillon, *Erasmo y Espag a: estudios sobre la historia espiritual del siglo xvi*, Mexico, 1966 (BATAILLON 1966), which analyses the impact of Erasmian ideas in the peninsula. To appreciate Erasmus's impact in Spain as part of a greater whole, see Richard J. Schoeck, *Erasmus and Europe: The Making of a Humanist*, Edinburgh University Press, Edinburgh, 1990 (SCHOECK 1990): the tip of the iceberg that is Erasmus studies. For recent perspectives on the Spanish Inquisition, see Henry Kamen, *The Spanish Inquisition: An Historical Revision*, Yale University Press, Newhaven and London, 1997 (KAMEN 1997b). The world of Italian *evangelismo* comes under scrutiny in Philip McNair, *Peter Martyr in Italy: An Anatomy of an Apostasy*, Clarendon Press, Oxford, 1967 (MCNAIR 1967), and in Dermot Fenlon, *Heresy and Obedience in Tridentine Italy*, Cambridge University Press, Cambridge, 1972 (FENLON 1972).

St Francis Borgia has not generated nearly as much interest as the strictly Italian branch of his family. See, for example, M. Yeo, *The Greatest of the Borgias*, Bruce Publishing Co., New York, 1936 (YEO 1936). St Francis' part in the early history of the Society of Jesus can be gleaned from John W. O'Malley, *The First Jesuits*, Harvard University Press, Cambridge, Mass., and London, 1993 (O'MALLEY 1993).

Like fifteenth-century popes, those of the sixteenth century have not tended to be the subjects of recent biographies. An exception is Julius II: see Ivan Cloulas, *Jules II*, Fayard, Paris, 1990 (CLOULAS 1990) and Christine Shaw, *Julius II: The Warrior Pope*, Blackwell, Oxford, 1993 (SHAW 1993). LOWE 1993 provides useful coverage of the first quarter of the century, particularly with regard to the Petrucci conspiracy against Leo X in 1517. The bulk of Hallman's study of Italian cardinals (HALLMAN 1985) falls in the post 1503 period. On the Sacred College, see also A.V. Antonovics, 'Counter-Reformation cardinals, 1534–1590', *European Studies Review* 2 (1970), pp 301–27 (ANTONOVICS 1970). For recent perspectives on the Roman Curia, see Gianvittorio Signorotto and Maria Antonietta Visceglia (eds), *Court and Politics in Papal Rome 1492–1700*, Cambridge University Press, Cambridge, 2002 (SIGNOROTTO AND VISCEGLIA 2002). The phenomenon of informal imperialism in the papal capital is explored by Thomas James Dandelet, *Spanish Rome 1500–1700*, Yale University Press, New Haven and London, 2001 (DANDELET 2001).

Relations between the papacy and the secular powers in the sixteenth century had previously concentrated on the sack of 1527: Judith Hook, *The Sack of Rome,* Macmillan, London, 1972 (HOOK 1972); André Chastel, *The Sack of Rome 1527*, Princeton University Press, Princeton, 1983 (CHASTEL 1983). For wider perspectives on urban life, PARTNER 1976 and PASCHINI 1940 remain useful, as do the works of D'AMICO 1983, O'MALLEY 1979 and STINGER 1985 for the city's cultural phenomena. For cultural patronage in sixteenth-century Rome and beyond, a useful starting point is Mary Hollingsworth, *Patronage in Sixteenth-Century Italy,* John Murray, London, 1996 (HOLLINGSWORTH 1996).

An interesting example of an early work I came across on a particular pope, Leo X, was *The Life and Pontificate of Leo X*, by Thomas Roscoe, Henry G. Bohn, London, 1846 (ROSCOE 1846). Generally favourable to the pope, in its two volumes, there are some barely known and/or long forgotten details about this pontiff.

As will readily be seen from the above, the wealth of literature available on the Renaissance period is considerable. Conspicuous for its absence, until now, has been the assembling in a single volume of the individual stories of the 18 diverse and amazing men covered by the description, 'Renaissance popes'.

A word must finally be said of the importance of J.H. Ignaz von Döllinger's work, *The Pope and the Council*, Rivingtons, London, 1869 (DÖLLINGER 1869). Döllinger, a Catholic archbishop, was professor of Church History in Munich; he revolutionized a whole school, age and thought on this subject. Döllinger was a scholarly and objective recorder of Church history. His resulting candour in admitting some irregularities in past papal affairs earned him excommunication from the reactionary and intolerant Pius IX. (At just that moment, papal infallibility was in the process of being defined). Döllinger, however, was scrupulously fair in his writings, which thus differed markedly from so many of the virulently anti-Catholic tracts starting to appear about this time.

The latter added fuel to the fire of the Borgia myth, which was showing signs of dying down. The Catholic historian Leopold von Ranke, some years later, did not help matters with his biography of Alexander VI: *The Ecclesiastical and Political History of the Popes of Rome, during the Sixteenth and Seventeenth Centuries,* trans. by Sarah Austin, 3 vols, John Murray, London, 1840 (RANKE 1840). A rival quipped that the inaccuracies in the book corresponded to something false in Ranke's own nature. (Perhaps this was because the aristocratic 'von' in his name was self-awarded.)

After so many years of a lack of positive effort to rehabilitate Alexander VI, there was now a move to put Ranke's book on the *Index*. This was resisted by Pope Leo XIII, whose view was that the Church had nothing to fear from a search for truth. How right he was.

Unfortunately, in the case of the Borgia pope there were, until Orestes Ferrara, all too few authors who followed his principle.

MISCELLANEOUS BIBLIOGRAPHY

The following books are listed alphabetically by title, since they either concern general topics in which could be found useful references to one or other of the Renaissance Popes or comprise collected short histories of the respective pontiffs.

April Blood, Florence and the Plot Against the Medici, by Lauro Martines. Jonathan Cape Ltd, London, 2003. (MARTINES 2003)

The Catholic Encyclopedia, Catholic Encyclopedia Press, New York, 1907. (CATHOLIC ENCYCLOPEDIA 1907). Although naturally overtaken historically by the later and thoroughly revised edition (see CATHOLIC ENCYCLOPEDIA 1966), the 1907 edition contained more information under certain headings than its successor. These included several of the popes of the Renaissance period.

A Dictionary of Popes, by Donald Atwater. London, 1939 (ATWATER 1939)

The Ecclesiastical and Political History of the Popes of Rome, during the Sixteenth and Seventeenth Centuries, by Leopold von Ranke (trans. by Sarah Austin). 3 vols, John Murray, London, 1840. (RANKE 1840)

Eunochs for the Kingdom of Heaven, by Cita Ranke. Heinemann, New York, 1990. (RANKE 1990)

A History of Orgies, by Burgo Partridge. Prion Books, London, 2002. (PARTRIDGE 2002)

A History of Terror, by Paul Newman. Sutton Publishing, Thrupp, 2000. (NEWMAN 2000)

A History of the Popes, by Sir Nicholas Cheetham. Dorset Press, New York, 1982. (CHEETHAM 1982). Originally published as *Keepers of the Keys: A History of the Popes from St Peter to John Paul II*.

Homosexuality and the Priesthood, edited by Jeannie Gramick. Crossroad, New York, 1990. (GRAMICK 1990)

The Inquisition, by Michael Baigent and Richard Leigh. Viking, London, 1999. (BAIGENT AND LEIGH 1999)

The Last Pope: The Prophecies of St Malachy for the New Millennium, by John Hogue. Element, Shaftesbury, 1998. (HOGUE 1998)

Liber Pontificalis, trans. by Raymond Davis. Liverpool University Press, Liverpool, 1992. (LIBER/DAVIS 1992)

The Lives of the Popes, B. Platina. London, 1645. (PLATINA 1645)

The Lives of the Popes in the Early Middle Ages, Horace K. Mann. Kegan Paul & Co, London, 1925. (MANN 1925)

The Medici, Godfathers of the Renaissance, by Michael Strathern. Jonathon Cape, London, 2003. (STRATHERN 2003)

Pageant of the Popes, by John Farrow. Sheed & Ward, New York, 1950. (FARROW 1950)

Papal Power, by Jean-Guy Vaillancourt. University of California Press, Berkeley, 1980. (VAILLANCOURT 1980)

Popery, by Cypriano de Valera. London, 1904. (VALERA 1904)

The Popes, by F. Gontard. Barrie & Rockliff, London, 1964. (GONTARD 1964)

The Popes: A Concise Biographical History, by J.M.W. Bean and others. Burns & Oates, New York, 1964. (BEAN ET AL 1964)

The Popes and the Jews in the Middle Ages, by Edward A. Synan. Macmillan, New York, 1965. (SYNAN 1965)

Renaissance Woman, by Gaia Servadio. I.B. Tauris, London and New York, 2005. (SERVADIO 2005). A valuable study of the feminine dimension to the Renaissance period.

Torture: The Grand Conspiracy, by Malise Ruthven. Weidenfeld & Nicolson, London, 1978. (RUTHVEN 1978)

The Triple Crown by Valerie Pirie. Sidgwick & Jackson, London, 1935. (PIRIE 1935). A valuable and industriously researched compendium of lesser known facts of papal history, particularly concerning conclaves.

A True History of the Lives of the Popes, by H.M. and R.T. London, 1679. (TRUE HISTORY 1679). A rare and curious volume, but useful if read with discretion and some scepticism.

Vicars of Christ, by Peter de Rosa. Bantam Press, London, 1988. (ROSA 1988). I found this book extremely useful. Despite some inaccuracies, it is the fruit of an unusually deep and wide search of sources and a positive mine of obscure facts, all fully investigated and authenticated.

Worldly Goods: The Wealth and Power of the American Catholic Church, the Vatican, and the Men Who Control the Money, by James Gollin. Random House, New York, 1971. (GOLLIN 1971). This unusual and frank study of Vatican finances through the ages was given to me by archbishop Marchinkus, the former controversial president of the Vatican Bank.

ART AND ARCHITECTURE BIBLIOGRAPHY

Fabio Benzi, *Palaces of Rome,* Thames & Hudson, London, 1997 (BENZI 1997).

Johann Burchard, *At the Court of the Borgias,* Folio Society, London, 1963 (BURCHARD 1963).

Richard Cocke, *From Magic to High Fashion: The Classical Tradition and the Renaissance of Roman Patronage, 1420–1600,* Mill Hill Publications, Norwich, 1993 (COCKE 1963).

Carlo Cresti, *Ville e Palazzi di Roma,* Magnus, Udine, 1998 (CRESTI 1963).

Eamon Duffy, *Saints & Sinners: A History of the Popes,* Yale University Press, London and New Haven, 1998 (DUFFY 1998).

Leopold David Ettlinger, *The Sistine Chapel Before Michelangelo: Religious Imagery and Papal Primacy,* Clarendon Press, Oxford, 1965 (ETTLINGER 1965).

R. Goffen, 'Article on Sixtus IV', *Renaissance Quarterly,* vol. xxxix (New York, 1986), pp 218–62 (GOFFEN 1986).

Anthony Grafton (ed.), *Rome Reborn: The Vatican Library and Renaissance Culture*, Yale University Press, New Haven & London, 1993 (GRAFTON 1993).

Pierre Grimal, *Churches of Rome,* Tauris Parke, London, 1997 (GRIMAL 1997).

George L. Hersey, *High Renaissance Art in St Peter's and the Vatican: An Interpretative Guide,* University of Chicago Press, Chicago, 1993 (HERSEY 1993).

Eunice D. Howe, *The Hospital of Santo Spirito and Pope Sixtus IV,* Garland Publishing, New York, 1978 (HOWE 1978).

Emilio Lavagnino, *Santa Maria del Popolo,* Treves Dell' Anonima Libreria Italiana, Rome, *c.*1920 (LAVAGNINO 1920a).

Emilio Lavagnino, *Santa Maria Maggiore,* Casa Editrice 'Roma', Rome, *c.*1920 (LAVAGNINO 1920b).

Egmont Lee, *Sixtus IV and Men of Letters*, Edizioni di Storia e Letteratura, Rome, 1978 (LEE 1978).

Roberto Luciani, *Santa Maria Maggiore e Roma*, Fratelli Palombi, Rome, 1996 (LUCIANI 1996).

Charles R. Mack, *Pienza: The Creation of a Renaissance City*, Cornell University Press, Ithaca, 1987 (MACK 1987).

Torgil Magnuson, *Studies in Roman Quattrocento Architecture*, Almqvist & Wiksell, Stockholm, 1958 (MAGNUSON 1958).

Michael Mallett, *The Borgias: The Rise and Fall of a Renaissance Dynasty*, Bodley Head, London, 1969 (MALLETT 1969).

Stefano Masi, *Rome and the Vatican*, Bonechi, Florence, 1999 (MASI 1999).

Georgina Masson, *The Companion Guide to Rome*, Collins, London, 1965 (MASSON 1965).

The New Catholic Encyclopaedia, McGraw-Hill, New York, 1966 (CATHOLIC ENCYCLOPEDIA 1966).

Ludwig von Pastor, *The History of the Popes from the Close of the Middle Ages*, 40 vols, London, 1901–53 (PASTOR 1901-53).

Carlo Pietrangeli, *The Vatican Museums: Five Centuries of History*, Quasar Biblioteca Apostolica Vaticana, Rome, 1993 (PIETRANGELI 1993).

Corrado Ricci, *Pintoricchio*, Heinemann, London, 1902 (RICCI 1902).

Georgio Vasari, *The Lives of the Artists*, trans Julia Conway Bondanella and Peter Bondanella, Oxford University Press, Oxford, 1998 (VASARI/BONDELLA 1998).

Carroll William Westfall, *In this Most Perfect Paradise: Alberti, Nicholas V and the Invention of Conscious Urban Planning in Rome, 1447–55*, Pennsylvania State University Press, Pennsylvania, 1974 (WESTFALL 1974).

INDEX